Maida Heatter's Best Dessert Book Ever

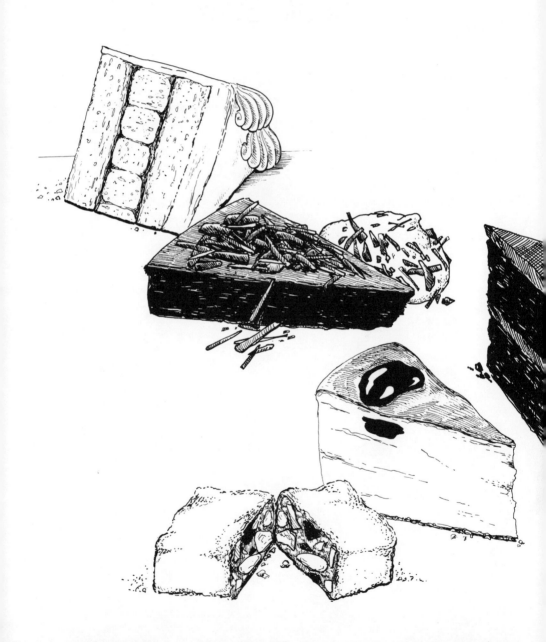

Also by Maida Heatter

Maida Heatter's Book of Great Desserts (1974)

Maida Heatter's Book of Great Cookies (1977)

Maida Heatter's Book of Great Chocolate Desserts (1980)

Maida Heatter's New Book of Great Desserts (1982)

Maida Heatter's Book of Great American Desserts (1985)

Maida Heatter's
BEST DESSERT
BOOK EVER

Drawings by Toni Evins

 RANDOM HOUSE NEW YORK

Copyright © 1990 by Maida Heatter
Illustrations copyright © 1990 by The Estate of Toni Evins

All rights reserved under International and Pan-American Copyright
Conventions. Published in the United States by Random House, Inc., New
York and simultaneously in Canada by Random House of Canada Limited,
Toronto.

Library of Congress Cataloging-in-Publication Data

Heatter, Maida.
    [Best dessert book ever]
    Maida Heatter's best dessert book ever / drawings by Toni Evins.
        p.   cm.
    ISBN 0-394-57832-5
    1. Desserts. I. Title. II. Title: Best dessert book ever.
TX773.H35 1990
641.8'6—dc20   90-8096

Manufactured in the United States of America
9 8 7 6 5 4 3 2
First Edition

Contents

Introduction

During a recent newspaper interview a reporter asked me why I had written another dessert book—my sixth. He seemed shocked.

My answer was, "Because that is what I do. I write dessert books, and I can't stop. The very day I delivered the manuscript for each of my books I started work on new recipes. I am lucky to be involved with something I love so much. I look forward to every new recipe as though it is my first. It is never boring."

The reporter asked, "Don't you run out of ideas?"

"On the contrary," I told him. "I run out of time, or butter and eggs—even chocolate—but not ideas."

"What are the trends in today's desserts?"

"There are many trends, and some of them contradict each other. But if there is one mood—one theme—throughout them all, it is simplicity."

In a recent *New York Times* article, current women's fashions were described as "natural, simple, undecorated, pure, never overdesigned." Those same words describe today's desserts. (Or maybe they describe the trend I like best.)

A dense, rich, flourless chocolate cake with no icing, and possibly just a bit of sauce or a few berries on the side. That's it. Simple, but classy. Simple, but full of flavor.

"What is your favorite dessert?"

"Chocolate ice cream. Or Tiramisu. But I love cheesecake and bread pudding. And apple tart and brownies. And *biscotti*. Glacéed Dried Fruit. *Panforte*. Prune Armagnac Ice Cream. White Chocolate Ice Cream. Crisp cookies like Cat's Tongues (especially when they are sandwiched with chocolate). Thin cookies like Tuiles aux Amandes. Thick meringue cookies, dry and crunchy, loaded with walnuts and chunks of chocolate. And whenever I make Banana Rum Terrine or Ethereal Chocolate Mousse Cake With Bittersweet Chocolate Sauce I love that the most.

These desserts not only make me happy, they make our friends and family happy. (As well as the butcher, the people who work in the post office, the people who work at the fish market, the garage mechanic, the people at the dry cleaner's and at the newsstand and the tree pruners and the air-conditioning man. And whoever else is near.)

As the reporter gathered his papers together to leave, I handed him a little bag of Santa Fe Brownies (huge, moist, soft, thick, dark, with a layer of a white cheesecake mixture running unevenly through the middle).

I said, "These are my newest brownies, and I am as excited about them as I was about the first brownies I ever made."

He tasted one, and swooned. (Don't miss them.)

Maida Heatter

Miami Beach

Maida Heatter's Best Dessert Book Ever

Ingredients

FLOUR

Many of these recipes call for sifted flour. That means that even if the package is labeled "presifted," you should sift the flour before measuring. If not, since flour packs down while standing, a cup of unsifted flour is liable to be a few spoonfuls more than a cup of just-sifted flour.

Sift the flour onto a piece of wax paper. Make sure there is no flour left in the sifter. Then transfer the sifter to another piece of wax paper. Lightly spoon the sifted flour into a metal measuring cup (from a set of graded cups), or lift it on a dough scraper and transfer it to the cup—do not pack or press the flour down—and scrape the excess off the top with a dough scraper or any flat-sided implement. If the sifted flour is to be sifted with other ingredients, return it to the sifter, add the ingredients to be sifted with it, and sift onto the second piece of paper. Again, make sure there is nothing left in the sifter.

It is never necessary to wash a flour sifter; just shake it out firmly and store it in a plastic bag.

I have switched to unbleached flour. I seldom, if ever, buy bleached flour anymore. But either one can be used in the recipes that call for unbleached flour.

SUGAR

All sugars should be measured in the graded measuring cups made for measuring dry ingredients.

Brown Sugar

Most brown sugars are made of white granulated sugar to which a dark syrup has been added. Dark brown sugar has a mild molasses, and light brown sugar has a milder, lighter syrup (which may also be molasses). Dark brown has a slightly stronger flavor, but dark and light brown may be used interchangeably. The label on Grandma's Molasses says, "You can easily make your own brown sugar as you need it by blending together ½ cup of granulated sugar with 2 tablespoons of unsulphured molasses. The yield is equivalent to ½ cup of brown sugar."

Brown sugar is moist; if it dries out it will harden, so it should be stored airtight. If it has small lumps it should be strained. The Savannah Sugar Refinery is now printing the following directions on its boxes of brown sugar: "If your brown sugar has been left open and becomes hard, place a dampened (not wet) paper towel inside the resealable poly bag and close the package tightly for 12 hours or more. A slice of apple can be used in place of the dampened towel."

Confectioners Sugar

Confectioners sugar and powdered sugar are the same. Both names refer to granulated sugar that has been pulverized and had about 3 percent cornstarch added to keep it powdery. Of the confectioners sugars, 4-x is the least fine and 10-x is the finest. They may be used interchangeably. Confectioners sugar should be strained; you can do several pounds at a time, if you wish. It does not have to be done immediately before using, as flour does. Store it airtight.

If directions say to sprinkle with confectioners sugar, place the sugar in a fine strainer over the top of the cake or dessert, and tap the strainer lightly with your hand to shake out the sugar.

Crystal Sugar

Crystal sugar, also called pearl sugar, or *Hagelzucker* in German, is generally used to sprinkle over certain cookies and pastries before baking. It is coarser than granulated sugar. It is available at Dean & DeLuca (see page 29).

WHIPPING CREAM

Plain old-fashioned whipping cream is scarce nowadays (although better restaurants and hotels manage somehow to get it). The kind that is generally available now, super- or ultrapasteurized (known as UHT—ultra-high-temperature pasteurized), is not as good; at least I don't think so. The reason dairies make it is that it has a six- to eight-week shelf life. This product is called "heavy whipping cream" or "heavy cream," depending on the manufacturer. Either one can be used in recipes that call for whipping cream.

The process of making ultrapasteurized cream involves heating the cream to 250 degrees for one second. It gives the cream a hint of caramel flavor (so mild you might not notice it) and makes it more difficult to whip (it takes longer), and once it is whipped it will not hold up as long. It is always advisable to chill the bowl and beaters in the freezer until very cold before whipping. And keep the cream in the refrigerator until you are ready to whip; do not let it stand around in the kitchen—it should be as cold as possible.

It seems to me that baked custards take longer to set if they are made with UHT cream, and ice creams take longer to churn. However, UHT is the kind I use.

How to Whip Cream

The best way to whip either plain old-fashioned or UHT cream is to place it in a large chilled bowl, set the bowl in a larger bowl of ice and water, and whip with a large, thin-wired balloon-type whisk. You get more volume this way, and it tastes better.

If that seems like more than you want to fuss with, use an electric mixer or an egg beater, and chill the bowl and beaters before using them. If the bowl does not revolve by itself, then move the beaters around the bowl to whip the cream evenly.

When I whip cream with an electric mixer I always—and I recommend this to everyone—finish the whipping by hand with a wire whisk; there is less chance of overwhipping. At this stage you can use a smaller whisk than if you were doing it all by hand.

Whipped cream, which can be heavenly, is not quite as delicious if it is whipped until it is really stiff. Softer is better.

NO BUTTERMILK?

If a recipe calls for buttermilk and you do not have any, here's how to make your own: Warm 1 cup of regular milk (sweet milk) over low heat to room temperature (about 70 degrees). Place 1 tablespoon of lemon juice in a 1-cup glass measuring cup, then fill to the 1-cup line with the room-temperature milk, stir, and let stand for 10 minutes. (The homemade version will have larger curds than commercial buttermilk has.)

Size

The size of eggs can be very important in certain recipes, especially when baking. All of these recipes call for eggs graded "large."

To Open Eggs

If directions call for adding whole eggs one at a time, they may all be opened ahead of time into one container and then poured into the other ingredients approximately one at a time. Do not open eggs directly into the ingredients—you would not know if a piece of shell had been included.

To Separate Eggs

A young bride was baking her first cake. When she came to the direction "Separate the eggs," she placed them on the counter and just stood there, puzzled—wondering how far apart they should be.

Eggs separate more safely—there is less chance of the yolk breaking—when they are cold. Therefore, if a recipe calls for separated eggs, it is usually the first thing I do when organizing the ingredients so that they are cold from the refrigerator.

The safest way to separate eggs is as follows: Place three small glass custard cups or shallow drinking glasses in front of you. One container is for the whites and one is for the yolks. The third might not be needed, but if you should break the yolk when opening an egg, just drop the whole thing in the third container and save it for some other use.

Tap the side of the egg firmly (but not too hard, or you might break the yolk) on the edge of the cup or glass to crack the shell, with luck, in a rather straight line. Then, holding the egg upright and with both hands, separate the halves of the shell (so that each half makes a cup), letting some of the white run into the cup or glass. Pour the yolk back and forth from one half of the shell to the other, letting all of the white run out. Then drop the yolk into the second cup or glass.

Many professional cooks simply open the egg into the palm of one hand, then hold their fingers, slightly separated, over a bowl. They let the white run through their open fingers, and then slide the yolk into a separate bowl.

As each egg is separated, the white should be transferred to another container (that is, in addition to the three), because if you place all the whites in one container, there is a chance that the last white may have some yolk in it, which could spoil all the whites.

Generally, a tiny bit of yolk or shell can be removed from the whites with an empty half-shell. Or try a piece of paper towel dipped in cold water.

To Beat Egg Whites

The success of many recipes depends on properly beaten whites. After you have learned how it becomes second nature.

First, the bowl and beaters must be absolutely clean. A little bit of fat (egg yolks are fat) will prevent the whites from incorporating air as they should and from rising properly.

Second, do not overbeat or the whites will become dry and you will not be able to fold them into the other ingredients without losing the air you have beaten in.

Third, do not beat them ahead of time. They must be folded in immediately after they are beaten; if they have to wait, they separate.

You can use an electric mixer, a rotary beater, or a wire whisk (a wire whisk and a copper bowl are said to give the best results).

If you use an electric mixer or a rotary beater, be careful not to use a bowl that is too large or the whites will be too shallow to get the full benefit of the beaters' action. If the bowl does not revolve by itself (as some bowls do in electric mixers on a stand), move the mixer or beater around the bowl to beat all the whites evenly.

If you use a wire whisk, it should be a large, thin-wired balloon-type whisk, at least 4 inches wide at the top. The bowl should be very large—the larger the better—to give you plenty of room for making large, circular motions with the whisk. An unlined copper bowl is the best (there is a good chemical reaction between copper and egg whites), or you can use glass, china, or stainless steel—but do not beat egg whites in aluminum, which might discolor the whites, or plastic, which is frequently porous and might be greasy from some other use.

A copper bowl should be treated each time before using as follows: Put 1 or 2 teaspoons of salt in the bowl and rub thoroughly with half a lemon, squeezing out a bit of the juice and mixing it with the salt. Then rinse with hot water (no soap) and dry. After using a copper bowl, wash it as you would any other, but be sure to treat it each time before beating egg whites.

When I beat egg whites with an electric mixer, if they do not have sugar added (sugar makes them more creamy and slightly lessens the chance of overbeating), I always—and I recommend this to everyone—finish the beating with a wire whisk. There is less chance of overbeating, and the whisk seems to give the whites a slightly creamy consistency. At this stage you can use a smaller whisk than the one mentioned above; use any whisk that seems right for the bowl the whites are in.

People often ask me if I bring whites to room temperature before beating them. If I do, it is a rare occasion and was not planned. They are usually cold when I beat them (because I do not plan ahead and do not have the patience to wait, and because I have had equally good results whether the whites were cold or at room temperature).

To Freeze Egg Whites or Yolks

Some of these recipes call for yolks and no whites, and some call for only whites.

Leftover egg whites can be kept covered in the refrigerator for a few days, or they can be frozen. I freeze them individually (or, occasionally, two or four together) in ovenproof glass custard cups. When frozen, hold the cup upside down under running hot water until the frozen egg white can be removed (but not until it melts). Quickly wrap each frozen egg white in plastic wrap or aluminum foil and return to the freezer. To use, unwrap, place in a cup or bowl, and let stand at room temperature to thaw. Or, to save time, place in a cup or bowl in a slightly warm oven or in a pan of shallow warm water.

To freeze egg yolks, stir them lightly just to mix, and, for each yolk, stir in ⅓ teaspoon of granulated sugar or ½ teaspoon of honey. Freeze them in a covered jar, labeling them so that you will know how many yolks and how much sugar or honey. When thawed, stir to mix well—they will not look exactly the same as before they were frozen (not as smooth), but they will work in recipes.

NUTS

Nuts can turn rancid rather quickly—walnuts and pecans more so than almonds. Always store all nuts airtight in the freezer or refrigerator. In the refrigerator nuts last well for nine months; in the freezer at zero degrees they will last for two years. Bring them to room temperature before using, smell and taste them before using (and, if possible, when you buy them)—you will know quickly if they are rancid. If you even suspect that they might be, do not use them. They would ruin a recipe.

To Toast Pecans

Pecans occasionally become limp after they are frozen, so I toast them. Toasted pecans are so great that now I toast all pecans (those that have been frozen and those that have not) before using them. Here's how: Place them in a shallow pan in the middle of a preheated 350-degree oven for 15 to 20 minutes, stirring occasionally, until they are very hot but not until they become darker in color.

To Blanch (or Skin) Almonds

Cover the almonds with boiling water. The skin will loosen almost immediately. Spoon out a few nuts at a time and, one by one, hold them under cold running water and squeeze them between your thumb and forefinger. The nuts will pop out and the skins will remain. Place the peeled almonds on a towel to dry. Then spread them in a shallow baking pan and bake in a preheated 200-degree oven for 30 minutes or so until they are completely dry.

If the almonds are to be split, sliced, or slivered, they should remain in the hot water longer to soften; let them stand until the water cools enough for you to touch it comfortably. Then, one at a time, remove the skin from each nut and immediately—while the nut is still soft—place it on a cutting board and cut with a small, sharp paring knife. Then bake to dry them as above. Sliced almonds are those that have been cut into very thin slices; slivered almonds are the fatter, oblong, julienne-shaped pieces. Don't expect sliced or slivered almonds that you have cut up yourself to be as even as store-bought ones. (Sometimes I think I like the uneven look better.)

To Blanch Hazelnuts

Spread the nuts on a jelly-roll pan and bake at 350 degrees for about 15 minutes or until the skins parch and begin to flake off. Then, working with a few at a time, place them on a large coarse towel (I use a terry-cloth bath towel). Fold part of the towel over to enclose the nuts. Rub firmly against the towel, or hold that part of the towel between both hands and rub back and forth. The handling and the texture of the towel will cause most of the skins to flake off. Pick out the nuts and discard the skins. Don't worry about the few little pieces of skin that may remain.

This is not as quick and easy as it sounds.

Pistachio Nuts

A light sprinkling of chopped unsalted green pistachio nuts is a nice touch. But don't overdo it; less is better than more. Fine pastries have about a teaspoon of them sprinkled in the center of the icing on a 9-inch cake.

Buy shelled unsalted green pistachio nuts. They are hard to find, but they keep for a long time in the freezer. They can be found at Paprikas Weiss, 1546 Second Avenue, New York, New York 10028.

Chop the nuts coarse or fine on a board using a long, heavy knife. Don't worry about the little pieces of skin that flake off; you can leave them with the nuts (or pick out the large pieces of skin, if you wish).

Wholesale Nuts

I often buy nuts from a wholesale nut company, where it is not necessary to buy huge amounts. Recently I bought a supply of toasted, blanched (skinned) hazelnuts, monster cashew nuts, macadamia nuts, and green pistachio nuts. They are available blanched or not, toasted or untoasted, salted or unsalted, whole or ground. I have often used a mixture of these exotic nuts (whole—not cut up) in brownie recipes. Biting into a dark, moist chocolate brownie and finding whole cashews and/or macadamias, et cetera, is fabulous. The company is The Barnard Nut Company, 8737 S.W. 132nd Street, Miami, FL 33176 (305-378-1111). They have a product list.

VANILLA BEANS

Tahitian vanilla beans (see page 31) are extraspecial, and many dessert chefs prefer them to other kinds. Whichever kind you use, the bean should be soft and moist, not dried out. I have tried many ways of storing them. The freezer is very good, although they seem to last as well wrapped airtight, placed in an airtight jar, and stored in a kitchen closet. They have remained perfectly fresh for many months both ways.

When a recipe calls for scraping the seeds out of a bean, you will find that the seeds tend to cling together in a lump no matter what you do.

Here's a great trick I learned from Paula Wolfert to prevent the seeds from lumping: On a plastic cutting board or a plate, slit the bean lengthwise. With a teaspoon, scrape down the length of the bean to scoop out all the seeds. Place the seeds in a little mound on the cutting board or plate. Add about a teaspoon of granulated sugar from the recipe, or as much as necessary, depending on the moisture of the bean. With the tip of your middle finger, work the sugar and seeds together, going round and round and back and forth until the sugar and seeds are totally mixed and the seeds are separated from each other by the sugar.

Once that is completed, the best way to get the most flavor from the seeds and the bean is to steep them in hot liquid from the recipe for about half an hour.

Incidentally, did you know that vanilla beans come from the fruit (the beans) of an orchid? They are green when harvested, then are cured to a mahogany brown. The flavor is in the tiny beans inside as well as in the pod itself.

INSTANT ESPRESSO OR COFFEE POWDER

Many of these recipes call for instant espresso or coffee powder—not granules. I use Medaglia D'Oro, which is powdered and is generally available at Italian or Cuban grocers. However, if you have only granular instant espresso or coffee, you can powder it in a food processor or blender and it will work just as well.

FRESH GINGER

Do not buy any that is soft and wrinkled—it should be firm and hard (like potatoes). To store: For a few days—or even weeks, if it is firm and fresh—it can stand at room temperature (like potatoes). For a longer time, it can be stored in the vegetable drawer of the refrigerator—wrapped or unwrapped does not seem to make any difference. Or it can be frozen, wrapped airtight in foil.

A chef at a famous San Francisco restaurant told me that he keeps fresh ginger for weeks at room temperature, lying on its side in a shallow dish filled with about half an inch of water (he adds water occasionally as it evaporates). About a month ago, when I had just bought some nice fresh ginger, I put one piece in water and another piece alongside it not in water. Now, a month later, the piece that is not in water looks healthier. The piece that is in water looks wrinkled—or is it my imagination? This experiment proves that if it is in good condition when you buy it, ginger is strong and hardy and lasts well almost in spite of what you do with it.

It is not necessary to peel ginger if the skin is pale and thin, but if it is old and tough, peel it with a vegetable parer. It can be grated on a standing metal grater on the side that has small round openings (rather than diamond-shaped openings). It can be grated if it is at room temperature, refrigerated, or frozen. At any temperature it is slow work to grate much. But it is quick and easy—actually a breeze—to grate it in a food processor. First slice it crosswise into very thin slices, about ⅛ inch (or less) thick.

Although the processor will grate the ginger very well, it will leave fibers in the mixture. Cutting it first into thin slices reduces the length of the fibers.

Fit the processor with the metal chopping blade. With the motor going, add the slices one or two at a time through the feed tube, pausing briefly between additions. Stop the machine once or twice to scrape down the sides of the bowl, and then process again for a few seconds.

If you plan to freeze the ginger and then grate it, frozen, in a food processor, it is best to slice it before you freeze it.

Incidentally, fresh-produce people tell me that Hawaiian ginger is the best.

CHOCOLATE

Chocolate comes from the pods of the cocoa tree, or *Theobroma cacao*, "the food of the gods" (I'll vote for that). After the pods are harvested, dried, processed, et cetera, the chocolates fall into two categories: unsweetened and sweetened.

If a recipe calls for unsweetened chocolate, there are very few to choose from. But if a recipe calls for sweetened chocolate, there is a large variety—semisweet, bittersweet, extrabittersweet, milk, or white chocolate.

Here are three of the best:

Valrhona Chocolate

Many of my friends who are professional pastry chefs say that Valrhona (made in France) is their favorite chocolate. A firm in Brooklyn called Van Rex Food (120 Imlay Street, Brooklyn, New York 11231 [718-376-4619]) sells it in large amounts ($100.00 is the minimum order). And I also know where you can get it in small amounts. A gorgeous kitchen shop in Santa Fe, New Mexico, cuts up the large bars and sells it in 6 ½-ounce pieces. They have bittersweet, semisweet, and white Valrhona chocolates. Write, call, or go to COOKWORKS, Inc., 316 Guadalupe Street, Santa Fe, New Mexico 87501 (505-988-7676). (COOKWORKS fills three separate buildings.)

I have used white, semisweet, and most bittersweet Valrhona chocolates with perfect results. But there is one bittersweet variety called Guanaja that I have had trouble with. Several professional pastry chefs have told me that they have also had trouble with it.

Callebaut Chocolate

Callebaut (made in Belgium) has as many devoted fans as Valrhona does. Dean & DeLuca (see page 29) carries Callebaut milk, semisweet, bittersweet, and white chocolates.

Maillard Chocolate

Maillard (made in America) is in the same class as the finest imported chocolates. If you use a lot of it and would like to buy it wholesale ($150.00 is the minimum order), their address is Box 1158, Bethlehem, Pennsylvania 18106. Dean & DeLuca (see page 29) also carries Maillard if you want to buy it in smaller amounts.

Dutch-Process Cocoa

This is not a brand name; it is so called because it was created in Holland by a Dutchman named Coenraad van Houten, who discovered the process of adding alkali very sparingly to cocoa to neutralize the acidity, make it less bitter, and deepen the color. The label will say either Dutch-process or "processed with alkali." I always use Dutch-process cocoa. Usually Droste.

Equipment

I use an electric mixer on a stand that comes with two different-sized bowls and a pair of beaters (rather than one beater, as some mixers have). Mine is a Sunbeam Mixmaster.

I think it is important, or at least extremely helpful, for many dessert recipes to use a mixer that:

    a. is on a stand;

    b. comes with both a small and a large bowl;

    c. has space to scrape the bowl with a rubber spatula while the mixer is going.

I especially recommend that you buy an extra set of bowls and extra beaters; they are generally available at the service center of the manufacturer of your mixer.

Incidentally, the new Cuisinart cordless hand mixer is remarkable. You will love it. I use mine often.

If you are using a hand-held mixer or an egg beater, when I say "small bowl of an electric mixer," that means one with a 7-cup capacity, and "large bowl of an electric mixer" means one with a 16-cup capacity.

THERMOMETERS

Oven Temperature

One of the most important and most overlooked requirements for good results in baking is correct oven temperature. The wrong temperature can cause a cake to fall, to be underdone, to refuse to rise; it can ruin a soufflé; it can turn cookies that should be deliciously crisp into pale, limp, soggy things; and it can be the cause of almost any other baking disaster that you might have experienced or heard about.

No matter how new or how good your oven is, *please* double-check the temperature every time you bake. Use a small portable oven thermometer from the hardware store or kitchen shop. Buy the mercury type—it is best. Light your oven at least 20 minutes ahead of time and place the thermometer on a rack close to the middle of the oven. Give the oven plenty of time to heat and cycle and reheat before you read the thermometer. If it does not register the heat you want, adjust the thermostat up or down until the thermometer registers the correct heat—no matter what the oven setting says.

When you put unbaked cakes or cookies in the oven, they reduce the temperature more than you would expect. If you check the temperature on a portable thermometer during the first 10 minutes of baking, don't think that your oven suddenly got sick; give it time to reheat.

Other Thermometers

Keep a freezer thermometer in your freezer and a refrigerator thermometer in your refrigerator—and look at them often. (Recently, an ice cream that I had successfully made before refused to set up and become firm enough. Since I was still working on the recipe, I thought it was my fault. It was, but only because I had failed to check the temperature in the freezer. After I did, and had the serviceman come to fix the freezer, the ice cream was spectacular. It was White Chocolate Ice Cream.)

Another thermometer that is essential is labeled "candy-jelly-frosting" or "sugar" thermometer. Even if you never use it for candy or jelly, you need it for making custard-type sauces. You won't have to wonder what it means when a recipe direction says, "Cook until it coats a spoon."

Always bend down to read a thermometer at eye level in order to get a correct reading.

DOUBLE BOILERS

Many of these recipes call for a double boiler. You can buy one in a hardware store or a kitchen shop. The thing to look for is one in which the upper section is not too deep and is smooth (no ridges). I like the Revere Ware double boilers; they come in two sizes, and I use both.

If necessary, you can create your own by placing a heat-proof bowl over a saucepan of shallow hot water. The bowl should be wide enough at the top to rest on the rim of the saucepan, keeping the bowl suspended over (but not touching) the water.

ROLLING PINS

If you have many occasions to use a rolling pin, you really should have different sizes and different shapes. Sometimes a very long, thick, and heavy pin will be best; for other doughs you will want a smaller, lighter one. The French-style rolling pin, which is extralong (20 inches), narrow, and tapered at both ends, is especially good for rolling dough into a round shape, while the straight-sided pin is better for an oblong shape. (I frequently use both shapes to roll out one piece of dough.)

AN 8-QUART MIXING BOWL

I have a large, heavy stainless-steel mixing bowl with an 8-quart capacity. There are several recipes in this book that call for folding in large amounts of beaten egg whites. This is the bowl I use. If you make some of these light and airy recipes (angelfood cake, et cetera), you will find this particular bowl (or another of the same size) extremely helpful. It is easier to fold in ingredients if the bowl is too large rather than too small (see page 31).

CAKE-DECORATING TURNTABLE

If you ice many cakes, or even a few, this is an important piece of equipment. Not that you can't ice a cake without it; you can, but it will not look the same. You will love the smooth, professional-looking results, and the ease of using a turntable. It works on the same principle as a lazy Susan, and although a lazy Susan can be used in place of a turntable, it usually does not turn as easily.

I put the cake on a plate, and then put the plate on a turntable. First put the icing on the sides, and then on the top. Hold a long, narrow metal spatula in your right hand with the blade at about a 30-degree angle to the side or the top of the cake. With your left hand slowly rotate the turntable counterclockwise. Hold your right hand still as the cake turns, and in just a few seconds you will have a smooth, sleek, neat-looking cake. It is easy. Fun. And exciting.

I also use the turntable when trimming and then fluting the edge of a pie crust. (You will wonder how you ever did without it.)

Dean & DeLuca carries cake-decorating turntables (see page 31).

PASTRY BAGS

For many years, the best pastry bags have been those that are made of canvas and are coated on one side only with plastic. Use them with the plastic coating inside. The small opening generally has to be cut a little larger to allow the metal tubes (tips) to fit.

The bags should be washed in hot soapy water, then just set aside to dry. (I usually stand them upright over a glass to dry.)

When filling a pastry bag, always fold down a deep cuff on the outside of the bag. Unless there is someone else to hold it for you, it is generally easiest if you support the bag by placing it in a tall, wide glass or jar. After the bag is filled, unfold the cuff and twist the top closed.

SMALL, NARROW METAL SPATULA

Many of these recipes call for this tool for smoothing the icing around the sides of a cake. Mine is 8 inches long; it has a 4-inch blade and a 4-inch wooden handle. The blade is ⅝ inch wide and has a rounded top. Although it can bend, it is more firm than flexible.

A table knife can sometimes be used in place of this spatula.

Metal spatulas are available in a variety of sizes at kitchen shops.

Techniques

Meticulously precise measurements are essential for good results in baking.

Glass or plastic measuring cups with the measurements marked on the side and the 1-cup line below the top are only for measuring liquids. Do not use them for flour or sugar. With the cup at eye level, fill carefully to exactly the line indicated.

Measuring cups that come in graded sets of four (1/4 cup, 1/3 cup, 1/2 cup, and 1 cup—as well as the 2-cup size that is pretty handy) are for measuring flour, sugar, and other dry ingredients—and for thick sour cream and peanut butter. Fill the cup to overflowing and then scrape or cut off the excess with a dough scraper, a metal spatula, or the flat side of a knife.

Standard measuring spoons must be used for correct measurements. Most come in sets of four (1/4 teaspoon, 1/2 teaspoon, 1 teaspoon, and 1 tablespoon). For dry ingredients, fill the spoon to overflowing and then scrape off the excess with a small metal spatula or the flat side of a knife.

TO ADD DRY INGREDIENTS ALTERNATELY WITH LIQUID

Begin and end with dry. The procedure is generally to add about one third of the dry, then half of the liquid, a second third of the dry, the rest of the liquid, and then the rest of the dry.

Use the lowest speed on an electric mixer (or it can be done by hand, stirring with a wooden or rubber spatula). After each addition, mix only until smooth. If your mixer is the type that allows you to scrape the sides of the bowl with a rubber spatula while the mixer is going, do so to help the mixing along. If the mixer does not allow room, or if it is a hand-held mixer, stop frequently and scrape the bowl with a rubber spatula. Do not beat any more than necessary.

ABOUT FOLDING INGREDIENTS
TOGETHER

Many of these recipes call for folding beaten egg whites and/or whipped cream into another mixture. The whites and/or cream have had air beaten into them, and folding rather than mixing is done in order to retain the air.

This is a very important step and should be done with great care. The knack of doing it well comes with practice and concentration. Remember that you want to incorporate the mixtures without losing any air. That means handle as little as possible.

And it means not to beat the whites or whip the cream until they are actually stiff. If you do, you will have to stir and mix rather than fold, thereby losing the air.

Other don'ts: Do not let beaten whites stand around or they will become dry and will separate. Do not fold whipped cream into a warm mixture or the heat will deflate the cream. Generally it is best to actually stir a bit of the beaten whites or whipped cream into the heavier mixture (to lighten it a bit) before you start to fold in. Then, generally (but not always), it is best not to add all of the remaining light mixture at once; do the folding in a few additions. The first additions should not be folded thoroughly.

For folding ingredients together it is best to use a rubber spatula, and a bowl with a rounded bottom. And it is better if the bowl is too large rather than too small.

Hold the spatula, rounded side toward the bottom and over the middle of the bowl, and cut through to the bottom of the bowl. Bring the spatula toward you against the bottom, then up the side and out, over the top, turning your wrist and the blade as you do this so that the blade is upside down when it comes out over the top. Return the spatula to its original position, then cut through the middle of the mixture again. After each fold, rotate the bowl slightly in order to incorporate all the ingredients as much as possible. Continue only until both mixtures are barely combined.

Occasionally a bit of beaten egg white will rise to the top. If just one or two small pieces rise, instead of folding more, simply smooth over the top gently with the spatula.

If the base mixture has gelatin in it, it should be chilled until it just starts to thicken before beaten whites or whipped cream are folded in, or the heavier mixture will sink.

When folding, it is ideal to have the gelatin mixture, the whipped cream, and/or the beaten whites all at the same consistency (although in some cases this is not possible).

TO MEASURE THE CAPACITY
OF A CAKE PAN

The correct way is by filling the pan to overflowing with a measured amount of water.

The important words are *to overflowing.* It does make sense. Otherwise, you might measure to 1/4 inch from the top and I might measure to 1/2 inch from the top. Therefore, when I give the capacity of a pan, I mean "filled with measured water until it just begins to overflow."

But a problem exists when the manufacturer of a Bundt pan calls it a 12-cup pan and it actually contains 14 cups of water. Therefore, I am referring to that pan, throughout this book, as a 10-inch Bundt pan with a 12- to 14-cup capacity. OK?

TO BUTTER A FANCY-SHAPED
TUBE PAN

If you spread the butter in a fancy tube pan with a piece of crumpled wax paper, it feels clumsy and seems inefficient. If you melt the butter and brush it on, most of the butter runs down to the bottom of the pan. It is best to let the butter stand at room temperature to soften, and then use a pastry brush or crumpled plastic wrap to brush or spread it carefully all over the pan.

TO CUT PAPER FOR LINING
THE BOTTOM OF A PAN

Place the pan right side up on a piece of baking-pan liner paper. With a pencil, trace around the bottom of the pan. Then, with scissors, cut carefully so that the paper will fit neatly, without wrinkling, in the bottom of the pan.

ABOUT PREPARING CAKE PANS

In many recipes, after buttering the pan, I dust it with bread crumbs because there is often less chance of sticking if you use crumbs rather than flour. The crumbs should be fine and dry. They may be homemade (see below), but I always have store-bought ones on hand. If you use store-bought crumbs, be sure to buy the ones marked "plain" or "unseasoned."

To prepare a tube pan: When directions call for buttering the pan and then coating it with crumbs, lift the crumbs with your fingers and sprinkle them around the tube.

In none of these recipes do I list in the ingredients the butter, flour, or crumbs that are used to prepare the cake pans. I don't think it is necessary to measure these ingredients.

TO PREPARE A COOKIE SHEET

For a cookie sheet it is best to use cold butter right from the refrigerator. You want only a thin layer, which is easier to make with cold butter. With a piece of crumpled plastic wrap, spread the butter all over the sheet.

Now, to flour the sheet, sift flour along a long side of the sheet. Then, over the sink, tilt the sheet toward the other long side and tap it to shake the flour down to cover the sheet. Shake off excess.

HOMEMADE BREAD CRUMBS

Use sliced white bread with or without the crusts. Place the slices in a single layer on cookie sheets in a 225-degree oven and bake until the bread is completely dry and crisp (if the bread is so stale that it is completely dry, it is not necessary to bake it). Break the slices into coarse pieces and grind them in a food processor or blender until the crumbs are rather fine, but not as fine as powder.

CHOCOLATE CRUMBS AND CHOCOLATE FLOUR

To coat a pan for a dark cake it is best to use dark crumbs or dark flour. Simply mix enough unsweetened cocoa powder into fine dry bread crumbs or flour to give the mixture a medium-brown color. It is handy to keep a jar of each of these already mixed. They last well.

TO WASH STRAWBERRIES

Remove them from their boxes as soon as possible. Place them in a single layer on a tray lined with paper towels and refrigerate until you are ready to wash them. They can be washed many hours before serving or shortly before.

Fill a large bowl with cool water. Place a wide strainer in the bowl so that the rim of the strainer rests on the rim of the bowl. Place the berries in the strainer, and raise and lower it into the water a few times to rinse the berries. Then lift the strainer, pour the water out of the bowl, and replace the strainer on the rim of the bowl.

If you are going to remove the green hulls, do it now; then place the berries in a single layer on a tray covered with paper towels and refrigerate uncovered.

TO FAN OUT A STRAWBERRY

This is a chic new way of cutting a berry when it is to be used for decoration. It does indeed look very pretty and dainty, and dressy.

Wash and drain the berry, but do not remove the green hull. Stand it on a cutting board, pointed end up. With a sharp knife cut down toward the bottom—without cutting through the bottom; cut into parallel vertical slices ⅛ inch wide.

And then, with your fingertips, fan out the slices at the top (without separating them at the bottom).

TO WASH BLUEBERRIES

They should be washed ahead of time to allow them to dry. Fill a large bowl with cold water. Place the berries in a wide strainer or a colander and lower it into the water; let the rim of the strainer or colander rest on the rim of the bowl. Pick out any loose stems and leaves or green berries. Raise the strainer or colander from the water to drain, and repeat as necessary with clean water until the water remains clean (no sand) after the berries are removed. Spread the berries in a single layer on a tray lined with paper towels and let stand, uncovered, at room temperature or in the refrigerator to drain and dry.

TO GRATE LEMON OR ORANGE RIND

It is best to use firm, deep-colored, thick-skinned fruit. And it is best if the fruit is cold; the rind is firmer and grates better. Use a standing metal grater—usually they have four sides, although some are round. Hold the grater up to the light and look at the shapes of the openings from the back or the inside. You should use the small holes that are round, not diamond-shaped. Place the grater on a piece of baking-pan liner paper or wax paper on the work surface. Hold the grater firmly in place with your left hand. With your right hand hold the fruit cupped in your palm at the top of the grater. Move your fingers back a bit so that the tips don't get scraped. Now, press the fruit down toward the bottom of the grater. Press firmly but don't overdo it—all you want is the zest (the thin, colored outside part). Do not work over the same spot on the fruit or you will be grating the white underneath; rotate the fruit in your hand as you press against the grater. Remove the gratings that stick to the inside of the grater with a rubber spatula.

It is easy. But it is easier with a food processor.

With a vegetable parer remove the thin, colored rind from the fruit, cut it into 1/2-inch pieces, and place the pieces in the bowl of a processor fitted with the metal chopping blade. Add some of the granulated sugar from the recipe (about 1/2 cup of sugar is enough for one or two pieces of fruit—but it does no harm if you use a bit more or less sugar). Process for 30 to 40 seconds, until the rind is fine.

ABOUT DECORATING CAKES

Cake decorating is an art, and it can be just as creative as painting. But to me, the pure, untouched simplicity of a smooth, shiny chocolate glaze—or a topping of barely firm whipped cream—is perfection, and adding anything to it would detract from an already perfect work of art. The same goes for an uniced pound cake or a loaf cake. Please don't feel that every cake needs decoration; simplicity is often decoration enough. Anything more might be gilding the lily.

Very often a few small, beautiful fresh flowers are a wonderful decoration. Either place them on the plate alongside the cake, or cut the stems short and place a few (or only one) directly on top of the cake, either resting on it or inserted into it.

A red rose on a chocolate cake is especially gorgeous.

HOW TO PREPARE THE PLATE BEFORE YOU ICE THE CAKE

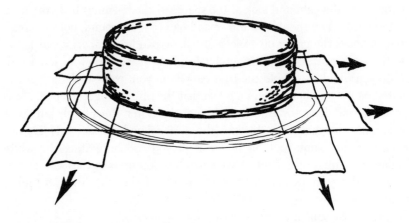

This is done to keep any icing off the plate. It will result in a clean, neat, professional-looking finished product.

Begin by tearing off a 10-inch piece of wax paper. Fold it crosswise into four equal strips (fold in half and then in half again), then cut through the folds with a sharp knife, making four 10-by-3-inch strips. (If the icing is very thick/sticky, like a marshmallow or 7-minute icing, it is better to use baking-pan liner paper instead of wax paper because it is stronger. It is also better if you cut the strips a bit longer and a bit wider, but not too large or they will get in the way while you are icing the cake.)

Lay the strips in a square pattern around the rim of a wide, flat cake plate. Then put the cake on the plate and check to be sure that the papers are under the cake all the way around.

After the cake is iced (before the icing hardens), remove the papers by slowly pulling each one out toward a narrow end.

IF YOU PLAN TO TRANSPORT A CAKE

To transport a cake that is iced, here's a trick I learned during the years when I made desserts at home and my husband took them in a station wagon or a boat to his restaurant: Melt about ½ ounce of semisweet chocolate and place it in the middle of the cake plate. Place the cake directly on the chocolate, which will act as a paste to keep the cake from sliding.

ABOUT WRAPPING COOKIES

Unless I am baking cookies to serve right away, I wrap them in clear cellophane. It gives them an attractive and professional look, keeps them fresh, and makes them easy to pack for the freezer, lunch box, or picnic basket, and easy to handle for mailing or to give as a gift.

Clear cellophane is hard to find. But you can get it from Dean & DeLuca (see page 31). It comes on a roll—20 inches wide and 100 feet long—in a box with a cutter edge.

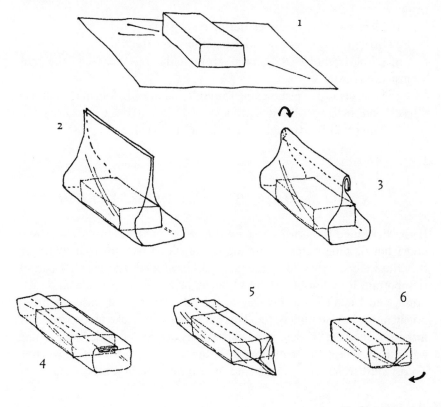

If you cannot get cellophane, wax paper or aluminum foil is easier to handle than plastic wrap (which will drive you crazy).

It is easier to cut cellophane with a knife than with scissors. First, cut off a long piece (on the cutting edge of the box), fold it in half crosswise, cut through the fold with a long knife, fold again and cut again, and continue to fold and cut until you have pieces the right width. Then fold and cut in the opposite direction. The final size of the pieces depends on the size of the cookies. If the size is close but a bit too long or too wide, do not cut the pieces individually (it takes too long). Instead, place the whole pile in front of you and fold one side of the entire pile to the size you want. Place your left hand firmly on the pile, holding the folded side down and at the same time holding the pile so that the papers do not slip out of place. With your right hand cut through the fold with the knife. (If the pile is very large, cut through about one or two dozen pieces at a time.)

Bar cookies should be wrapped individually. Small drop cookies, thin rolled cookies, and some ice-box cookies may be wrapped two to a package, placed with their bottoms together.

Wrap one cookie as a sample to be sure the papers are the right size.

Spread out as many pieces of cellophane as you have room for, or as many as you have cookies for.

1. Place a cookie in the center of each paper.

2. Bring the two narrow sides together over the top.

3, 4. Fold over twice so that the second fold brings the cellophane tight against the cookie.

5. Now, instead of just tucking the ends underneath, fold in the corners of each end, making a triangular point.

6. Then fold the triangles down under the cookie.

HOW TO WASH A PASTRY BRUSH

If you have used the brush for a sugar glaze or preserves, just rinse it well under hot running water, separating the bristles a bit with your fingers so that the water reaches all of them. If you have used it to butter a pan, it is important to remove every bit of butter or it will become rancid on the brush, and I don't know any way to get rid of that. First rinse the brush briefly under hot running water. Then rub it well on a cake of soap, rubbing first one side of the bristles and then the other. Rinse well under hot running water, then repeat the soaping and rinsing once or twice more to be sure. To dry, just let it stand, bristles up, in a dish drain or a glass.

ABOUT FREEZING CAKES

I don't think that any baked cake tastes as good after freezing as when it is fresh (except cheesecakes). However, if it is frozen for only a short time (a few days or weeks), the difference might be infinitesimal. If it is a big help to you to prepare it ahead, do. But if you have your choice, fresh is best.

If you want to ice a cake first and then freeze it, it may be frozen directly on the cake plate and left on the plate. Or, to keep the cake from sticking to the plate, it may be placed on a round of wax paper or baking-pan liner paper (cut to fit the bottom of the cake) on the plate, and then removed from the plate and wrapped when it is frozen. Freeze until the icing is firm, then wrap the cake airtight with plastic wrap and, if you wish, rewrap it in foil or in a freezer bag.

Everything should be thawed completely before it is unwrapped. (Foods sweat while thawing. If they thaw while they are still wrapped, the moisture will form on the outside of the wrapping; if they are unwrapped before they thaw, the moisture will form on the food itself, and that could spoil the looks of a beautiful smooth icing.)

However, if you have a cake in the freezer and you want some right away, unwrap it, cut it, and serve it. Many cakes are delicious frozen (especially chocolate cakes with little or no flour—and brownies). Just don't let the rest of the cake stand around uncovered; rewrap it immediately.

Label packages—if not, you might wind up with a freezer full of UFOs (Unidentified Frozen Objects).

ABOUT FREEZING COOKIES

Most cookies freeze quite well (but, like cakes, for a limited time only). It is always extremely handy (it is a luxury) to have cookies in the freezer for unexpected company; they usually thaw quickly, and many can be served frozen.

(Almost always, when I need a quick—or not so quick—gift for someone, my first thought is cookies. And if they are in the freezer, individually wrapped in clear cellophane, all I have to do is plan some attractive packaging for them.)

The same rule about thawing cakes applies to cookies—thaw before unwrapping (if possible).

Any cake or cookie that can be frozen can be thawed and refrozen—even several times. I do it often, because I would rather refreeze it than let it stand around and get stale.

ABOUT CUTTING CAKES, PIES, AND BAR COOKIES

Cakes and cookies should be cut carefully and neatly with a very sharp knife that is long enough. You might not use the full length of the blade, but it gives leverage. Some cakes cut best with a sawing motion—try it. Some cut best with a serrated knife—try that also.

If it is a round cake or a pie, always start cutting each pie-shaped wedge from the exact center. Mark the center with the tip of the knife. Or, to find the exact center, lightly score the cake or pie in half first in one direction and then in the opposite direction. Then, if you don't trust yourself to cut freehand, mark each quarter lightly with the tip of the knife, marking the outside edge into 2 to 6 portions, depending on the size of the cake or pie and the size of the portions. But always keep your eye on the center so that the slices all radiate out from there.

If it is a loaf cake or a square cake, it may be a big help to use a ruler and toothpicks to mark the portions.

Brownies and many other bar cookies cut best if they are very cold or almost frozen. Work on a cutting surface that is too large rather than too small. Use a very sharp knife. Or a serrated one.

Occasionally, for certain cakes that stick to the knife, it is best if the blade is hot and wet. In the kitchen, work next to the sink and hold the blade under hot running water before making each cut. In the dining room, have a tall pitcher of hot water and dip the blade into it before each cut. Sometimes it is best to wipe the blade after each cut.

Most important, take your time. And if it isn't going well, remember all the options—try a different knife, or a wet blade, or simply wipe the blade.

A FINAL WORD

I once put a cake in the oven and then realized that I had forgotten to use the baking powder the recipe called for. (The cake had beaten egg whites in it, and there was no way I could still add the baking powder.) I learned the hard way (more than once) that it is necessary to organize all the ingredients listed in a recipe—line them up in the order called for—before actually starting to mix. As you use an ingredient, set the jar or box aside. That way, nothing should be left on the work surface when you are through. A quick look during and after mixing will let you know if something was left out; if you are lucky, before it is too late.

Dean & DeLuca is a wonderful shop in New York City that carries specialty foods and housewares (especially for the kitchen and dining room). I am happy to say that my friends at Dean & DeLuca have agreed to carry every cake pan I used in the recipes in this book, plus several hard-to-find kitchen and food items that I especially like.

Either go there, call them, or write to them.

Dean & DeLuca, 560 Broadway, New York, New York 10012 (1-800-221-7714 or 212-431-1691).

Here is a list of every item mentioned in this book that they carry:

Loaf pans: (5-cup cap.) 8 by 4 by 2½ inches
        (6-cup cap.) 8½ by 4½ by 2¾ inches (by
          Chicago Metallic)
        (8-cup cap.) 9 by 5 by 3 or 2¾ inches
        (8-cup cap.) 10¼ by 3¾ by 3¼ inches
        (8-cup cap.) black metal—9 by 5 by 3½ inches
          with a 7-by-3-inch base (I use this for brioche)
        (9-cup cap.) 10½ by 4½ by 3 inches
        (10-cup cap.) 13¾ by 4¼ by 2¾ inches
Tube pans: (10-cup cap.) 8½ by 3¾ inches (Kugelhopf by
          Kaiser)
        (12- to 14-cup cap.) 10 by 3¾ inches (One piece
          nonstick Bundt)
        (12-cup cap.) 10 by 4 inches (Swirl design)
        (13½-cup cap.) 8½ by 4½ inches (One-piece
          nonstick Bundt by La Forme)
        (18-cup cap.) 10 by 4¼ inches (One piece;
          nonstick; no design)
        (18-cup cap.) 10 by 4¼ inches (Two-piece
          angelfood pan; no design)

LA FORME BUNDT PAN

12-CUP TUBE PAN
WITH A SWIRL DESIGN

Round layer-cake pans: 8 or 9 inches by 2 inches
Square cake pan: 8 by 8 by 2 inches
9 by 9 by 2 inches (Magic Line)
Oblong pan: 13 by 9 by 2 inches (Magic Line)
13 by 9 by 2 inches (Wear-Ever)
Jelly-roll pan: 15½ by 10½ by 1 inch
Cheesecake pan: 8 by 3 inches (round; one piece)
Springform pan: 8 by 3 inches
9 by 3 inches
Pyrex pie plate: 9 inches round
Individual black metal tartlet pans: 4⅝ by ¾ inch
Giant muffin pan: for 6 muffins, each 4 by 2 inches (Rowoco)
Paper liners for giant muffin pan (Rowoco)
Miniature muffin pans: 12 muffins, each 1¾ by ¾ inch
(Nonstick, by Foley—"Great Cooks")

Cherry pitter
Stainless steel mixing bowl: 8-quart cap.
Individual white porcelain soufflé dishes: (⅔-cup cap.) 3¼ by
1½ inches (Pillivuyt)
Clear glass soufflé dish: (8-cup cap.) 6½ by 3½ inches
Clear cellophane
Baking-pan liner (a.k.a. baking parchment)
Cake-decorating turntables
5-inch round cookie cutter
Chocolate-roll board
Slicer knife: serrated 12-inch blade

Food Items:
Tahitian vanilla beans
Mascarpone cheese
Callebaut chocolate
Valrhona chocolate
Maillard chocolate
Crystal sugar
Crystallized ginger
Mixed diced candied fruit (for Panforte) available all year
Dried sour cherries

Chocolate Cakes

Rum Chocolate Truffle Roll

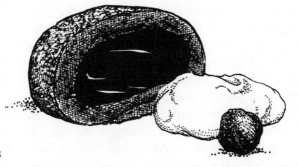

ABOUT 12 PORTIONS

When I serve this the words I hear between moans and groans (of joy) are illegal, immoral, sexual, sensuous, *and* more, more, more. *A dark-colored, light-textured, moist sponge cake is rolled around a dense, intense chocolate-truffle mixture that is loaded with rum. It is served with whipped cream, a chocolate truffle or two (which are part of this recipe), and possibly some fresh berries. An exciting chocolate experience.*

CHOCOLATE SPONGE ROLL

¼ cup sifted unsweetened cocoa powder
    (preferably Dutch-process)
2 tablespoons sifted cake flour
2 tablespoons sifted cornstarch
4 eggs graded "large," separated
¼ cup granulated sugar
1 teaspoon dry instant espresso or coffee
½ teaspoon vanilla extract
¼ teaspoon salt
¼ teaspoon cream of tartar
Additional cocoa powder (to be used after
    the cake is baked)

Adjust an oven rack to the center of the oven and preheat the oven to 350 degrees. Line a 15½-by-10½-by-1-inch jelly-roll pan (see page 30) as follows: Place the pan upside down on a work surface. Tear off a length of regular-weight aluminum foil about 18 inches long. Center the foil shiny side down over the pan. With your hands, press down on the sides and corners of the foil to shape it to the pan. Remove the foil. Turn the pan right side up, let water run into the pan, pour out the water but do not dry the pan (a wet pan holds the foil in place), and carefully place the shaped foil in the pan, pressing it gently to fit the pan. To butter the foil, use room-temperature (not melted) butter and spread it with crumpled plastic wrap all over the bottom and sides. Set the pan aside.

Sift together the cocoa, flour, and cornstarch (from one piece of wax paper to another) five or six times, and then set the mixture aside in the sifter on a piece of wax paper.

In the small bowl of an electric mixer, beat the yolks to mix well. Gradually add about half (⅛ cup) of the sugar (reserve remaining sugar), the espresso or coffee, and the vanilla, and continue to beat for several minutes until the mixture is pale, thick, and forms a wide ribbon when the beaters are raised. Remove the bowl from the mixer.

If you do not have an additional small bowl and an additional set of beaters for the mixer, transfer the yolk mixture to a similar-sized bowl and set aside. Wash and dry the bowl and beaters.

In the clean small bowl of the mixer, with clean beaters beat the egg whites with the salt until foamy. Add the cream of tartar and beat at high speed until the whites hold a soft point when the beaters are raised. On moderate speed gradually add the remaining ⅛ cup of sugar. Then beat on high speed again until the whites hold a straight point when the beaters are raised, but not until they are dry.

Remove the bowl from the mixer and with a rubber spatula—in three additions—briefly fold the whites into the yolks without being thorough. Turn into a larger bowl. Sift the dry ingredients over the top about one-third at a time, and gently fold together with a rubber spatula. Do not handle any more than necessary. When the dry ingredients are just incorporated (although the color will still be uneven), turn the mixture into the prepared pan, forming several large mounds rather than just one (the less you have to spread the batter the better). Then, with the back of a large spoon, gently smooth the batter.

Bake 12 to 13 minutes until the top springs back when gently pressed with a fingertip. Do not overbake.

When you remove the pan from the oven, immediately cover it with aluminum foil. (I use heavy-duty foil here, although regular weight may be used. The heavy-duty foil will rest on the sides of the pan, suspended above the cake; regular weight sinks and touches the cake, which might cling slightly when the foil is removed. But if so, that is no problem.) Use pot holders and fold the foil down securely around the rim to make the pan airtight. (This keeps the steam in the pan and keeps the cake moist.)

Let stand until cool.

Then remove the foil from the top of the pan. Through a fine strainer, strain cocoa generously over the top of the cake. Cover the cake with a length of plastic wrap, and over that place a flat-sided cookie sheet. Turn the pan and the sheet upside down. Remove the pan and gently peel off the foil. Cover the bottom of the cake with another length of plastic wrap.

Gently roll the cake with both pieces of plastic wrap, rolling from one long side to another. The cocoa side of the cake will be on the outside of the roll. The seam should be on the bottom. Let stand.

RUM CHOCOLATE TRUFFLE MIXTURE

16 ounces semisweet chocolate
¾ cup heavy cream
3 ounces (¾ stick) unsalted butter at room
    temperature
½ cup dark rum

Chop the chocolate medium-fine and set aside. In a 2½- to 3-quart heavy saucepan over moderate heat, bring the cream just to a boil. Add the chocolate, remove from the heat, and whisk until melted and smooth. Add the butter and stir until melted. Gradually mix in the rum.

Let stand at room temperature, stirring occasionally with a rubber spatula until cool.

Then place in the refrigerator and stir and scrape the bottom and sides frequently for about 25 minutes until the mixture thickens enough to be spread. It should be firm enough not to run but not so firm that it will be difficult to spread on the tender cake. If you clear a path with a rubber spatula on the bottom of the pan and it just stays clear, it is ready.

Remove and reserve ½ cup of the mixture (for truffles).

Unroll the cake and remove the plastic wrap that was inside the roll, leaving the cake cocoa side down on the plastic wrap. Spoon the remaining truffle mixture along the long edge of the cake that was on the inside of the roll (it should be the edge that is closest to you). Then spread the mixture toward the farther long side, making a very thin layer for the last inch or so, and actually stopping it just short of the farther side.

Using the plastic wrap under the cake to help roll it, start at the long side close to you and roll the cake until it is rolled just past the farther long side (the seam should be on the bottom). Let the cake stand, and shape the truffles now (see below), before the mixture hardens.

Let the cake stand at room temperature for about an hour until it is firm enough to be transferred to a long platter or a chocolate-roll board (see page 31). I find it easiest to transfer the cake roll with my hands, but you might prefer to use a flat-sided cookie sheet as a spatula.

Then sprinkle the top of the roll generously with unsweetened cocoa powder through a fine strainer. Brush excess cocoa off the platter or board. Let stand at room temperature.

Serve at room temperature.

To slice, dip a sharp knife into hot water before cutting each slice. Each portion may be a slice about 1 inch thick or two thinner slices.

Serve with a generous mound of whipped cream (see below) alongside each portion and place a truffle on each plate.

TRUFFLES
(ABOUT 12)

Spoon the reserved mixture by slightly rounded teaspoonfuls onto wax paper. Let stand at room temperature until just dry enough to be handled (although it will be soft and tender).

Meanwhile, place a mound of cocoa powder on a length of wax paper and have another piece of wax paper ready for the finished truffles.

With your fingers, or with a wide metal spatula, pick up a mound, press it with your fingertips into an uneven truffle shape, roll it in the cocoa, and then place it on wax paper for several hours to set and dry. Do not refrigerate.

WHIPPED CREAM

2 cups whipping cream
⅓ cup confectioners sugar
1½ teaspoons vanilla extract

In a chilled bowl with chilled beaters whip the cream with the sugar and vanilla only until it holds a soft shape. Do not whip until stiff.

If you whip the cream ahead of time, cover and refrigerate. Just before serving, if the cream has separated a bit, whisk it briefly with a wire whisk only until incorporated.

The Hôtel de Crillon's Chocolate Cake

10 TO 12 PORTIONS

Cake? It looks like a cake—a shallow single-layer cake—but it tastes like the best-ever fudge candy. Plain, pure chocolate fudge.

This is famous at the Hôtel de Crillon, one of the grandest hotels in Paris. It could not be more simple, more sophisticated, more chic, or more chocolate. And—would you believe?—it is ridiculously easy to make. (It is all mixed in the top of a double boiler.) It must be made a day ahead, refrigerated overnight, and served cold.

8 ounces bittersweet or semisweet chocolate
8 ounces (2 sticks) unsalted butter
1 cup granulated sugar
4 eggs graded "large"
Unsweetened cocoa powder (to be sifted on top after the cake is baked and chilled)
About 1 ounce bittersweet or semisweet chocolate (to make chocolate shavings)

Adjust a rack one-third up from the bottom of the oven and preheat the oven to 325 degrees. Butter a 9-inch round layer-cake pan (see page 30). Line the bottom with a round of baking-pan liner paper cut to fit. Butter the paper. Dust all over with chocolate flour (see page 21) and turn upside down over paper to shake out excess. Set aside.

On a chopping surface, with a long and heavy knife cut the chocolate into medium-sized pieces and place in the top of a large double boiler. Cut each stick of butter into four pieces and add to the chocolate. Add the sugar. Place over hot water on moderate heat and stir frequently until the chocolate and butter are melted and the mixture is smooth. (You will still see the grains of sugar.)

Remove the top of the double boiler from the hot water and, one at a time, add the eggs, mixing them in with a heavy wire whisk.

Pour the mixture into the prepared cake pan. Place the pan in a jelly-roll pan and place in the oven. Then add a scant inch of hot water to the jelly-roll pan.

Bake for 1 hour and 15 minutes. Then, carefully (using a flat-sided cookie sheet as a spatula), remove the pan from the hot water and let stand for a few hours until completely cool.

With a small sharp knife, carefully cut around the rim to loosen the sides of the cake from the pan.

To remove the cake from the pan, cover the pan with a flat cake plate or a serving board and turn the pan and plate or board upside down. It will most probably be necessary to bang the pan and the plate or board several times, firmly, on the work surface. The cake will finally come out of the pan. Do not remove the paper lining, and do not worry if the sides look a bit ragged. (The cake will be less than an inch high, and the inside of the cake will still be quite soft.)

Refrigerate overnight.

Then peel off the paper lining. If necessary, to smooth the sides, let the cake stand at room temperature for 30 to 45 minutes, until the sides are soft enough to be smoothed with a table knife or a small metal spatula, and return the cake to the refrigerator.

To sprinkle cocoa over the top (this can be done hours before serving if you wish, or just before), it is best first to transfer the cake to a large piece of wax paper or baking-pan liner paper. Use a large metal spatula or a flat-sided cookie sheet as a spatula, and transfer the cake, placing it crust side down. Then, through a fine strainer, sprinkle a solid layer of cocoa over the cake. Return the cake to the plate or board and refrigerate.

ESPRESSO CREAM

1 cup whipping cream
3 tablespoons confectioners sugar
3 teaspoons instant espresso or coffee powder
½ teaspoon vanilla extract

In a chilled small bowl of the electric mixer, with chilled beaters whip the cream with the sugar, espresso or coffee powder, and vanilla only until the cream holds a soft shape. Think "sauce," not whipped cream.

If you whip the cream ahead of time, refrigerate it and then, just before serving, whisk it a bit with a small wire whisk to ensure a smooth texture.

To make chocolate shavings, work with a vegetable parer over a piece of paper. Shave about an ounce of chocolate into uneven shavings. (If you wish, this can be done ahead of time and can wait either at room temperature or, if the room is warm, in the refrigerator.)

When serving the cake, place a mound of the cream on each plate alongside each portion of cake.

With a large spoon or a wide metal spatula, sprinkle the shaved chocolate generously onto the cake, and also sprinkle just a bit of it onto the cream and even onto the plate itself. (If you are serving the cake at the table, the shaved chocolate can be served in a small pitcher and poured on. Or it can be served in a small bowl and spooned on.)

Sonrisa Chocolate Cake

8 TO 10 PORTIONS

In beautiful Rancho Santa Fe in Southern California, there is a charming little bakery named Sonrisa. It would be the dream place of everyone who says, "I would like to have my own little bakery." (Me too.) The young couple who own Sonrisa, our good friends Linn Hadden and Bruce Munter, do almost everything themselves. Bruce makes the cakes and breads; Linn makes the bran muffins, brownies, and cookies, and she makes the gorgeous flower arrangements with flowers from their own garden. Sitting there in that delightful spot with a cup of cappuccino and a delicious pastry and watching the action is one of my favorite pastimes.

This flourless chocolate cake is one of Sonrisa's most popular cakes. Although it is never on display, the customers know about it and ask for it, and Bruce cannot keep up with the demand. It is a single-layer cake, dense, rich, moist, and fudgy. (Actually, it is a chocolate mousse that is baked in a cake pan.)

Bruce and I both use Callebaut bittersweet chocolate for this. It is available from many specialty shops (see page 13).

You will need an 8-by-3-inch springform pan (see page 30).

10 ounces bittersweet or semisweet chocolate
4 ounces (1 stick) unsalted butter
6 eggs graded "large," separated
1 cup granulated sugar
1 tablespoon dark rum
Confectioners sugar (to be sifted on top after the cake is baked)

Adjust a rack one-third up from the bottom of the oven and preheat the oven to 375 degrees. Butter an 8-by-3-inch springform pan. Line the bottom of the pan with a round of baking-pan liner paper cut to fit. Butter the paper and dust the pan all over with flour or chocolate flour (see page 21), invert over paper, and tap lightly to shake out excess. Then, with your fingertips, sprinkle a thin layer of fine dry bread crumbs over the bottom of the pan (to make it easier to remove the cake from the pan).

The cake will be baked in a larger pan of shallow hot water; to prevent the water from leaking into the pan, it is necessary to wrap the pan in heavy-duty aluminum foil. Cut two 15-inch squares of heavy-duty foil. Place one on top of the other. Place the pan in the middle of the foil. With your hands, bring up the foil all around the pan, gathering it at the top and pressing it firmly to fit the pan. Then fold down any foil that extends above the rim of the pan, folding it onto itself on the outside of the pan. Or with scissors cut away the foil that extends above the top of the pan. Set the pan aside.

On a board, with a long and heavy knife cut the chocolate into medium or small pieces, and cut the butter into six or eight pieces.

Place the chocolate and butter in the top of a large double boiler over warm water on moderate heat, and let cook until partially melted. Then stir until completely melted and smooth. Remove the top of the double boiler and set aside.

In the small bowl of an electric mixer, beat the egg yolks with ¾ cup of the sugar (reserve the remaining ¼ cup sugar) on high speed for several minutes until the mixture forms a wide ribbon when the beaters are raised.

Transfer the mixture to the large bowl of the electric mixer. On low speed add the chocolate (which may still be warm) and the rum and beat, scraping the bowl with a rubber spatula, until smooth. Remove the bowl from the mixer and set aside.

If you do not have an additional small bowl and beaters for the mixer, wash and dry the bowl and beaters (or use another bowl and portable beaters). In the clean small bowl with clean beaters, beat the egg whites until they hold a soft shape. On moderate speed gradually add the remaining ¼ cup of sugar, and then, on high speed, beat until the whites just hold a straight shape when the beaters are raised. Do not beat any more than necessary.

Stir one fourth of the whites into the chocolate mixture. Then, in two additions, fold in the remaining whites (with a large rubber spatula, if possible) only until just barely blended. Do not fold any more than necessary.

Transfer the batter to the prepared pan. Place the pan in another pan that is wider but not deeper. Place in the oven and pour hot water 1 inch deep into the wider pan.

Bake for 15 minutes. Reduce the temperature to 350 degrees and bake for 15 minutes more. Then reduce the temperature to 275 degrees and bake for 30 minutes more (total baking time is 1 hour).

Turn off the oven and prop open the oven door a few inches. Let the cake stand in the oven for 30 minutes.

Then remove the pan from the water, remove the foil, and let stand for several hours at room temperature until completely cool.

Removing this cake from the pan is delicate work. Be very careful. First use a sharp knife with a firm blade to cut around the cake, always pressing the blade against the pan. Then remove the sides of the pan and, immediately, use a small and narrow metal spatula or a table knife to smooth the sides of the cake. Cover the cake with an inverted cake plate and carefully turn the cake and the plate upside down. Very carefully remove the bottom of the pan and slowly peel off the paper lining. Leave the cake upside down.

To decorate the top, cut seven strips of baking-pan liner paper or wax paper ½ inch wide and slightly more than 8 inches long. Place the papers evenly in one direction ½ inch apart on the top of the cake. Sprinkle confectioners sugar generously through a fine strainer onto the cake. Carefully remove the papers, leaving a striped pattern. Brush excess sugar off the plate.

Let the cake stand at room temperature, and serve it at room temperature, with a mound of cold whipped cream on the side.

WHIPPED CREAM

1 cup whipping cream
½ teaspoon vanilla extract
2 tablespoons confectioners sugar

In a chilled bowl with chilled beaters whip the cream with the vanilla and sugar until it holds a soft shape; it should not be stiff. Refrigerate the whipped cream until serving time. If the cream has separated a bit while standing, whisk it slightly with a wire whisk before serving.

NOTE: At Sonrisa the cake is baked without the water bath, and the results are radically different. Without the water, the cake rises high, forms a hard crust, and then cracks and sinks unevenly. It looks as though it had been in an earthquake. Therefore, at Sonrisa, this is called Chocolate Earthquake.

Gustaf Anders's Chocolate Cake

12 TO 16 PORTIONS

From Gustaf Anders's outstanding restaurant in Santa Ana, California. (At one dinner there we had a memorable parsley salad—one I had never heard of before—of fresh, crisp parsley leaves mixed with chopped sun-dried tomatoes and fresh basil, with a sharp Roquefort and garlic dressing. Delicious.) His cake is sensational enough to serve at the chocolate lovers' annual hoedown but incredibly easy and foolproof (no folding in beaten egg whites). It is a shallow single layer—dense, dark, rich, moist, and fudgelike (almost like chocolate truffles)—covered with a dark chocolate icing and chocolate shavings.

At the restaurant they make this with Callebaut bittersweet chocolate (see page 13); I have made it several times with a variety of chocolates and it is always great.

The cake can be served as it is, but such dense chocolate is always better with whipped cream and, if possible, fresh berries on the side.

8 ounces semisweet chocolate
8 ounces (2 sticks) unsalted butter
1 cup granulated sugar
⅛ teaspoon salt
1 teaspoon vanilla extract
6 eggs graded "large"
½ cup sifted unbleached flour

Adjust a rack one-third up from the bottom of the oven and preheat the oven to 375 degrees. Butter a 9-inch springform pan, which may be either 2 or 3 inches deep (see page 30) although the cake will be only 1¼ inches high. Line the bottom of the pan with a round of baking-pan liner paper cut to fit, butter the paper, and dust all over with chocolate bread crumbs (see page 21). Shake out excess crumbs over paper and set the pan aside.

Cut or break the chocolate into pieces and cut the butter into pieces. Place them together in a heavy saucepan over low heat and stir almost constantly until melted.

Transfer the mixture to the large bowl of an electric mixer and beat until smooth. Then beat in the sugar, salt, vanilla, and—one at a time—the eggs, beating well after each addition. On low speed add the flour and beat only until incorporated.

Turn into the prepared pan. Bake for 30 minutes or until the middle of the cake barely moves when you shake the pan a bit. Do not overbake.

Turn the heat off, open the oven door, and let the cake cool in the open oven for 10 minutes. Then finish cooling in the room. (The top of the cake will crack—it is OK.)

The cake is tender and delicate at this stage; if you can let it stand a little longer after it has cooled it will become a bit stronger.

With a narrow metal spatula or a table knife, carefully cut around the sides of the cake, cutting up and down and pressing the blade against the pan. Release and remove the sides of the pan. Cover the cake with a flat cake plate or a serving board. Turn the plate or board and the cake upside down. Remove the bottom of the pan and the paper lining. Leave the cake upside down. With a pastry brush, brush away loose crumbs from the sides of the cake and the plate. (The sides of the cake will not be perfectly straight—it is OK.)

To protect the plate while icing the cake, slide five or six strips of baking-pan liner paper (each about 7 by 3 inches) under the edges of the cake (you can gently raise the edges a bit with a wide metal spatula as you slide the papers under). The cake should touch the papers all around. If you have a cake-decorating turntable, place the cake plate on it.

ICING

1½ cups whipping cream
6 ounces semisweet chocolate
1 tablespoon unsalted butter
3 to 4 ounces milk chocolate (for shavings)
Confectioners sugar (for topping)

Pour the cream into a heavy 1½- to 2-quart saucepan. Bring to a low boil over moderate heat, uncovered. Adjust the heat to let the cream simmer, and let simmer, stirring occasionally (stir more frequently toward the end to prevent burning), until it is reduced to ¾ cup—this can take 30 to 40 minutes. Meanwhile, cut or break the chocolate into pieces. After the cream is reduced, add the chocolate and butter and stir until melted. Transfer to the small bowl of an electric mixer.

Place the bowl in the freezer for about 10 minutes until the mixture is cold and starts to set around the rim (but it must still be soft in the center).

Beat the icing at high speed until it is about as firm as soft whipped cream. Do not overbeat. The icing will continue to thicken as it stands.

Remove the bowl from the mixer and, with a small, narrow metal spatula or a table knife, spread the icing on the sides of the cake to fill in any hollows and make the sides straight, and then form a smooth layer of icing all around the sides.

Then, with a long, narrow metal spatula, spread the remaining icing over the top of the cake. The sides and the top may be smooth or swirled.

The shavings may be made now or later, although it is easier if they are made ahead of time and refrigerated. Either way, work over wax paper or baking-pan liner paper. With a vegetable parer scrape the milk chocolate into uneven shavings.

With a large serving spoon sprinkle the shavings all over the top of the cake.

Then, through a fine strainer, sprinkle confectioners sugar all over the shavings.

Gently remove the paper strips by pulling each one slowly toward a narrow end.

Let stand at room temperature until serving time. Make the portions small.

WHIPPED CREAM AND BERRIES

2 cups whipping cream
¼ cup confectioners sugar
1 teaspoon vanilla extract
Optional: 2 pints fresh raspberries, or washed,
    hulled, and cut-up fresh strawberries

In a chilled bowl with chilled beaters whip the cream with the sugar and vanilla only until the cream holds a soft shape—it should not be stiff. If you whip the cream ahead of time, refrigerate it. And then, before serving, if it has separated a bit, whisk it slightly with a wire whisk until incorporated.

To serve, place a spoonful of the cream on one side of each portion of cake, and a spoonful of the berries on the other side.

French Chocolate Cake with Two Sauces

This is 1-inch high, coal black, rich/dense/fudgelike, with a dark and shiny chocolate glaze. It is served with two sauces, one white (white chocolate) and one red (cranberry). It is gorgeous to look at, and tantalizing to taste. This is all quite quick and easy, but is appropriate for the fanciest dinner party.

8 PORTIONS

6 ounces semisweet chocolate
4 ounces (1 stick) unsalted butter
3 eggs graded "large"
¾ cup granulated sugar
1 teaspoon vanilla extract
½ cup plus 2 tablespoons sifted cake flour

Adjust an oven rack one-third up from the bottom and preheat the oven to 350 degrees. Butter an 8-inch springform pan that does not have to be (but may be) more than 1½ inches deep (see page 30). Line the bottom of the pan with a round of baking-pan liner paper cut to fit, butter the paper, and dust the pan all over with chocolate flour (see page 21). Tap the pan lightly over paper to shake out excess, and set aside.

Chop the chocolate rather fine and place it, and the butter, in the top of a small double boiler over warm water on moderate heat. Stir occasionally with a small wire whisk until melted and smooth. Remove the top of the double boiler and set aside to cool for 5 to 10 minutes.

Meanwhile, place the eggs and the sugar in the small bowl of an electric mixer and beat at high speed for about 5 minutes until the mixture is pale and forms a ribbon when the beaters are raised. Transfer the mixture to the large bowl of the mixer. Add the vanilla, the chocolate mixture, and the flour and beat on low speed briefly only until the ingredients are just incorporated. Remove the bowl from the mixer.

Turn into the prepared pan. Rotate the pan briskly in opposite directions to level the batter.

Bake for 28 to 30 minutes until a toothpick inserted in the middle just comes out dry. The top will be domed and cracked; it will flatten as it cools. Let the cake cool in the pan.

When the cake is cool, release and remove the sides of the pan. Cover the cake with a cake plate and turn the cake and the place upside down. Remove the bottom of the pan and the paper lining.

Cut four or five strips of baking-pan liner paper, each about 9 by 2½ inches. Gently slide the papers under the edge of the cake. (Use a wide metal spatula to raise an edge of the cake gently while you slide in a strip of the paper.) The cake should touch the papers all around. If you have a cake-decorating turntable, place the cake plate on it.

HONEY CHOCOLATE GLAZE

2 ounces unsweetened chocolate
2 ounces semisweet chocolate
2 ounces (½ stick) unsalted butter
2 teaspoons honey

Place both chocolates, the butter, and the honey in the top of a small double boiler over warm water on moderate heat. Stir occasionally until melted and smooth. Remove from the heat. Let stand until cool. (Stir over ice and water if you wish to save time.)

Pour the cooled glaze onto the top of the cake. With a long, narrow metal spatula smooth the top, allowing a very little bit of the glaze to run down the sides of the cake. Then, with a small, narrow metal spatula, smooth the glaze around the sides.

Remove the strips of paper by slowly and gently pulling each strip out toward a narrow end.

Let the cake stand at room temperature.

Serve the cake with the following two sauces. After placing a portion of the cake on an individual plate, pour one sauce on one side of the cake and the other sauce on the other side.

WHITE CHOCOLATE SAUCE
1¼ CUPS

6 ounces white chocolate
½ cup whipping cream

On a board, with a long and heavy knife shred/chop the chocolate fine.

Place the cream in a 1-quart heavy saucepan over moderate heat until it just comes to a low boil. Remove the pan from the heat, add the white chocolate, and whisk until melted and smooth. Let stand until cool. If the sauce thickens too much before serving, warm it slightly in the top of a double boiler.

CRANBERRY SAUCE
1 1/4 CUPS

6 ounces (1 cup) fresh or frozen cranberries
1/2 cup granulated sugar
1 cup orange juice

Rinse the berries and place them in a 6-cup heavy saucepan. Add the sugar and orange juice. Stir over moderate heat until the mixture comes to a low boil. Let boil, uncovered, for 5 to 10 minutes, stirring occasionally.

Remove from the heat. Let cool. Puree in a blender or a food processor and then strain. Or work the mixture through a food mill.

Chocolate Intrigue

2 SMALL LOAVES, ABOUT
8 PORTIONS EACH

Gloria and Jacques Pépin and some of their friends came to our home for a visit one afternoon while I was working on this recipe. They all said yes, they would like some. When it was served they all raved about it, more than I expected since it is a plain little loaf. They all asked what the exotic flavor was. I asked them to guess. Jacques guessed many spices—a mixture of spices—some of which I had never heard of. And they never did guess what it is. When I told them that it is just a little bit of black pepper, they thought I was kidding; they thought that there must be more to it. Incidentally, they all loved the cake and had seconds.

It is a moist cake with a fine texture and an extremely generous amount of chocolate. It keeps well (preferably in the refrigerator), slices beautifully, and is quick and easy to make.

You need two small loaf pans, preferably 8-by-4-by-2½-inch pans (see page 29) with a 5-cup capacity, but I have also used 8½-by-4½-by 2¾-inch pans with a 6-cup capacity; the cakes were equally delicious in the larger pans, although not quite as high.

3 ounces semisweet chocolate
2 ounces unsweetened chocolate
1 tablespoon dry instant espresso or coffee
1⅓ cups boiling water
1¾ cups sifted unbleached flour
¼ cup unsweetened cocoa powder
    (preferably Dutch-process)
1½ teaspoons baking powder
1 teaspoon salt
½ teaspoon black pepper, ground fine
4 ounces (1 stick) unsalted butter
1½ teaspoons vanilla extract
2 cups granulated sugar
3 eggs graded "large"

Adjust an oven rack one-third up from the bottom and preheat the oven to 325 degrees. Butter two 5-cup loaf pans (see above) and dust all over with chocolate bread crumbs (see page 21), tap over paper to remove excess crumbs, and set aside.

In a small saucepan over moderate heat place both chocolates with the espresso or coffee and water. Whisk frequently until the chocolates are melted and the mixture is smooth. Transfer to a small pitcher that will be easy to pour from (i.e., a 2-cup measuring cup) and set aside to cool to lukewarm.

Sift together the flour, cocoa, baking powder, salt, and pepper and set aside.

In the large bowl of an electric mixer beat the butter until soft. Beat in the vanilla and then gradually add the sugar and beat well until incorporated. Add the eggs and beat until smooth. Then, on low speed, alternately add the dry ingredients in three small additions with the chocolate mixture in two large additions. Scrape the bowl as necessary and beat until smooth.

Pour the mixture (which will be very liquid) into the prepared pans.

Bake both pans on the same rack for 1 hour and 10 to 15 minutes; cover the pans loosely with foil after about 40 minutes of baking. Bake until a cake tester gently inserted comes out clean; since the cake forms a hard crust on top, it is best to insert the cake tester on the side of the top edge, where there is no crust.

Let the cakes cool in the pans for about 15 minutes. Then cover each pan with a rack, invert pan and rack, remove pan, and let the cake cool upside down (the bottom of the cake is moist and tender at this stage).

It is best to wrap the cakes in plastic wrap and refrigerate them for several hours or overnight.

Serve plain. Or, as an important dessert, serve with Bittersweet Chocolate Sauce with Cocoa (see page 357) and, if you wish, with ice cream also. Pour the sauce on one side of a portion of cake and place the ice cream on the other side.

New York City Brown- stone Front Cake

12 PORTIONS

I have seen recipes named Brownstone Front Cake since I was a child. Some were chocolate, some were caramel, some were loaf cakes, and some were layer cakes. I never got to know one of them well until recently (now we're best friends). This one is a large loaf cake, intensely and densely and seductively chocolate, with a thin layer of dark chocolate glaze poured over the top. The cake itself is amazingly dark, deliciously moist, very chocolate, and not too sweet. It is easy to make and keeps well. It slices beautifully.

You need a loaf pan with a 9-cup capacity.

2 ounces unsweetened chocolate
1 cup boiling water
1 teaspoon dry instant coffee
1 ¾ cups unsifted unbleached flour
¼ cup unsweetened cocoa powder
   (preferably Dutch-process)
1 teaspoon baking soda
⅛ teaspoon salt
4 ounces (1 stick) unsalted butter
1¾ firmly packed cups light brown sugar
2 eggs graded "large"
1 teaspoon vanilla extract
½ cup sour cream

Adjust a rack one-third up from the bottom of the oven and preheat the oven to 325 degrees. You need a loaf pan with a 9-cup capacity; mine measures 10½ by 4½ by 3 inches (see page 29). This pan is not as wide as some and it makes a gorgeous cake. Butter the pan. Then dust it all over with chocolate bread crumbs (see page 21). Invert over paper and tap lightly to shake out excess. Set the pan aside.

Chop the chocolate into coarse pieces and place it in a small saucepan off the heat. Add the boiling water and instant coffee. Stir until the chocolate is melted. (The mixture is in a saucepan so that, if necessary, it can be placed over low heat until the chocolate is melted.) Stir to mix and set aside.

Sift together the flour, cocoa, baking soda, and salt and set aside.

In the large bowl of an electric mixer beat the butter until soft. Add the sugar and beat until well mixed. Beat in the eggs one at a time, and then beat in the vanilla. On low speed add about half of the dry ingredients and beat to mix. Beat in the sour cream and then the remaining dry ingredients. Still on low speed, gradually add the melted chocolate mixture, scraping the bowl as necessary with a rubber spatula and beating until thoroughly mixed.

Pour the batter into the prepared pan.

Bake for about 1½ hours or until a cake tester gently inserted in the middle comes out dry.

Cool the cake in the pan for about 15 minutes. Then cover with a rack, turn the pan and rack upside down, and remove the pan, leaving the cake upside down to cool on the rack.

Prepare a flat serving tray or a board as follows: Cut a length of wax paper slightly longer than the bottom of the cake. Fold it in half lengthwise and cut on the fold. Then fold each piece in half lengthwise. Place the two papers on the serving tray or board, folded edges meeting in the center of the tray or board.

Carefully transfer the cake to the lined tray or board.

BROWNSTONE ICING

2 ounces unsweetened chocolate
1½ ounces (3 tablespoons) unsalted butter
¼ cup whipping cream
1 cup strained or sifted confectioners sugar
½ teaspoon vanilla extract
Tiny pinch of salt

Chop the chocolate into coarse pieces and place it in a small heavy saucepan with the butter and cream. Stir over moderate heat until perfectly smooth. Mix in the sugar, vanilla, and salt and remove from the heat.

Let stand at room temperature for 5 to 10 minutes, stirring frequently, until the mixture just begins to thicken a bit.

Then pour the icing in a wide ribbon, back and forth, over the length of the cake. Allow the icing to run down the sides of the cake in a few places, but do not spread it over the sides.

When the icing is set, remove the papers by gently pulling each one toward a narrow end of the cake.

Sour Cream Black Fudge Loaf Cake

ABOUT 12 PORTIONS

From one to ten, this gets a ten for dense-dark-moist-rich-fudgelike deliciousness. And it is easy to make. It can be served as is, or—preferably—with its chocolate sour cream icing, which is one of the very best and easiest of all chocolate icings. The icing can be spread as smooth as satin, or it can be swirled and rippled, or, if you wish, it can also be used with a pastry bag to form a design. Whatever, it will be gloriously semi-soft and perfect.

> 1 cup plus 3 tablespoons sifted unbleached flour
> 3 tablespoons unsweetened cocoa powder (preferably Dutch-process)
> 1 tablespoon baking powder
> ½ teaspoon salt
> 3½ ounces semisweet chocolate
> 2 ounces unsweetened chocolate
> 2 tablespoons dry instant espresso or coffee
> 2 tablespoons boiling water
> 4 ounces (1 stick) unsalted butter
> 1 teaspoon vanilla extract
> 1 firmly packed cup light brown sugar
> 2 eggs graded "large"
> ½ cup sour cream

Adjust a rack one-third up from the bottom of the oven and preheat the oven to 350 degrees. Butter an 8-cup loaf pan, preferably one that is long and narrow as opposed to one that is short and wide. The pan that measures 10¼ by 3¾ by 3¼ inches (see page 29) makes a beautifully shaped cake.

Dust the pan with chocolate bread crumbs (see page 21), tap over paper to remove excess crumbs, and set aside.

Sift together the flour, cocoa, baking powder, and salt and set aside.

Place both of the chocolates in the top of a small double boiler over warm water on moderate heat. Cover the pan with a folded paper towel (to absorb steam) and the pan cover. Cook until the chocolate is almost melted, then remove the top of the double boiler and stir until melted and smooth, and set aside.

In a small cup stir the espresso or coffee with the boiling water and set aside.

In the large bowl of an electric mixer beat the butter until soft. Beat in the vanilla and sugar and then the eggs, one at a time. Add the chocolate (which may still be slightly warm) and beat to mix. On low speed beat in half of the sifted dry ingredients, then the sour cream and espresso or coffee, and finally the remaining dry ingredients. Scrape the sides of the bowl as necessary with a rubber spatula and beat only until smooth.

Turn into the prepared pan. Smooth the top. Bake for about 1 hour and 5 minutes until a cake tester gently inserted in the middle comes out dry. Remove from the oven and let stand for 10 minutes. While standing the cake will settle down slightly, but it will be OK.

Cover the pan with a rack, turn the pan and rack upside down, remove the pan, and let the cake stand upside down to cool.

Prepare a serving board or flat tray as follows: Cut a length of wax paper slightly longer than the cake. Fold the paper in half lengthwise and cut on the fold. Then fold each piece in half lengthwise. Place the two strips on the serving board or tray, folded edges meeting in the center of the board or tray. Carefully transfer the cake to the lined board or tray.

SOUR CREAM CHOCOLATE ICING

6 ounces semisweet chocolate
Pinch of salt
½ cup sour cream

Place the chocolate in the top of a small double boiler over warm water on moderate heat, cover the pan with a folded paper towel (to absorb steam) and with the pan cover, and cook until the chocolate is almost melted. Then stir until melted and smooth. Remove the top of the double boiler and stir in the salt and the sour cream.

Spread the icing over the top and sides of the cake. Either smooth the icing with a long, narrow metal spatula or form it into swirls with the underside of a spoon. Or, if you wish, reserve some of the icing, smooth the balance all over the cake, and then, with a pastry bag and a fluted tube, decorate the cake as you wish.

Remove the strips of paper by slowly pulling each one out toward a narrow end.

Bishop's Bread

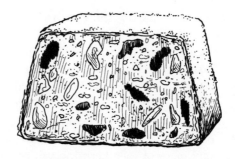

ABOUT 10 PORTIONS

This is great. It is not bread; it is a delicious coffee or tea cake. The story is that Bishop's Bread—an old Austrian-German recipe (Bischofsbrot)— was served when the bishop came to call. It is a light, moist sponge cake (this version is considerably lighter than the classic recipe). The cake has a generous amount of sweet and chewy dates and raisins, crisp and crunchy almonds, and chopped chocolate throughout. It is surprising that since the cake is so light, the fruit and nuts do not sink. And it is surprising that since the cake is so light, it slices beautifully—you can cut it into thin slices.

Traditionally the cake is white and contains pieces of cut-up dark chocolate. This cake is chocolate color and the pieces of cut-up chocolate are white.

You need a loaf pan with a 10-cup capacity. It is preferable to use a long and narrow pan rather than a short and wide one; the cake will look better and will be easier to slice. The pan that measures 13¾ by 4¼ by 2¾ inches is perfect for this (see page 29). The pan should not have a dark finish, as the cake tends to bake with a dark crust anyhow and a dark pan will make a too-dark crust.

It is best to bake this a day before serving.

4 ounces (½ packed cup) pitted dates
2½ ounces (½ cup) unblanched almonds
3 to 4 ounces white chocolate
2 tablespoons plus ¼ cup unsifted
    unbleached flour
2½ ounces (½ loosely packed cup) raisins
2 tablespoons unsweetened cocoa powder
5 eggs graded "large," separated
3 tablespoons plus ⅓ cup granulated sugar
Pinch of salt
Confectioners sugar (to sprinkle on top
    before serving)

Adjust an oven rack one-third up from the bottom and preheat the oven to 350 degrees.

Line a 10-cup loaf pan with aluminum foil as follows: Place the pan upside down on the work surface. Measure the bottom of the pan. Cut two pieces of aluminum foil, one for the length of the pan and the two short sides and another for the width of the pan and the two long sides. Place one piece of foil shiny side down over the pan, fold the foil over the sides of the pan to shape it to the pan, remove, and set aside. Repeat to shape the second piece of foil. Turn the pan right side up. Carefully place one piece of the shaped foil in the pan, pressing it into place, and then place the second piece of foil in the pan and press that into place also. (You now have a double layer of foil on the bottom and a single layer on each side.) If the foil extends above the sides of the pan, fold it down over the rim.

To butter the foil, it is best to place a piece of butter in the lined pan, place the pan in the oven briefly until the butter is melted, and then, with a pastry brush or crumpled plastic wrap, spread the butter all over the foil and the corners of the pan that are not covered with foil. To coat the pan with crumbs, place some fine dry bread crumbs in the pan, tilt the pan from side to side until all the surfaces are crumbed, and then turn the pan upside down over a piece of paper to allow excess crumbs to fall out (do not tap the pan; the crumb coating should be generous). Set the prepared pan aside.

With scissors cut each date into about five pieces and set aside. On a board, with a heavy knife chop the almonds into medium-large pieces and set aside. On the board, with the heavy knife cut the white chocolate into about 1/4-inch pieces and set aside.

Sift 2 tablespoons of the flour into a large mixing bowl (reserve the remaining 1/4 cup flour). Add the dates and, with your fingers, toss and separate the pieces of dates until they are thoroughly floured. Add the raisins and repeat tossing and separating. Finally, add the chopped nuts and chocolate and toss again to flour all the ingredients. Set aside.

Sift together the remaining 1/4 cup of flour and the cocoa. Place the sifter over a piece of wax paper, place the sifted flour mixture into the sifter, and set aside.

In the small bowl of an electric mixer, beat the egg yolks and the 3 tablespoons of sugar (reserve remaining sugar) at high speed for 5 minutes until pale and thick. Remove the bowl from the mixer, pour the yolk mixture over the floured-fruit mixture, and with a rubber spatula fold together until incorporated. Set aside.

In a clean small bowl of the electric mixer, with clean beaters beat the egg whites with the salt, first at low speed and then at high speed, until the whites hold a soft shape. On moderate speed add the remaining 1/3 cup sugar, one tablespoon at a time. Then increase the speed to high again and beat only until the whites hold a semifirm (not stiff) point when the beaters are raised. Do not overbeat.

Remove the bowl from the mixer. Let it stand for a moment while you sift the reserved flour and cocoa mixture over the fruit mixture (do not fold together), and then turn all of the egg-white mixture over the top of the sifted-flour mixture. With a large rubber spatula, fold all the ingredients together until just incorporated.

Turn the mixture into the prepared pan. Smooth the top.

Bake for about 1 hour and 10 minutes until the top springs back when gently pressed with a fingertip.

Let the cake cool in the pan for 40 to 50 minutes. Then cover the cake with a rack, turn the pan and rack upside down, remove the pan and the foil, and let the cake finish cooling upside down. Wrap in plastic wrap and let stand at room temperature overnight.

To serve, sift confectioners sugar generously over the top of the cake. Cut with a sharp straight-edged knife into slices about ½ inch thick.

White Chocolate and Banana Cake

2 SMALL
LOAVES—ABOUT 8
PORTIONS EACH

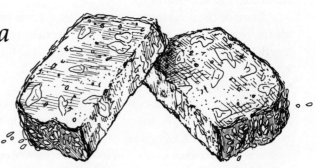

With nuts, coconut, and rum; the combination is tropical, exotic, intriguing, and delicious. The loaves are gorgeous. The technique is a little unusual, and easy.

6 ounces white chocolate
4 ounces (1 cup) walnuts
8 ounces (2 sticks) unsalted butter
2¾ cups unsifted unbleached flour
1¼ teaspoons baking soda
1 teaspoon salt
4 to 6 fully ripened bananas (to make 2 cups mashed)
1½ cups granulated sugar
2 eggs graded "large"
3 tablespoons dark rum (or brandy)
1 teaspoon vanilla extract
3½ ounces (1 firmly packed cup) shredded coconut
Optional: sesame seeds (to sprinkle on top)

Adjust an oven rack one-third up from the bottom and preheat the oven to 350 degrees. Butter two 6-cup loaf pans, preferably pans that measure 8½ by 4½ by 2¾ inches (see page 29). Dust the pans with fine dry bread crumbs or toasted or untoasted wheat germ (the wheat germ makes an especially nice crust) and turn them upside down over paper to allow excess to fall out. Set the pans aside.

On a board, with a long and heavy knife cut the chocolate into ¼- to ½-inch pieces and set aside. Break or chop the walnuts into medium-small pieces and set aside.

Melt the butter in a small frying pan or saucepan over moderate heat; then transfer it to the large bowl of an electric mixer and let stand briefly.

Sift together the flour, baking soda, and salt and set aside.

Peel the bananas. On a wide plate, with a table fork mash the bananas; the texture should be coarse, not pureed. Set aside.

Add the sugar to the butter (which may still be warm) and beat to mix well. Then add the eggs, rum (or brandy), and vanilla and beat at high speed for 5 minutes until pale and thick. Add the bananas and beat just to mix. Then, on low speed, gradually add the sifted dry ingredients and beat only until thoroughly incorporated (the mixture does not have to be smooth—it will be lumpy because of the bananas).

Remove the bowl from the mixer. Stir in the coconut, chocolate, and walnuts.

Place half of the batter in each of the prepared pans. Smooth the tops. Sprinkle the optional sesame seeds generously on the tops (they are a delicious addition to this recipe).

Bake for about 1 hour and 15 minutes until a cake tester gently inserted in the middle of each loaf comes out dry and the tops of the loaves spring back when they are gently pressed with a fingertip. During baking, if the tops are not browning evenly, reverse the pans, front to back. Cover the pans loosely with aluminum foil for the last 20 minutes of baking to prevent overbrowning. The tops will crack during baking—they are supposed to.

Cool the loaves in the pans for about 15 minutes. Then cover a pan with a pot holder or a folded towel, gently turn the pan upside down onto the palm of your hand, remove the pan, cover the loaf with a cake rack, and turn the loaf and rack upside down, leaving the loaf right side up on the rack. Set aside. Repeat to remove the second loaf from the pan. Let cool.

Irish Whiskey Chocolate Cake

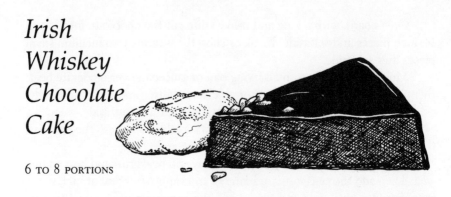

6 TO 8 PORTIONS

Amazingly moist and light, but with a punch from the generous amount of whiskey. Although the cake is not too large and is only 1 1/2 inches high and is not a tremendous amount of work and looks quite plain and simple, it is a very important dessert cake. The texture and the flavor are most unusual and they put this cake way above the crowds up into the stratosphere. Chocolate lovers describe this in one word, perfect.

> 4 ounces (1 stick) unsalted butter, cut into 6 pieces
> 4 ounces semisweet chocolate, chopped or broken into coarse pieces
> 1/2 cup Irish whiskey
> 1 cup minus 2 tablespoons sifted unbleached flour
> 3 tablespoons unsweetened cocoa powder (preferably Dutch-process)
> 3 eggs graded "large," separated
> 1 cup granulated sugar
> Pinch of salt

Butter a 9-by-1 1/2- or 2-inch round layer-cake pan (see page 30), line it with a round of baking-pan liner paper cut to fit, butter the paper, and dust all over with chocolate flour (see page 21). Turn the pan upside down over paper and tap lightly to shake out excess. Set aside.

Place the butter, chocolate, and whiskey in the top of a large double boiler over warm water on moderate heat. Stir frequently with a wire whisk until melted and smooth. Remove the top of the double boiler and set aside to cool. Sift together the flour and cocoa and set aside.

In the small bowl of an electric mixer beat the egg yolks with ⅔ cup of the sugar (reserve remaining ⅓ cup sugar) for several minutes until very pale.

On moderate speed gradually add the melted-chocolate mixture and beat to mix. On low speed gradually add the sifted dry ingredients and beat only to mix. Remove the bowl from the mixer. Transfer the mixture to a large mixing bowl and set aside.

If you do not have an additional small bowl and additional beaters for the mixer, wash and dry the ones you just used. In a clean small bowl of the mixer, with clean beaters beat the egg whites with the salt until they hold a soft shape. Then on moderate speed gradually add the remaining ⅓ cup of sugar. Continue to beat on high speed until the whites just hold a straight shape when the beaters are raised—but not until they are dry.

Remove the bowl from the mixer and add the whites all at once to the chocolate mixture. With a rubber spatula gently fold together only until the color is almost, but not completely, smooth.

Turn into the prepared pan. Smooth the top.

Bake for 30 minutes. During baking the cake will rise above the top of the pan and a crack may form across the top of the cake—it is OK.

There is really no way to test this cake; just be sure of your oven temperature and time the baking carefully.

Remove the pan from the oven and let the cake stand in the pan for 10 minutes. While cooling, the top of the cake will settle back to the height of the pan. The cake will have a hard and crusty top and will be sumptuously soft, moist, and tender inside.

Cover the cake with a rack and carefully turn the cake pan and the rack upside down. Remove the pan and the paper lining. Let the cake continue to cool upside down.

Because the cake is so tender, when it has cooled completely place it in the freezer for about 15 minutes before transferring it to a cake plate; use a flat-sided cookie sheet as a spatula in order to transfer the cake safely.

When the cake is on the cake plate, cut about six strips of baking-pan liner paper or wax paper that measure about 8 by 3 inches. The papers will be slipped under the edges of the cake to protect the plate while icing the cake; use a wide metal spatula to raise a small edge of the cake and slide a strip of the paper partly under the edge. Continue all around the cake until the plate is covered under the edges all around.

If you have a cake-decorating turntable, place the cake plate on it.

ICING

1 tablespoon unsalted butter
1/4 cup heavy cream
4 ounces semisweet chocolate, cut or broken
   into medium-sized pieces
Optional: about 2 tablespoons unsalted green
   pistachio nuts, chopped fine

Place the butter and cream in a small heavy saucepan over moderate heat. Let the mixture just come to a simmer. Add the chocolate, stir to melt, and remove from the heat and let stand, stirring occasionally, for 10 to 15 minutes or more until cool.

Stir well and then pour all of the icing onto the cake. With a long, narrow metal spatula spread the icing to the edges, and allow a little bit of it to run down the sides. Smooth the top and then smooth the sides.

Sprinkle the optional pistachio nuts in the center of the cake.

Let stand for 10 or 15 minutes for the icing to set up a bit. Then remove the paper strips by slowly pulling each one out toward a narrow end.

Let the cake stand at room temperature. Serve at room temperature with whipped cream on the side.

WHIPPED CREAM

1 1/2 cups heavy cream
3 tablespoons confectioners sugar
1 teaspoon vanilla extract

In a small chilled bowl, with chilled beaters whip the cream with the sugar and vanilla until the cream is semifirm, not stiff. If the cream is whipped ahead of time, cover and refrigerate it. It may separate a bit. If so, just before serving whisk it briskly with a small wire whisk to reincorporate.

Serve a mound of the cream alongside each portion of the cake.

Creole Chocolate Layer Cake

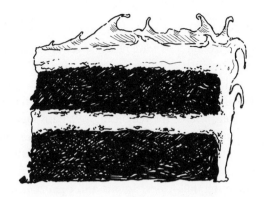

12 PORTIONS

A festive, impressive, important (4½ inches high) layer cake to make for a celebration. Not too sweet—or too rich—although it is intensely chocolate, with a light and fluffy marshmallowlike icing that shines like satin. This is not difficult to make.

The cake uses egg yolks; the icing uses the egg whites. You will need a sugar thermometer for the icing. It is best to ice this cake the day it will be served.

> 4 ounces unsweetened chocolate
> 1 ounce (¼ stick) unsalted butter
> 4 egg yolks graded "large" (reserve the whites for the icing)
> 2 cups granulated sugar
> 1 teaspoon vanilla extract
> Optional: 3 teaspoons instant espresso or coffee powder
> ½ teaspoon salt
> 1¾ cups milk
> 1 teaspoon baking soda
> 2 cups sifted cake flour

Adjust a rack to the center of the oven and preheat the oven to 350 degrees. Butter two 9-by-1½- or 2-inch round layer-cake pans (see page 30). Line the bottoms with rounds of baking-pan liner paper cut to fit. Butter the papers. Dust all over the bottoms and sides of the pans with chocolate bread crumbs (see page 21); invert over paper and allow excess crumbs to fall out (do not tap the pans or you might remove too much of the crumb mixture). Set the pans aside.

Place the chocolate and the butter in the top of a small double boiler over hot water on moderate heat. Cover until partially melted, then uncover and stir frequently until melted and smooth. Remove the top of the double boiler and set aside.

Place the egg yolks in the small bowl of an electric mixer. Add ½ cup of the sugar (reserve the remaining 1½ cups sugar), the vanilla, the optional espresso or coffee powder, and the salt and beat at high speed for about 3 minutes until pale and thick. Add the chocolate mixture, which may still be slightly warm, and then, gradually, add about half of the milk (reserve the remaining milk). Beat to mix and then transfer to the large bowl of the electric mixer.

In a small cup, mix the baking soda with about ¼ cup of the milk. On low speed add the baking-soda mixture to the chocolate mixture, then add the remaining sugar and milk. Then add the flour and beat on low speed only until incorporated. It will be a thin mixture.

Divide the batter evenly between the two pans. (If you don't trust your eye, measure 3 cups for each pan.)

Bake the two pans on the same rack for 40 to 45 minutes or until the cake just barely begins to come away from the sides of the pans. (Watch carefully for the first sign of a space between the cake and the pan—do not overbake.)

Without waiting, cut around a cake with a small sharp knife to be sure that it is not sticking to the pan. Cover the pan with a rack. Turn the pan and rack upside down. Remove the pan and paper lining. Cover the cake with another rack and turn both racks and the cake upside down, leaving the cake right side up to cool. Remove the second cake from the pan the same way. Let the cakes cool.

Brush the sides of the cakes with a pastry brush to remove loose crumbs.

Prepare a large, flat cake plate by placing four 10-by-3-inch strips of wax paper around the rim of the plate.

Place one of the cakes upside down on the plate; check to be sure that the papers touch the cake all around.

If you have a cake-decorating turntable, place the cake plate on it.

CREOLE ICING

This will hold its shape and remain soft and luscious—it will not become crusty. But the cake must be served the day it is iced; the following day the icing becomes sticky and difficult to serve.

4 egg whites graded "large"
⅛ teaspoon salt
1½ firmly packed cups light brown sugar
¼ teaspoon cream of tartar
½ cup water
1 teaspoon vanilla extract

Place the whites and the salt in the small bowl of an electric mixer and let stand. In a 6-cup saucepan place the sugar, cream of tartar, and water. Stir over moderate heat until the sugar is dissolved. Raise the heat to high, and when the mixture comes to a boil cover the pan for ½ minute (the steam will dissolve any sugar granules clinging to the sides of the pan). Then uncover, insert a sugar thermometer, and let the mixture cook over high heat until the thermometer registers 234 degrees (the thread stage).

Meanwhile, since the sugar syrup and the beaten whites should both be ready at the same time, start to beat the whites when the thermometer registers 228 to 230 degrees. (For both the syrup and the whites to be ready at the same time, it might be necessary to adjust the speed of the mixer or the heat under the syrup.)

Moments before the syrup is ready, transfer the whites to the large bowl of the mixer and continue to beat. Then, when the whites are stiff and the thermometer registers 234 degrees, slowly pour the syrup in a thin stream into the whites, holding the saucepan 6 to 8 inches above the bowl of whites.

When the syrup is all added, add the vanilla and continue to beat for 5 to 10 minutes at high speed, scraping the bowl frequently, until the mixture is thick enough to be spread on the cake and will hold a straight peak when the beaters are raised.

With a long, narrow metal spatula, spread a layer of the icing about ⅓ inch thick on the top of the first cake. Cover with the other cake right side up (bottoms together).

Spread the icing on the sides and then on the top of the cake. Smooth the sides and then the top. And then, with the bottom of a spoon, form swirls and peaks in the icing. (This icing behaves like a charm.)

Remove the papers by slowly pulling each one out toward a narrow end.

It is best to serve this cake on wide plates. And it is best, when serving this, to dip the knife blade into hot water before making each cut; cut with a hot and wet blade. Place each portion on a cut side rather than standing up; it will be easier to eat.

Mexican Chocolate Layer Cake

12 TO 14 PORTIONS

A gorgeous cake for an important event; incredibly delicious, and truly easy. Two thick and dark, moist and luscious chocolate layers (made with ice water—an unusual step). With a chocolate mousse icing simply too good to be true. Both the cake and the icing are well flavored with espresso, and the cake also has a hint of cinnamon and cloves.

The layers can be made a day ahead if you wish. The icing should be completed early in the day for that night; the finished cake should be refrigerated for at least a few hours and should be served cold.

2¼ cups sifted cake flour
½ cup unsweetened cocoa powder
  (preferably Dutch-process)
1 tablespoon baking powder
1 tablespoon instant espresso powder (I use
  Medaglia D'Oro)
1 teaspoon cinnamon
¼ teaspoon cloves
½ teaspoon salt
6 ounces (1½ sticks) unsalted butter
2 teaspoons vanilla extract
1¼ cups granulated sugar
3 eggs graded "large," separated
1 cup ice water

Adjust two racks to divide the oven into thirds and preheat the oven to 325 degrees. Butter two 9-inch layer-cake pans (see page 30), line them with baking-pan liner paper cut to fit, and butter the paper. Then dust the pans all over with chocolate flour (see page 21), invert and tap the pans over paper to shake out excess flour, and set aside.

Sift together the flour, cocoa, baking powder, espresso powder, cinnamon, cloves, and salt and set aside.

In the large bowl of an electric mixer beat the butter until soft. Beat in the vanilla and 1 cup of the sugar (reserve the remaining ¼ cup sugar). Add the egg yolks all at once and beat to mix. Then, on low speed, alternately add the sifted dry ingredients in three additions with the ice water in two additions. Beat to mix. Remove the bowl from the mixer and set aside.

In the small bowl of the electric mixer with clean beaters beat the egg whites until they hold a soft shape. Reduce the speed to moderate and gradually add the remaining ¼ cup of sugar. Then, on high speed, continue to beat briefly only until the whites just hold a straight point when the beaters are raised slowly. Remove the bowl from the mixer.

With a rubber spatula fold about one fourth of the beaten whites into the chocolate mixture. Then add all of the remaining beaten whites and fold gently until just barely incorporated.

Pour half of the batter into each of the prepared pans and smooth the tops.

Bake one pan on each rack for 30 to 35 minutes. After about 20 minutes, quickly and carefully reverse the pans, top to bottom, to ensure even baking. The cakes are done when a toothpick gently inserted in the middle of each comes out clean and the rims of the cakes spring back when gently pressed with a fingertip.

Let the cakes stand in the pans for about 10 minutes. Then, with a small sharp knife, carefully cut around the sides of the cakes to release. Cover each pan with a rack, invert pan and rack, remove the pan, cover with another rack, and invert again, leaving cakes right sides up (with the paper linings still on the bottoms).

Let cool to room temperature, and then place in the freezer to chill and firm up a bit (because the layers are tender and fragile at room temperature).

Meanwhile, cut four strips of baking-pan liner paper, each about 10 by 2½ inches, and place them in a square pattern on a wide serving plate. Prepare the icing.

MEXICAN CHOCOLATE MOUSSE ICING

5½ ounces semisweet chocolate
4 teaspoons instant espresso powder
¼ cup hot water
1 teaspoon unsweetened cocoa powder
¼ cup granulated sugar
3 egg yolks graded "large"
1¾ cups whipping cream
1 teaspoon vanilla extract

On a board, with a long and heavy knife shred/chop the chocolate until fine and let stand. In a small, heavy saucepan stir the espresso, water, and cocoa to mix. Stir in the sugar. Stir over moderate heat until the sugar dissolves and the mixture just comes to a boil. Add the chopped chocolate. Stir until melted and smooth. Remove from the heat and continue to stir for 2 minutes. Stir in the egg yolks, and then stir in 4 tablespoons of the cream (reserve the remaining cream) and the vanilla.

Transfer to a bowl and stir occasionally until cool. (If you wish, stir over ice and water to save time; the mixture must cool.)

Meanwhile, in a small chilled bowl with chilled beaters whip the remaining cream until it holds a shape when the beaters are raised.

Fold about one fourth of the whipped cream into the cooled chocolate syrup. Then fold in the remaining whipped cream.

Remove the paper lining from the bottom of one of the chilled layers. Place the layer upside down on the serving plate (check to be sure that the strips of paper touch the cake all around).

With a long, narrow metal spatula spread a layer of the icing a scant ½-inch thick on the bottom layer. Remove the paper lining from the remaining chilled cake and place the cake right side up (bottoms together) over the icing.

Brush loose crumbs off the sides of the cake and spread a very thin layer of the icing on the sides. Cover the sides with another layer of icing.

Either use all the remaining icing on the top of the cake or reserve some to decorate the cake with and spread the balance on top. With a long metal spatula smooth the icing on the top, and with a small metal spatula smooth the icing on the sides.

To decorate the cake you may, if you wish, use a pastry bag and a number 5 star-shaped tube and form large rosettes all around the rim of the cake with the reserved icing. Or, without a pastry bag, you can form swirls in the icing with the bottom of a spoon. Or you can leave it smooth and place a beautiful fresh rose on top right before serving.

Refrigerate, and serve cold.

Hazelnut and Bourbon Chocolate Cake

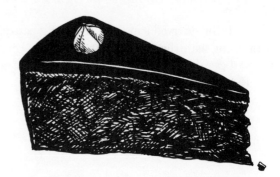

12 PORTIONS

A chic and classy single layer of dense, intense chocolate-coffee-bourbon cake, with a shiny, dark chocolate glaze. There are many chocolate cakes with ingredients similar to these, but this one has more chocolate per square inch than any other I know. The cake can be made a day before it will be served, but it is best to ice it the same day you will serve it.

> 12 ounces semisweet chocolate
> ¼ cup bourbon
> ¾ cup sifted unbleached flour
> 1 tablespoon unsweetened cocoa powder
> 2 teaspoons instant espresso or coffee powder (I use Medaglia D'Oro)
> 2 ½ ounces (½ cup) blanched and toasted hazelnuts (see page 9)
> ½ cup granulated sugar
> 4 ounces (1 stick) unsalted butter
> 3 eggs graded "large," separated
> Pinch of salt

Adjust a rack one-third up from the bottom of the oven and preheat the oven to 350 degrees. Butter an 8-inch springform pan, which may be 2 or 3 inches deep (see page 30) although the cake will be only 1 ½ inches deep, line the bottom with a round of baking-pan liner paper cut to fit, butter the paper, and dust the pan all over with chocolate bread crumbs (see page 21). Then, over paper, shake out excess crumbs, and set the pan aside.

On a board, with a long and heavy knife shred/chop the chocolate fine. Place the chocolate and bourbon in the top of a large double boiler over warm water on low heat. Cover and let cook until partly melted. Then uncover and stir until completely melted and smooth. Remove and set aside the top of the double boiler.

Sift together the flour, cocoa, and espresso or coffee powder. Let stand.

Place the hazelnuts in the bowl of a food processor fitted with the metal chopping blade. Add about one third of the sugar (reserve the remaining sugar) and 2 generous tablespoons of the sifted dry ingredients (reserve the remaining sifted ingredients).

Process for 30 seconds, scraping the sides once, until the nuts are fine. Set aside.

In the small bowl of an electric mixer beat the butter with one third of the sugar (reserve the remaining sugar) until thoroughly mixed. Add the egg yolks all at once and beat until mixed. Then beat in the chocolate mixture, which may still be warm (the mixture might look curdled, but it will be OK). Then add the ground-nut mixture and beat until incorporated.

Remove the bowl from the mixer and transfer the ingredients to the large bowl of the mixer.

Wash the small bowl of the mixer and the beaters (unless you have an additional bowl and additional beaters), and beat the egg whites with the salt until they barely hold a soft shape. On moderate speed gradually add the remaining sugar. Then, on high speed, beat until the whites just barely hold a straight point when the beaters are raised. Remove the bowl from the mixer.

Sift the remaining sifted ingredients over the chocolate mixture, and turn the beaten egg-white mixture over the sifted ingredients. With a rubber spatula fold everything together, folding only until you do not see any more dry ingredients (you may see a bit of egg white that is not blended). Do not handle any more than necessary.

Turn into the prepared pan. Tilt the pan slightly to smooth the top.

Bake for 30 minutes. The center will still feel soft; the rim will just spring back when gently pressed with a fingertip.

Place the pan on a rack and let stand until cooled to room temperature.

Then remove the sides of the pan. If the rim of the cake is higher than the center, it should be trimmed. If so, it is best to chill the cake (for only 10 to 15 minutes) in the freezer before trimming. And if you have a cake-decorating turntable, place the cake (still on the bottom of the pan) on the turntable, and use a long thin knife (such as a ham slicer) to level the top.

To place the cake upside down on a cake plate, cover it with a wide and flat plate, turn the cake and the plate upside down, and then remove the bottom of the pan and the paper lining.

If the cake is going to wait overnight before being iced, cover it airtight with plastic wrap.

ICING

6 ounces semisweet chocolate
4 tablespoons whipping cream
1 tablespoon unsalted butter
Optional: 12 blanched and toasted hazelnuts
(to be used as decoration—see page 9)

On a board, with a long and heavy knife shred/chop the chocolate fine. Place the chocolate, cream, and butter in the top of a double boiler over warm water on low heat. Cover until partly melted, then uncover and stir until melted and smooth. Remove the top of the double boiler and set aside for about 10 minutes, stirring occasionally.

Meanwhile, to protect the plate while icing the cake, slide four strips of baking-pan liner paper (each about 2½ by 9 inches) under the edges of the cake (you can gently raise the edge a bit with a wide metal spatula as you slide the papers under). The cake should touch the papers all around. If you have a cake-decorating turntable, place the cake plate on it.

Stir the icing and pour it all onto the top of the cake. With a long, narrow metal spatula smooth the icing over the top of the cake, allowing a bit of it to run down the sides. Then, with a small, narrow metal spatula, smooth the icing (in a thin coat) on the sides.

Place the optional hazelnuts in a ring close to the rim around the top.

Remove the paper strips by pulling each one out toward a narrow end of the strip.

Serve each portion with a large spoonful of the following whipped cream.

WHIPPED CREAM

If you plan to serve fewer than 10 or 12 portions, judge the amount of cream accordingly.

2 cups whipping cream
1 teaspoon vanilla extract
¼ cup confectioners sugar

In a chilled bowl with chilled beaters whip the cream with the vanilla and sugar only until it holds a soft shape—it should not be stiff. If you whip the cream ahead of time, cover and store it in the refrigerator. If it separates a little, whisk it a bit with a wire whisk just before serving.

Chocolate Date Cake

6 to 8 portions

A small and simple cake. Quick and easy.

Cakes that contain a puree of fruit have a wonderful texture and are especially moist. This one has a puree of dates and it is remarkably moist and delicious. You won't recognize the flavor of dates; you will simply know that there is something special—and different.

> 4 ounces (½ packed cup) pitted dates
> ⅓ teaspoon baking soda (see Note)
> ¼ cup boiling water
> 1 ounce unsweetened chocolate
> 1 ounce semisweet chocolate
> ¾ cup unsifted unbleached flour
> ¼ teaspoon salt
> 4 ounces (1 stick) unsalted butter
> ½ teaspoon vanilla extract
> ⅔ cup granulated sugar
> 1 egg graded "large"
> ⅓ cup sour cream

Adjust a rack one-third up from the bottom of the oven and preheat the oven to 350 degrees. Line and butter an 8-by-8-by-2-inch square cake pan (see page 30) as follows: Place the pan upside down. Center a 12-inch square of aluminum foil, shiny side down, over the pan. With your hands, fold down the sides and the corners to shape the foil to the pan. Remove the foil. Run cold water into the pan and pour it out, but do not dry the pan (a wet pan holds the foil in place). Place the pan right side up on the work surface, place the shaped foil in the pan, and, with a pot holder or a folded towel, press the foil into place all over the pan. The edges of foil that extend over the top of the pan should be folded over the outside of the pan. To butter the pan use room-temperature butter, and brush it all over the foil with a pastry brush or crumpled plastic wrap. Butter thoroughly and set the pan aside.

Place the dates in a small bowl. Add the baking soda and the boiling water. Stir to mix. Transfer to the bowl of a food processor fitted with the metal chopping blade. Process for 10 seconds or until the dates are a coarse puree. Set aside.

Place both chocolates in the top of a small double boiler over warm water on moderate heat. Cover the pot with a folded paper towel (to absorb steam) and the pot cover and let the chocolate cook until almost melted. Then uncover, remove the top of the double boiler, stir until melted and smooth, and set aside.

Sift together the flour and salt and set aside.

In the large bowl of an electric mixer beat the butter until soft. Add the vanilla and sugar and beat to mix. Beat in the egg, the melted chocolate, and then the pureed-date mixture.

On low speed beat in half of the sifted ingredients, then all of the sour cream, and finally the remaining dry ingredients, beating only until incorporated.

Transfer to the prepared pan. Smooth the top.

Bake for 45 minutes or until the top just barely springs back when gently pressed with a fingertip.

Let the cake cool in the pan for 20 to 30 minutes. Then cover with a cake plate or a serving board. Turn the plate or board and the pan upside down. Remove the pan and the foil. Let stand while you prepare the icing.

ICING

4 ounces semisweet chocolate
4 tablespoons whipping cream

On a board, with a long and heavy knife shred/chop the chocolate rather fine. Place it in the top of a small double boiler over warm water on moderate heat and stir until melted. Add the cream and stir until smooth.

Set the icing aside for a few minutes, stirring it occasionally.

Then transfer all the icing to the top of the cake. With a long, narrow metal spatula smooth the icing over the top only (not the sides), and then, going from left to right—back and forth—with the spatula on an angle, make ridges in the icing about half an inch apart.

Let stand at room temperature.

NOTE: To measure ⅓ teaspoon, first measure 1 teaspoon. Then cut away and return to the box ⅔ teaspoon of the baking soda.

Panforte Cioccolato

16 SLICES

Panforte *was originally made in Siena, Italy, about one thousand years ago—and it is still made there. The religious crusaders carried it with them on their expeditions not only because it is so good and so satisfying but also because it lasts so very well. Nowadays you will see* panforte *in better food stores, especially at Christmastime (it does make a perfect gift), but make it anytime; it is always a special treat. Simple, but sophisticated and elegant. Chewy, crunchy, and caramel candylike. Not too sweet. Slightly spicy.*

Although the translation of panforte *is "strong bread," this is a fruit cake. It is shallow (a scant 1 inch high), almost solid fruits and nuts, with barely enough batter (a chocolate honey batter) to hold it all together. It is wonderful.*

You will need a sugar thermometer.

5 ounces (1 cup) blanched or unblanched
    (natural) almonds
4 ounces (½ loosely packed cup) diced
    glazed orange peel (see Notes)
4 ounces (½ loosely packed cup) diced
    glazed lemon peel (see Notes)
4 ounces (½ loosely packed cup) diced
    glazed citron (see Notes)
½ cup unsifted unbleached flour
⅓ cup unsweetened cocoa powder
    (preferably Dutch-process)
1 teaspoon cinnamon
¼ teaspoon allspice
¼ teaspoon white pepper
1½ teaspoons powdered instant espresso or
    coffee
5 ounces (1 cup) blanched and lightly toasted
    hazelnuts (see Notes)
½ cup mild honey
½ cup granulated sugar
Confectioners sugar (to sprinkle on after
    baking)

To toast the almonds: Preheat the oven to 350 degrees. Place the almonds in a shallow cake pan and bake in the center of the oven, stirring once or twice, for 12 to 15 minutes. Set aside.

Adjust a rack one-third up from the bottom of the oven and preheat the oven to 325 degrees. You will need a 9-inch springform pan that can be either 2 or 3 inches deep (see page 30). Cut a round of baking-pan liner paper to fit the bottom of the pan and cut a strip (or two shorter strips) about 1½ inches wide to go around the sides of the pan. Butter the sides and bottom of the pan. First place the strip (or strips) around the sides of the pan just touching the bottom and covering only part of the way up on the sides. Then place the round in the bottom of the pan. Butter the papers on the bottom and the sides, dust all over with fine dry bread crumbs, invert over paper to shake out excess crumbs, and set the pan aside.

Place all of the glazed fruits in a large mixing bowl. Sift together, onto the fruit in the bowl, the flour, cocoa, cinnamon, allspice, white pepper, and instant espresso or coffee powder. With your hands, mix the fruits with the dry ingredients, thoroughly separating and coating the pieces. Add the almonds and hazelnuts and mix again. Set aside.

Place the honey and sugar in a saucepan with a 6-cup capacity over moderate heat. Stir with a wooden spatula until the sugar is dissolved and the mixture comes to a boil. Then insert a sugar thermometer in the pan and let the mixture boil without stirring until the thermometer registers 248 degrees (stiff-ball stage); the mixture will reach this temperature soon after it comes to a boil.

Now you must work very quickly before the hot syrup cools and hardens. Pour the syrup onto the fruit-and-nut mixture, stir with a heavy wooden spatula to mix, and—without waiting—transfer the mixture to the prepared pan. (There will be just barely enough of the syrup to wet the dry ingredients.)

Immediately cover with a piece of plastic wrap and press down on the top with your hands to press the mixture into an even layer. Then use a can or a small saucepan or any round and flat piece of equipment to press down very firmly on the top to form a compact layer, and quickly remove the plastic wrap.

Bake for 40 minutes. (You will not know by looking or testing that the cake is done; it will become firm as it cools.) Do not overbake.

Set aside to cool. When completely cool and firm, remove the sides of the pan and the paper strip (or strips) on the sides. Cover the cake with a rack and turn upside down. Remove the bottom of the pan and the paper lining on the bottom.

Place the cake upside down on a length of wax paper. Through a fine strainer, generously sprinkle on confectioners sugar, forming a thick coating. Then, carefully, turn the cake right side up and sprinkle sugar on that side also. There should be a generous amount of sugar on both sides.

Wrap airtight in plastic wrap and let stand at room temperature for days if you wish—or a week or two (or freeze).

To cut into portions, unwrap the room-temperature cake, resugar if necessary, and using a long, sharp, heavy knife, cut straight down across the top. Then cut each half into 8 wedges.

NOTES: You can use glazed fruit that you buy already diced, or you can buy the large pieces and dice it yourself. If you dice it yourself, cut the pieces about ¼-inch square.

You can blanch and toast the hazelnuts yourself (see page 9). Or you can buy them already blanched and toasted (see page 9).

Loaf Cakes and a Giant Muffin

Black Pepper and Black Fig Ginger Cake

12 TO 16 SLICES

Sharp, spicy, and gingerful. A perfectly beautiful loaf with an intense, exotic flavor. A delicious coffee cake. Serve either plain or with cream cheese.

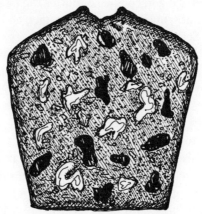

8 ounces (1 packed cup) black mission figs (see Note)
4 ounces (½ cup) crystallized ginger (see page 31)
1½ cups sifted unbleached flour
½ cup sifted whole wheat flour
1 teaspoon baking powder
½ teaspoon salt
2 teaspoons ground ginger
2 teaspoons cinnamon
½ teaspoon nutmeg
1 teaspoon freshly ground black pepper, ground fine
1 tablespoon unsweetened cocoa powder
4 ounces (1 stick) unsalted butter
2 teaspoons vanilla extract
¾ firmly packed cup light brown sugar
3 eggs graded "large"
¼ cup milk
Finely grated rind of 1 large, firm orange
6 ounces (1½ cups) walnuts, broken into large pieces

Adjust a rack one-third up from the bottom of the oven and preheat the oven to 350 degrees. You need a loaf pan with an 8-cup capacity. Either the standard 9-by-5-by-3-inch pan or, preferably, a longer, narrower, and deeper pan. The 10¼-by-3¾-by-3¼-inch pan (see page 29) made of shiny metal makes a gorgeous cake. Butter the pan, dust it all over with fine dry bread crumbs, invert the pan over paper, and tap lightly to shake out excess crumbs. Set the pan aside.

With scissors, cut the stems off the figs and then cut the figs into slices ¼ inch wide, and set aside. (If you dip the blade in cold water occasionally, it will prevent the pieces of figs from sticking to each other.)

Place the crystallized ginger on a large board. With a long, heavy knife, cut it into uneven coarse pieces, ⅛ to ¼ inch in size. Set aside.

Sift together both flours, the baking powder, salt, ginger, cinnamon, nutmeg, black pepper, and cocoa powder and set aside. Any of the ingredients that are too coarse to go through the sifter should be stirred back into the sifted ingredients.

In the large bowl of an electric mixer beat the butter until soft. Add the vanilla and sugar and beat until well mixed. Beat in the eggs one at a time (the mixture might appear curdled—it is OK). On low speed add half of the sifted dry ingredients, beat only to mix, beat in the milk, and then add the remaining dry ingredients. Beat to mix and then remove the bowl from the mixer.

Stir in the grated rind and then the figs, ginger, and nuts.

Turn into the prepared pan and smooth the top.

Bake for about 1 hour and 20 minutes until a cake tester gently inserted in the middle (all the way to the bottom) comes out clean (it should be moist, not dry, but clean).

Cool the cake in the pan for 15 minutes. Then cover the cake with a large pot holder or a folded kitchen towel, turn the pan upside down into the palm of your hand, remove the pan, cover the cake with a rack, and turn the cake and rack upside down, leaving the cake right side up on the rack to cool.

NOTE: Although the figs are dried, they must be soft and moist, not dry and hard.

Irish Whiskey Gingerbread

Black pepper, a double shock of ginger, and a shot of whiskey; it's an old Irish custom. A sharp spice cake with a tantalizing flavor and a moist and yummy texture.

8 PORTIONS

4 ounces (½ cup) crystallized ginger (see page 31)
1½ cups sifted unbleached flour
½ teaspoon cream of tartar
½ teaspoon baking soda
½ teaspoon ground ginger
½ teaspoon cinnamon
½ teaspoon nutmeg
½ teaspoon mace
1 tablespoon unsweetened cocoa powder
¼ teaspoon salt
2 ounces (½ stick) unsalted butter
½ teaspoon black pepper, ground fine
¼ firmly packed cup dark brown sugar
1 egg graded "large"
½ cup molasses
¼ cup milk
½ cup Irish whiskey

Adjust a rack one-third up from the bottom of the oven and preheat the oven to 350 degrees. You need a loaf pan with a 5-cup capacity; the 8-by-4-by-2½-inch pan (see page 29) makes a nicely shaped loaf. If you use a larger pan the loaf will not be as high, but the flavor will be fine nevertheless. Butter the pan and dust it all over with chocolate bread crumbs (see page 21), invert over paper to shake out excess crumbs, and set aside.

Place the crystallized ginger in the bowl of a food processor fitted with the metal chopping blade and process for about 15 seconds until the ginger forms a thick, pastelike puree. You should have a generous ⅓ cup of the puree. Set aside.

Sift together the flour, cream of tartar, baking soda, ground ginger, cinnamon, nutmeg, mace, cocoa, and salt and set aside.

In the large bowl of an electric mixer beat the butter until soft. Add the black pepper and the brown sugar and beat to mix well. Beat in the ginger puree. Add the egg and beat to mix. Then add the molasses and beat until well mixed. On low speed add about half of the sifted dry ingredients and beat only until incorporated. Then beat in the milk and ¼ cup of the whiskey (reserve remaining ¼ cup of whiskey to brush on top of the cake after baking). Finally add the remaining dry ingredients and beat only until completely mixed. (The mixture might not be perfectly smooth because of tiny pieces of crystallized ginger; it is OK.)

Turn into the prepared pan. Move the pan back and forth a bit to level the batter.

Bake for 1 hour and 5 minutes or until a cake tester gently inserted in the middle comes out dry and the top springs back when gently pressed with a fingertip.

Remove from the oven. Without waiting, slowly brush the remaining ¼ cup of whiskey all over the top.

Let cool in the pan for 10 to 15 minutes. Then cover the pan with a rack. Turn the pan and rack upside down. Remove the pan, leaving the cake upside down to cool on the rack.

Cut into thin slices.

Pepper Cake with Pumpkin and Prunes

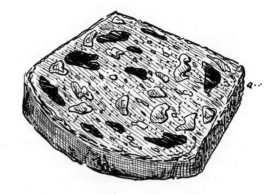

ABOUT 20 SLICES

This has pepper and ginger (and several other flavors); the combination is HOT! Wonderfully sharp and spicy. Sophisticated. Divine with a cup of tea or coffee, delicious with a tall glass of cold milk, or with a short glass of sherry or dessert wine. Easy to make. It calls for long, slow baking. Keeps well. Slices nicely.

1½ cups sifted unbleached flour
1 teaspoon baking soda
1 teaspoon cinnamon
1 teaspoon ginger
½ teaspoon nutmeg
¼ teaspoon cloves
¼ teaspoon salt
6 ounces (1 cup) soft and moist dried, pitted
      prunes
3 ounces preserved stem ginger in syrup (to
      make ⅓ cup sliced or diced)
4 ounces (generous 1 cup) walnuts
4 ounces (1 stick) unsalted butter
1 teaspoon black pepper, ground fine (see
      Note)
½ packed cup light brown sugar
½ cup granulated sugar
2 eggs graded "large"
1 cup canned unsweetened solid-pack
      pumpkin (not pumpkin-pie filling)

Adjust a rack one-third up from the bottom of the oven and preheat the oven to 325 degrees. You will need a loaf pan with an 8-cup capacity. This cake is especially attractive in a long and narrow pan that measures 10¼ by 3¾ by 3¼ inches (see page 29). Butter the pan, dust it all over with chocolate bread crumbs (see page 21), turn the pan upside down over paper and shake out excess crumbs, and set aside.

Sift together the flour, baking soda, cinnamon, ginger, nutmeg, cloves, and salt and set aside. With scissors cut the prunes into ¼-inch slices and set aside. Drain the ginger lightly and, on a cutting board, with a small sharp knife, cut it into very thin slices or small dice and set aside. Break the nuts into coarse pieces and set aside.

In the large bowl of an electric mixer beat the butter until soft. Add the black pepper and then both sugars and beat to mix well.

Beat in the eggs and then the pumpkin (the mixture might look curdled—it is OK). Beat in the prunes, ginger, and walnuts. Then, on low speed, add the sifted dry ingredients and beat only until incorporated.

Turn into the prepared pan. Smooth the top.

Bake for about 1 hour and 40 minutes until a cake tester gently inserted in the middle comes out dry. Cool the cake in the pan for about 15 minutes.

Then cover the cake with a pot holder, turn it out onto the palm of your hand, remove the pan, gently cover the cake with a rack, and turn the rack and the cake upside down, leaving the cake right side up to cool on the rack. (The cake will be rather tender when you turn it out of the pan. If you are not very sure of yourself, simply cover the pan with a rack, turn the pan and rack upside down, remove the pan, and leave the cake upside down on the rack.)

NOTE: Use only ½ teaspoon of pepper to make a cake that is equally delicious but less peppery-hot.

Caraway Raisin Pound Cake

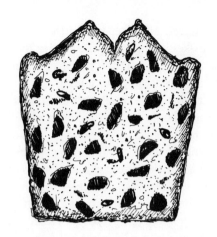

12 TO 16 SLICES

This is no ordinary, run-of-the-mill pound cake. Moist, dense, intense, compact, satisfying, chewy, with a fantastic crust that is divinely crisp (when the cake is fresh). It is old-fashioned, and I would say it is homey—but home was never like this. Loaded with raisins (two or three times as many as are usually used in a cake this size) and flavored with lemon, orange, nutmeg, caraway seeds, and brandy. The cake bakes for almost 2 hours.

12 ounces (2½ cups) raisins
3 large and firm lemons
1 large and firm orange
¾ cup granulated sugar
2 cups sifted unbleached flour
1 teaspoon baking powder
½ teaspoon salt
2 teaspoons nutmeg
8 ounces (2 sticks) unsalted butter
1 tablespoon vanilla extract
3 tablespoons brandy or cognac
½ firmly packed cup light brown sugar
4 eggs graded "large"
1½ tablespoons caraway seeds

Adjust a rack one-third up from the bottom of the oven and preheat the oven to 350 degrees. You will bake this in a loaf pan with an 8-cup capacity. That could be the standard 9-by-5-by-3-inch loaf pan, or, preferably, a longer, narrower, and deeper pan; the 10¼-by-3¾-by-3¼-inch pan (see page 29) makes a gorgeous cake. Butter the pan, dust it all over with fine dry bread crumbs, invert the pan over paper, and tap lightly to shake out excess crumbs. Set the pan aside.

The raisins get special treatment in this cake to keep them from sinking; they should be heated and cooled as follows: Tear off a strip of aluminum foil about 24 inches long. Place the raisins in the center of the foil, covering an area about 8 by 5 inches. The raisins should not be mounded high. Bring the two narrow ends of the foil together on top and fold together. Then fold the sides together to close securely. Place the package in the hot oven for about 15 minutes until very hot. Then let the package cool to room temperature. (To save time you may, if you wish, place the hot package in the freezer for a few minutes, and then let it stand at room temperature until you are ready to use the raisins.)

With a vegetable parer peel the thin colored rind of the lemons and orange. (You will not use the rest of the fruit for this recipe.)

Place the rind and the granulated sugar in the bowl of a food processor fitted with the metal chopping blade. Process for 30 seconds or until the rind is chopped fine. Set aside. (See Note.)

Sift together the flour, baking powder, salt, and nutmeg and set aside.

In the large bowl of an electric mixer beat the butter until soft. Beat in the vanilla and brandy or cognac, and then add the light brown sugar and the processed rind mixture and beat until well mixed. Add the eggs, two at a time, beating until smooth after each addition. On low speed add the caraway seeds and the sifted dry ingredients, scraping the bowl and beating only until incorporated. Remove the bowl from the mixer.

Open the package of raisins and, with your fingers, separate the raisins (which will be sticky now) to prevent them from sticking to each other. Then fold them into the batter.

Turn into the prepared pan and smooth the top.

Cover the top of the pan with a length of aluminum foil, folding the foil tightly around the sides (this causes the cake to steam, making it moist, and it prevents the top from overbrowning). After 30 minutes remove the foil from the top of the pan and continue to bake the cake. Total baking time is about 1¾ hours in the pan that is 10¼ inches long, and almost 2 hours in the pan that is 9 inches long. If necessary to prevent overbrowning, place a piece of foil loosely on the pan for about the final 30 minutes of baking. Bake until a cake tester gently inserted in the middle comes out clean and the cake just barely begins to come away from the sides of the pan.

Let the cake cool in the pan for about 15 to 20 minutes. Then cover the pan with a large pot holder or a folded kitchen towel, turn the pan upside down into the palm of your hand, remove the pan, cover the cake with a rack, turn rack and cake right side up, and let stand until cool.

NOTE: To make this without a food processor, do not pare the rind of the lemons and orange. Grate the rinds of the whole fruit on a metal grater, using the side of the grater that has small round openings rather than diamond-shaped openings. Do not mix the grated rind with the granulated sugar. Add the granulated sugar to the batter along with the brown sugar. Stir the grated rind into the batter after removing the bowl from the mixer, just before adding the raisins.

Espresso Date-Nut Loaf

12 TO 16 SLICES

A moist and dark loaf, loaded with soft dates, raisins, and crisp walnuts. Generously flavored with espresso. Serve as a not-too-sweet coffee cake, or use this for unusual cream cheese sandwiches. Easy. And exceptionally delicious.

It is best to buy whole pitted dates, not the diced kind. The diced ones are liable to be too hard and dry.

10 ounces (1¼ firmly packed cups) pitted dates
1 teaspoon baking soda
1 cup boiling water
2 cups sifted unbleached flour
½ teaspoon salt
½ teaspoon baking powder
2 tablespoons unsweetened cocoa powder
3 tablespoons instant espresso powder (see Note)
2 eggs graded "large"
⅓ cup vegetable oil (I use canola, safflower, or corn oil)
1 firmly packed cup light brown sugar
1 teaspoon vanilla extract
2½ ounces (½ cup) raisins
6 ounces (1½ cups) walnuts, broken into large pieces

Adjust a rack one-third up from the bottom of the oven and preheat the oven to 350 degrees. You will bake this in a loaf pan with an 8-cup capacity. It could be the standard 9-by-5-by-3-inch pan, or, preferably, a longer, narrower, and deeper pan. The 10¼-by-3¾-by-3¼-inch pan (see page 29) makes a gorgeous cake. Butter the pan, dust it all over with fine dry bread crumbs, invert the pan over paper, and tap lightly to shake out excess crumbs. Set the pan aside.

With scissors cut the dates crosswise into slices ¼ to ½ inch wide. Place the dates in a bowl. Stir the baking soda into the boiling water, pour onto the dates, and stir to mix. Let stand until cool or lukewarm.

Sift together the flour, salt, baking powder, cocoa, and espresso and set aside.

In the large bowl of an electric mixer beat the eggs to mix. Add the oil, sugar, and vanilla and beat to mix. Add the date mixture and beat only to mix. Then, on low speed, add the sifted dry ingredients and beat only until incorporated.

Remove the bowl from the mixer and stir in the raisins and nuts.

Turn into the prepared pan.

Bake for about 1 hour and 10 minutes until a cake tester gently inserted in the middle—all the way down—comes out clean. Once during baking reverse the pan, front to back, to ensure even browning. And watch the color of the cake during baking; if the top shows signs of darkening too much, cover the pan loosely with aluminum foil.

Let the baked cake cool in the pan for about 15 minutes. Then cover with a rack, invert the pan and rack, remove the pan, and let the cake cool upside down on the rack.

NOTE: If you do not have instant espresso powder, you can use instant espresso granules; simply add the granules to the hot-water-and-date mixture and stir to dissolve.

Napa Valley Prune Cake

2 SMALL LOAVES OR 1
LARGE TUBE PAN

*This is a plain whole wheat cake, dark and spicy, loaded with moist
stewed prunes and crisp toasted walnuts. Delicious. Not too sweet. Wonderful with tea or coffee. And it is easy.*

8 ounces (generous 2 cups) walnuts
1 1-pound-9-ounce jar stewed prunes (see
    Note)
1 cup unsifted unbleached flour
1 cup unsifted whole wheat flour
1 teaspoon baking soda
½ teaspoon salt
1½ teaspoons powdered instant espresso or
    coffee
1½ teaspoons cinnamon
1½ teaspoons ground ginger
1 teaspoon allspice
1 teaspoon nutmeg
1 teaspoon ground cloves
3 eggs graded ''large''
1¾ firmly packed cups dark brown sugar
1 teaspoon vanilla extract
1 cup salad oil (I use sunflower, corn, or
    canola oil)
½ cup unflavored yogurt

Adjust a rack one-third up from the bottom of the oven and preheat the oven to 350 degrees. Butter two 8½-by-4½-by-2¾-inch loaf pans, each with a 6-cup capacity (see page 29). Or butter a 10-inch Bundt pan or any other tube pan with a 12- to 14-cup capacity (see page 29); butter the pan even if it has a nonstick finish. Then dust the pan (or pans) all over with chocolate bread crumbs (see page 21). Shake out excess crumbs over paper and set pan (or pans) aside.

Place the nuts in a single layer in a wide, shallow pan and bake for about 10 minutes until they are hot to the touch. Let stand to cool and then break the nuts into large pieces and set aside.

In a wide strainer over a bowl, drain the prunes. With scissors or a small sharp knife remove the pits and cut the prunes into coarse pieces, cutting each prune into three or four pieces (do not mash or puree the prunes). You should have a scant 2 cups of prunes. Set aside.

Sift together the two flours, baking soda, salt, instant espresso or coffee, cinnamon, ginger, allspice, nutmeg, and cloves and set aside.

In the large bowl of an electric mixer beat the eggs to mix. Beat in the sugar, then the vanilla and the oil. On low speed add half of the sifted dry ingredients and beat only until mixed. Then beat in the yogurt, and finally the remaining dry ingredients, beating only until smooth. Add the chopped prunes and beat to distribute them. Remove the bowl from the mixer and stir in the nuts.

Pour the batter into the prepared pan (or pans) and place in the oven.

Two loaf pans take about 1 hour and 15 minutes; one large tube pan seems to take a few minutes less time. Bake until a cake tester gently inserted in the middle comes out dry and the top of the cake springs back when gently pressed with a fingertip. Cover the pan (or pans) loosely with aluminum foil for about the last 20 minutes of baking to prevent overbrowning.

Let cool in the pan (or pans) for 15 or 20 minutes. Then cover each cake with a pot holder or folded kitchen towel, turn the pan upside down onto the palm of your hand, remove the pan, cover the cake with a rack, and turn upside down again, leaving the cake right side up to cool on the rack. (If you have used a fancy tube pan, the cake should be cooled upside down.)

NOTE: If you want to stew the prunes yourself, you will need 12 ounces of dried pitted prunes.

Port Wine, Prune, and Pistachio Loaf

A beautifully shaped and mildly spiced loaf with chunks of moist, wine-flavored prunes and pistachio nuts.

Allow about an hour or more for the prunes to marinate.

A LARGE LOAF—ABOUT
12 SLICES

12 ounces (1½ packed cups) moist-packed
    dried pitted prunes
½ cup port wine
1 tablespoon Irish whiskey or cognac
2 cups unsifted unbleached flour
1 teaspoon salt
1 teaspoon baking soda
½ teaspoon baking powder
2 tablespoons unsweetened cocoa powder
1¼ teaspoons cinnamon
1 teaspoon ground ginger
½ teaspoon allspice
2 ounces (½ stick) unsalted butter
¾ firmly packed cup dark brown sugar
1 egg graded "large"
1 cup sour cream
6 ounces (generous 1 cup) unsalted green
    pistachio nuts

With scissors cut the prunes into ⅓- to ½-inch chunks and place in a jar with a leak-proof cover. Add the wine and whiskey or cognac, cover, and let stand for 1 hour or more, turning the jar occasionally from end to end.

Before baking, adjust a rack one-third up from the bottom of the oven and preheat the oven to 350 degrees. Butter a loaf pan with an 8-cup capacity. It can measure 9 by 5 by 2¾ or 3 inches, or 10¼ by 3¾ by 3¼ inches (see page 29). Dust the pan all over with chocolate crumbs (see page 21), invert the pan over paper and tap gently to remove excess, and set aside.

Sift together the flour, salt, baking soda, baking powder, cocoa, cinnamon, ginger, and allspice and set aside.

In the small bowl of an electric mixer beat the butter until soft. Add the sugar and egg and beat until mixed. Transfer to the large bowl of the mixer. On low speed add the dry ingredients in three additions alternately with the sour cream in two additions, beating only until mixed after each addition.

Add the prunes along with any remaining liquid and beat briefly only until barely mixed. Remove the bowl from the mixer and stir in the nuts.

Turn into the prepared pan and smooth the top.

Bake for about 1 hour and 20 minutes until a cake tester gently inserted in the middle of the cake comes out clean; for about the last half hour cover the loaf loosely with aluminum foil to prevent overbrowning.

Cool in the pan for about 20 minutes. Then cover the loaf with a large pot holder or a folded kitchen towel, turn the pan upside down into the palm of your hand, remove the pan, cover the loaf with a rack, and turn upside down again, leaving the loaf right side up on the rack to cool.

Apricot and Walnut Applesauce Cake

Applesauce cakes are deliciously moist. This one also has the crisp crunch of walnuts, the tantalizing tartness of dried apricots, and the lovely flavor of cinnamon and cloves. This can be served as a sweet bread (plain or with cream cheese) or as a most special plain cake.

ABOUT 10 PORTIONS

6 ounces (1 packed cup) dried apricots (see Notes)
6 ounces (1½ cups) walnuts
2 cups sifted unbleached flour
1 teaspoon baking soda
1¼ teaspoons baking powder
1¼ teaspoons cinnamon
½ teaspoon ground cloves
½ teaspoon salt
4 ounces (1 stick) unsalted butter
1½ teaspoons vanilla extract
1 cup granulated sugar
2 eggs graded "large"
2 cups unsweetened applesauce (I use Mott's Natural)

Adjust a rack one-third up from the bottom of the oven and preheat the oven to 350 degrees. Butter a loaf pan with a 9-cup capacity; I use the 10½-by-4½-by-3-inch pan (see page 29). Then dust the pan all over with fine dry bread crumbs or with toasted or untoasted wheat germ, invert the pan over paper, and tap lightly to shake out excess. Set the pan aside.

With scissors cut the apricots into slices ¼-inch wide, place in a large bowl, and set aside.

Cut or break the walnuts into medium-sized pieces and set aside.

Sift together the flour, baking soda, baking powder, cinnamon, cloves, and salt.

Add 2 to 3 tablespoons of the sifted dry ingredients to the apricots. With your fingers toss and mix to separate and coat each piece of apricot thoroughly. Then add the walnuts and toss and mix again. Set aside.

In the large bowl of an electric mixer beat the butter until soft. Add the vanilla and sugar and beat well until thoroughly mixed. Beat in the eggs one at a time. Then, on low speed, add about one third of the sifted dry ingredients and beat to mix. Add all of the applesauce and beat to mix. Finally add the remaining sifted ingredients and beat only until completely mixed.

Remove the bowl from the mixer and stir in the apricot-and-walnut mixture (along with any remaining sifted dry ingredients).

Turn into the prepared pan and smooth the top.

Bake for 1 hour and 25 to 30 minutes until a cake tester gently inserted in the middle, all the way to the bottom, comes out clean but not dry. Do not underbake.

Cool in the pan for 15 minutes.

Then cover the pan with a rack, turn the pan and the rack upside down, remove the pan, cover with another rack, and turn upside down again, leaving the cake right side up to cool.

When the cake is completely cool, wrap it in plastic wrap or wax paper and refrigerate for a few hours or overnight before slicing. Serve the cake either cold or at room temperature.

NOTES: The apricots should not be hard and dry; they should be soft and moist.

During baking the cake rises with a flat top. This is due to the moisture in the large amount of applesauce (which is also responsible for making this such an outstanding cake).

Rum-Raisin and Nut Gingercake

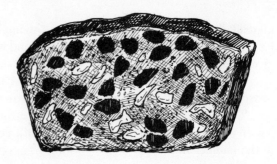

Made with fresh ginger, this has a light color, as opposed to gingerbread, which is usually dark. It is almost solid raisins and nuts, with a hint of rum and an irresistible flavor of ginger and lemon scrumptious. Although this is especially appropriate at Christmastime, it is equally delicious all year. It keeps wonderfully.

The raisins have to be soaked in the rum overnight or longer before you make the cake (see Note).

12 ounces (2⅓ cups) raisins
⅓ cup dark rum
8 ounces (generous 2 cups) walnuts
1½ ounces (a piece about 1 by 3 inches)
    fresh ginger
1 cup granulated sugar
1½ cups sifted unbleached flour
1½ teaspoons baking powder
½ teaspoon salt
2 ounces (½ stick) unsalted butter
3 eggs graded "large"
Finely grated rind of 2 large lemons

Place the raisins and rum in a jar with a leak-proof cover. Let stand overnight or longer, turning the jar upside down occasionally to marinate all the raisins (see Note).

When you are ready to make the cake, adjust an oven rack one-third up from the bottom and preheat the oven to 325 degrees. This should be baked in a loaf pan that measures 9 or 10 by 5 by 3 inches (see page 29) and has at least an 8-cup capacity. The cake will not reach the top of the pan, but this cake should not be any deeper. Butter the pan (even if it is a nonstick pan), dust all over with fine dry bread crumbs, shake out excess crumbs over paper, and set aside.

Break or cut the nuts into medium-sized pieces and set aside.

Peel the ginger with a vegetable parer (unless the ginger is very young and fresh and has a pale and thin skin, in which case it is not necessary to peel it). On a board, with a sharp knife slice the ginger against the grain almost paper thin. Fit a food processor with the metal chopping blade and, with the motor running, add the ginger through the feed tube and process for a few seconds, scraping down the sides once if necessary. Then add ¼ cup of the sugar (reserve the remaining ¾ cup sugar) and process for 5 seconds. Set aside.

Sift together into a large mixing bowl the flour, baking powder, and salt and set aside.

In the small bowl of an electric mixer beat the butter until soft. Add the remaining ¾ cup of sugar and beat to mix well. Then add the eggs one at a time, scraping down the sides as necessary and beating until smooth after each addition. Remove the bowl from the mixer. Add the processed ginger and the grated lemon rind and stir to mix. Then add the raisins along with any remaining rum and stir to mix.

Pour the mixture over the sifted dry ingredients and stir until the dry ingredients are moistened. Mix in the nuts.

Turn into the prepared pan and smooth the top.

Bake for 1 hour and 20 to 25 minutes until a cake tester gently inserted in the middle comes out clean and the top springs back when gently pressed with a fingertip.

Cool the cake in the pan for 15 to 20 minutes. Then cover the pan with a rack, turn the pan and rack upside down, and remove the pan. Cover the cake with another rack and gently and carefully turn the cake and both racks upside down, leaving the cake right side up to cool.

When the cake has cooled to room temperature, refrigerate it for a few hours (or longer), or freeze it for about half an hour if you plan to slice it immediately. This slices best when it is cold. The cake, sliced or unsliced, may be wrapped and stored in the refrigerator for several days, or in the freezer for longer.

NOTE: To save time, place the raisins and rum in a small heavy saucepan, covered, over low heat and stir occasionally until the rum is absorbed and/or evaporated. Uncover and cook.

Fig and Piñon Loaf

2 SMALL LOAVES

With dried figs, nuts, seeds, whole wheat flour, bran, and honey. Chewy, dense, wheaty, richly browned, and beautifully shaped loaves. Not very sweet. Delicious with tea or coffee, or at the table with or without butter or cheese.

7 ounces (2 cups) pecans or walnuts
10 ounces (1¼ firmly packed cups) dried
 black and/or brown figs, soft and moist
1½ cups sifted unbleached flour
1½ cups sifted whole wheat flour
2 teaspoons baking powder
¾ teaspoon baking soda
½ teaspoon salt
1¼ teaspoons cinnamon
1 egg graded "large"
½ cup mild honey
4 ounces (1 stick) unsalted butter, melted
1½ cups milk
⅔ cup All-Bran cereal
⅓ cup untoasted unsalted sunflower seeds
⅓ cup pine nuts (piñons)
Optional: additional pine nuts (piñons), for
 topping

Adjust a rack one-third up from the bottom of the oven and preheat the oven to 350 degrees. Butter two 5-cup loaf pans that measure 8 by 4 by 2 1/2 inches (see page 29). Dust them generously with wheat germ, oatmeal, or fine dry bread crumbs. Invert them over paper and tap lightly to shake out excess. Set the pans aside.

To toast the pecans or walnuts, place them in a single layer in a jelly-roll pan and bake for about 10 minutes until very hot to the touch. Set aside to cool. Then break into large pieces and set aside.

With scissors (wet the blades with cold water if necessary) cut the stems off the figs, and cut the figs into 1/2-inch chunks. To steam the figs, place them in a vegetable steamer or a strainer over hot water, covered, on high heat, for about 10 minutes until very soft. Then set aside and let stand, covered.

In the large bowl of an electric mixer sift together both of the flours, the baking powder, baking soda, salt, and cinnamon and set aside. Any of the whole wheat flour that is too coarse to go through the sifter should be stirred back into the sifted ingredients.

In the small bowl of the electric mixer (or in any small bowl) beat the egg to mix, then beat in the honey, melted butter, and milk.

Add the liquid ingredients to the dry ingredients and beat briefly only until incorporated. Remove the bowl from the mixer and stir in the All-Bran, figs, pecans or walnuts, seeds, and pine nuts (piñons).

Turn into the prepared pans. Smooth the tops. Sprinkle the tops with the optional pine nuts (piñons).

Bake for about 50 minutes, reversing the pans, front to back, once during baking to ensure even browning. Bake until a cake tester gently inserted into each loaf comes out clean.

Let the loaves stand in the pans for 10 to 15 minutes. Then cover a loaf with a pot holder or a folded kitchen towel and turn the pan upside down into the palm of your hand. Remove the pan, cover with a rack, and turn upside down again, leaving the loaf right side up on the rack to cool. Remove and cool the remaining loaf.

This slices best when it is refrigerated.

Texas Muffins

6 GIANT MUFFINS—SEE
NOTES

*Bakeries and restaurants all across the country are competing with each
other to see who can make the largest muffins. Pan manufacturers are
making muffin pans larger and larger. ("Nothing succeeds like excess.")
Standard muffin pans have a ½-cup capacity; these giant pans have a
1¼-cup capacity. Each muffin made of this batter in a standard pan
weighs a scant 2 ounces, but made in this giant pan each one weighs almost 8 ounces. This pan, as well as liner papers that fit it, is made by
Rowoco (see page 30).*

*These are whole wheat–applesauce muffins, moist and spicy. They
are large in size and flavor. Delicious with tea or coffee. Serve these anytime—all year—but they always make me think of Christmas.*

1½ cups sifted whole wheat flour
1 cup sifted unbleached flour
2 teaspoons baking soda
¾ teaspoon salt
1 teaspoon cinnamon
¼ teaspoon ground ginger
¼ teaspoon nutmeg
¼ teaspoon ground cloves
¼ teaspoon mace
4 ounces (1 stick) unsalted butter
1 teaspoon vanilla extract
1¼ firmly packed cups light brown sugar
2 eggs graded "large"
1½ cups applesauce, smooth or chunky,
    sweetened or not (see Notes)
5 ounces (1 cup) raisins
6 ounces (1½ cups) walnuts, broken into
    large pieces

Adjust an oven rack one-third up from the bottom and preheat the oven to 350 degrees. Line six 4-by-2-inch muffin pans (see above) with liner papers, or butter the pans. Set aside.

Sift together the flours, baking soda, salt, cinnamon, ginger, nutmeg, cloves, and mace. (Any whole wheat flour that is too coarse to go through the sifter should be stirred back into the sifted ingredients.) Set aside.

In the large bowl of an electric mixer beat the butter until soft. Add the vanilla and sugar and beat to mix. Beat in the eggs and then, on low speed, add the sifted dry ingredients in three additions alternately with the applesauce in two additions.

Remove the bowl from the mixer and stir in the raisins and walnuts.

Spoon the mixture into the prepared pan. (The forms will be filled almost to the top.)

Bake for about 45 minutes, reversing the pan once, front to back, to ensure even baking. The muffins are done if they spring back when gently pressed with a fingertip.

Cool in the pan for 5 to 10 minutes. Then cover the pan with a large rack, turn the pan and rack upside down, remove the pan, and turn the muffins right side up to finish cooling on the rack.

NOTES: This recipe can be used to make 28 standard-sized muffins (that is, two pans of 12 muffins each, and four of the forms in a 6-muffin pan). The pans can be lined with liner papers or they can be buttered. Line or butter the pans even if they are nonstick. For these pans adjust two racks to divide the oven into thirds. Bake one pan on one rack and two pans on another. After about 20 minutes of baking, reverse the pans, top to bottom and front to back. Total baking time for these standard pans is about 25 minutes.

I have made these muffins many times and they have always been a treat, but I think I have had the best results when I used Mott's Natural (unsweetened) applesauce.

Cakes Baked in Tube Pans

Light Pound Cake

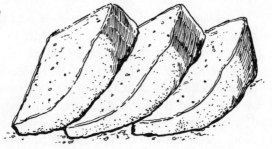

10 PORTIONS

This wonderful plain cake is about halfway between a sponge cake and a pound cake. The texture is light and airy and moist; the crust is a gorgeous golden-honey-amber color. Although I think this is easy, you can spoil it, easily, by underbeating the eggs at the beginning and/or overbeating after adding the butter and flour. So be careful. Good luck.

This stays moist and fresh for several days if wrapped airtight.

You will need a tube pan with a fancy design and a 12-cup capacity; it should measure 10 inches in diameter and 4 inches in depth (see page 29).

> 4 ounces (1 stick) unsalted butter
> 1 cup unsifted unbleached flour
> 1 1/4 teaspoons baking powder
> 1/4 teaspoon salt
> 6 eggs graded "large"
> 2 teaspoons vanilla extract
> 1 cup granulated sugar
> Optional: confectioners sugar (to sprinkle on
>   before serving)

Adjust a rack one-third up from the bottom of the oven and preheat the oven to 350 degrees. Generously butter a 10-by-4-inch tube pan with a fancy design. Dust it all over with fine dry bread crumbs (using your fingers to sprinkle the crumbs on the tube), and invert over paper to allow excess crumbs to fall out. Set the pan aside.

Place the butter in a small pan over low heat until melted, and then set aside to cool.

Meanwhile, sift together the flour, baking powder, and salt and set aside.

In the large bowl of an electric mixer beat the eggs with the vanilla and sugar at high speed for 25 minutes or until the mixture is pale and falls in a slow ribbon when the beaters are raised.

Mixing in the butter and dry ingredients should take only seconds. On low speed add the cool melted butter and beat only until incorporated. Still on low speed, add the sifted dry ingredients and beat only until incorporated, scraping the sides frequently with a rubber spatula. Do not overbeat.

Pour the mixture into the prepared pan. Bake for 50 to 55 minutes until the top springs back sharply when gently pressed with a fingertip. If the top becomes too dark, cover it loosely with foil for the last 10 or 15 minutes. The top of the cake will sink slightly toward the end of baking and while cooling. It is OK.

Let cool in the pan for about 10 minutes. Cover with a rack and turn the pan and the rack upside down. Remove the pan. Let stand until cool.

If you wish, generously sprinkle the top of the cake with the optional confectioners sugar through a fine strainer.

Transfer to a cake plate or a cutting board.

It is better to serve three thin slices as a portion rather than one thick slice.

Walnut Buttermilk Lemon Cake

12 TO 16 PORTIONS

The lemon flavor is intense. Walnuts and lemons complement each other. If you have ever had trouble with a buttermilk lemon cake (as many of us have had), your troubles (and mine) are over with this recipe. This very well may be the best lemon cake of them all.

It is plain—but gorgeous. It is a knockout.

7 ounces (2 cups) walnuts
Finely grated rind of 2 or 3 large and firm
      lemons
⅓ cup lemon juice
3 cups sifted cake flour
2 teaspoons baking powder
½ teaspoon salt
8 ounces (2 sticks) unsalted butter
2 cups granulated sugar
1 teaspoon vanilla extract
5 eggs graded "large"
⅔ cup buttermilk

Adjust a rack one-third up from the bottom of the oven and preheat the oven to 350 degrees. Butter a 10-by-3¾-inch Bundt pan with a 12- to 14-cup capacity (see page 29). Dust it all over with fine dry bread crumbs, using your fingers to sprinkle crumbs on the tube. Tap the pan upside down to shake out excess crumbs and set aside. (Butter and crumb the pan even if it has a nonstick finish.)

On a large board, with a long and heavy knife chop the walnuts into medium-small pieces (¼ to ½ inch) and set aside.

Mix the grated rind and lemon juice and set aside. Sift together the flour, baking powder, and salt and set aside.

In the large bowl of an electric mixer beat the butter until soft. Add the sugar and vanilla and beat to mix well. Add the eggs one at a time, beating until incorporated after each addition. Then, on low speed, add half of the sifted ingredients and beat to mix. Then add all of the buttermilk, beat to mix, and finally add the remaining dry ingredients and beat to mix.

Remove the bowl from the mixer. Stir in the lemon rind and juice and then the walnuts.

Turn into the prepared pan, pouring half on one side of the tube and half on the other side. Smooth the top.

Bake for about 1 hour until a cake tester inserted in the middle comes out clean and the top of the cake springs back when gently pressed with a fingertip. (The cake will not quite reach the top of the pan.)

The glaze should be mixed as soon as the cake is put in the oven.

GLAZE

⅓ cup lemon juice
½ cup granulated sugar

Mix the juice and sugar and let stand, stirring occasionally, while the cake is baking.

When the cake is done, remove the pan from the oven and let stand for 10 minutes.

Meanwhile, spread out a length of aluminum foil a little longer than the diameter of the cake.

Cover the pan with a rack, turn the pan and rack upside down, and place over the aluminum foil. Then remove the pan.

With a pastry brush, brush the glaze all over the hot cake until it is absorbed. If much glaze runs down on the foil, move the cake and rack off the foil, lift the foil, and pour the excess glaze onto the cake. Let stand until dry and cool.

When the cake has cooled completely, use a cookie sheet with three flat sides as a spatula and transfer the cake to a serving plate.

For each portion, two thin slices are nicer than one thick slice.

Carrot Fruit Cake

12 TO 16 PORTIONS

Gorgeous and delicious, moist and yummy, loaded with fruit (all dried—no candied fruit) and nuts. Made in a fancy pan, this is festive and looks like the Christmas season—but you will enjoy it anytime. If you make this (as I do) in the 8½-inch diameter nonstick La Forme Bundt pan with a 13½-cup capacity (see page 29), the finished cake will stand 4½ inches high and will look spectacular. Incidentally, the cake weighs 5 pounds, and makes a wonderful Christmas present.

No matter how many carrot cakes you have tried, don't miss this one.

4 ounces (½ packed cup) pitted dates
4 ounces (about 25 large) dried apricots
4 ounces (½ packed cup) dried pitted prunes
4 ounces (generous ¾ cup) raisins
8 ounces (2¼ cups) walnuts
2½ cups sifted unbleached flour
2 teaspoons baking soda
2 teaspoons baking powder
½ teaspoon salt
3 teaspoons cinnamon
½ teaspoon ground ginger
¼ teaspoon powdered cloves
¼ teaspoon allspice
¼ teaspoon nutmeg
1 pound carrots (to make 4 packed cups, grated)
4 eggs graded "large"
2 cups granulated sugar
1½ cups vegetable oil (I use safflower, canola, or corn oil)
Confectioners sugar (to sprinkle on top after the cake is baked)

Adjust a rack one-third up from the bottom of the oven and preheat the oven to 350 degrees. Butter a tube pan (preferably one with a fancy design) with at least a 13½-cup capacity. Dust all over with fine dry bread crumbs. Use your fingertips to sprinkle the crumbs on the tube. Tap upside down over paper to remove excess crumbs, and set the pan aside.

With scissors cut the dates, apricots, and prunes into ¼- to ½-inch slices or chunks. Place them, along with the raisins, in a medium-large mixing bowl and set aside.

Cut or break the walnuts into medium-sized pieces and set aside.

Sift together the flour, baking soda, baking powder, salt, cinnamon, ginger, cloves, allspice, and nutmeg.

Add 2 to 3 tablespoons of the sifted dry ingredients to the bowl of dried fruit. With your fingers toss the fruit well to separate and coat each piece thoroughly. Turn into a large strainer over the sifted dry ingredients and shake out excess dry ingredients. Set aside the floured fruit and the sifted dry ingredients.

Cut off the stem ends of the carrots. Then, under running water, scrub them well with a brush. It is not necessary to peel the carrots. Grate the carrots on a medium-sized grater. Set aside.

In the large bowl of an electric mixer beat the eggs to mix. Add the sugar and beat to mix. Then, gradually, beat in the oil. On low speed gradually add the sifted dry ingredients and beat only to mix, scraping the bowl as necessary.

Remove the bowl from the mixer.

Stir in the walnuts and the floured fruit. Transfer to a larger bowl and stir in the shredded carrots.

Turn into the prepared pan. Smooth the top.

Bake for about 1 hour and 20 minutes until a cake tester gently inserted in the middle of the cake comes out clean.

Let the cake cool in the pan for 15 to 20 minutes. Then cover the pan with a rack, turn the pan and rack upside down, remove the pan, and let the cake cool upside down on the rack.

When the cake has cooled, sprinkle confectioners sugar through a fine strainer over the top and transfer to a serving plate.

Tahini Carrot Cake

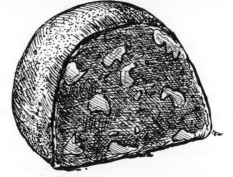

12 TO 16 PORTIONS

This simple-looking cake is out of this world. It has a subtle blend of spices, a rich mixture of flavors, and a moist and crunchy texture.

Tahini is a puree of lightly roasted sesame seeds with its own distinctive, nutty flavor. It is available in health-food stores and Middle Eastern grocery stores. The sunflower, pumpkin, and sesame seeds are from a health-food store.

You need a fancy tube pan with a 10- to 12-cup capacity. A 10-by-4-inch Kugelhopf pan with a 12-cup capacity makes a beautiful cake (see page 29).

Sesame seeds (to prepare the pan and to sprinkle over the top of the cake)
¾ cup unsifted whole wheat flour
½ cup unsifted unbleached flour
1 teaspoon baking powder
1 teaspoon baking soda
½ teaspoon salt
1 teaspoon cinnamon
1 teaspoon allspice
12 ounces carrots (to make a scant 3 packed cups, grated)
4 eggs graded "large"
1⅓ firmly packed cups light brown sugar
1 teaspoon vanilla extract
¾ cup vegetable oil (I use safflower, canola, or corn oil)
¾ cup tahini (see Note)
4 ounces (generous 1 cup) walnuts, in medium-sized pieces
⅓ cup unsalted sunflower seeds
⅓ cup unsalted pumpkin seeds
Optional: confectioners sugar (to sprinkle on top before serving)

Adjust a rack one-third up from the bottom of the oven and preheat the oven to 350 degrees. Butter a 10- or 12-cup tube pan that has a design (butter it even if it is a nonstick pan). Dust it all over with raw or toasted wheat germ or with fine dry bread crumbs; turn the pan upside down over paper to allow excess to fall out. Sprinkle the bottom of the pan lightly with sesame seeds and set the pan aside.

Sift together the whole wheat flour, unbleached flour, baking powder, baking soda, salt, cinnamon, and allspice and set aside. (Any whole wheat flour that is too coarse to go through the sifter should be stirred back into the sifted ingredients.)

Scrub the carrots under running water, trim the stem ends, and grate them medium or medium-fine to make a scant 3 cups, firmly packed. Set aside.

In the large bowl of an electric mixer beat the eggs, sugar, and vanilla to mix. Beat in the oil and tahini. Then, on low speed, add the sifted dry ingredients and beat only to mix. Add the nuts and sunflower and pumpkin seeds and beat only to mix.

Remove the bowl from the mixer and stir in the carrots until thoroughly mixed.

Turn into the prepared pan. Sprinkle the top lightly with sesame seeds.

Bake for about 1 hour and 15 minutes until a cake tester gently inserted in the middle comes out dry. Cool in the pan for 15 minutes.

Then cover the pan with a rack and turn the pan and rack upside down. Remove the pan, leaving the cake upside down to cool.

Sprinkle with the optional confectioners sugar through a fine strainer before serving.

NOTE: Tahini settles in two layers as it stands; it should be stirred until mixed before using.

Dartmouth Apple Cake

10 TO 12 PORTIONS

*Moist, crunchy, luscious, and loaded with ginger and spices, apples, wal-
nuts, and raisins that have been marinated in Frangelico liqueur (which
is made of wild hazelnuts). It is baked in a Bundt pan and looks gorgeous. Great for the holidays—for serving or gift-giving. Great anytime.*

*Granny Smith apples are crisp and sour. They are the right kind to
use for this. When you see perfect ones, fresh and firm, remember this
cake.*

The raisins have to be marinated overnight.

> 3½ ounces (¾ cup) raisins
> ¼ cup Frangelico liqueur
> 7 ounces (2 cups) walnuts
> 6 large knobs stem ginger in syrup, drained
>   (to make ⅓ cup chopped)
> About 10 ounces (2 medium) firm and tart
>   apples (i.e., Granny Smith)
> 1 cup unsifted unbleached flour
> 1 cup unsifted whole wheat flour
> 1 teaspoon baking soda
> 1 teaspoon nutmeg
> 1 teaspoon allspice
> 1 teaspoon cinnamon
> 1 tablespoon unsweetened cocoa powder
> ½ teaspoon salt
> 3 eggs graded "large"
> 1 cup granulated sugar
> 1 cup vegetable oil (I use safflower or corn
>   oil)
> 1 teaspoon vanilla extract
> 1 cup buttermilk
> Optional: confectioners sugar (for sifting on
>   top before serving)

Soak the raisins in the Frangelico in a small leak-proof jar for at least 12 hours, turning the jar from end to end occasionally.

Adjust a rack one-third up from the bottom of the oven and preheat the oven to 350 degrees. Butter a 10-by-3¾-inch Bundt pan with a 12- to 14-cup capacity (see page 29) (butter the pan even if it has a nonstick finish). Dust all over with chocolate bread crumbs (see page 21), and tap over paper to remove excess crumbs.

Place the walnuts in a wide, shallow pan and bake for 8 to 10 minutes until very hot to the touch. Cool, then break into coarse pieces and set aside.

Chop the ginger medium-fine (I use a small round wooden bowl with a half-moon chopping knife that just fits the bowl. You could also chop the ginger on a board with a long, heavy sharp chef's knife). Set aside.

To prepare and dice the apples: Peel them with a vegetable parer. Cut in half vertically. With a melon baller remove the core. With a small sharp knife cut a groove above and below the core to remove the stem and blossom end of each apple. Place the apples flat side down. Cut into slices a scant ¼-inch wide. Then cut as necessary to form julienne sticks a scant ¼-inch wide. Finally cut in the opposite direction to make a scant ¼-inch dice. Set aside.

Sift together the flours, baking soda, nutmeg, allspice, cinnamon, cocoa, and salt and set aside. (Any of the whole wheat flour that is too coarse to go through the sifter should be stirred back into the sifted ingredients.)

In the large bowl of an electric mixer beat the eggs to mix. Beat in the sugar, oil, and vanilla. Beat in the ginger. Then, on low speed, add the sifted dry ingredients in three additions alternately with the buttermilk in two additions.

When mixed, remove the bowl from the mixer. Stir in the raisins along with any remaining Frangelico, the walnuts, and the diced apples.

Turn into the prepared pan, pouring half on one side of the tube and half on the other side.

Bake for about 1 hour until a cake tester gently inserted in the middle comes out clean.

Remove the pan from the oven. Let the cake cool in the pan for 15 to 20 minutes. Then cover with a rack. Turn the pan and rack upside down. Remove the pan and let the cake cool upside down. Serve it upside down.

Before serving, sprinkle with the confectioners sugar through a fine strainer, if you wish.

Apple Cake from the Catskills

12 PORTIONS

This gorgeous cake is made in a tube pan with a fancy pattern. A generous amount of diced apples, walnuts, raisins, and spiced cinnamon-sugar are layered in and over the batter before baking. The result is a moist and crunchy cake with a variety of flavors and textures. Serve it plain as a wonderful coffee cake or with ice cream as a luscious dessert. This is easy to make. Once you have made it you will want to make it again and again.

3 cups sifted unbleached flour
3 teaspoons baking powder
1 teaspoon salt
2⅓ cups granulated sugar
2 teaspoons cinnamon
½ teaspoon nutmeg
½ teaspoon ground ginger
1¾ pounds (5 to 6 medium-sized) tart apples
    (preferably Granny Smith)
4 eggs graded "large"
1 cup vegetable oil (I use safflower, canola, or
    corn oil)
2 teaspoons vanilla extract
⅓ cup Calvados, applejack, brandy, or apple
    juice
2 ounces (generous ½ cup) walnuts, cut into
    medium-sized pieces
2½ ounces (½ cup) raisins
Confectioners sugar (to sprinkle on top
    before serving)

Adjust a rack one-third up from the bottom of the oven and preheat the oven to 350 degrees. You need a large tube pan with a fancy pattern and a 13- to 14-cup capacity. This is especially beautiful made in the large La Forme Bundt pan (see page 29). Or you can use the standard 10-inch Bundt pan. Butter the pan (even if it has a nonstick finish). Then dust the pan all over with fine dry bread crumbs. Use your fingertips to sprinkle the crumbs on the tube. Turn the pan upside down over paper to tap out excess crumbs. Set the pan aside.

Sift together the flour, baking powder, and salt and set aside.

Mix ⅓ cup of the sugar (reserve the remaining 2 cups sugar) with the cinnamon, nutmeg, and ginger and set aside.

Peel the apples with a vegetable parer. Cut them in half from top to bottom. Remove the cores with a melon baller. With a small sharp knife cut a groove above and below each core to remove the stem and fiber. Then cut into ⅓-inch dice and set aside.

In the large bowl of an electric mixer beat the eggs to mix. Then beat in the oil, vanilla, Calvados (or applejack, brandy, or apple juice), and the remaining 2 cups of sugar. Then, on low speed, add the sifted dry ingredients and beat only until smooth.

Pour half the batter (or a generous 2 cups) into the prepared pan, smooth the top, sprinkle with half the walnuts, half the raisins, half the apples, and half the cinnamon sugar. Then repeat with the remaining batter, nuts, raisins, apples, and cinnamon sugar.

Cover the top of the pan with aluminum foil and fold down the sides of the foil to make it airtight.

Bake for 25 minutes (see Note), remove the foil, and continue to bake for an additional 1 hour and 15 to 25 minutes (total baking time is 1 hour and 40 to 50 minutes). Cover the pan loosely with foil for about the last half hour to prevent overbrowning. Bake until a cake tester gently inserted in the middle of the cake comes out clean.

Let the cake cool in the pan for about 20 minutes. Then cover with a wide, flat cake plate and turn the pan and plate upside down. Remove the pan and let the cake cool completely.

Then sprinkle confectioners sugar generously over the cake through a fine strainer.

NOTE: Covering the cake with foil for the first 25 minutes of baking causes it to steam, which moistens the top layer of apples and prevents them from drying out.

Raisin Date-Nut Prune Cake

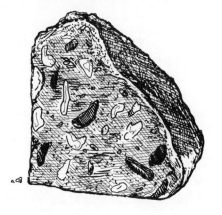

12 PORTIONS

This sour cream cake is dark, moist, chewy, and not too sweet; it keeps well, looks lovely, and is easy to make. You will need a 10- to 12-cup tube pan with a design; the cake is especially gorgeous in the 12-cup tube pan that has a simple swirl design (see page 29).

> 8½ ounces (2⅓ cups) walnuts
> 4 ounces (½ cup) pitted dates
> 8 ounces (1 packed cup) pitted stewed prunes
>   (see Note)
> 2 cups sifted all-purpose flour
> 2 teaspoons nutmeg
> 1½ teaspoons cinnamon
> 1 teaspoon baking powder
> 1 teaspoon baking soda
> ½ teaspoon salt
> 4 ounces (1 stick) unsalted butter
> 1 teaspoon vanilla extract
> 1⅓ cups granulated sugar
> 3 eggs graded "large"
> 5 ounces (1 cup) raisins
> 1 cup sour cream

Adjust a rack one-third up from the bottom of the oven and preheat the oven to 350 degrees. Generously butter a 10- to 12-cup tube pan with a design (butter it even if it is a nonstick pan). To coat the pan with chopped nuts, place ⅔ cup of the walnuts (reserve the remaining 1⅔ cups of the nuts) in the bowl of a food processor fitted with the metal chopping blade. Process for 8 seconds or until fine but not until buttery, or chop them fine any other way. Turn the chopped nuts into the buttered pan. Over a piece of paper tilt and turn the pan from side to side to coat it all over. To coat the tube it is necessary to sprinkle the nuts directly onto the tube with your fingers. Invert the pan over the paper to allow loose nuts to fall out, but do not tap the pan; the nut coating should be as heavy as possible. (When the cake is baked, the nut coating not only looks attractive but tastes crisp, crunchy, and delicious.) Reserve any nuts that fell out of the pan to add to the batter (or sprinkle a few of them back into the bottom of the pan). Set the pan aside.

Break or cut the remaining 1⅔ cups of nuts into rather large pieces and set aside.

With scissors cut each date crosswise into three or four slices and set aside.

Place the pitted stewed prunes in a wide strainer or colander set over a bowl and let stand to drain.

Sift together the flour, nutmeg, cinnamon, baking powder, baking soda, and salt and set aside.

In the large bowl of an electric mixer beat the butter until soft. Beat in the vanilla and sugar. Then add the eggs one at a time, beating after each addition until incorporated. Add the drained prunes and beat. (It is not necessary to cut the prunes; beating will break them up enough.) Beat in the dates and raisins.

On low speed add half of the sifted dry ingredients and beat to mix, then beat in the sour cream, and finally add the remaining dry ingredients, beating only until mixed. Remove the bowl from the mixer.

With a heavy wooden spatula stir in the nuts that are in large pieces plus any of the remaining nuts that were chopped fine.

Turn into the prepared pan, pouring half on one side of the tube and half on the other side.

Bake for 1 hour and 20 minutes until a cake tester gently inserted into the cake comes out clean and the top springs back when lightly pressed with a fingertip. Cool the cake in the pan for about 15 minutes.

Then cover the pan with a rack, turn the pan and the rack upside down, remove the pan, and let the cake stand until cool.

It is best to chill this cake in the freezer or refrigerator before slicing; it slices best when it is cold.

NOTE: If you want to stew the prunes yourself, you will need an 8-ounce box or bag. If you buy them already stewed, you will need a 16-ounce jar.

Cranberry Pumpkin Cake

12 PORTIONS

A large, dark cake made in a large, plain tube pan. It has a moist texture, a gloriously spicy flavor, chunky walnuts, and sharp and tart cranberries. The flavors, textures, and perfume are spectacular. Make it for Thanksgiving, and then you will make it all year. This is easy, and the nuts and berries do not sink.

6 ounces (1½ cups) walnuts
12 ounces (2 cups) fresh or frozen cranberries (see Note)
3 cups sifted unbleached flour
2 teaspoons baking soda
2 teaspoons baking powder
3 teaspoons cinnamon
1 teaspoon salt
½ teaspoon ground ginger
½ teaspoon finely ground black pepper
¼ teaspoon cloves
¼ teaspoon nutmeg
¼ teaspoon allspice
1 1-pound can (scant 2 cups) solid-pack pumpkin
2 cups granulated sugar
1¼ cups vegetable oil (I use safflower or corn oil)
4 eggs graded "large"

Adjust a rack one-third up from the bottom of the oven and preheat the oven to 350 degrees. Butter a one-piece 10-by-4¼-inch tube pan with an 18-cup capacity and no design (see page 29). Butter the pan even if it has a nonstick finish, and dust it all over with chocolate bread crumbs (see page 21). Use your fingertips to crumb the center tube. Turn upside down over paper and tap lightly to remove excess crumbs. Set the pan aside.

Spread the nuts out in a single layer in any wide pan and bake for about 10 minutes until very hot to the touch. Cool, and then break into medium-sized pieces and set aside.

Wash and drain the cranberries if they are fresh (see Note).

Sift together the flour, baking soda, baking powder, cinnamon, salt, ginger, pepper, cloves, nutmeg, and allspice and set aside.

In the large bowl of an electric mixer beat the pumpkin, sugar, and oil to mix. Add the eggs and beat until incorporated. On low speed gradually add the sifted dry ingredients, beating only until smooth. Remove the bowl from the mixer. Fold in the nuts and cranberries.

Turn into the prepared pan, pouring half on one side of the tube and half on the other side. Smooth the top.

Bake for about 1 hour and 10 minutes (if the cranberries were frozen when they were added, the baking time might be as much as 15 minutes longer) or until a cake tester gently inserted in the middle of the cake—all the way to the bottom—comes out clean.

Cool the cake in the pan for 15 to 20 minutes.

Then cover the pan with a rack and turn the pan and the rack upside down. Remove the pan. Cover the cake with another rack and carefully turn the cake and both racks upside down, leaving the cake right side up to cool on a rack.

Serve plain or with ice cream.

NOTE: If you are using fresh cranberries, place them in a wide strainer or colander, rinse under running cold water, shake to drain, and then spread out the berries in a single layer on an absorbent towel. Dry the tops lightly with a towel and let stand to air and dry until you are ready to use them.

If you are using frozen cranberries, which should not be washed before they are frozen because if they are damp before freezing they become mushy, wait until you are ready to add them to the batter before washing. Then turn the frozen berries into a wide strainer or colander, rinse quickly under running cold water, shake briskly to drain, and use immediately before the berries start to thaw.

Light, Lighter, and Lightest Cakes

Mile-high Sponge Cake

Gorgeous! Plain, simple, and sensational. The best sponge cake I know, as light as angelfood, more than 4 inches tall, moist, fine-grained, with a wonderful flavor of lemon and mace. This can be baked a day ahead if you wish. You will need a sugar thermometer.

10 LARGE PORTIONS

1¼ cups granulated sugar
½ cup water
8 eggs graded "large," separated
1 cup sifted cake flour
¼ teaspoon salt
¼ teaspoon mace
1 teaspoon vanilla extract
Finely grated rind of 2 or 3 large, firm
    lemons
1 teaspoon cream of tartar
Optional: confectioners sugar (to sprinkle on
    after baking)

Adjust a rack one-third up from the bottom of the oven and preheat the oven to 325 degrees. You will need a 10-by-4¼-inch two-piece angelfood pan that does not have a nonstick finish (see page 29). Nothing should be done to the pan; just have it ready.

Combine 1 cup of the sugar (reserve remaining ¼ cup sugar) with the water in a small, narrow saucepan (if the pan is too large or too wide, the thermometer will not be able to work). If possible, use a saucepan with a spout for pouring. Stir the sugar and water with a wooden spatula over moderate heat until the sugar is dissolved and the mixture comes to a boil. Cover the saucepan and let the mixture boil for 1 minute (to allow the steam to melt any granules of sugar sticking to the sides of the pan). Then uncover, insert a sugar thermometer, and let boil over high heat without stirring until the thermometer registers 230 to 234 degrees (thread stage).

Meanwhile, in the small bowl of an electric mixer beat the egg yolks at high speed for about 5 minutes until they are pale and thick.

When the sugar syrup is ready, pour it in a thin, threadlike stream into the yolks while continuing to beat at high speed.

After the syrup is added, continue to beat for about 5 minutes more until the mixture is completely cool and very thick. (If necessary to prevent splashing, reduce the speed slightly.)

Meanwhile, sift together the flour, salt, and mace seven or eight times. Then let stand.

When the yolk mixture has cooled, beat in the vanilla and transfer to a large mixing bowl other than the large bowl of the mixer (if you have an 8-quart bowl [see page 16], use it now). Fold in the grated lemon rind. Then, in several small additions, sift the dry ingredients over the top and, with a large rubber spatula, fold together just until incorporated. Set the bowl aside.

Now, with clean beaters, in the large bowl of the electric mixer, beat the egg whites until they are foamy. Add the cream of tartar and beat on high speed until the whites hold a soft shape. Then, gradually, on moderate speed, add the remaining ¼ cup of sugar. Increase the speed to high again and continue to beat until the whites hold a straight shape when the beaters are raised.

Add 1 to 2 cupfuls of the whites to the yolks and, with a large rubber spatula, fold together. Then add the remaining whites all at once and fold only until just incorporated. Do not handle any more than necessary.

Transfer the mixture to the cake pan, pouring half on one side of the tube and half on the other side. Gently smooth the top.

Bake for 55 to 60 minutes until the top just springs back when it is gently pressed with a fingertip.

When done, gently turn the pan upside down and either let it rest on its little feet or its elongated center tube, or suspend the tube of the pan over an inverted funnel or the neck of a bottle.

Let cool completely upside down. You can remove the cake from the pan now or you can cover it airtight and let it stand (right side up) overnight.

To remove the cake from the pan, insert a knife with a sharp and firm blade about 6 inches long between the side of the cake and the pan. Press the blade toward the pan and, with an up-and-down sawing motion, cut around the cake. Then pull up on the tube (and/or press up from under the bottom of the pan) to remove the sides of the pan. Then cut around the tube. And finally (always pressing the blade toward the pan), cut around the bottom of the cake.

Cover the cake with a wide and flat cake plate. Turn the bottom of the pan with the cake and the plate upside down. Lift off the bottom of the pan.

Let the cake stand upside down.

If you wish, generously sprinkle the optional confectioners sugar through a fine strainer over the cake; brush excess sugar off the plate.

Angelfood Cake

ABOUT 12 PORTIONS

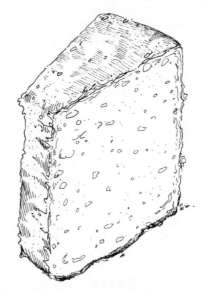

Although this is an old-fashioned cake, it is chic and popular today; there is no fat (butter, oil, or egg yolk) in angelfood cake. And although it is easy, correctly beating the egg whites and correctly folding dry ingredients into them are essential. The result is a glorious cake that is both plain and elegant. An accomplishment to be proud of.

You need a two-piece 10-by-4¼-inch angelfood pan (see page 29)— it must not have a nonstick finish—a very large mixing bowl (preferably with about an 8-quart capacity), and a large-sized rubber spatula (for folding in the large volume of beaten whites).

> 1 cup unsifted cake flour
> 1½ cups superfine sugar (see Note)
> 2 cups egg whites (from about 16 eggs
>   graded "large"; they may be whites that
>   were frozen and then thawed)
> ½ teaspoon salt
> 1½ teaspoons cream of tartar
> 2 teaspoons vanilla extract

Adjust a rack one-third up from the bottom of the oven and preheat the oven to 375 degrees. Have the cake pan (see above) standing by; do not butter it.

Sift together four times the flour and ¾ cup of the sugar (reserve remaining ¾ cup sugar) and set aside.

In the large bowl of an electric mixer beat the egg whites on moderate speed for 1 minute. Then add the salt, cream of tartar, and vanilla, increase the speed to high, and beat until the mixture holds a soft shape (that is, it should hold a point that will curl over) when the beaters are raised. Reduce the speed to moderate and start to add the remaining ¾ cup sugar as follows: Add 1 rounded tablespoon at a time, slowly sprinkling it all over the surface and beating briefly between additions.

After all the sugar has been added, increase the speed to high again and beat briefly until the whites hold a firm shape when the beaters are raised. But do not beat until dry—the whites should remain shiny.

Transfer the whites to a larger mixing bowl (preferably with about an 8-quart capacity).

Then, gradually—in about eight small additions—sift the reserved dry ingredients over the whites and, at the same time, gently fold the dry ingredients and whites together with a large rubber spatula. Do not handle any more than necessary.

Turn the mixture into the cake pan, placing half on one side of the tube and half on the other side.

With a long, narrow metal spatula cut through the mixture in a circular fashion, going around the pan two or three times to cut through any large air pockets. Smooth the top.

Bake for about 45 minutes until the top of the cake springs back when gently pressed with a fingertip.

The cake must cool in the pan upside down. If the pan does not have small feet or a raised center tube to keep the cake raised from the surface, it should be hung upside down over an inverted funnel or the neck of a bottle (any bottle will do if it has a neck that will fit inside the tube).

Cool completely.

Then, with a sharp knife that has a firm blade about 6 inches long, carefully cut around the outside of the cake, pressing the blade against the pan and cutting with an up-and-down sawing motion. Remove the outside of the pan. Then cut around the center tube and around the bottom of the cake (always pressing the blade against the pan).

Cover the cake with a flat cake plate, turn the cake and the plate upside down, and remove the bottom of the pan.

To serve, cut carefully in order not to squash the cake. Use a sharp knife and cut with a back-and-forth sawing motion. There are special cutters for angelfood cake, but with enough care a plain sharp knife will do just as well.

I have often read that angelfood cake should not be frozen because it will become tough. I believed what I read. But I recently tried it. I froze part of a cake and left part at room temperature; each part was wrapped airtight in plastic wrap. The next day I thawed the frozen piece and tasted both and could not tell the difference.

NOTE: To use plain granulated sugar, process it for 20 to 30 seconds in a food processor fitted with the metal chopping blade.

VARIATIONS: Mocha Angelfood Cake

> *Follow the above recipe with the following changes.*

Use only ¾ cup of unsifted cake flour. Add ½ cup unsweetened cocoa powder (preferably Dutch-process) and 3 tablespoons instant espresso or coffee powder. Sift the cocoa and espresso or coffee with the flour.

(When you fold the dry ingredients into the whites, you will think that the whites will not absorb them all. But they will.)

During baking the cake will rise very high and will form deep and wild-looking cracks; it is OK.)

This is glorious.

Optional—Before serving, sprinkle the top generously with confectioners sugar through a fine strainer, and then sprinkle with a generous layer of unsweetened cocoa powder through a strainer (on top of the sugar).

Spiced Angelfood Cake

> *Follow the above recipe, adding the following ingredients to the flour and sugar before sifting.*

1 teaspoon cinnamon
1 teaspoon unsweetened cocoa powder
    (preferably Dutch-process)
1 teaspoon instant coffee powder
½ teaspoon nutmeg
½ teaspoon ginger
¼ teaspoon cloves
¼ teaspoon allspice

Black-and-White Angelfood Cake

This is a production. It takes great care and finesse—as well as a sure hand and self-confidence—to fold together all the ingredients without losing any of the air that has been beaten into the whites. It is a high, moist, tender, spongy angelfood cake in which half the batter is chocolate and the other half is white. The two batters are placed alternately by large spoonfuls in the pan. The result is a dramatic, spectacular, picturesque cake; the height of elegance.

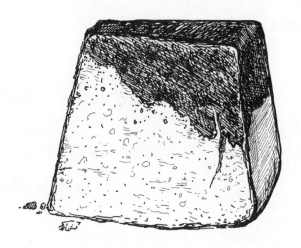

Follow the above recipe for Angelfood Cake (see page 131) with the following changes:

Use only ¾ cup plus 2 tablespoons of flour. Before sifting the flour with half of the sugar, remove and set aside 2 tablespoons of the flour and 4 tablespoons of the sugar.

Now, for the white part of the cake, sift together several times the 2 tablespoons of the reserved flour with 2 tablespoons of the reserved sugar and set aside.

And for the dark part, sift together several times the remaining 2 tablespoons sugar with 3 tablespoons unsweetened cocoa powder and an optional 1 tablespoon powdered instant espresso and set aside.

When you have followed the Angelfood Cake recipe through the step of folding the flour and sugar into the whites, transfer half of the mixture to a large bowl (it can be the bowl in which you beat the egg whites).

Into one of the bowls, in two additions, sift the reserved 2 tablespoons sugar and 2 tablespoons flour (that have been sifted together) and fold together carefully.

Into the other bowl, in two additions, sift the 2 tablespoons sugar with 3 tablespoons cocoa and optional espresso (that have been sifted together) and fold together carefully. (It is better if this is not thoroughly blended than if it is handled too much.)

Use two large serving spoons, one for each of the batters. Place 3 large spoonfuls (mounded high) of the white mixture in the bottom of the pan—leaving spaces between them for the dark mixture.

Then place 3 large spoonfuls of the dark mixture in the spaces. Continue, placing dark over light and light over dark.

Cut through the batter, cutting around and around two or three times with a long, thin metal spatula to cut through any large air pockets. Smooth the top.

Bake as above.

Layered Lemon Angelfood Cake

ABOUT 10 PORTIONS

This is made with the plain Angelfood Cake *(see page 131)*, which is cut into layers and filled with the following lemon filling. It is then covered with whipped cream. It is a grand and glorious, impressive and important dessert. You will be proud of it. The cake and filling can be made and put together the day before serving; the whipped cream can be put on the cake a few hours before serving. The cake should be refrigerated until serving time.

If fresh strawberries are available, they do go well with this cake.

After the cake is removed from the pan, let it stand while you prepare the following filling.

The cake and filling will be layered together in the pan that the cake was baked in; have the pan handy.

You need a sugar thermometer for the lemon filling.

LEMON FILLING

1 envelope unflavored gelatin
¼ cup cold water
6 eggs graded "large," separated
Finely grated rind of 2 lemons
¾ cup lemon juice
1½ cups granulated sugar

In a small custard cup sprinkle the gelatin over the water, stir, and then let stand to soften. In the top of a large double boiler off the heat whisk the egg yolks (reserve the egg whites) just to mix. Whisk in the lemon rind and juice and then ¾ cup of the sugar (reserve the remaining ¾ cup sugar).

Place over hot water in the bottom of the double boiler on moderate heat. Stir constantly, and scrape the bottom and sides with a rubber spatula until the mixture thickens enough to coat a spoon (at this point it will register 180 degrees on a sugar thermometer).

Remove the top of the double boiler, add the gelatin, stir for a few moments until the gelatin is dissolved, and then transfer the mixture to a mixing bowl. Place the bowl in a larger bowl of ice and water and stir constantly with a rubber spatula until the mixture is cold but not until it starts to set. Remove the bowl of the mixture and set aside.

In the small bowl of an electric mixer beat the egg whites at moderate speed for about 1 minute. Increase the speed to high and beat until the whites hold a soft point (one that bends over) when the beaters are raised. Then, gradually, at moderate speed, add the remaining ¾ cup sugar, 1 spoonful at a time. Transfer to the large bowl of the electric mixer and, on high speed again, continue to beat until the whites stand in straight peaks when the beaters are raised (the mixture will resemble a marshmallow cream). Remove the bowl from the mixer and set aside.

Now return the bowl of the lemon mixture to the ice water and stir constantly until the mixture just starts to thicken—do not allow it to actually set. Remove the bowl from the ice water and, without waiting, gradually— in small additions—fold about half of the lemon mixture into the whites. Then fold the egg whites into the last of the lemon mixture. Set aside briefly.

With a long, serrated knife, cut the top fourth off the cake to make one layer.

Brush the cake pan with tasteless oil. Place the layer of cake upside down in the oiled pan.

Pour one third of the lemon mixture on the cake in the pan and spread smooth. Cut another fourth off the cake, place it upside down over the layer of filling, and cover that with another layer of filling.

Continue to make a four-layer cake with three layers of filling. The top and bottom layers should be cake.

Refrigerate for at least 6 hours, or overnight.

To remove the cake from the pan, cut around the rim with a straight sharp knife. Cut around the tube. Cover the cake pan with a large flat cake platter, carefully centering the pan. Turn the pan and platter upside down. Lift and remove the sides of the pan, and then lift and remove the bottom of the pan.

Refrigerate.

WHIPPED CREAM

2 cups whipping cream
3 tablespoons confectioners sugar
1 teaspoon vanilla extract

In a chilled bowl with chilled beaters whip the cream with the sugar and vanilla until it holds a shape. It should be firm enough to use with a pastry bag if you wish, but no stiffer than necessary.

With a long, narrow metal spatula spread a rather thin layer on the sides and then spread a thicker layer on top. If you wish, decorate the cake with some of the cream in a pastry bag fitted with a star-shaped tube. Or the cream can all be spread with the spatula and then lightly swirled with the back of a spoon.

NOTES: It is best, when serving this, to place each portion on its side (not upright). Serve on plates 8 or 9 inches in diameter.

I made this recently to serve to an important food editor. I reserved some of the whipped cream to decorate the cake with. The rest of it I smoothed all over the top and sides. Then, with a large pastry bag and a number 7 star-shaped tube, I made a ring of large rosettes around the rim of the top. And sprinkled chopped green pistachio nuts on the rosettes. It was gorgeous, and a huge success.

Apricot Rum Cake

12 PORTIONS

You will bake three layers of heavenly sponge cake. After they have cooled, one of the layers will be cut into small pieces, marinated in dark rum, and then used as a filling (along with a generous amount of tart homemade apricot preserves) between the other two layers. To top it all, there is an inch-thick coating of light and fluffy marshmallowlike icing (some of which may be used—if you wish—with a pastry bag to decorate the cake).

All in all it is fantastic—with a powerful amount of rum. Mildred Knopf, in one of her wonderful cookbooks, said about a dessert that contained a generous amount of liquor, that when it was served it stood up and declared, "I can lick any man in the house." Ditto, this dessert.

None of this is difficult. The layers can be baked a day ahead if you wish. (This type of sponge cake, made without baking powder, does not dry out quickly.) But it is best to serve the cake the day it is filled and iced. If the finished cake stands overnight, the icing develops a slightly resistant, sticky quality—it is better when it is fresh.

This is a gorgeous dessert for a dinner party.

Making this calls for a large mixing bowl (preferably one with an 8-quart capacity—see page 16) and a large-sized rubber spatula.

SPONGE LAYERS
(3 9-INCH LAYERS)

12 eggs graded "large," separated
3/4 cup granulated or superfine sugar
1 teaspoon lemon juice
3/4 cup sifted unbleached flour
1/4 teaspoon salt
1/2 teaspoon cream of tartar

Preparing the pans is a bit of a bore, but I've tried every other way I could think of and this is the best. On three pieces of baking-pan liner paper trace around the bottom of a 9-inch layer-cake pan (see page 30); there should be at least a 1-inch border around the circles. With a piece of crumpled plastic wrap spread butter over each circle and slightly beyond the pencil lines. Sift flour over the buttered sections. Then, over paper or over the sink, shake off loose flour. Now, one at a time, cut out the circles by cutting just barely inside the pencil lines. Try not to handle the buttered and floured sections. Place each buttered and floured round into a cake pan, buttered and floured side up. (The sides of the pans must be dry; the cake must cling to the sides. Otherwise, the sides of the cake will buckle.)

Set the prepared pans aside.

Adjust two racks to divide the oven into thirds and preheat the oven to 350 degrees.

In the small bowl of an electric mixer beat the yolks to mix well. Gradually add 1/2 cup of the sugar (reserve remaining 1/4 cup sugar). Then beat on high speed for 5 minutes until pale, thick, and increased in volume. Beat in the lemon juice. On lowest speed gradually add the flour, scraping the sides with a rubber spatula as necessary and beating only until incorporated.

Transfer the egg-yolk mixture to a large mixing bowl (preferably one with an 8-quart capacity) and set aside.

In the large bowl of the electric mixer, with clean beaters beat the egg whites with the salt until foamy. Then, while beating, add the cream of tartar through a fine strainer. On high speed beat until the whites hold a soft shape. Reduce the speed to moderate and gradually add the remaining 1/4 cup sugar, 1 or 2 teaspoonfuls at a time. When all the sugar has been added, increase the speed to high again and beat until the whites hold a firm shape when the beaters are raised, but care beful—do not overbeat.

With a large-sized rubber spatula, gradually, in about three additions, fold the whites into the yolk mixture. Do not be thorough until the end. Do not fold even once more than necessary.

Divide the batter into the prepared pans. Smooth the tops with the underside of a large spoon.

Bake for 45 minutes or until the tops spring back when gently pressed with a fingertip and are richly browned.

As soon as the cakes are removed from the oven, turn each one upside down on a cake rack. (If the cakes are allowed to cool right side up, the tops will sink in the middle). During cooling, lift each pan briefly several times to be sure that the cake is not sticking to the rack.

When the cakes have cooled, cut around each with a small sharp knife, cutting carefully and gently, always pressing the blade against the pan and cutting with an up-and-down motion. Do not try to cover too much space with each cut.

When the sides of the cakes are released, place each pan upside down onto a rack. Now the cakes should come out of the pans easily. If you missed a spot while cutting, you may have to recut. Remove the pans. Do not remove the paper linings until you are ready to finish the cake. Cover each cake with another rack and turn upside down, letting the cakes stand right side up now.

If you are going to wait overnight before finishing the cake, wrap each layer in plastic wrap and let stand at room temperature (or freeze for longer storage).

HOMEMADE APRICOT PRESERVES

6 ounces (loosely packed, generous 1 cup)
   dried apricots
1/2 cup water
1/3 cup apricot preserves

Place the apricots and water in a small heavy saucepan and cover. Bring to a boil over moderate heat. Stir occasionally and cook, covered, until the apricots are tender. Uncover and cook for a few minutes until only 1 to 2 tablespoons of water remain. Add the preserves and stir to mix.

Transfer to the bowl of a food processor fitted with the metal chopping blade and process until smooth, or work the mixture through a food mill.

You will have 1 cup of preserves. Divide into three equal amounts.

Now peel the paper linings off the bottoms of the cakes.

Place one layer of cake upside down on a large, flat cake plate. Spread one part of the preserves on the top (which was the bottom) of the cake. Place another layer of the cake upside down on the work table and spread it also with one part of the preserves. Let stand.

Cut the remaining layer into 1-inch cubes and place in a wide bowl.

MARINADE

¾ cup dark rum

Pour the rum over the cubed cake and toss gently with a rubber spatula. The cubes should stay whole; do not allow them to break up. The cubes should absorb all the rum.

You will use the rum-soaked cubes to form a middle layer of the cake. Place the pieces carefully, one at a time, starting around the outer edge of the cake, on top of the cake on the cake plate. The pieces may be placed any which way, either side up, but they must be pushed very close to each other. When you have covered the entire surface, you will probably still have some of the rum-soaked pieces left over. You can use every one by just pushing them close enough to each other. You can always push two pieces apart a bit and squeeze another one in.

When they are all in place, lift the second layer with your hands and, by lining up the farther edges of both layers, place it, apricot side down, over the rum-soaked pieces.

Now, while you make the icing, place something flat and lightweight on top of the cake to weight it down very slightly. I use a clear plastic board that weighs 10 ounces. You could use one or two empty layer-cake pans. Or a round cake rack. Whatever, it must not be heavy or it will squash the cake too much, and/or press it out of shape.

Prepare Creole Icing (see page 68).

If you have a cake-decorating turntable, place the cake plate on it.

Spread the remaining preserves around the sides of the cake, especially to fill in any hollows. Then spread a thin layer of the icing around the sides to cover completely. Then add more icing on the sides, forming a smooth layer about ½ inch thick. Next, if you plan to decorate the cake with a pastry bag, reserve about a cup or so of the icing and pile the rest of it on top of the cake. Spread smooth. If you are not going to decorate the cake with a pastry bag, pile all the remaining icing on top, smooth the top and sides, and then form deep, gorgeous swirls and peaks with the bottom of a spoon. (I don't know any other icing that forms swirls and peaks as beautifully as this one does.) If you are going to use a pastry bag, be doubly sure that the icing on the cake is perfect—smooth, even, and neat. Then, with a pastry bag fitted with a star-shaped tube, decorate to your heart's content. This icing is divine to decorate with.

Let cake stand at room temperature.

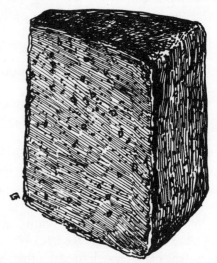

Rum Mocha Chiffon Cake

ABOUT 12 PORTIONS

The most glorious of all chiffon cakes! About 5 inches tall (that is very tall indeed), the color is deep mahogany, the texture is fine-grained, light, moist, spongy, and the flavor is espresso–rum–semisweet-chocolate. Ecstasy. It is a highly sophisticated cake. Not really difficult to make, but an achievement to be proud of. And you will be.

This remains moist and does not dry out even after several days.

(The difference between a chiffon and an angelfood cake is that angelfood uses only egg whites while chiffon uses the whites plus the yolks and vegetable oil.)

This is delicious as it is, as finger food, with tea or coffee. But for a spectacular dessert serve it with ice cream, fresh berries, and chocolate sauce.

You need a really large mixing bowl for folding in the large volume of beaten egg whites, a large rubber spatula, and an angelfood cake pan.

½ cup unsweetened cocoa powder
(preferably Dutch-process)
3 tablespoons dry instant espresso or coffee
¼ cup boiling water
½ cup dark rum (see Notes)
1¾ cups twice-sifted cake flour
1¾ cups superfine sugar (see Notes)
1½ teaspoons baking soda
7 eggs graded "large," separated, plus 2 to 3
additional egg whites to make 1⅓ cups
whites (the additional whites may have
been frozen and thawed)
½ cup vegetable oil (I use safflower, canola,
or corn oil)
2 teaspoons vanilla extract
1 teaspoon salt
½ teaspoon cream of tartar
Optional: confectioners sugar (to sprinkle on
top before serving)

Adjust an oven rack one-third up from the bottom and preheat the oven to 325 degrees. You will need a 10-by-4¼-inch angelfood pan. It must be a two-piece pan (the bottom and tube in one piece, the sides in a separate piece), and it must not have a nonstick finish (see page 29). The pan must not be buttered.

In a small bowl whisk the cocoa and espresso or coffee with the boiling water. Then stir in the rum and set aside.

Into the large bowl of an electric mixer sift together the flour, 1¼ cups of the sugar (reserve remaining ½ cup sugar), and the baking soda. Set aside.

In the small bowl of an electric mixer beat the egg yolks (reserve the egg whites) until well mixed. Beat in the oil, vanilla, and then the cocoa mixture.

Remove the bowl from the mixer (but do not remove the beaters). Add the egg yolk and cocoa mixture to the large bowl of the mixer (which contains the sifted dry ingredients) and beat until smooth, scraping the bowl occasionally with a rubber spatula.

If you do not have an additional large bowl and additional beaters for the mixer, transfer the mixture to another large bowl (if possible, use one larger than the large mixer bowl; see "An 8-quart Mixing Bowl," page 16). Wash and dry the used bowl and beaters.

Place the egg whites and salt in the clean large bowl of the electric mixer and, with clean beaters, beat at moderate speed until foamy. Add the cream of tartar, increase the speed to high, and beat until the whites hold a soft shape (a peak that bends over) when the beaters are raised. Then, on moderate speed, add the remaining ½ cup sugar, sprinkling 1 rounded tablespoonful at a time all over the surface.

When the sugar is all added, increase the speed to high again and beat until the whites hold a straight, firm peak when the beaters are raised. (For this recipe the whites should be a little more firm than usual.) Then remove the bowl from the mixer.

With a large rubber spatula briefly fold about one third of the cocoa mixture into the whites without being too thorough. Briefly fold in another third of the cocoa mixture without being too thorough.

If you have not already transferred the cocoa mixture to a bowl larger than the mixer bowl, and if you have one that is larger, transfer it now. (If you do not have one that is larger it will be OK. It is just easier to fold ingredients together in a bowl that is a little too large.)

Add the whites to the remaining cocoa mixture and fold together only until just barely blended. Do not handle a bit more than necessary.

Turn the batter into the angelfood pan, pouring half of it on one side of the tube and half on the other side. Tilt the pan a bit to level the batter.

Bake for 65 to 70 minutes until the top springs back when gently pressed with a fingertip. (The top will form deep and wild-looking cracks, but the cake will be served upside down and the cracks will not show.)

Remove the pan from the oven. The cake must cool upside down in the cake pan, but it will be too high to simply turn the pan upside down, even if the pan has three little legs or a raised center tube. Therefore, hang the cake upside down over an inverted funnel or the neck of a bottle, and let hang until cool.

The cake will shrink slightly while cooling.

To remove the cake from the pan, with a knife that has a firm (not flexible), sharp blade about 6 inches long and is narrow (not wide), cut around the sides of the cake. Cut with an up-and-down motion and, while cutting, always press the blade against the pan in order not to cut into the cake. Remove the sides of the pan. Then cut around the center tube, and between the bottom of the cake and the bottom of the pan.

Cover the cake with a wide, flat cake plate. Turn the bottom of the pan (and the cake) and the cake plate upside down. Remove the bottom of the pan.

Optional: Sprinkle confectioners sugar generously over the top of the cake through a fine strainer.

NOTES: An interesting aside about this cake: If you use water in place of rum, the cake does not rise as high and the top does not crack during baking. However, you can, if you wish, use whiskey or cognac in place of rum.

If you do not have superfine sugar, use granulated sugar, but first process it in a food processor fitted with the metal chopping blade for 20 to 30 seconds.

Cider-Jelly Jelly Roll

8 TO 10 PORTIONS

Everything old is new again. One of the most delicious foods I know—one that is totally new to me—has actually been made for more than one hundred years on the same farm with the same equipment by the same family. It is sugarless cider jelly, which is simply boiled cider with no sweeteners, preservatives, or additives. The cider from about fifty apples is boiled down to make one pound of wonderful, tart-sweet jelly. It is made on a small general farm in southern Vermont. I buy it by the case because I never want to be without it. I eat it with cottage cheese on crisp toast for lunch almost every day. I tell all our friends about it.

Frankly, because I wanted to tell you about this jelly, I made up this recipe. It is a light and tender jelly roll (as far as the recipe is concerned, you can surely use any jelly you like) covered with a smooth and shiny dark-chocolate glaze. The combination of the tart-sweet jelly and the chocolate glaze is tantalizing.

To buy the jelly by mail, send for a price list from Wood's Cider Mill, RFD #2, Box 477, Springfield, Vermont 05156 (802-263-5547). The jelly comes in different-sized jars; I buy the 10-ounce size.

4 eggs graded "large," separated
½ cup granulated sugar
1 teaspoon vanilla extract
¼ teaspoon salt
⅛ teaspoon cream of tartar
½ cup sifted unbleached flour
Confectioners sugar (to be used after the cake is baked)
8 ounces (about ⅔ cup) cider jelly or any other jelly (to be used after the cake is baked)

Adjust an oven rack to the center of the oven and preheat the oven to 400 degrees. Line a 15½-by-10½-by-1-inch jelly-roll pan (see page 30) as follows: Place the pan upside down on the work surface. Tear off a length of regular-weight aluminum foil about 18 inches long. Center the foil shiny side down over the pan. With your hands press down on the sides and corners of the foil to shape it to the pan. Remove the foil. Turn the pan right side up. Let water run into the pan, pour out the water but do not dry the pan (a wet pan holds the foil in place), and carefully place the shaped foil in the pan, pressing it gently to fit. To butter the foil use room temperature (not melted) butter and spread it with crumpled plastic wrap all over the bottom and sides. Sift flour all over the pan. Then, over the sink, tilt and shake the pan to spread the flour all over and to shake out excess.

In the small bowl of an electric mixer beat the yolks to mix well. Gradually add half (¼ cup) of the sugar (reserve the remaining ¼ cup sugar) and beat for a few minutes until the mixture is pale and thick. Beat in the vanilla. Remove the bowl from the mixer, transfer the yolk mixture to a large mixing bowl, and set aside.

If you do not have an additional small bowl and additional beaters for the mixer, wash and dry the bowl and beaters. In the clean bowl with clean beaters beat the whites with the salt until they are foamy. Add the cream of tartar and beat on high speed until the whites hold a soft point when the beaters are raised. On moderate speed gradually add the reserved ¼ cup of sugar, and then, on high speed, beat until the whites hold a straight point when the beaters are raised—but do not beat until dry.

Remove the bowl from the mixer. Sift the flour over the yolk mixture, place the beaten whites on top, and, with a rubber spatula, fold all the ingredients together, only until you do not see any dry flour; even though the mixture looks lumpy and uneven, do not fold anymore.

Turn the mixture into the cake pan, forming several large mounds rather than just one (the less you have to spread this airy mixture the better). Then, with the bottom of a large spoon, smooth the batter gently.

Bake for 12 to 13 minutes until the top springs back when pressed gently with a fingertip (test carefully in several spots). Do not underbake.

Remove the pan from the oven. Through a strainer sift a generous layer of confectioners sugar on the cake (this will prevent the cake from sticking to wax paper), cover with a length of wax paper, and then with a cookie sheet. Turn the pan and the cookie sheet upside down. Remove the pan and the foil lining. Cover the cake (this is the bottom of the cake) with another length of wax paper. Using the wax papers to encourage the cake to roll, roll it up with both pieces of wax paper, rolling from one long side to another. Holding the ends of the papers will make it easier to roll the cake. The seam should be on the bottom of the cake. Let stand until cool.

In a small bowl with a wire whisk beat the jelly until soft.

Unroll the cake. Remove the top piece of wax paper. Spread the jelly all over the cake, making it a bit heavier on the close side (which will be the inside of the roll) and thinner on the farther side; actually, stop the jelly about ½ inch before the farther side.

Now, with your hands, reroll the cake. At the end of the roll, lift the cake and place it, seam down, on a chocolate-roll board (see page 31) or any long and narrow platter.

To protect the board or platter while icing the roll, prepare two strips of baking-pan liner paper or wax paper, each about 16 by 5 inches. Fold each paper in half the long way. Slide each paper, folded side forward, slightly under a side of the roll. Set aside.

CHOCOLATE GLAZE

4 ounces semisweet chocolate
2 tablespoons heavy cream
1 tablespoon unsalted butter

Chop or break the chocolate into coarse pieces and place it in the top of a small double boiler over hot water on moderate heat. Add the cream and the butter. Cover and cook, stirring occasionally, until smooth. If necessary, whisk or beat the glaze to make it totally smooth. Remove the top of the double boiler.

Let the glaze stand, stirring occasionally, until it is cool and has a bit of body, but not until it actually thickens or becomes firm.

Then pour it slowly over the length of the roll. With a narrow metal spatula spread the glaze to cover the top and the upper parts of the sides. Then, to form an attractive rippled pattern in the glaze, make little up-and-down waves about half an inch apart with the spatula, first on the very top of the roll and then on the left and right sides.

Remove the strips of paper by pulling each one out toward a narrow end.

It is best, if possible, to let the jelly roll stand for several hours before serving; the slices will be more clean-cut than if it is sliced too soon. Let the roll stand at room temperature and serve at room temperature.

Because the cider jelly is tart, the roll really wants to be served with whipped cream on the side (a great combination).

WHIPPED CREAM

1½ cups heavy cream
1 teaspoon vanilla extract
3 tablespoons confectioners sugar

In a chilled bowl with chilled beaters whip the cream with the vanilla and sugar until it just holds a shape but not until it is really stiff. If the cream must stand, refrigerate it and whisk briefly just before serving.

VARIATION: Rum Apricot Jelly Roll

> *Follow the above recipe but use the following Rum Apricot Preserves for the filling. Delicious.*
>
> *Serve with whipped cream.*

RUM APRICOT PRESERVES
1 CUP

6 ounces dried apricots
½ cup water
⅓ cup apricot preserves
5 tablespoons dark rum

Place the apricots and water in a small, heavy saucepan. Cover. Over moderate heat bring to a boil. Stir occasionally and cook until the apricots are tender. Uncover and cook until only 1 to 2 tablespoons of water remain. Stir in the preserves. Transfer to the bowl of a food processor fitted with the metal chopping blade, add the rum, and process until smooth. Or add the rum and work the mixture through a food mill.

After the mixture cools, if it becomes too thick, thin it as necessary with rum and/or water.

Coffee
Pavlova

8 PORTIONS

Anna Pavlova was a world-famous Russian prima ballerina. Her perform-
ance in Swan Lake *was legendary; this dessert was most likely inspired*
by Pavlova's interpretation of the dying swan. Incredibly light. Both Aus-
tralia and New Zealand claim to have been the birthplace of this recipe.

The classic Pavlova is a vanilla meringue topped with whipped
cream and fresh fruit (strawberries and raspberries—or pineapple and pas-
sion fruit).

In this recipe the meringue is coffee-flavored. It is covered with
whipped cream and served with a simple chocolate sauce and a few op-
tional berries.

This meringue is amazing. It is dry and crisp on the outside, and
soft, moist, tender, and marshmallowlike (but not sticky) on the inside.
Even the next day.

The meringue can be made a few hours before serving (it takes an
hour to bake and a little more than an hour to cool) or the day before. It
will be shaped free-form with a long, narrow metal spatula on a lined
cookie sheet.

1 cup strained granulated sugar

3 teaspoons powdered (not granular) instant
    espresso or coffee

½ teaspoon cinnamon

½ teaspoon unsweetened cocoa powder

4 egg whites graded "large" (they may be
    whites that were frozen and thawed)

⅛ teaspoon salt

1 teaspoon cider vinegar or white vinegar

½ teaspoon vanilla extract

Confectioners sugar (to sprinkle on before
    baking)

Adjust a rack one-third up from the bottom of the oven and preheat the oven to 325 degrees. Prepare a cookie sheet as follows: First cut a piece of baking-pan liner paper to line the sheet. Trace a 7-inch circle in the center of the paper. Butter the sheet. Place the baking-pan liner paper pencil side down on the sheet. Then butter the traced area in the center of the paper, and about 1 to 2 inches beyond the pencil line (the meringue will spread). Sift flour onto the buttered paper and tilt and tap the sheet over the sink to shake off excess flour. If you have a cake-decorating turntable, place the sheet on it. Let stand.

In a bowl stir the sugar, espresso or coffee powder, cinnamon, and cocoa until completely mixed. Set aside.

Place the egg whites, salt, and vinegar in the small bowl of an electric mixer. Beat briefly on low speed and then on high speed until the whites hold a firm shape (but not until they are dry). Beat in the vanilla and then, on high speed, add 3 teaspoons of the sugar mixture, 1 at a time, beating for 10 seconds between additions. After the last addition beat longer if necessary until the meringue is really stiff (but not dry).

Now you must work very quickly to shape the meringue and get it into the oven before it softens and deflates. Turn the meringue into the large bowl of the mixer (or any other bowl approximately that size), add the remaining sugar mixture, and fold together only until you do not see any more dry ingredients (even if the meringue does not look smooth, do not handle it anymore).

Without waiting, turn the mixture out onto the buttered and floured section of the cookie sheet and, with a long, narrow metal spatula, spread the meringue to fill in the circle, smooth the top and sides, and shape the sides on an angle, making the top of the meringue about an inch narrower than the base. It will be about 2 inches high.

Through a fine strainer sprinkle confectioners sugar over the top and place it in the oven.

Bake for 1 hour. Then turn off the heat but do not open the oven door. Let the meringue stand in the oven for 1 hour.

During baking the meringue will expand and form several cracks on top. Then, during cooling, it will sink. Maybe the top will sink and the sides will not. Any of these conditions are OK.

Remove the sheet from the oven and, with a flat-sided cookie sheet, transfer the meringue to a cake plate and let cool.

Serve, or let stand, loosely covered, for several hours or overnight.

WHIPPED CREAM

1½ cups whipping cream
2 tablespoons confectioners sugar
1 teaspoon vanilla

In a chilled bowl with chilled beaters whip the cream with the sugar and vanilla until it holds a shape. If you whip the cream ahead of time, refrigerate it and then whisk a bit with a small wire whisk just before using.

SIMPLE CHOCOLATE SAUCE
¾ CUP

It is simple and easy, but rich, thick, and delicious.

6 ounces semisweet chocolate
½ ounce unsweetened chocolate
¼ cup warm water
1 tablespoon dark rum

Chop both chocolates into rather fine pieces, and place in the top of a small double boiler over warm water on moderate heat. Cover with a folded paper towel (to absorb steam) and the pot cover. Let the chocolate cook until almost melted. Then remove from the heat and whisk until smooth. Add the warm water all at once and whisk until smooth. Then whisk in the rum. Set aside until serving time.

This should be tepid or at room temperature when served. It can be reheated slightly in the double boiler if it thickens too much. However, if it becomes really firm, whisk it after heating to restore its original smoothness.

Shortly before serving, spread the whipped cream over the top of the meringue. At serving time, pour some of the chocolate sauce alongside each portion.

Tarts, a Pie, and Individual Strudels

Apple Tart

A jelly-roll pan is lined with a dough somewhat like a butter or sugar-cookie dough, which is filled with sliced apples, cinnamon sugar, raisins, and nuts, baked, and then covered with apricot glaze. Simple looking, but gorgeous. And delicious. And easy.

You need a jelly-roll pan that measures 15 1/2 by 10 1/2 by 1 inch (see page 30).

The crust can be made and shaped a day ahead if you wish, or it can be made just before using.

Serve the tart, cut into squares, either warm or at room temperature (it can be reheated). Serve it plain or with vanilla ice cream and/or Butterscotch Sauce (see page 407) or Clear Caramel Sauce (see page 408).

PASTRY

This should not be refrigerated before it is rolled out.

2 1/2 cups unsifted unbleached flour
1/3 cup granulated sugar
1/2 teaspoon salt
Finely grated rind of 2 large and firm lemons
5 ounces (1 1/4 sticks) cold and firm unsalted
    butter
1 egg plus 2 egg yolks graded "large"
1 tablespoon lemon juice

Place the flour, sugar, salt, and lemon rind in the bowl of a food processor fitted with the metal chopping blade. Pulse once or twice to mix.

Cut the butter lengthwise into quarters. Cut the pieces, all together, into 1/4-inch slices.

Add the butter to the processor and pulse the machine six times.

Place the egg, yolks, and lemon juice in a small cup and, with the motor running, pour through the feed tube and process for about 30 seconds until the ingredients barely begin to hold together (but not until they form a ball).

Turn out onto a large board or work surface. With your hands press the ingredients together to form a mound. Then "break" the dough as follows: Start at the farther side of the dough and, with the heel of your hand, push off a small amount (about ¼ cupful), smearing it against the work surface and away from you. Continue until all the dough has been pushed off.

Then form the dough into an 8-by-4-inch oblong.

Place the dough on a floured pastry cloth. With a floured rolling pin roll the dough carefully into an oblong about 18 by 13 inches (to fit in the 15½-by-10½-by-1-inch pan). Keep the sides reasonably straight and the corners reasonably square (although this dough can be patched and mended as necessary).

Trim the edges of the dough (most easily done with a pizza wheel).

To transfer the dough to the unbuttered jelly-roll pan, roll it up on the rolling pin and unroll it over the pan. Use your fingertips (or, if your fingernails cut into the dough, use the second joint of your bent finger) to press the dough into place. You can cut off excess dough and use it to patch and fill in wherever necessary. With a small sharp knife trim the edge even with the top of the pan.

Refrigerate. (You can cover the pan with plastic wrap and refrigerate overnight if you wish.)

FILLING

2½ ounces (¾ cup) walnuts
½ cup granulated sugar
2 teaspoons cinnamon
¼ teaspoon nutmeg
⅛ teaspoon ground cloves
About 3 pounds (about 6 large) tart apples
    (preferably Granny Smith)
2½ ounces (½ cup) raisons
2 ounces (½ stick) unsalted butter

Adjust a rack one-third up from the bottom of the oven and preheat the oven to 450 degrees.

Cut or break the walnuts into medium-sized pieces and set aside. Mix the sugar, cinnamon, nutmeg, and cloves and set aside. Peel the apples with a vegetable parer, cut them in half vertically, and, with a melon baller, remove the cores. With a small sharp knife cut a groove above and below the cores to remove the stems and fibers.

Place the apples flat side down on a cutting board. Slice the apples crosswise (not lengthwise—and not into wedges) into ⅛-inch slices. As you slice, keep the sliced apple halves intact (it will be easier to place the slices on the pastry).

Sprinkle all the raisins and then the nuts onto the pastry. Place the apple slices overlapping each other over the raisins and nuts lengthwise in the pan. (You will probably make three rows of apples if you have used large apples.) Leftover slices may be diced and sprinkled between the rows of apple slices.

Melt the butter in a small pan and drizzle it all over the apples. Sprinkle the cinnamon sugar evenly over the top.

Bake at 450 degrees for 10 minutes, then reduce the temperature to 350 degrees and bake for about 45 minutes longer (total baking time is about 55 minutes). Once during baking reverse the pan, front to back, to ensure even baking.

APRICOT GLAZE

Prepare the glaze when the tart has about 15 minutes more to bake.

½ cup apricot preserves
2 tablespoons Calvados or applejack

In a small pan over low heat melt the preserves. Stir in the Calvados or applejack. Strain through a fine strainer set over a small cup. Return to the saucepan over low heat. Bring to a simmer and let simmer slowly, uncovered, for about 10 minutes.

When you remove the pan from the oven, the glaze should be simmering hot. Slowly and carefully drizzle the glaze all over the tart, covering the apples as well as you can.

Serve hot or at room temperature. Cut into oblongs and with a wide metal spatula transfer to plates.

NOTE: Trimmed scraps of this dough make delicious cookies. Press the scraps together, roll rather thin, brush with milk, and sprinkle with crystal sugar or granulated sugar. With a knife cut into squares or strips, and bake until the cookies are golden brown on the bottoms.

Cheese and Fruit Tartlets

6 INDIVIDUAL TARTLETS

These have a crisp crust, a layer of cream-cheese filling, and a fresh-fruit topping. It takes time to make individual crusts, but they can be made and frozen (baked or unbaked) way ahead of time—or you can do it all shortly before serving.

The finished tartlets are fancy and festive; plan them for an important occasion.

You will need individual metal tartlet pans (preferably black metal) with fluted rims and loose bottoms. Mine measure 4⅝ inches in diameter and ¾ inch in depth (see page 30), although pans of a slightly different size or shape may be substituted.

PASTRY

Because of the egg yolks this is different from standard pie crust. It is easy, you don't have to be afraid of handling it too much, and it does not get soggy.

This pastry should be used as soon as it is prepared; it should not be refrigerated before it is rolled out.

1¼ cups unsifted unbleached flour
¼ cup granulated sugar
½ teaspoon salt
Finely grated rind of 1 large lemon
4 ounces (1 stick) cold and firm unsalted butter
2 egg yolks graded "large" (reserve 1 egg white to use below)
2 teaspoons lemon juice
1 egg white (for brushing on the crusts toward the end of baking)

Place the flour, sugar, salt, and lemon rind in the bowl of a food processor fitted with the metal chopping blade. Pulse once or twice to mix. On a board, with a long and heavy knife cut the butter into lengthwise quarters, and then cut the pieces—all together—into 1/4-inch slices. Add the butter to the processor bowl and pulse the machine six to eight times until the mixture resembles coarse crumbs.

Stir the yolks and lemon juice to mix, uncover the processor, sprinkle the yolk mixture all over the surface, and then pulse the machine again eight times—no more. The ingredients will not hold together.

Turn the ingredients out onto a large board or work surface. With your hands press the ingredients together to form a mound. Then "break" the dough as follows: Start at the farther side of the dough and, with the heel of your hand, push off a small amount (a scant 1/4 cupful), smearing it against the work surface and away from you.

Continue until all the dough has been pushed off, form it into a mound again, and "break" it a second time.

Form the dough into a fat sausage shape with flat ends. Cut the dough into 6 equal pieces. Cover with plastic wrap.

On a floured pastry cloth, with a floured rolling pin roll out one piece of the dough until it is about 6 1/2 inches in diameter. Roll the dough up loosely on the rolling pin and then unroll it over one of the tartlet pans, centering it carefully. Gently ease down the sides of the dough, making it fit the pan without being stretched, and at the same time forming the sides a little thicker than the bottom.

The dough can be patched if it tears or breaks. (But it will not stick if there is much flour on one of the pieces. Brush off the flour and/or wet the piece very slightly with water.)

Then trim the top of the pastry, making it even with the top of the pan, by cutting it with a small sharp knife.

Repeat to form all the crusts. It is not necessary to prick these with a fork. Place in the freezer until firm.

Before baking, adjust an oven rack one-third up from the bottom and preheat the oven to 450 degrees. Tear regular-weight (not heavy-weight) aluminum foil into squares about 6 inches in diameter. With scissors cut the squares casually (they do not have to be perfect) into round shapes 6 inches in diameter.

When the crusts are frozen firm, line each one with a round of the foil, placing the shiny side against the crust. With your fingers, press firmly against the bottom and sides. And, to keep the pastry from puffing up, fill each shell with dried beans (reserved for this purpose) or with aluminum pie pellets.

Place the crusts on a large cookie sheet and bake for 10 minutes. Then remove the sheet and pans from the oven, reduce the temperature to 325 degrees, and carefully remove the foil and beans or pellets by lifting opposite sides of the foil.

Return the pans to the cookie sheet and continue to bake at 325 degrees for about 5 to 8 minutes more (total baking time is about 15 to 18 minutes).

While the crusts are baking, beat the egg white slightly just until foamy. During the last few minutes of baking, brush the crusts with the egg white (this seals the crust and keeps it crisp). Bake until the rims are golden and the bottoms are sandy-colored.

Remove from the oven and let stand until cool. Then remove the crusts from the pans.

If these are made a day or two ahead, they may be stored airtight at room temperature. For longer storage they may be frozen (in a freezer box).

CREAM CHEESE FILLING
ENOUGH FOR 6 TARTLETS

8 ounces cream cheese (at room temperature)
3 tablespoons honey
3 tablespoons whipping cream

In the small bowl of an electric mixer beat the cheese with the honey and cream until soft and smooth.

With a small spoon spread about 3 tablespoons of the filling 1/4 to 1/3 inch thick over the bottoms of the pastry shells.

STRAWBERRY TOPPING
FOR 6 TARTLETS

You will need about 2 quarts of fresh medium-sized strawberries. Wash, hull, and drain them. Reserve 1 whole berry for each tartlet and cut the remaining berries in half the long way. Place the berry halves on top of the cheese filling as follows: First place a ring of berries around the outer edge, placing each berry half on its flat (cut) side, with its wide end (stem end) around the outside. The berries should be touching each other. Then repeat with a second row (unless the berries are so large that only one row will fit). In the center place 1 berry standing upright.

APPLE TOPPING
FOR 6 TARTLETS

You will need about 3 pounds (6 medium-sized) tart apples (preferably Granny Smith). Peel the apples with a vegetable parer, cut them in half the long way, and with a mellon baller remove the cores. With a small sharp knife cut a small groove above and below the cores to remove the stems and fibers. Cut the apples into 1/2-inch dice. In a wide frying pan melt 2 ounces (1/2 stick) unsalted butter, then add about 5 tablespoons granulated sugar and the apples. Stir, cover, and cook over high heat for a few minutes. Then cook uncovered, stirring occasionally, until the apples are tender. Cool.

This apple mixture may stand overnight, refrigerated, or it may be used as soon as it has cooled.

Fill the crusts with the apples, mounding them high.

CHERRY TOPPING
FOR 6 TARTLETS

Because these cherries are cooked, they become juicy and it is best not to put them on top of the cheese filling too far ahead of time; 1 hour is about the longest they should stand. You need fresh black Bing cherries, and a cherry pitter (see page 31).

One and a half pounds of large cherries should be enough. With a cherry pitter, pit the cherries.

Place the cherries with 4 tablespoons of kirsch and 4 tablespoons of granulated sugar in a wide frying pan over high heat. Stir constantly for 2 to 3 minutes until the cherries are barely tender. Do not overcook or the cherries will wrinkle too much. Pour into a strainer set over a bowl. (There will be a few tablespoons of syrup remaining; reserve it for some other use—for instance, over ice cream or mixed with a fresh fruit cup.)

Cool and then chill the cherries. Shortly before serving, place them on top of the cheese filling. Start at the outside of the tartlets and place them, touching each other, to fill in the tops.

GLAZE

For the strawberry or cherry tartlets, use bright-red currant jelly. (Both Crosse & Blackwell and Robertson's have great color and stay clear and shiny.) For the apple tartlets, use apricot preserves. Use a scant 1/2 cup of preserves. Place in a small pan over low heat and stir frequently to melt. Apricot preserves should be strained; currant jelly does not have to be strained. Brush the warm preserves generously all over the fruit, covering the fruit and also any spaces between pieces of fruit.

Refrigerate and serve cold.

VARIATIONS: Other fruits may be substituted in place of those mentioned. Or you can use a combination; for instance, blueberries with raspberries or strawberries.

Free-form Apple Tartlets

4 INDIVIDUAL TARTLETS   BAKED

I think it is easier to make these than a standard apple pie. Most of the work can be done a day ahead if you wish. The tartlets can be served piping hot right out of the oven (you can reheat them), or at room temperature.

The delicious pastry is quickly made in a food processor. It will be chilled, then divided into pieces, rolled into rounds, wrapped, and refrigerated until you are ready to bake. The apples will be cut, sautéed with the filling ingredients, and cooled. They may be used at this stage or refrigerated for a day or two. You can make and bake the tartlets all at one time, or, if you wish, you can bake only one or two and reserve the remaining pastry and apples. Or you can divide the recipe in half and make only two. Or multiply it to make more. You can prepare either the pastry or the filling first.

Serve the tartlets plain or with Butterscotch Sauce (see page 407) or Clear Caramel Sauce (see page 408).

PASTRY

> 4 ounces (1 stick) cold and firm unsalted
>   butter
> 1 cup unsifted unbleached flour
> ½ teaspoon salt
> 1 tablespoon granulated sugar
> 3 tablespoons ice water

Cut the butter lengthwise into quarters. Cut the pieces—all together—into ¼-inch slices. Refrigerate.

Place the flour, salt, and sugar in the bowl of a food processor fitted with the metal chopping blade. Add the cold butter and pulse the machine four or five times—no more. With the motor running add the ice water all at once through the feed tube and process only for 7 or 8 seconds—no longer. The ingredients will not (should not) hold together now.

Turn out onto a large board or work surface. With your hands quickly press the ingredients together, and then form the dough into a fat sausage shape with flat ends. Tiny pieces of butter should remain visible in the dough. Wrap in plastic wrap and refrigerate for about 30 minutes.

Then cut the dough into fourths, rewrap, and refrigerate for 30 minutes or longer.

FILLING

> 2 pounds of tart apples (about 4
>   medium-large), preferably Granny Smith
> 3 tablespoons unsalted butter
> ¼ cup granulated sugar
> 1 teaspoon cinnamon
> Pinch of nutmeg
> 4 tablespoons water
> Finely grated rind of 1 large lemon
> ¼ cup raisins
> ⅓ cup walnuts, cut or broken into
>   medium-sized pieces

Peel the apples with a vegetable parer. Cut the apples in half vertically and with a melon baller remove the cores. With a small sharp knife cut grooves above and below the cores to remove the stems and fibers. Cut each piece into 4 to 6 wedges (depending on the size of the apples). Then cut each piece crosswise into 4 to 6 pieces (depending on the size), cutting through 2 or 3 pieces at a time.

In a wide nonstick frying pan, place the butter, sugar, cinnamon, nutmeg, water, and lemon rind. Stir over high heat to melt the butter and mix the ingredients. Add the apples, stir, and cook, covered, for 5 minutes. Then stir in the raisins, and cook uncovered, stirring frequently, for about 5 minutes more until all the liquid has completely evaporated and the apples are tender—but not falling apart.

Set aside to cool completely. If you are not ready to complete the tartlets now, the filling can be refrigerated.

Just before using, stir in the nuts.

GLAZE AND TOPPING

1 egg yolk
1 teaspoon water, plus additional water (for
    brushing)
Crystal sugar (see page 4) or granulated sugar
    (to sprinkle on top)
Apricot preserves (to brush on after baking)

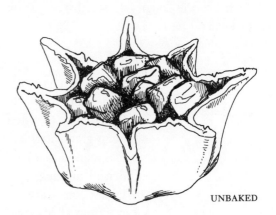

UNBAKED

In a small cup mix the yolk and 1 teaspoon of water to make a glaze and set aside.

When you are ready to bake, adjust a rack one-third up from the bottom of the oven and preheat the oven to 450 degrees.

On a floured pastry cloth, with a floured rolling pin pound a round of the dough until it is soft enough to be rolled out. Then roll it into a round shape 6½ to 7 inches wide. It is all right if it is not a perfect circle. However, if the edges are ragged they can be trimmed just a bit with a pizza wheel (preferably) or with scissors. The rolled out rounds of pastry should be stacked with plastic wrap between the rounds and should be refrigerated.

Place one fourth of the cooked and cooled filling in the center of one round, mounding it high and leaving a 1½-inch border. Brush the border with water and, with your fingers, raise the border and pinch deep pleats in it about 1 to 1½ inches apart, making it stand up straight (see illustration). Then, with your fingertip, press down on the spaces between the pleats (pressing them against the filling), and fold down the pleats (they can be folded either to the left or the right).

Repeat filling and shaping all the rounds of dough. Work quickly before the dough softens. As you shape each tartlet, with a wide metal spatula transfer it to an unbuttered cookie sheet. Four tartlets will fit on one sheet. If you have a dark or nonstick sheet, use it (a dark or nonstick sheet helps the bottom crust brown).

Brush the glaze on the sides of the tartlets and then sprinkle the pastry and the exposed filling with the crystal or granulated sugar.

Bake for 5 minutes, and then reduce the temperature to 400 degrees and continue to bake for 25 to 30 minutes more (total baking time is about 30 to 35 minutes) until golden. Do not underbake.

While the tartlets are baking, prepare the apricot preserves. You will use about a tablespoon or so for each tartlet. In a small saucepan over moderate heat stir the preserves until melted. Strain through a small strainer set over a cup, and then return to the saucepan. Just before the tartlets are finished, heat the preserves to a simmer.

As soon as the tartlets are baked, loosen them from the cookie sheet with a wide metal spatula and transfer them to a rack. Brush the hot preserves on the sides of the hot tartlets, and drizzle some of it over the filling.

Serve as soon as possible. Serve plain or with ice cream.

NOTE: Due to a change of plans, I was obliged to serve these in the evening instead of at noon, as I had planned. I was not optimistic about them, since they had waited so long after they were baked. Just before serving I warmed them for about 5 minutes in a 400-degree oven on a cookie sheet, and they were as crisp and delicious as when they were just baked.

These can also be frozen after they are baked, wrapped individually in foil. To serve, place them directly from the freezer—still wrapped in foil—in a 400-degree oven for 30 minutes. Then open the package and continue to bake for 5 minutes more.

Joe's Chocolate Fudge Pie

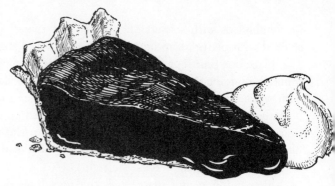

8 TO 10 PORTIONS

Shortly after I met Bob Andrews, an Associated Press editor in Washington, D.C., he asked me if I ever get tired of chocolate. I answered, "Never."

"Do you really love it?"

"Yes, I really love it."

Why did he sound suspicious? My guess was that he himself was not crazy about chocolate.

I asked, "Do you like chocolate?"

He broke into a wide grin, his eyes sparkled, and slowly he said, "Yes, I like chocolate very much—I love it."

Although we were almost strangers, we suddenly had a deep bond. And then, to seal the bond, Bob offered to send a wonderful chocolate recipe to me.

It arrived promptly with this memo: "This pie is very easy to prepare and it will knock your socks off. It creates ecstacy."

Yes, it knocked my socks off. Yes, it creates ecstacy.

It has a crisp pie crust, and a chocolate-fudge filling that is about halfway between a dense fudge sauce and fudge candy. When timed carefully the filling is almost—but not completely—firm. An irresistible quality. Smooth as silk.

You need a 9-inch Pyrex pie plate (see page 30).

Prepare the pastry for Free-form Apple Tartlets (see page 163). After the ingredients are removed from the processor bowl, press them together until they hold together and form a ball. Wrap and refrigerate for 30 minutes.

On a floured pastry cloth, with a floured rolling pin roll out the dough into a 13-inch circle. Roll it up loosely on the rolling pin and unroll it over the pie plate, centering it carefully.

If you have a cake-decorating turntable, place the pie plate on it. Carefully, ease the dough down on the sides of the plate, making it a little thicker on the sides—and making it fit the plate all over.

Trim, fold, and flute the edge as you wish. I like to make a zigzag pattern as follows: With scissors trim the edge of the pastry, leaving an even 1 inch beyond the top of the plate. Then, with your fingers (floured as necessary), fold the edge to the outside, and under itself, to make a hem that extends about ½ inch higher than the rim. Press the hem lightly together, making it stand upright. To flute the hem, leave it upright, lightly flour the thumb and index finger of your right hand, and pinch the dough from the outside so that the outer edge of the raised wall forms a horizontal V (or a V that has the point facing outward). It seems easiest to me to start this at the right side (three o'clock) of the plate. Use the index finger of your left hand to support the inside of the crust while you pinch it.

Pinch again 1 inch away from the first. Continue to pinch and form V's all around the outside of the rim, 1 inch apart.

Then do the same thing on the inside of the rim, this time starting at the left side of the plate (nine o'clock), pinching between two outpointing V's on the outside and forming a nice, neat zigzag pattern all around, standing about ½ inch straight up.

With a fork prick holes ¼-inch apart in the bottom and sides of the pastry.

Place the shell in the freezer for 15 minutes or more until it is firm. (Wrapped airtight after it is frozen, it may be kept in the freezer for months if you wish.)

About 20 minutes before baking, adjust a rack one-third up from the bottom of the oven and preheat the oven to 450 degrees.

To keep the pastry from puffing up, cut a 12-inch square of aluminum foil and place it, shiny side down, in the frozen shell. Press it into place all over. Do not fold the corners of the foil over the rim; let them stand up. Fill the foil at least three-quarters full with dried beans or pie weights.

Bake the frozen shell at 450 degrees for about 13 minutes until it is set and slightly colored on the edges. Remove the plate from the oven. Reduce the heat to 400 degrees. Gently, remove the foil and beans or pie weights by lifting the four corners of the foil.

Return the plate to the oven and continue to bake for 8 to 10 minutes. If the shell starts to puff up anywhere, reach into the oven and pierce the shell with a cake tester to release trapped air. Bake until the edges are golden and the bottom is dry.

Place on a rack and let cool.

FILLING

4 ounces (1 stick) unsalted butter
4 ounces unsweetened chocolate
4 eggs graded "large"
3 teaspoons light corn syrup
1½ cups granulated sugar
¼ teaspoon salt
½ teaspoon nutmeg
1 teaspoon vanilla extract
¼ cup milk

Adjust an oven rack one-third up from the bottom and preheat the oven to 350 degrees.

In the top of a small double boiler over warm water on moderate heat melt the butter and chocolate, stirring occasionally, until melted and smooth. Set aside.

In a bowl beat the eggs to mix. Add the corn syrup, sugar, salt, nutmeg, vanilla, and milk. Stir or beat to mix. Then add the chocolate mixture (which may still be warm) and beat well.

Pour into the prepared crust.

Bake for about 33 minutes until a small sharp knife gently inserted near the edge (all the way to the bottom) comes out barely—but not completely—clean. If you bake this until the knife comes out truly clean, the pie will be overbaked.

Cool to room temperature. Serve at room temperature or chilled.

Serve with whipped cream, which may be piled on top of the pie or served separately.

WHIPPED CREAM

2 cups whipping cream
1 teaspoon vanilla extract
4 tablespoons confectioners sugar

In a chilled bowl with chilled beaters whip the cream with the vanilla and sugar until it holds a soft shape, but not until it is really stiff.

If you plan to place the cream on top of the pie, it is best to whip it and place it on the pie no more than an hour or so ahead (the closer to serving time the better).

Individual Apple Strudels with Dried Fruits

6 STRUDELS

This pastry dough, called phyllo (or filo), which you can buy ready-made in most supermarkets, is as thin as onion skin. It is the lightest, flakiest, and most ethereal. The pastry is rolled around a soft, moist, mildly spiced apple filling that is mixed with rum-flavored raisins, figs, dates, and prunes.

Poetry. Ecstacy. Joy. You're going to love it.

Strudels were originally created in Austria or Hungary when both countries were part of the Hapsburg Empire and Vienna was the capital. But the inspiration comes from Turkish baklava, originally made in the 1500s. (Baklava is baked in layers—not rolled like strudel—with a filling of walnuts or almonds and a topping of sugar syrup.)

In Vienna it is said that you should be able to read the newspaper through not only one layer of strudel dough but three layers. (That is only true when the dough is freshly made.)

Strudels are best hot, right out of the oven. No problem. Make these whenever you wish and refrigerate them for a day or two or freeze them for weeks before baking.

Both of my grandmothers made sensational strudels and they made their own strudel dough. I use commercial phyllo from the supermarket and I think it is just as good. Handling the bought dough and shaping the strudels is not difficult; it is easy and great fun after you have done it once and you know how. But you must be careful to keep the unused dough covered airtight at all times or it will dry out (quickly) and become too brittle to work with.

Serve strudels as a luncheon or dinner dessert or as a fabulous coffee cake with tea or coffee between meals.

I serve these with a small sharp knife and a fork, but generally the knife is used only to cut the strudel in half, and then the halves become finger food. Using a fork for cutting strudel squashes and destroys the fragile and delicate pastry.

Phyllo is stored in the frozen-food section of food stores. It should be thawed in the refrigerator for one or two days (if you thaw it at room temperature the sheets will stick together). An unopened package of phyllo will keep in the refrigerator for three or four weeks. Once the package has been opened it will keep for a week or two in the refrigerator if it is sealed airtight. However, follow the directions on the package to thaw and then to store.

Bought phyllo sheets should preferably measure about 14 by 18 inches; 12 by 17 inches is OK, but a bit more trouble to shape because it is narrower.

This recipe is written for six individual strudels; you can multiply the recipe if you wish. Freeze extras. To bake frozen strudels, thaw at room temperature for about 1 hour or overnight in the refrigerator, wrapped, before baking. Strudels can go directly from the refrigerator into the oven.

1 thick slice dense brioche or 2 slices
    home-style (compact) white bread
3 to 4 ounces unsalted butter
¼ cup granulated sugar
½ teaspoon cinnamon
¼ teaspoon ground cloves
Finely grated rind of 1 small lemon
¼ cup raisins
1 large black or brown dried fig ⎫ to total 3
4 large pitted dates   ⎬ to 4 ounces
4 large pitted prunes   ⎭
¼ cup dark rum
About ¾ pound (2 medium-large) Granny
    Smith apples
Optional: ⅓ cup walnuts, in medium-sized
    pieces
6 sheets thawed phyllo
Confectioners sugar (to sprinkle on after
    baking)

Break the bread into coarse pieces or cut into small squares and place in the bowl of a food processor fitted with the metal chopping blade. Process to make 1 cup of crumbs (they may be coarse crumbs).

In a wide frying pan over moderate heat melt 1 ounce ($\frac{1}{4}$ stick) of the butter (reserve the remaining butter). Add the crumbs and stir until they are dry and lightly toasted. Set aside.

In a small bowl mix the granulated sugar, cinnamon, and cloves. Stir in the lemon rind and set aside.

Place the raisins in a small frying pan. Cut the fig, dates, and prunes in thin strips and add to the raisins. Add the rum. Place over low heat, cover, and let cook briefly, stirring once or twice, until the rum is absorbed and/or evaporated. Set aside.

Peel the apples with a vegetable parer, cut them in half from top to bottom, with a melon baller remove the cores, and with a small sharp knife cut a groove above and below the cores to remove the stems and fibers. Place an apple half flat side down and, holding the apple together, cut it into $\frac{1}{4}$-inch slices in one direction, and then in the opposite direction, forming thin julienne sticks. Finally, cut the sticks into small dice. Dice all the apples and place in a mixing bowl.

Stir in the toasted bread crumbs, cinnamon sugar, dried fruits, and the optional walnuts.

In a small pan over low heat melt 2 ounces of the remaining butter (reserve remaining 1 ounce of butter, which you may or may not need). Place the melted butter next to your work space.

Work as quickly as possible. Place the 6 sheets of thawed phyllo on a large tray and cover it completely with plastic wrap. Keep the pile covered, except when you are removing a sheet, and do that quickly.

Place one sheet on a pastry cloth or a smooth towel with the narrow end of the dough closest to you. With a large pastry brush, very lightly brush butter on the top half of the dough. (Always use a small amount of butter; if you use more than that the strudel will be greasy.)

Fold the unbuttered half of the dough onto the buttered half. Then butter the half that is facing up.

Use a $\frac{1}{3}$-cup metal measuring cup (the kind that is meant for dry ingredients) to measure a firmly packed $\frac{1}{3}$ cup of the apple filling. Place it about 1$\frac{1}{2}$ inches from the narrow end facing you and from the two long sides. With your fingers push the filling into a mound that has a flat top and is no closer than 1 to 1$\frac{1}{2}$ inches from the three sides.

Fold a 1- to 1$\frac{1}{2}$-inch hem on both of the long sides all the way to the farther end; the hem should cover the sides of the filling. Butter both of the long hems. Then make a similar hem on the narrow end that is facing you. Butter that hem.

Lift the pastry cloth or towel at the end where the filling is and, with the help of the cloth, roll the strudel jelly-roll fashion. Just before you reach the end of the strudel, butter the top of the roll. Then lift the rolled strudel and hold it in one hand while you lightly brush butter all over it.

Place on an unbuttered jelly-roll pan.

Continue to shape all the strudels, and, if you need it, melt the remaining butter.

Bake, or wrap individually in plastic wrap for the refrigerator or freezer.

To bake, adjust a rack one-third up from the bottom of the oven and preheat the oven to 375 degrees. Bake for 5 minutes and then reduce the temperature to 350 degrees and continue to bake for about 40 to 45 minutes more (total baking time is about 45 to 50 minutes) until golden brown all over. Do not underbake.

With a wide metal spatula transfer to a brown paper bag and let drain for a few minutes. Then sprinkle confectioners sugar generously over the tops through a fine strainer.

Serve while hot (or at least within half an hour). Serve plain or with vanilla ice cream.

NOTE: It is always better to bake strudels at a moderate or low temperature for a long time. At a higher temperature the pastry might darken and even burn on the outside while it is still raw on the inside.

Yeast Recipes

Fruit and Nut Brioche Loaf

1 1½-POUND LOAF, 6
INCHES HIGH IN THE
CENTER

According to some authorities the first brioches were made centuries ago in Brie, France (some recipes actually contained Brie cheese in the ingredients).

This is a most delicious sweet bread or coffee cake. I have never seen a fruit and nut brioche in a bakery; as far as I know the only way to have it is to make your own. The rising takes hours, but the actual work in making this is quick and easy—and fun.

Although this can be baked in any loaf pan with an 8-cup capacity, I use a particular 9-by-5-by-3½-inch pan (for this and many other yeast breads) that is made in France and is not necessarily intended for brioche. The pan is made of a black metal that guarantees a beautifully browned crust, never too pale. The pan is a loaf shape generously flared at the top, which seems to encourage the yeast dough to rise like the space shuttle (see page 29).

Serve brioche plain or lightly toasted, either with or without butter, whipped cream cheese, or chèvre, and jelly or marmalade, if you wish.

4 ounces (1 stick) cold and firm unsalted
    butter
3 tablespoons granulated sugar
¼ cup warm water (105 to 115 degrees)
1 envelope active dry yeast
3 cups plus about 3 to 4 tablespoons
    additional unsifted bread flour (if
    necessary)
¾ teaspoon salt
3 eggs graded "large"
4 ounces (1 loosely packed cup) pitted dates
    (see Note)
2 ounces (⅓ cup) raisins
3 ounces (½ cup) unsalted pistachio nuts
    (see Note)
2 ounces (½ cup) walnuts, cut into
    medium-sized pieces

Cut the butter lengthwise into quarters, and then slice through the four quarters all at once into ¼-inch slices. Place in the refrigerator for a few minutes. Place the sugar in a small cup. Pour the warm water into a 1-cup glass measuring cup, add 2 teaspoons of the sugar (reserve the remaining sugar) and the yeast, stir with a table knife, and let stand for about 10 minutes until the mixture rises to just above the ½-cup line.

Fit the food processor with the metal chopping blade. Place 3 cups of the flour in the processor bowl. Add the salt and the remaining sugar, and pulse the machine once or twice to mix the dry ingredients. Add the cold cut-up butter and process for 5 seconds or until the mixture forms crumbs.

Then, through the feed tube, with the motor running, add the yeast mixture and the eggs. (If you pour the eggs into the cup that the yeast mixture was in, it will help you get every bit of the yeast mixture.) Process until the dough is mixed. The dough should not be wet or sticky. If it is, add the remaining flour 1 tablespoonful at a time through the feed tube. Process until the dough begins to clear the side of the bowl. After the dough forms a ball, process for 30 seconds. (If the machine stalls or stops, chances are that you need a bit more flour.)

Lightly flour a large board or work surface. Turn the dough out and knead for 1 minute.

Place the dough in a well-buttered bowl with about a 10-cup capacity. Cover with plastic wrap, and place in a warm (about 80 degrees), draft-free spot. Let rise for 2 hours or longer (this seems to take forever to start to rise) until the dough is more than doubled in volume. (In a 10-cup bowl the dough will almost reach the top of the bowl.)

Meanwhile, while the dough is rising, cut the dates with scissors or a small sharp knife into crosswise slices 1/4 inch wide. Have ready the raisins, pistachios, and walnuts.

Butter an 8-cup loaf pan, preferably with a dark finish.

Flour a large board or work surface. Turn out the risen dough. With a floured rolling pin roll the dough to deflate it and to spread it out until it is an oval or oblong shape about 12 by 15 inches.

Sprinkle the cut dates all over the surface, and with the floured rolling pin roll over the dates to press them into the dough. Then sprinkle on the raisins and roll them into the dough. And, finally, sprinkle on the pistachio nuts and roll them into the dough.

Fold the dough in thirds, folding from the narrow sides.

Sprinkle with the walnuts, and roll them into the dough.

And then, from a narrow side, roll up the dough like a jelly roll and place it seam down in the buttered pan.

Cover the top of the pan with a piece of buttered plastic wrap. Place in a warm (about 80 degrees), draft-free spot.

Let rise for about 1 1/2 hours until the dough has risen to almost 2 inches above the pan (in the middle of the loaf).

About 20 minutes before baking, adjust a rack one-third up from the bottom of the oven and preheat the oven to 400 degrees.

When you are ready to bake, with sharp scissors cut slits in the top of the loaf as follows: Place the loaf in front of you so that the short ends are parallel to the edge of the counter in front of you. You will make five or six cuts down the length of the loaf, each cut parallel to the short sides of the loaf and about 1/2 inch deep in the center of each cut. Start at the farther end of the loaf. Hold the scissors at a 45-degree angle to the top of the loaf and cut.

Bake at 400 degrees for 15 minutes. Then cover the loaf loosely with aluminum foil shiny side down, reduce the temperature to 350 degrees, and continue to bake 25 minutes more (total baking time is about 40 minutes).

To test the loaf, turn it out on its side onto a cake rack and tap the bottom of the loaf sharply with your fingertips. If the tapping makes a hollow sound, the loaf is done. If it needs more baking, place it directly on the oven rack without the pan for a few minutes more, but be careful that you do not overbake or the loaf will become dry.

When done, cool on a rack.

NOTE: If you wish, you can vary the fruit by using a 6-ounce mixture of dates, figs, prunes, and dried apricots (all cut into 1/4-inch slices) instead of only 4 ounces dates. (The apricots are special—their tart flavor in this sweet and rich loaf is spectacular.)

And you can substitute walnuts or pecans (cut into medium-sized pieces) for the pistachios.

Mile-high Cinnamon Bread

1 9-INCH LOAF

This spectacular loaf deserves some special words of praise. In the middle of the loaf the slices are about 7 inches high. Each slice has a round-and-round-and-round spiral of a dark and spicy cinnamon-sugar mixture. And the texture of the bread is so light and delicious that I can't believe there is not some strange secret ingredient—but there is not. Have your camera ready for this.

1/2 teaspoon plus 1/4 cup granulated sugar
1/4 cup warm water (105 to 115 degrees)
1 envelope active dry yeast
1 cup milk
3 tablespoons unsalted butter, cut up
4 cups unsifted bread flour
1 teaspoon salt
1 egg graded "large"
Additional granulated sugar (to sprinkle on
     top after the loaf is shaped)

In a 1-cup glass measuring cup stir 1/2 teaspoon of the sugar (reserve the remaining 1/4 cup sugar) into the warm water, sprinkle on the yeast, and stir with a small knife. Let stand at room temperature for 10 minutes.

Meanwhile, in a small saucepan over moderate heat, heat the milk and butter to 90 to 100 degrees (it is not necessary for the butter to melt).

Place the flour, the remaining 1/4 cup of sugar, and the salt in the bowl of a food processor fitted with the metal chopping blade. Pulse just to mix. Then, with the motor running, through the feed tube add the yeast mixture, the milk-and-butter mixture, and the egg (if you pour the milk mixture into the cup that the yeast was in and then add it, you will be sure to get every bit of the yeast into the dough).

Process until the mixture forms a ball, and then continue to process for 30 seconds more. If the dough is too stiff, add a few drops of water. If the machine slows down, remove about half of the dough and process the two halves separately. Then knead them together.

On a large board or work surface, knead the dough for about 1 minute. Then place it in a buttered large bowl, turn to butter all sides of the dough, cover loosely with plastic wrap, and place in a warm, draft-free spot to rise for about 1½ hours until well risen and thoroughly doubled in bulk.

Then lightly flour a large board or work surface. Turn the dough out onto the floured area. Press down on the dough to deflate it. Fold in two opposite sides to meet in the middle; then fold in the remaining two opposite sides to meet, forming the dough into a square. Press down on the dough to flatten it slightly, cover loosely, and let stand for 10 minutes.

Meanwhile, butter a 9-by-5-by-3½-inch loaf pan with an 8-cup capacity and a dark finish (I use the same pan as for the previous brioche recipe, see page 29) and set it aside.

Prepare the following Vanilla Water and Cinnamon Sugar and set them aside.

VANILLA WATER

3 tablespoons water
1 teaspoon vanilla extract

Mix the water and vanilla in a small cup and set aside.

CINNAMON SUGAR

⅓ cup granulated sugar
1 tablespoon plus 1 teaspoon cinnamon
1 tablespoon plus 1 teaspoon unsweetened
    cocoa powder
½ teaspoon nutmeg

Mix the sugar, cinnamon, cocoa, and nutmeg and set aside.

With a floured rolling pin roll out the dough to form a rectangle 12 by 22 inches—with corners that are as square as possible and with straight sides. (If the dough is elastic and shrinks back, just pause briefly and then roll again.)

With a wide pastry brush, brush about two thirds of the Vanilla Water all over the dough (be very sure that you do not miss any spots—this is important). If necessary, use 1 to 2 teaspoons of additional water.

Then sprinkle two thirds of the Cinnamon Sugar slowly and carefully in a thin layer all over the wet dough. (If you sprinkle too much in any one spot, you will not have enough to cover all the dough—so care beful).

Now, one at a time, fold the two long sides of the dough in to meet each other in the middle. Pinch them together a bit to seal. Gently roll over the surface with a rolling pin to flatten the folded dough to about 7 by 25 inches (see Note).

Then use the remaining Vanilla Water to wet the dough, and sprinkle on the remaining Cinnamon Sugar (again, carefully).

Now, starting at the narrow end closest to you, roll up the dough like a jelly roll. Just before you reach the farther end, brush a little plain water on the roll at the spot where it will meet the end of the roll. Pinch the end a bit to seal.

Carefully and gently place the roll, seam down, in the buttered pan. The roll of dough will almost fill the pan.

Sprinkle about 1 tablespoon of granulated sugar over the top of the loaf.

Cover loosely with plastic wrap. Place in a warm, draft-free spot and let the loaf rise for about 1 hour until almost doubled and about 2 inches above the top of the pan.

Meanwhile, adjust a rack one-third up from the bottom of the oven and preheat the oven to 350 degrees.

Just before baking the bread, cut slits in the top as follows: You must use either a new single-edge razor blade or a very sharp knife. First cut a slit along each long side of the loaf—level with the top of the pan—only ¼ inch deep. (If you cut the slits any deeper, you will expose the Cinnamon Sugar and it will run over—but that is not a disaster.) Then cut four more slits—only ¼ inch deep—about an inch apart, parallel with and between the first two slits.

Bake for 45 to 50 minutes. Cover the top loosely with foil toward the end of the baking to prevent overbrowning. Bake until the loaf, when removed from the pan, sounds hollow when tapped sharply on the bottom with your fingertips.

Cool on a rack.

NOTE: The bottom of my pan measures 7 inches long (the pan flares at the top). Therefore, I shape the loaf into a roll that is 7 inches long. However, if the bottom of your pan is longer, the loaf can be longer.

Hungarian Coffee Cake

I was invited to a fabulous luncheon in Palm Beach. It was served formally by butlers in a private ocean-front beachhouse. It was the mostest. Lobster and champagne were only the beginning. One of the many delicious desserts was a light, moist, rich yeast cake with the texture of a sponge cake, layered before baking with a chewy brown sugar, cinnamon, walnut, and lemon mixture. I told the hostess that it was the very cake I had wanted to make for years. She graciously told me that her Hungarian cook made it and that she would have the recipe for me before I left. She did. This is it. It is a very special "plain" cake.

10 TO 12 PORTIONS

This is best the day it is made. It dries out if it stands longer, but leftovers may be wrapped and frozen, and they will still be wonderful.

It needs 2 1/2 hours of rising time.

You must use a nonstick tube pan with a design. The La Forme Bundt pan with a 13 1/2-cup capacity (see page 29) is perfect for this and makes a stunning cake.

2 tablespoons warm water (105 to 115 degrees)
2 teaspoons active dry yeast
2 ounces (1/2 stick) unsalted butter
2/3 cup milk
6 egg yolks graded "large"
1/4 cup granulated sugar
1/2 teaspoon salt
1/2 teaspoon vanilla extract
2 cups unsifted bread flour (or unbleached flour)

Pour the water into a small cup. Sprinkle on the yeast, stir with a fork to mix, and let stand for 15 minutes.

Meanwhile, in a small saucepan over low heat, melt the butter. Add the milk and heat briefly only until warm (105 to 115 degrees). Set aside briefly.

Place the yolks, sugar, salt, and vanilla in the large bowl of an electric mixer and beat just to mix. Beat in the warm milk, then the yeast mixture and 1 cup of the flour (reserve the remaining 1 cup flour). Beat to mix well. Then cover and let stand for 30 minutes.

Generously butter a nonstick tube pan with a 13½-cup capacity (see above) and set aside.

Prepare the Walnut Mixture.

WALNUT MIXTURE

3½ ounces (1 cup) walnuts
½ firmly packed cup light brown sugar
Finely grated rind of 2 firm lemons
1½ teaspoons cinnamon

On a large board, with a long and heavy knife chop the nuts until rather fine and set aside. In a small bowl mix the sugar, lemon rind, and cinnamon. Then stir in the nuts and set aside.

When the dough is ready, add the remaining 1 cup of flour and beat to mix. Then beat on medium-to-low speed for 5 to 7 minutes, scraping the bowl with a rubber spatula almost constantly, until the dough becomes very elastic and crawls up on the beaters even at lowest speed. (This beating is actually kneading the dough.) If the dough crawls up on the beaters too soon, force it down with a rubber spatula—or beat with a dough hook. Remove the bowl from the mixer.

(This is the most rubbery and elastic dough I have ever used; it has a mind of its own.)

Spoon or pour about half (a scant 1 cup) of the dough into the buttered pan. Smooth the dough with the bottom of a teaspoon. Sprinkle half (1 cup) of the nut mixture over the dough (it will be a generous layer). Then spoon or pour the remaining dough on top, smooth with a teaspoon, and sprinkle the remaining nut mixture over the dough. (If the dough does not cling to the sides of the pan all around, it is OK.)

(This mixture will fill the La Forme pan only about one-third up from the bottom, but during rising and baking it will rise to the top.)

Cover the pan with buttered plastic wrap and place in a warm, draft-free spot (70- to 80-degree temperature) to rise for about 2 hours until doubled in bulk. (The cake might or might not rise up to touch the plastic wrap. It will rise a bit more during baking.)

About 20 minutes before you are ready to bake, adjust a rack one-third up from the bottom of the oven and preheat the oven to 375 degrees.

When the dough has risen, remove the plastic wrap and bake the cake for 25 minutes. Cover the top of the pan loosely with foil for the last 10 minutes of baking time. The top of the cake will be richly browned. (Do not underbake.) I don't know any way to test this for baking time. Just be sure your oven temperature is correct, and watch the clock carefully.

Remove the pan from the oven, let stand for 2 minutes, then cover the pan with a rack, turn pan and rack upside down, and remove the pan. Let the cake stand upside down to cool.

Preferably serve two or three thin slices rather than one thick slice.

Sourdough Chocolate Cake

12 TO 16 PORTIONS

I learned this recipe from a Swiss bread baker in Aspen, Colorado, who made it with the same sourdough starter he had used for making breads for many years.

You will make your own sourdough starter (easy) 24 hours ahead. Then you will make the cake in two steps—2 to 3 hours apart. It is a large, thick single-layer cake baked in a square or oblong pan. The color is dark brown, the texture is light and moist, the flavor is intensely chocolate. Devilish. Fun, fascinating, interesting, unusual, easy, and superdelicious. With a scrumptious chocolate icing.

It looks and tastes like a plain, nonyeast (and nonsour) chocolate cake.

Although this contains yeast, there is no kneading.

You will need a shallow square or oblong cake pan with a 12-cup capacity. Generally, that means a 10-inch square pan. But lately I have been using a wonderful 9-inch square pan with a 12-cup capacity. The sides are straight, not flared, and the corners are perfectly square, not rounded. It makes a gorgeous cake. It is a Magic Line pan (see page 30).

SOURDOUGH STARTER

⅔ cup unsifted bread flour or unbleached
    flour
1 teaspoon active dry yeast
⅔ cup lukewarm water (105 to 115 degrees)

In a small bowl made of glass, pottery, or stoneware, stir the flour and yeast to mix. Stir in the water only until the flour is barely moistened; it will be a lumpy mixture.

Cover the bowl loosely with a cloth napkin and let stand for 24 hours at a temperature of 70 to 80 degrees. There will be about 1¼ cups of the starter when it is mixed. As it stands it will increase in volume to about 2½ cups and then it will sink back to its original size. It will develop a strong sourdough odor. Stir the starter well to mix just before using it.

CAKE

½ cup sourdough starter (you will not need
    the remainder)
¼ cup nonfat dry milk powder
1½ cups unsifted bread flour or unbleached
    flour
1 cup lukewarm water (105 to 115 degrees)

In the small bowl of an electric mixer (with about a 7-cup capacity) beat the sourdough starter, dry milk powder, flour, and water until smooth. Remove the bowl from the mixer. Cover with plastic wrap and let stand at 70 to 80 degrees for 2 to 3 hours until the mixture rises almost to the top of the bowl.

3 ounces unsweetened chocolate
4 ounces (1 stick) unsalted butter
1 teaspoon vanilla extract
2 tablespoons unsweetened cocoa powder
Optional: 2 to 3 teaspoons powdered instant
    espresso or coffee
½ teaspoon salt
1 cup granulated sugar
1½ teaspoons baking soda
2 eggs graded "large"

Adjust an oven rack one-third up from the bottom and preheat the oven to 350 degrees. Butter a square or oblong cake pan with a 12-cup capacity (see above), dust it all with chocolate bread crumbs (see page 21), shake out excess crumbs over paper, and set aside.

Place the chocolate in the top of a small double boiler over warm water on moderate heat. Cover with a folded paper towel (to absorb steam) and the pot cover. When the chocolate is almost melted, stir until smooth and set aside to cool briefly.

In the large bowl of an electric mixer beat the butter with the vanilla, cocoa, optional espresso or coffee, salt, and sugar until mixed. Beat in the baking soda and then the eggs one at a time. Add the melted chocolate, scrape the bowl as necessary, and beat to mix. Now add the sourdough mixture and beat until smooth.

Turn into the prepared pan and smooth the top.

Bake for 40 to 45 minutes until a cake tester gently inserted in the middle comes out clean and the top springs back when gently pressed with a fingertip. (The top will crack.) Do not overbake.

If you wish, you can let the cake cool in the pan and then ice it, and serve it directly from the pan.

Or you can let it stand for 10 to 15 minutes, cover with a rack, turn pan and rack upside down, remove the pan, cover with another rack and turn upside down again, leaving the cake right side up on a rack to cool.

The cake is tender and fragile. To transfer it to a flat cake plate or a serving board, it is safest to do as follows: Cover the cake with a rack, turn upside down, remove the bottom rack, cover the cake with the cake plate or serving board, and turn upside down again, leaving the cake right side up.

PEANUT BUTTER CHOCOLATE ICING

Spectacular—and easy. It will be spread almost 3/4 inch thick, and then formed into swirls and peaks.

⅔ cup unsweetened cocoa powder
 (preferably Dutch-process)
2 cups confectioners sugar
2 ounces (½ stick) unsalted butter
4 ounces cream cheese (at room temperature)
¼ cup smooth peanut butter
3 tablespoons milk
Pinch of salt
1 teaspoon vanilla extract

Sift together the cocoa and sugar and set aside. In a small pan over low heat, melt the butter. Meanwhile, in the small bowl of the electric mixer, beat the cream cheese and peanut butter until soft and smooth. Gradually add the warm melted butter and beat until smooth. On low speed gradually add about one third of the sifted dry ingredients and beat to mix. Beat in the milk, salt, and vanilla, and then, gradually, the remaining dry ingredients.

When thoroughly mixed, increase the speed to high and beat for 5 minutes.

Remove the bowl from the mixer and, without waiting, transfer all the icing to the top of the cake. With a long, narrow metal spatula smooth the icing over the top only (if a little runs down on the sides, just leave it—do not spread the icing on the sides), and then, with the spatula, form deep swirls and peaks.

Is this gorgeous?

Cookies with Chocolate

All cookies—no matter which—suffer if they are left unwrapped and exposed to the air for any length of time. Crisp cookies become limp, meringues become wet, brownies dry out, et cetera. Wait only until they cool, and then wrap or package them airtight.

Santa Fe Brownies

32 LARGE BROWNIES

In Santa Fe, New Mexico, at the wildly popular Plaza Bakery/Häagen Dazs Ice Cream Shoppe (which is on The Plaza), people stand in line not only for the ice cream and frozen yogurt, mud pies, bagels, bread and rolls, cakes and cookies of all kinds, but also—and especially—for these spectacular brownies.

These are about two inches thick—it takes only six of them to make a pound. Dark-chocolate brownies with a ribbon of a white cream-cheese mixture through the middle. As dense as fudge, not cakelike. After baking, it is best to refrigerate this overnight before cutting it into brownies.

CHOCOLATE MIXTURE

1½ cups unsifted unbleached flour
1½ teaspoons baking powder
¾ teaspoon salt
6 ounces unsweetened chocolate
6 ounces semisweet chocolate
8 ounces (2 sticks) unsalted butter
5 eggs graded "large"
1¼ cups granulated sugar
1½ firmly packed cups dark brown sugar
1 tablespoon vanilla extract
8 ounces (2¼ cups) walnuts, in large pieces

Adjust a rack one-third up from the bottom of the oven and preheat the oven to 350 degrees. Prepare a 9-by-13-by-2-inch pan (see Note) as follows: Turn the pan upside down. Carefully center a 17- to 18-inch length of aluminum foil, shiny side down, over the pan. With your hands press down on the sides and corners to shape the foil to fit the pan. Remove the foil. Run water into the pan and then pour it out; do not dry the pan (a wet pan holds the foil in place). Place the shaped foil in the pan and gently press it into place. To butter the foil, place a piece of butter in the lined pan, place the pan in the oven to melt the butter, and then, with crumpled plastic wrap, spread the butter all over the bottom and sides of the foil. Set the pan aside.

Sift together the flour, baking powder, and salt and set aside.

Place both of the chocolates and the butter in the top of a large double boiler over warm water on moderate heat, cover, and stir occasionally until melted and smooth. Then remove the top of the double boiler and set aside briefly.

In the large bowl of an electric mixer beat the eggs just to mix. Add both of the sugars and the vanilla and beat only until mixed.

On low speed beat in the melted-chocolate mixture (which should still be warm), and then the sifted dry ingredients, scraping the bowl with a rubber spatula and beating only until incorporated. Remove the bowl from the mixer.

Remove and set aside 2¼ cups of the mixture.

Add about two thirds of the nuts (reserve remaining nuts) to the mixture in the large bowl and stir to mix.

Spread the chocolate-and-nut mixture evenly in the prepared pan. Set aside.

CREAM CHEESE MIXTURE

12 ounces cream cheese (at room temperature)
3 ounces (¾ stick) unsalted butter (at room temperature)
1½ teaspoons vanilla extract
¾ cup granulated sugar
3 eggs graded "large"

In the small bowl of the electric mixer, with clean beaters beat the cream cheese and butter until smooth. Beat in the vanilla and sugar. Then add the eggs one at a time and beat only until smooth.

Pour the cheese mixture slowly, in a wide ribbon, all over the chocolate mixture in the pan. With the bottom of a spoon, spread the cheese mixture to the edges of the pan.

Stir the remaining chocolate mixture well to soften it a bit (but it will be quite thick) and then pour it in a wide ribbon—or in globs—over the cheese layer. The top chocolate layer does not have to cover all of the cheese layer and it does not have to reach the sides of the pan.

With a table knife cut through the top chocolate layer and the cheese layer in a zigzag pattern to marbelize the mixtures slightly; don't overdo it.

Sprinkle the remaining nuts evenly all over the top.

Bake for 1 hour and about 15 minutes until the cake tests done. Once during baking reverse the pan, front to back, to ensure even browning. For this recipe—and only this recipe—I use a broom straw for testing. (A toothpick is too short and a metal cake tester tests done while the cake is still too wet.) As soon as the straw, inserted in the middle, comes out just barely clean, remove the pan from the oven. Do not overbake.

Cool in the pan. Then cover the pan with a board or cookie sheet and turn the pan and board or sheet upside down. Remove the pan and the foil lining.

Cover the cake with wax paper or plastic wrap and then with another board or sheet and turn upside down, leaving the cake right side up.

Refrigerate overnight, or at least for several hours.

Then, with a ruler and toothpicks, mark the cake into quarters. With a long and sharp knife (I used a serrated knife, called a slicing knife, with a 12-inch blade—originally intended for slicing meat—see page 31), cut the cold and firm cake into quarters. Then cut each quarter into eight brownies.

Wrap individually in clear cellophane or wax paper. Or place in an airtight box with wax paper between the layers.

Serve at room temperature. Or refrigerated. Or almost frozen.

NOTE: You can use a traditional 9-by-13-by-2-inch pan (i.e., a Wear-Ever pan) or the Magic Line pan with straight (not flared) sides and square (not rounded) corners. If you use the traditional pan, use regular-weight aluminum foil to line the pan. And if you use the Magic Line pan, use heavy-duty foil. The sharp, square corners might tear regular-weight foil.

Espresso Brownies

24 LARGE BROWNIES

Dark, rich, incredibly chocolate. The sour cream is most unusual in brownies; it makes them especially moist and fudgelike. (These are thinner than many other brownies, but no less delicious.)

10 ounces (2½ cups) walnuts
5 ounces unsweetened chocolate
6 ounces (1½ sticks) unsalted butter
4 eggs graded "large"
2 cups granulated sugar
⅔ cup sifted unbleached flour
⅓ cup sifted unsweetened cocoa powder
    (preferably Dutch-process)
½ teaspoon salt
5 teaspoons powdered instant espresso or
    coffee (I use Medaglia D'Oro instant
    espresso)
1 teaspoon vanilla extract
⅓ cup sour cream

Adjust a rack one-third up from the bottom of the oven and preheat the oven to 400 degrees. Prepare a 15½-by-10½-by-1-inch jelly-roll pan (see page 30) as follows: Place the pan upside down on a work surface. Place a 19-inch length of 12-inch-width aluminum foil, shiny side down, over the pan, centering it carefully so that the borders are all the same. Fold down the sides and the corners to shape the foil to fit the pan. Remove the foil. Run cold tap water into the pan; pour out the water but do not dry the pan (the wet pan holds the foil in place). Place the shaped foil in the wet pan. To butter the foil, place a piece of butter in the pan and place the pan in the oven to melt the butter. Then spread the butter with a piece of crumpled plastic wrap or wax paper to coat the foil all over. Set the pan aside.

To toast the nuts: Spread them in a single layer in a large shallow pan and bake for 8 to 10 minutes in a 400-degree oven until they are just about too hot to touch. Cool. Break into large pieces and set aside.

Place the chocolate and butter in the top of a large double boiler over hot water on moderate heat. Cover and let cook until the chocolate and butter are almost melted. Then uncover and stir until smooth. Then remove the top of the double boiler and set aside.

In the small bowl of an electric mixer beat the eggs to mix. On low speed add the sugar, increase the speed to high, and beat for 15 minutes.

Meanwhile, sift together the flour, cocoa, salt, and espresso or coffee and set aside.

In a small cup stir the vanilla into the sour cream. Add to the egg mixture and mix only briefly. Transfer the egg mixture to the large bowl of the electric mixer. Then, all at once, add the slightly warm chocolate mixture and the sifted dry ingredients on low speed, scraping the bowl frequently with a rubber spatula and beating only until just barely mixed—no longer.

Remove the bowl from the mixer, add the walnuts, and fold them in with a rubber spatula.

Turn into the prepared pan and spread as smooth as possible.

Bake for about 20 minutes until a toothpick gently inserted in the middle comes out dry. Do not overbake or underbake.

Remove the pan from the oven. Let stand for 5 minutes. Then cover the pan with a large rack and turn the pan and the rack upside down. Remove the pan and the foil. Let the cake cool upside down.

When cool, chill the cake for about 45 minutes in the freezer or longer in the refrigerator. Cover the cold cake with a large rack or a flat-sided cookie sheet and turn over, leaving the cake right side up. Transfer the cold cake to a cutting board and, with a ruler and toothpicks, mark it into quarters. With a long-bladed sharp knife or a serrated French bread knife it cut into quarters. Then cut each quarter into six brownies.

Wrap individually in clear cellophane, wax paper, or foil.

VARIATION: Prune Armagnac Espresso Brownies

Prepare Prunes in Armagnac (see page 396). When the prunes are ready to be used, place about 15 (1 cup), lightly drained, in the bowl of a food processor or blender. Add about 1 tablespoon of the prune juice. Process or blend the mixture for 5 to 10 seconds to make a thick, chunky puree; you should have about ½ cup of puree.

Follow the above brownie recipe. Stir the prune puree into the brownie mixture just before adding the sour cream.

While this cake is baking, prepare a rack that is slightly larger than the cake pan: Lightly butter the rack to prevent the cake from sticking to it (otherwise this cake might stick—slightly).

Chocolate-Ginger Sandwich Cookies

24 SANDWICHED
COOKIES

Crisp, crunchy, sharp-flavored cookies made with fresh ginger and pepper, sandwiched together with semisweet or bittersweet chocolate. Ginger, pepper, and chocolate are a great combination. Many of our friends say these are the best cookies I ever made. They are indeed sensational!

These are freezer cookies and have to be frozen for a few hours (or longer) before they are sliced and baked.

Do not plan these cookies for a picnic or any event in warm weather; the chocolate filling might melt.

2 ounces (a piece about 1½ by 2½ inches) fresh ginger
8 ounces (2 sticks) unsalted butter
1 teaspoon vanilla extract
¼ teaspoon salt
⅛ teaspoon white pepper, ground fine
1 packed cup dark brown sugar
2 egg yolks graded "large"
1½ cups sifted unbleached flour
1 cup yellow cornmeal (preferably stone-ground from a health-food store—see Note)
Finely grated rind of 2 large lemons
8 ounces semisweet or bittersweet chocolate (to be used as filling after the cookies are baked)

If the ginger is fresh and young and has a pale and tender skin, it is not necessary to remove the skin; if it is older and has a tough or dark skin, pare it with a vegetable parer. Slice the ginger across the grain about ⅛ inch thick. Fit a food processor with a metal chopping blade. With the motor running, add the slices of ginger through the feed tube and process until pureed, scraping the sides of the bowl once or twice as necessary. You should have about ⅓ cup of lightly packed ginger puree. Set it aside. (To grate the ginger without a food processor you can use a standing metal grater. Do not slice the ginger. Grate on the side of the grater that has round, rather than diamond-shaped, openings.)

In the large bowl of an electric mixer beat the butter until soft. Add the vanilla, salt, pepper, and sugar, and beat until thoroughly mixed. Add the egg yolks and the pureed or grated ginger and beat to mix. On low speed beat in the flour and then the cornmeal.

Remove the bowl from the mixer and, with a wooden spoon or spatula, stir in the lemon rind.

The dough will be soft. Turn it out onto a well-floured surface. Flour all sides of the dough and, with your hands, form it into a smooth and even shape about 10 inches long, 3½ inches wide, and 1 to 1¼ inches high. Place a length of plastic wrap alongside the dough. Flip the dough over onto the plastic wrap. Slide a flat-sided cookie sheet under the dough, and transfer to the freezer until firm enough to be wrapped. Then wrap the dough in the plastic and freeze until frozen hard (or longer).

Before baking adjust two racks to divide the oven into thirds and preheat the oven to 350 degrees. Line cookie sheets with baking-pan liner paper.

With a sharp knife cut the frozen dough into 48 slices ³⁄₁₆ inch thick, and place them at least 1 inch apart on the lined cookie sheets.

Bake for 15 to 17 minutes, reversing the sheets, top to bottom and front to back, once or twice during baking to ensure even browning. The cookies are done when they are lightly colored all over.

Remove from the oven and let stand for about 1 minute. Then, with a wide metal spatula, transfer the cookies to racks to cool.

Chop or break the chocolate rather fine and place it in the top of a small double boiler over warm water on low heat. Cover with a folded paper towel (to absorb steam) and with the pot cover, and let cook until the chocolate is partially melted. Then uncover and stir until completely melted. Remove the top of the double boiler and let the chocolate cool for a few minutes. Then stir just to mix and, with a small spoon, place the chocolate ⅛ to ¼ inch thick, down the middle, on the flat side of one of the cookies. Keep the chocolate about ¼ inch away from the edges of the cookie. Place another cookie over it, flat sides together. Place on a flat tray. Continue to make all the sandwiches.

Refrigerate or freeze only until the chocolate becomes firm. Store airtight.

These can be kept airtight at room temperature for several days, or they can be frozen for longer storage. If frozen, let the cookies thaw completely before unwrapping, or before opening the container.

NOTE: I have also used whole-grain cornmeal from a health-food store. The baked cookies are even more coarse and crunchy. Delicious both ways.

Meringues with Walnuts and Chocolate

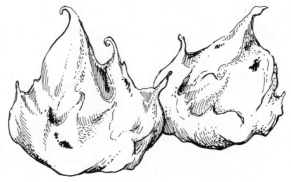

24 VERY LARGE COOKIES

In 1720 a Swiss baker in the tiny town of Meiringen discovered a delicate confection made of beaten egg whites and sugar. It was not long before meringues became popular. As the story goes, Marie Antoinette made them herself in the royal kitchens at Trianon.

I can't resist these. They are gorgeous—huge meringues loaded with walnuts and chopped chocolate. Light and airy, dry, crisp, crunchy. You will never again wonder what to do with leftover egg whites. Serve these with tea or coffee, or pass a bowl or basket of them when you serve ice cream or fruit for dessert.

You must have an airtight container (I suggest a Rubbermaid freezer box) ready to use as soon as these are removed from the oven. If they are exposed to humidity, they may become sticky. Pick a dry day to make meringues. These take 2 hours of baking and then 1 hour more in the oven with the heat off. But after that they will last for weeks in an airtight container at room temperature.

2 ½ ounces (¾ cup) walnuts

3 ounces semisweet or bittersweet chocolate

4 egg whites graded "large" (to measure ½
cup; they may be whites that were
frozen and then thawed)

⅛ teaspoon salt

¼ teaspoon cream of tartar

1 teaspoon vanilla extract

1 cup granulated sugar

Adjust two racks to divide the oven into thirds and preheat the oven to 225 degrees. (Some ovens balk at such a low temperature; it is always best to check the temperature with a portable oven thermometer.) Cut aluminum foil to fit two cookie sheets, and set aside.

Break or cut the nuts into coarse pieces and set aside. Cut the chocolate into pieces a little larger than chocolate morsels. The pieces will be uneven; it is OK. Set aside.

Place the egg whites, salt, cream of tartar, and vanilla in the small bowl of an electric mixer. Beat on moderate speed for a minute or two until the whites are foamy and hold a soft point (one that bends over) when the beaters are raised. Continue to beat on moderate speed and start adding the sugar, 1 rounded tablespoonful at a time. Beat for about half a minute between additions. After all the sugar is added, increase the speed to high and continue to beat for 5 to 7 minutes more until the meringue is very stiff and the sugar is completely dissolved—test it by rubbing a bit between your fingers. (Total beating time from start to finish is 15 to 18 minutes.)

Remove the bowl from the mixer. To hold the aluminum foil in place on the cookie sheets, spread a bit of the meringue near each corner of the cookie sheets. Cover the sheets with the foil, shiny side up, and press firmly on the corners.

Transfer the meringue to a larger bowl. Fold in the walnuts and the chocolate.

Use a heaping (mounded high) tablespoon of the meringue for each cookie. Use one spoon for picking up with and another for pushing off with. Place the meringues about an inch apart on the lined cookie sheets. Let the meringues form exotic swirls and peaks—the more the better. Gorgeous.

Bake for 2 hours, reversing the sheets, top to bottom and front to back, once during baking to ensure even baking. The meringues should not color—or only barely (see Note). They should feel dry. You should be able to lift one off the foil. (Lift slowly. If some of the meringue sticks to the foil, bake longer as necessary.)

Then turn off the heat but do not open the oven door. Let the meringues stand in the oven with the heat off for 1 hour until completely dry.

Then lift the meringues with your fingers and transfer to a completely airtight container. Cover each layer of the meringues loosely with plastic wrap before covering the container.

NOTE: During baking a little bit of melted sugar may run out of the meringues and caramelize a bit. It is OK.

Very Small Chocolate Cakes

24 PETITS FOURS

Petite, darling, adorable, bite-sized flourless chocolate cakes with chocolate icing. French, elegant, and classy. Tender and soft, light and moist, and ultraspecial. Serve these at a tea party, or with coffee after a dinner party, or as a luncheon dessert. But they are not too elegant or sophisticated to be in great demand by young children; they are perfect for a children's party. Candylike, but not too sweet or too rich.

Although these can probably be made in any small tartlet pan, I do recommend this one—a nonstick pan for miniature muffins. Each opening has a 2-tablespoon capacity and measures 1 3/4 by 3/4 inch (see page 30). Each pan makes 12 cakes; you need two pans for this recipe. Incidentally, this pan can be used for any muffin or cupcake recipe.

2 ounces unsweetened chocolate

2½ ounces (½ cup) blanched and toasted
   hazelnuts (see page 9—blanched and
   toasted almonds may be substituted)

½ cup granulated sugar

3 egg whites graded "large" (they may be
   whites that were frozen and thawed)

Pinch of salt

¼ teaspoon almond extract, or ½ teaspoon
   vanilla extract

Adjust a rack to the center of the oven and preheat the oven to 350 degrees. Lightly butter two of the above miniature muffin pans. Strain a generous amount of chocolate flour (see page 21) all over the pans (if you miss any spots, the cakes will stick even though it is a nonstick pan). Turn each pan upside down over paper and tap to shake out excess. Set the pans aside.

On a board, with a long, sharp, heavy knife shred and then chop the chocolate as fine as possible; pieces should be no larger than ¹⁄₁₆ inch (see Note). Place in a large mixing bowl and set aside.

Place the nuts and about three fourths of the sugar (reserve remaining sugar) in the bowl of a food processor fitted with the metal chopping blade. Process for about 15 seconds until fine, but not until oily or moist.

Add the processed nuts and sugar to the chocolate and fold/stir with a rubber spatula until mixed. Set aside.

Place the egg whites and the salt in the small bowl of an electric mixer and beat on moderate speed until foamy, then on high speed until the whites hold a soft shape when the beaters are raised. On moderate speed add the reserved sugar 1 rounded teaspoonful at a time. Then add the almond or vanilla extract and beat on high speed only until the whites barely hold a straight shape when the beaters are raised; do not beat until stiff and dry.

Add the beaten whites all at once to the nut mixture, and with a rubber spatula fold together until incorporated; do not handle any more than necessary. Transfer to a small bowl for ease in handling.

With two teaspoons (one for picking up with and one for pushing off with) place the mixture in the prepared pans. The forms will be slightly mounded. Do not smooth the tops.

Bake for 18 to 20 minutes until the tops barely spring back when gently pressed with a fingertip (do not overbake).

As soon as you remove a pan from the oven, cover it with a rack, turn the pan and rack upside down, remove the pan, and let the cakes cool upside down (they will shrink a little as they cool—it is OK). Place each rack of cakes over a length of aluminum foil. The cakes should be close to each other but not touching. The icing will be poured over the cakes.

ICING

The icing can be made while the cakes cool or later, but it must be used as soon as it is made.

¼ cup granulated sugar
¼ cup water
1 ounce unsweetened chocolate, chopped fine or medium
1 teaspoon light corn syrup (i.e., Karo)
1 teaspoon unsalted butter
2 ounces milk chocolate, broken or chopped into medium-sized pieces
About 2 tablespoons unsalted green pistachio nuts or blanched almonds, chopped fine (to be used on top of the icing)

Place the sugar and water in a small (about 3-cup) heavy saucepan over high heat. Stir with a wooden spatula until the sugar is dissolved and the mixture comes to a boil. Cover for 1 minute to allow steam to wash down any sugar granules from the sides of the pan, and then boil uncovered for 3 minutes (total boiling time is 4 minutes).

Remove the pan from the heat and stir in the unsweetened chocolate, corn syrup, and butter. Then add the milk chocolate and stir with a wire whisk until smooth.

Cool and stir for about 5 to 10 minutes until the icing thickens slightly. Chill briefly if necessary.

Transfer to a small pitcher (a 1-cup plastic measuring cup with a spout works well), and slowly pour the icing over the tops of the cakes, letting it run down unevenly on the sides.

You can move the rack, scrape up the icing that ran off (use a wide metal spatula), and use it again.

The icing sets quickly. Before it sets sprinkle the chopped nuts over the tops. (If the icing has already started to set, tap the nuts a bit with a fingertip to be sure they hold.)

Let stand for an hour or so until set. These may be served immediately or the next day, although the icing loses its gorgeous shine after a few hours.

NOTE: If you add the chocolate to the nuts and sugar in the processor, there is a chance that by the time the nuts are fine enough the fat in the chocolate will make the mixture oily and lumpy; it must be dry in order to fold in the egg whites.

McMaida's Shortbread

8 TO 16 WEDGES

I thought of making a shortbread cookie. It occurred to me to roll out the dough, spread half of it with melted chocolate, and sandwich it with the remaining dough—before baking. It seemed like a new idea. I wondered what would happen. Would the chocolate seep down through the bottom layer of dough? Would it run out on the edges and burn? I anticipated trouble. But the cookie fairy was watching over the experiment, and it worked like magic.

You will have a chocolate sandwich on shortbread; the chocolate is bittersweet or semisweet, and the vanilla-flavored shortbread is golden brown, crisp, and crunchy. The cookies are cut into wedges after baking. They are simple and gorgeous, delicious, unusual, and very special.

It takes longer to describe this (almost) than it does to make it. It is an unusual procedure, but quick, easy, and fun.

1 1/4 cups sifted unbleached flour

1/3 firmly packed cup light brown sugar

4 ounces (1 stick) unsalted butter, cold and
firm, cut into 1-inch pieces

1/2 teaspoon vanilla extract

3 ounces bittersweet or semisweet chocolate

Adjust a rack one-third up from the bottom of the oven and preheat the oven to 325 degrees.

To prepare the pan: Cut a round of baking-pan liner paper to fit the bottom of an 8-inch layer-cake pan (see page 30) and set it aside. Also cut two strips of baking-pan liner paper, each 11 by 2 inches, and set aside. Butter the bottom and sides of the pan. Carefully place one of the long strips in the middle of the pan; press it onto the bottom and up the two sides. Butter the middle two inches of the strip. Then place the other strip at a right angle to the first—on top of the first—forming a cross. Press it on the bottom and up the two sides of the pan. Now place the round piece of paper in the pan, press it into place, and butter the round and the exposed parts of all four strips on the sides of the pan (the strips will act as handles to help remove the cake after it is done).

Place the flour and sugar in the bowl of a food processor fitted with the metal chopping blade. Add the butter and start the machine. Add the vanilla through the feed tube and process for about 25 seconds until the mixture just holds together and forms a ball. Turn the dough out onto a work surface and knead once or twice to be sure the mixture is smooth.

On a lightly floured surface, with lightly floured hands form the dough into a short, fat sausage (only about 3 inches long) with flat ends. Cut it into two equal pieces. Set one piece aside.

On a lightly floured pastry cloth, with a lightly floured rolling pin roll the other piece of dough carefully and slowly into as perfect a round shape as you can, to just fit the bottom of the pan (most 8-inch pans measure 7 1/2 inches across the bottom).

If you try to transfer the dough to the pan at this point it will probably be impossible. But if you freeze the dough until it is firm, it will be easy. Here's how: Cover the round of dough with a piece of plastic wrap and any flat utensil (the bottom of a two-piece quiche or tart pan works well). Slide your left hand under the pastry cloth and flip the dough upside down onto the flat utensil. Transfer to the freezer.

Repeat with the second round of dough.

Cut the chocolate into pieces, place in the top of a small double boiler over warm water on moderate heat, cover with a folded paper towel (to absorb steam) and the pot cover. Let cook until slightly melted. Then uncover and stir until completely melted and smooth. Remove the top of the double boiler and set aside.

Remove one of the firm rounds of dough from the freezer. Place the cake pan right side up on top of the dough and, with a small sharp knife, trim around the rim of the pan. Then lift the round of dough and place it in the prepared pan; the dough should fit in the pan perfectly.

The dough may still be almost frozen and the chocolate may still be slightly warm. Pour the chocolate onto the center of the dough in the pan. With the underside of a spoon spread the chocolate slowly and carefully, stopping it 1/2 inch from the edge of the dough and making the last 1/2 inch of the chocolate thinner than the rest.

Now trim around the edges of the second round of dough and place it, while still firm, over the chocolate. The sides should just fit the pan. Do not press down on the middle of the dough or you will force the chocolate out toward the edges. Let stand for a few minutes for the dough to soften slightly. Then, with floured fingertips, press gently around the rim. And with the floured prongs of a fork, press around the rim to seal the edges and to form a design.

Bake for about 50 minutes until well browned.

Remove from the oven and let stand for 1 hour until just barely cool. If the cookie cools completely, it will crumble when you cut it. It is best if the chocolate filling is still slightly soft when you cut it.

Then, using the strips of paper to help release the cake, gently lift each strip a bit until the cake is loose from the pan. Then cover with a rack, turn pan and rack upside down, remove pan and paper lining, cover with another rack, and turn upside down again, leaving the cake right side up.

Transfer to a board and, with a long, thin, sharp knife, cut the cake in half, and then cut each half into four to eight wedges. Cut slowly and carefully.

Store airtight. These keep well.

Chocolate Sandwich Cookies

Thin and crisp, brown sugar ice-box cookies (yummy) sandwiched together after baking with chocolate between them (double yummy). The dough must be frozen for at least several hours before it is sliced and baked.

32 SANDWICHED
COOKIES

2 cups unsifted unbleached flour
1/4 teaspoon salt
1/4 teaspoon baking soda
1/4 teaspoon cinnamon
4 ounces (1 stick) unsalted butter
1/2 teaspoon vanilla extract
2/3 cup firmly packed light brown sugar
1 egg graded "large"
6 ounces semisweet or bittersweet chocolate
    (to be used as filling after the cookies
    are baked)

Sift together the flour, salt, baking soda, and cinnamon and set aside.

In the large bowl of an electric mixer beat the butter until soft. Beat in the vanilla and then the sugar. When thoroughly mixed add the egg, and then, gradually, on low speed, add the sifted dry ingredients, beating until incorporated.

Turn out onto a lightly floured board or work surface. Press the dough together and then form it into a smooth and even oblong about 10 inches long, 3 inches wide, and 1 inch high.

Place a 15-inch length of plastic wrap on a cookie sheet. Carefully transfer the oblong of dough to the plastic wrap and, gently, wrap the dough in the plastic wrap. Transfer the wrapped dough on the cookie sheet to the freezer. Freeze for several hours or overnight.

Before baking, adjust two racks to divide the oven into thirds and preheat the oven to 400 degrees.

Unwrap the dough and, with a sharp knife, carefully cut it into slices 1/8 inch thick—or less. Place the cookies 3/4 inch apart on unbuttered cookie sheets.

Bake for 10 to 12 minutes, reversing the sheets, top to bottom and front to back, once during baking to ensure even browning. The cookies should be lightly browned when done. Do not underbake.

If you bake only one sheet at a time, bake it in the center of the oven. One sheet might bake in a little less time.

With a wide metal spatula carefully transfer the warm cookies to a rack to cool.

Cut or break the chocolate into pieces. Place it in the top of a small double boiler. Cover with a folded paper towel (to absorb condensation) and the pot cover. Place over hot water on moderate heat and let cook until partially melted. Then uncover and stir until completely melted.

Remove the top of the double boiler, and transfer the chocolate to a small cup or bowl for ease in handling. Hold a cookie bottom side up. With a small spoon gently place about ½ teaspoon (see Note) of the melted chocolate on the cookie, placing it the long way, in the middle. Do not spread the chocolate near the edges. Do not use so much chocolate that it runs out the sides. Place another cookie on the chocolate, bottoms together. Press the cookies together very gently to spread the chocolate slightly.

Place the sandwiched cookies on a tray and chill briefly in the refrigerator or freezer only until the chocolate is set.

Store and serve at room temperature.

NOTE: A demitasse spoon holds about the same amount as a ½-teaspoon measuring spoon.

Two-tone Hazelnut Cookies

28 COOKIES

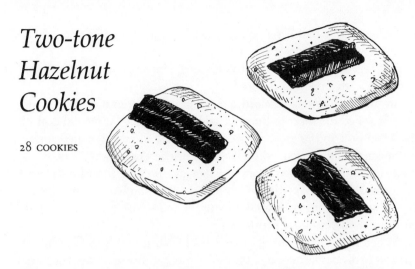

These are made with two doughs. One is a hazelnut mixture that is shaped like an ice-box cookie, then chilled and sliced. The other is a rich and dark chocolate mixture that is pressed out of a pastry bag fitted with a star-shaped tube; it is formed into long strips that are chilled and then cut into short lengths. Each hazelnut cookie is topped, before baking, with a short length of the chocolate mixture. During baking the chocolate bakes into the hazelnut cookie, leaving a dark strip with just a hint of the original star shape. Unusual and exotic-looking. Tender, delicate, fragile, fancy, and very delicious. Fun to make, and easy.

HAZELNUT DOUGH

2 ounces (½ cup) blanched and toasted hazelnuts (see page 9 for a source for blanched and toasted hazelnuts)
¾ cup sifted unbleached flour
¼ teaspoon salt
½ teaspoon baking soda
½ teaspoon cinnamon
Optional: ½ teaspoon powdered instant espresso or coffee
3½ ounces (1 stick minus 1 tablespoon) unsalted butter
¼ cup granulated sugar

To grind the hazelnuts to a powder: Either use a nut grinder or place the nuts in the bowl of a food processor fitted with the metal chopping blade.

In a processor it is best if you add the sugar to the nuts and process them together until powdery. Set the nuts aside.

Sift together the flour, salt, baking soda, cinnamon, and the optional espresso or coffee powder. Set aside.

In the small bowl of an electric mixer beat the butter until soft. If you have not added the sugar to the nuts, add it now to the butter and beat to mix. Then beat in the ground hazelnuts and the sifted dry ingredients.

Spoon the mixture out onto a length of plastic wrap or wax paper. Bring up the sides of the plastic wrap or wax paper and, pressing against the plastic wrap or wax paper, shape the dough into a roll or an oblong 7 or 8 inches long. Wrap in the plastic wrap or wax paper and refrigerate for at least an hour (or overnight, if you wish).

When the hazelnut dough is chilled and you are ready to bake, adjust two racks to divide the oven into thirds and preheat the oven to 350 degrees. Line two cookie sheets with baking-pan liner paper or aluminum foil shiny side up.

Unwrap the roll of hazelnut dough and cut it into ¼-inch slices. Place the slices 1 inch apart on the lined cookie sheets. Set aside.

CHOCOLATE DOUGH

¾ cup less 2 tablespoons sifted unbleached
    flour
3 tablespoons unsweetened cocoa powder
    (preferably Dutch process)
2 ounces (½ stick) unsalted butter
½ teaspoon vanilla extract
1 tablespoon sugar

Sift together the flour and cocoa and set aside. In the small bowl of an electric mixer beat the butter, vanilla, and sugar. On low speed add the sifted dry ingredients and beat to mix.

Fit a pastry bag with a star-shaped tube that is about number 4 (one with about a ½-inch opening at the widest point). Place the chocolate mixture in the bag. Twist the top of the bag closed.

Line a cookie sheet or a tray with wax paper. Press out the chocolate mixture onto the wax paper, forming long strips about ½ inch wide. This chocolate mixture will be quite stiff. Place in the freezer or refrigerator briefly until firm enough to handle.

With a small sharp knife cut the chocolate strips into pieces a little shorter than the length of the hazelnut cookies. Place a chocolate strip lengthwise on each hazelnut cookie.

Bake two sheets at a time for about 15 minutes, reversing the sheets, top to bottom and front to back, once during baking to ensure even browning. When done the cookies will be only lightly colored.

With a wide metal spatula transfer the baked cookies to racks to cool. Store airtight.

Miami Vice

12 TO 16 LARGE
COOKIES

Jim Nassikas, a friend of ours in San Francisco, recently raved to me about a fantastic chocolate cookie he had had at a friend's house. When I asked what it was like, he could only say, "Chocolate-chocolate-chocolate. I never had anything like it."

I wanted the recipe.

Jim called the friend who had served the cookies, and she referred us to The Model Bakery in St. Helena, California, where she had bought the cookies. When I called the bakery I was told that the recipe was the secret of their French pastry chef, who had brought it with him from France.

I ordered some of the cookies from the bakery.

When they arrived at our home in Miami Beach, I knew right away that they were Mulattoes, a recipe I had made up for my first book in 1974. But the technique of shaping them was radically different.

Since the bakery wouldn't tell, I had to guess how to make them. Now I think that these are not exactly like those from the bakery—these are better!

Mulattoes are drop cookies, but these are ice-box cookies—like you never had before. Very dark chocolate—almost fudge candy—chunky, nutty, a mouthful. A hunk. When you taste these you will see why I named them Miami Vice. The Model Bakery calls them Rads (short for radical, I think. Surprisingly, according to William Safire, who writes about the English language, rad is currently used to mean "great, wonderful, remarkable").

These are best when they are very fresh, preferably within hours of baking. Since they are ice-box cookies they can easily be sliced and baked whenever you wish. It is no problem to have them fresh.

> 1 ounce unsweetened chocolate
> 7 ounces Baker's semisweet chocolate (some other brands don't work as well in this recipe)
> 1 ounce (¼ stick) unsalted butter
> ¼ cup sifted all-purpose flour
> ¼ teaspoon baking powder
> ⅛ teaspoon salt
> 2 eggs graded "large"
> ¾ cup granulated sugar
> 2 teaspoons instant espresso or coffee powder
> ½ teaspoon vanilla extract
> 6 ounces (1 cup) semisweet chocolate morsels
> 7 ounces (2 cups) walnuts, in large pieces (I use them just as they come)

In the top of a large or small double boiler over hot water on moderate heat melt the unsweetened chocolate, semisweet chocolate, and butter. Stir to mix and then remove the top of the double boiler from the heat and set it aside to cool slightly.

Sift together the flour, baking powder, and salt and set aside to cool.

In the small bowl of an electric mixer beat the eggs, sugar, espresso or coffee, and vanilla at high speed for about 1 minute. Remove the bowl (but not the beaters) from the mixer.

Pour the melted-chocolate mixture into the large bowl of the mixer. Beat in the egg mixture, and then, on low speed, add the sifted dry ingredients and beat only until incorporated.

Remove the bowl from the mixer and stir in the chocolate morsels and the nuts.

Spread out a 16-inch length of wax paper. Place the dough by large spoonfuls in a 10-inch length down the middle of the paper. It will be a thick, high, and wide strip. Bring the long sides of the paper over the dough and press down gently with your hands to make a smooth and even shape about 2 inches high, 2½ inches wide, and 10 to 12 inches long, with flat ends. (If the dough is too soft for you to shape it, slide a cookie sheet under the wax paper and transfer the dough, as is, to the freezer for about 10 minutes or as necessary for it to firm up just a bit, and then continue to shape the dough.)

When the dough is shaped, slide a flat-sided cookie sheet under the roll of dough and place it in the refrigerator for a few hours or overnight. (The roll of dough can be refrigerated for a few days if you wish.)

Before baking, adjust an oven rack to the middle of the oven and preheat the oven to 350 degrees. Line a cookie sheet with baking-pan liner paper or aluminum foil, shiny side up.

Unwrap the firm dough and, with a ruler and the tip of a small sharp knife, mark the dough into ¾-inch widths. With a very sharp and heavy knife carefully cut the slices. If you have any trouble slicing these, hold the knife under hot running water for 5 to 10 seconds before making each cut. Shake the water off the knife but do not dry it. Place the slices cut side down about an inch apart on the lined sheet; these will barely spread or change shape during baking. Let the sliced cookies stand at room temperature for about 20 minutes so they are not too cold when they go into the oven.

Bake for 11 minutes—NO LONGER. After 11 minutes the cookies will not look or feel done, but they will be. Actually, they will look almost the same as when they went into the oven. They will be a little wet in the centers but will become firmer as they cool.

When just baked these will be too gooey to transfer. Let stand on the sheet until firm enough to be moved, and then, gently and carefully, with a wide metal spatula, transfer them to a rack to cool.

Let stand at room temperature for about an hour before serving. If they must wait any longer, wrap them airtight—do not let them dry out. I wrap these individually in clear cellophane and serve them as soon as possible.

Pennsylvania Dutch Chocolate Cookies

ABOUT 15 HUGE OR 36 MEDIUM-SIZED COOKIES

This is one of only very few chocolate recipes that are traditional for Christmas. It is customary to serve these after dark on Christmas Eve. They are plain, intensely chocolate, crisp wafers. (Divine anytime.)

1 cup sifted whole wheat flour
1½ cups sifted unbleached flour
1 teaspoon baking soda
1 teaspoon cinnamon
Scant ½ teaspoon salt
1 cup unsweetened cocoa powder (preferably Dutch-process)
8 ounces (2 sticks) unsalted butter
1 teaspoon vanilla extract
2 cups granulated sugar
1 egg graded "large"
1 tablespoon water
Additional granulated sugar (to sprinkle on just before baking)

Adjust two racks to divide the oven into thirds and preheat the oven to 400 degrees. Line cookie sheets with baking-pan liner paper or aluminum foil, shiny side up; or, if you wish, these can be baked on unlined and unbuttered sheets—they will not stick. Set aside.

Sift together both flours, the baking soda, cinnamon, salt, and cocoa and set aside.

In the large bowl of an electric mixer beat the butter until soft. Beat in the vanilla and 2 cups of sugar. Then beat in the egg and water. On low speed gradually add the sifted dry ingredients, scraping the bowl with a rubber spatula as necessary and beating until incorporated.

Turn the mixture out onto a large board or countertop and knead until perfectly smooth. Then work with half of the dough at a time.

On a lightly floured pastry cloth, with a floured rolling pin roll out the dough just a bit. Then, to flour both sides, turn the dough upside down and roll the dough until it is ¼ inch thick (no thinner).

Traditionally these are cut with a very large plain round cutter about 5 inches in diameter (see page 31). These are indeed gorgeous when large, but make them any size or shape you want.

Cut out the cookies, first cutting right up against the edge of the rolled dough, and cut them just touching each other. Use a wide metal spatula to transfer them to the cookie sheets, placing them about 1 inch apart. If the cookies are 5 inches wide, place only three or four on each sheet.

Reflour the cloth only slightly before rolling the second half of the dough. Reserve the scraps from both halves of the dough, knead them together, and reroll. Do not incorporate any more flour than necessary.

Sprinkle the tops of the cookies generously with additional sugar.

Bake for 9 to 10 minutes, reversing the sheets, top to bottom and front to back, once during baking to ensure even baking. Do not overbake; these are so dark that they can burn and you wouldn't know it by looking. They will not feel firm to the touch when they are done, but they will become firm when they cool.

With a wide metal spatula transfer the cookies to racks to cool.

Store airtight.

Chocolate Hazelnut Macaroons

16 MACAROONS

The ultimate and most irresistible nut macaroon—chewy and moist—you can't stop eating them.

I stumbled on these purely by accident. I thought I was making meringues with ground nuts incorporated into the mixture, but they came out macaroons. The ingredients are almost identical; the techniques are different.

5 ounces (1 cup) plus 16 blanched and
    roasted hazelnuts (see Note)
1½ tablespoons unsweetened cocoa powder
¾ cup granulated sugar
4 egg whites graded "large" (they may be
    whites that were frozen and thawed)
¼ teaspoon almond or vanilla extract

Lightly butter a cookie sheet and flour it as follows: Work over the sink. Sift flour along one long side of the sheet, then tilt and tap the sheet to cover the entire surface with flour (allow excess flour to fall into the sink). Set the sheet aside.

Place 1 cup of the hazelnuts (reserve remaining hazelnuts), the cocoa, and half of the sugar (reserve remaining sugar) in the bowl of a food processor fitted with the metal chopping blade. Process for 30 to 40 seconds until fine, scraping down the sides once or twice as necessary. Set aside.

In the top of a large double boiler off the heat beat the egg whites and the almond or vanilla extract until foamy. Stir in the ground-hazelnut mixture and the remaining sugar.

Place over hot water in the bottom of the double boiler on moderate heat and stir and scrape the pan almost constantly for 15 minutes or until the consistency resembles soft mashed potatoes. It is ready when, if you scrape a path in the bottom of the pan with a rubber spatula, it stays clear for a few seconds.

Remove the top of the double boiler. Work quickly before the mixture stiffens. Transfer the mixture to a shallow bowl for ease in handling.

To shape the cookies use two teaspoons (one for picking up with and one for pushing off with) and carefully, neatly, form round drop cookies on the prepared sheet. Use a rounded teaspoonful of the dough for each cookie. Place them about an inch apart.

Place one of the remaining hazelnuts on the top of each macaroon, pressing it down gently; only about half of the nut should remain exposed.

Let stand uncovered for 1 hour.

Before baking adjust an oven rack to the center of the oven and preheat the oven to 350 degrees.

Bake the macaroons for about 15 minutes until they feel slightly resistant—or dry but soft—to the touch. Break one open to test it; it should be moist inside. Do not turn off the oven.

With a wide metal spatula transfer the macaroons to a rack. Place the rack over foil or wax paper. The following glaze should be applied immediately while the cookies are hot; therefore it is best to prepare the glaze while the cookies are still baking.

GLAZE

3 tablespoons confectioners sugar
2 teaspoons hot water

In a small saucepan over moderate heat stir the sugar and water until the mixture comes to a boil.

With a small, soft brush, brush the boiling-hot glaze over the right-out-of-the-oven cookies. Place the rack on the cookie sheet and return to the oven to bake for 1 minute more. Then let cool on the rack.

It is best if these are stored only loosely covered. If they are stored airtight, they become too moist after a few days.

NOTE: See page 10 for a source for blanched and roasted hazelnuts.

The Newest Chocolate-Chocolate Chunk Cookies

32 RATHER LARGE COOKIES

Thin and crisp, buttery, and very dark. With more chocolate than usual, and in larger chunks. They also have walnuts in halves or pieces as large as they come, plus the additional soft chewiness of raisins. The best ever.

8 ounces semisweet or bittersweet chocolate
1¾ cups sifted unbleached flour
¼ teaspoon baking soda
¼ teaspoon salt
⅓ cup unsweetened powdered cocoa
    (preferably Dutch-process)
8 ounces (2 sticks) unsalted butter
1 teaspoon vanilla extract
1 cup granulated sugar
½ firmly packed cup dark brown sugar
1 egg graded "large"
2 tablespoons milk
5 ounces (1 cup) raisins
4 ounces (generous 1 cup) walnut halves
    and/or large pieces, plus 32 additional
    halves or pieces (to top the cookies with)

Adjust two racks to divide the oven into thirds and preheat the oven to 350 degrees. Line cookie sheets with baking-pan liner paper or aluminum foil, shiny side up. Set aside.

On a board, with a heavy and sharp knife cut the chocolate into rather large pieces. (If the chocolate is in thin bars, it may be cut or broken into 1/2-inch pieces; but if it is a thick slab, first slice it about 1/4 inch thick and then cut in the opposite direction into pieces about 1/2 inch wide—or larger.) Set aside.

Sift together the flour, baking soda, salt, and cocoa and set aside.

In the large bowl of an electric mixer beat the butter until soft. Add the vanilla and both of the sugars and beat until mixed. Beat in the egg and milk. Then, on low speed, gradually add the sifted dry ingredients, scraping the bowl as necessary with a rubber spatula and beating only until incorporated.

Remove the bowl from the mixer. With a heavy wooden spatula stir in the raisins, chopped chocolate, and 1 cup of the walnuts (reserve the remaining walnuts). The mixture will be thick and stiff. (Since the mixture is so stiff, you will be surprised at how much it will run during baking, and how thin the cookies will become.)

Use a heaping tablespoon of the dough for each cookie; place only six mounds on each cookie sheet.

After placing the mounds on the sheets, flatten them slightly as follows: Dip a fork into cold water and, with the underside of the wet fork, flatten the tops of the cookies only slightly, making the cookies about 1/2 inch thick. Dip the fork again as necessary.

Place an additional piece of walnut on the top of each cookie. The dough is so stiff you will not be able to actually press the nut into the cookie; it is OK.

Bake two sheets at a time for 14 to 15 minutes, reversing the sheets, top to bottom and front to back, once during baking to ensure even baking.

When done, the cookies will still feel soft, but do not overbake them or they will become too hard, or actually burn.

Let the cookies cool on the sheets for a few minutes until they are firm enough to be moved. With a wide metal spatula transfer the cookies to racks to cool. They will become crisp and less fragile as they cool. Store airtight.

Chocolate Chunk Peanut Cookies

15 HUGE COOKIES

Tremendous, stupendous, and easy. With just barely enough batter to hold the generous amount of chocolate chunks and peanuts together. They are 4 to 5 inches wide, rather thin, with a crisp but tender texture and a seductive flavor (both sweet and salty).

1 8-ounce bar milk chocolate
1 cup sifted unbleached flour
¾ teaspoon baking soda
4 ounces (1 stick) unsalted butter
½ cup smooth peanut butter
½ teaspoon vanilla extract
½ cup granulated sugar
½ firmly packed cup dark brown sugar
1 egg graded "large"
4 ounces (1 cup) salted peanuts

Adjust two racks to divide the oven into thirds and preheat the oven to 350 degrees. Line cookie sheets with baking-pan liner paper or aluminum foil, shiny side up, and set aside.

On a board, with a long and heavy knife cut the chocolate in both directions to make ½-inch pieces and set aside.

Sift together the flour and baking soda and set aside.

In the large bowl of an electric mixer beat the butter, peanut butter, and vanilla until soft and smooth. Add both sugars and beat to mix. Beat in the egg. On low speed gradually add the sifted dry ingredients and beat only until incorporated.

Remove the bowl from the mixer and stir in the peanuts and chocolate. It will be a thick mixture.

Place mounds of the dough—each about ¼ cupful—about 3 inches apart (no more than five mounds on a cookie sheet). Wet a fork under cold running water or in a glass of cold water and, with the underside of the wet prongs, flatten each mound to about ¾-inch thickness.

Bake two sheets at a time, reversing the sheets, top to bottom and front to back, once during baking to ensure even baking.

The timing of these is tricky. You can't tell if they are done by feeling them (they will still feel much too soft when they are done). And you can't tell by looking (they will color only slightly). They take about 17 to 18 minutes. They will rise during baking and just barely begin to sink a little bit when done. (They will really flatten as they cool.)

When you remove the sheets from the oven, the cookies will be too soft and fragile to be transferred. Let them stand until they are firm enough to be moved, and then, with a wide metal spatula, transfer to a rack to cool.

If you are going to bake only one sheet at a time, adjust the rack to the middle of the oven.

Handle gently. These may be placed very carefully in a cookie jar or wrapped two together—bottoms together—in clear cellophane.

Raisin and Peanut Butter Chocolate Cookies

24 LARGE COOKIES

These have oatmeal that is ground to a powder in a food processor. It gives the cookies a different look and a moist and chewy texture. Especially rich, yummy, and delicious. Loaded with raisins.

2 ounces unsweetened chocolate

1½ cups plus 2 tablespoons "old-fashioned" (not "instant") rolled oats

1 cup sifted all-purpose flour

¼ teaspoon salt

½ teaspoon baking powder

½ teaspoon baking soda

1 tablespoon plus 1 teaspoon unsweetened cocoa powder

4 ounces (1 stick) unsalted butter

¼ cup smooth peanut butter

1½ teaspoons vanilla extract

½ cup granulated sugar

½ firmly packed cup light brown sugar

1 egg graded "large"

6 ounces (1¼ cups) raisins

Adjust two racks to divide the oven into thirds and preheat the oven to 375 degrees. Line cookie sheets with baking-pan liner paper or aluminum foil, shiny side up, and set aside.

Place the chocolate in the top of a small double boiler over warm water on low heat, then cover the pan with a folded paper towel (to absorb steam) and the pot cover. Let cook until just melted. Then uncover and remove the top of the double boiler and set aside.

Place the oats in the bowl of a food processor fitted with the metal chopping blade. Pulse the machine a few times and then process for about 25 seconds until the oatmeal is fine and powdery. Set aside.

Sift together the flour, salt, baking powder, baking soda, and cocoa and set aside.

In the large bowl of an electric mixer beat the butter until soft. Add the peanut butter and beat until smooth. Beat in the vanilla and both of the sugars. Add the melted chocolate and the egg and beat until smooth. Then, on low speed, gradually add the sifted dry ingredients and the ground oatmeal and beat just until mixed. (It will be a thick mixture.)

Remove the bowl from the mixer and, with a heavy wooden spatula, stir in the raisins.

Place a large piece of aluminum foil next to the sink. To shape the dough use two tablespoons, one for picking up with and one for pushing off with, and place the dough by mounds—each mound being a well-rounded tablespoon of the dough—any which way on the foil.

Wet your hands with cold water, shake them off—do not dry them—pick up a mound of the dough, roll it between your wet hands into a ball shape, and then flatten until the round of dough is about ⅓ inch thick. Continue to shape the cookies, wetting your hands as necessary and placing the cookies about 2 inches apart on the lined sheets. Place eight cookies on a sheet.

Optional: If you wish, dip a fork in cold water and press the bottom of the prongs down on the top of each cookie, in one direction only—just for looks.

Bake two sheets at a time for 8 minutes, reversing the sheets, top to bottom, once during baking to ensure even baking. When you open the oven door, work quickly. When the 8 minutes are up, the cookies will still feel soft, but they will firm up as they cool, and they should remain moist and chewy.

To bake only one sheet, adjust a rack to the center of the oven.

Let the cookies stand on the sheets for a few minutes until they are firm enough to be transferred. Then, with a wide metal spatula, transfer to a rack to cool.

Store airtight, preferably in a shallow box. Since these cookies will remain soft, it is best to store them two together—flat sides together—to keep them from losing their shape.

Double Chocolate Banana Cookies

20 HUGE COOKIES

Recently, while baking a batch of drop cookies, I was called away from the kitchen for a few hours. Some of the cookies were baked and some were not. The unbaked cookies were already shaped on sheets of aluminum foil. I worried about what might happen if the unbaked cookies waited at room temperature while I was away. As a safety precaution I slid cookie sheets under the sheets of foil and placed them in the refrigerator.

Then, when I came home and baked the cookies, I made a wonderful discovery. These same cookies that had previously run too much and lost their shape now held their shape and baked beautifully.

This recipe is a result of that experience.

The cookies are rich, dark chocolate, with mashed bananas, walnuts, and large chunks of white chocolate. They are soft, moist, and cakelike. Their flavor depends on bananas that are ripe enough; the banana skins should have a generous amount of dark markings. The cookies measure almost 4 inches in width, and at the center they are about 1 inch thick. They are shaped with a standard-sized ice cream scoop (when filled level, the scoop holds 1/3 cup).

These have a tendency to burn. Therefore they are baked on double cookie sheets, and the racks must not be too high or too low in the oven.

6 ounces semisweet chocolate

10 ounces white chocolate

6 ounces (1½ cups) walnuts

2 cups plus 2 tablespoons sifted unbleached flour

¼ cup unsweetened cocoa powder (preferably Dutch-process)

2 teaspoons baking powder

¼ teaspoon baking soda

½ teaspoon salt

2 large fully ripe bananas (to make 1 cup mashed)

6 ounces (1½ sticks) unsalted butter

1 teaspoon vanilla extract

½ cup granulated sugar

½ firmly packed cup light brown sugar

2 eggs graded "large"

Adjust two racks to divide the oven into thirds (see Note) and preheat the oven to 375 degrees. Line several cookie sheets with aluminum foil, shiny side up. (Do not use baking-pan liner paper on the sheets for these cookies; they will stick.) If you do not have enough sheets to shape the cookies all at once, the dough can wait in the bowl.

Chop or break the semisweet chocolate into coarse pieces and place in the top of a small double boiler over hot water on moderate heat. Cover with a folded paper towel and the pot cover, and cook until almost melted. Then remove the top of the double boiler and stir until completely melted. Set aside.

On a board, with a sharp and heavy knife cut the white chocolate into chunks a generous ½ inch in diameter. Set aside.

Chop or break the walnuts into coarse pieces and set aside.

Sift together the flour, cocoa, baking powder, baking soda, and salt and set aside.

Mash the bananas on a plate with a fork (they should not be liquefied) and set aside.

In the large bowl of an electric mixer beat the butter until soft. Add the vanilla, both sugars, and the mashed bananas, and beat well. Add the melted semisweet chocolate and beat until pale in color. Then add the eggs and beat to mix. Finally, on low speed, add the sifted dry ingredients and beat only to mix.

Remove the bowl from the mixer and stir in the white chocolate and walnuts.

Using a standard-sized ice cream scoop, shape the cookies and place them at least 2 inches apart on the foil-lined sheets (place only four on a sheet).

Before baking, place each sheet in the refrigerator for 20 to 25 minutes (not longer or the cookies will take too long to bake all the way through—and they might burn on the outside).

Then place each cookie sheet on another cookie sheet and bake two sheets at a time for 20 to 23 minutes, reversing the sheets, top to bottom and front to back, once during baking. Watch the cookies carefully—do not overbake. To test for doneness, gently press the top of a cookie with your fingertip; when the cookie just resists the pressure and springs back, it is done.

Remove from the oven, let stand for a minute or two, and then, with a wide metal spatula, transfer the cookies to racks to cool.

To store, place two cookies bottoms together, and wrap in clear cellophane or place in plastic sandwich bags.

NOTE: Depending on your oven, if the racks are so high or so low that the cookies burn, it might be best to bake only one sheet at a time on the middle rack (but try two racks first, and watch carefully).

Cookies Without Chocolate— and Candy

Raisin Sandwich Cookies

18 LARGE COOKIE
SANDWICHES

Each cookie sandwich consists of two delicious brown sugar–butter cookies, filled—before baking—with a generous layer of raisins. They're terrific, and important. Making these is a craft (they take time). Having them, giving them, eating them, is a special joy. This is happiness.

DOUGH

2 1/4 cups unsifted unbleached flour
1/4 teaspoon baking soda
1/2 teaspoon cinnamon
1/4 teaspoon salt
7 ounces (1 3/4 sticks) unsalted butter
1 teaspoon vanilla extract
2/3 firmly packed cup light brown sugar
1 egg plus 1 egg yolk graded "large"

Sift together the flour, baking soda, cinnamon, and salt and set aside. In the large bowl of an electric mixer beat the butter until soft. Add the vanilla and sugar and beat to mix. Beat in the egg and yolk and then, on low speed, add the sifted dry ingredients and beat until thoroughly mixed.

The mixture will be soft and sticky. Turn it out onto a well-floured surface. Flour your hands and quickly form the dough into a ball. Turn it to flour all sides. Then, with your hands, carefully form the dough into an 8-by-4-inch rectangle with square corners. Cut the rectangle into two 4-inch squares. Handle the squares carefully and wrap each piece individually in plastic wrap. (The squares will lose their shape a bit.) Refrigerate for 1 to 2 hours or longer; the dough may be refrigerated overnight if you wish.

FILLING AND TOPPING

1 egg plus 1 egg yolk graded "large" (do not mix these together)
10 to 12 ounces (about 2 cups) soft, moist, fresh raisins (see Note)
1 teaspoon water
Crystal sugar (see page 4) or granulated sugar

Place one square of the refrigerated dough on a floured pastry cloth. With a floured rolling pin pound the dough slightly until it is flexible enough to be rolled out; if the dough is too firm, it should stand at room temperature until it can be pounded and softened. Turn the dough upside down once or twice to flour both the top and the bottom, and reflour the cloth if necessary. Carefully roll out the dough into a 10½-inch square, with square corners; if the dough cracks on the edges, pinch it together.

To straighten the sides, hold a ruler on edge and push it up against each side until the dough is almost completely straight (a few uneven spots are OK).

Line a cookie sheet with baking-pan liner paper or wax paper. Place the cookie sheet right next to the rolled-out dough and transfer the dough by rolling it loosely on the rolling pin and then unrolling it onto the sheet. Straighten the edges again if necessary.

Place in the freezer until firm.

Meanwhile, repeat the directions to roll the second square of dough into a 10½-inch square; straighten the sides with a ruler. With a rolling pin transfer this square to another lined cookie sheet; do not freeze this square.

Beat the whole egg (reserve the additional yolk) just to mix and, with a pastry brush, brush about half of the beaten egg generously over the second square of dough. Sprinkle the raisins evenly all over the dough, right up to the sides (it should be a generous layer of raisins, almost completely covering the dough).

Now remove the firm dough from the freezer and brush it generously with the beaten egg (if any beaten egg remains, drizzle it over the raisins) and, without waiting (without letting the egg dry), place the square of firm dough egg side down over the raisins. Press down firmly on the dough with your hands to make a compact sandwich. If necessary, straighten the sides again.

Place in the freezer for 20 to 30 minutes (or longer, even overnight if you wish—the dough cuts most easily and neatly when frozen).

At about this time adjust two racks to divide the oven into thirds and preheat the oven to 350 degrees. Line two cookie sheets with baking-pan liner paper (preferably) or aluminum foil, shiny side up.

With a ruler and the tip of a small sharp knife mark the dough in half in one direction and in thirds in the opposite direction. With the ruler and the tip of the knife score the dough lightly just to mark it.

Cutting these cookies takes care and patience. Work next to the sink. Hold a long-bladed sharp knife under hot running water for a few seconds. Just shake off the water, and with the wet and hot blade cut the cold and firm dough into six pieces. Repeat wetting and heating the blade before each cut. Finally cut each piece into three bars.

Place the bars 1 inch apart on the lined cookie sheets.

Stir the reserved egg yolk with the water to mix well and strain through a fine strainer into a small cup. Brush the tops of the cookies generously with the egg wash and then sprinkle them generously with the crystal or granulated sugar.

Bake two sheets at a time for about 20 minutes, reversing the sheets, top to bottom and front to back, once during baking to ensure even browning. Bake until golden brown. (The cookies will lose their shape slightly during baking.)

Transfer the cookies to racks to cool.

NOTE: If fresh and moist seeded muscat raisins are available, use them; they are more moist and chewy than regular seedless raisins. However, because muscat raisins stick together, placing them in a thin layer takes much more time and patience than placing seedless raisins.

Honey Biscotti

ABOUT 30 *BISCOTTI*

Biscotti, *in Italian, means cookies. But most of us think of one particular cookie when we hear the word. Traditionally it is a long, narrow cookie, dry, crisp, crunchy, and hard. It is baked twice, once in an oval free-form shape, and then again after it is sliced into narrow cookies somewhat like zwieback (which means twice-baked in German). They have been making varieties of this in Italy—and other countries—since the thirteenth century. Biscotti have recently become popular in America. Many pasta/pizza shops, chic kitchen shops, and Italian restaurants have a tall glass jar of biscotti on display, and they sell like hotcakes.*

Biscotti may be served almost anytime, with fruit, ice cream, coffee, or alone. Italians often have them at breakfast. Or after a casual dinner (especially after a pasta or pizza dinner) with a sweet red wine—a Vin Santo, or "holy wine" (a Marsala or port may be used). Traditionally, the biscotti are dunked into wine or cappuccino, coffee, or cafe latte (café au lait). Some people (I am one of them) like these best dry, not dunked.

If you buy biscotti in a gourmet food shop you will probably pay from one to two dollars each, and they will probably not be as good or as large as these.

These biscotti—the addition of honey was suggested by my editor, Jason Epstein—are

*new and original, and markedly different from
and better than any others I have ever had.*

*Although this recipe is quick and easy to
make, it does require two lengthy periods of
baking, and for one brief moment it calls for
confidence and courage.*

7 ounces (1 1/4 cups) whole unblanched (skins
    on) almonds
3 eggs, graded "large"
1/2 cup mild and light honey
1 teaspoon vanilla extract
1/2 teaspoon almond extract, or 1/4 teaspoon
    bitter almond extract
3 cups plus 1 tablespoon sifted unbleached
    flour
1 1/2 teaspoons baking powder
1/4 teaspoon salt
1 1/4 teaspoons white pepper, ground fine
1 1/4 teaspoons ground ginger
1/2 cup granulated sugar

First toast the almonds: Preheat the oven to 375 degrees and bake the almonds in a wide, shallow pan, in the center of the oven, stirring once, for 13 minutes. Set aside to cool.

Adjust two racks to divide the oven into thirds and reduce the oven temperature to 300 degrees. Line two 12-by-15 1/2-inch cookie sheets with baking pan liner paper or aluminum foil, shiny side up, and set aside.

In a small bowl beat the eggs with the honey and the vanilla and almond extracts to mix well, and set aside.

Into the large bowl of an electric mixer sift together the flour, baking powder, salt, pepper, ginger, and sugar.

Add the beaten egg mixture all at once to the dry ingredients and beat on low speed, scraping the bowl as necessary with a rubber spatula until the mixture holds together. Slowly beat in the nuts. The mixture will be thick, gooey, and rubbery.

Lightly flour a large work surface and turn the dough out onto the floured area. Lightly sift flour over the top of the dough.

Cut the dough in half. With a wide dough scraper (or with a wide spatula or pancake turner) turn one piece of the dough a few times to lightly flour all sides of it and form the dough into an elongated oval about 10 inches long. Place a lined cookie sheet next to the oval of dough.

Now is the time when you need confidence. The dough will be soft and will lose its shape when you transfer it. (If you use more flour and make a dough that will hold its shape, it will then be too firm to spread out as it should during baking.) With both hands or with a wide dough scraper (or with a wide spatula or pancake turner) pick up the dough and quickly transfer it to the cookie sheet, placing it diagonally on the sheet. However the dough flops on the sheet, it will be OK. Reshape it with your fingers and/or press the dough scraper (or spatula or pancake turner) against the sides of the dough to straighten the shape. (It should be only about 2 ½ to 3 inches wide in the middle and only ½ to ¾ inch high.)

Repeat with the remaining half of the dough and the second cookie sheet.

With a wide pastry brush, brush excess flour off the dough.

Bake two sheets at a time for 50 minutes, reversing the sheets top to bottom and front to back once during baking to insure even browning. (The shapes will flatten and spread a bit during baking.)

Remove the sheets from the oven. Reduce the oven temperature to 275 degrees. Peel the paper away from the back, or with a large spatula, or using a flat-sided cookie sheet as a spatula, release the baked strips and transfer to a large cutting board.

Cutting the strips into narrow finger-shapes should be done slowly and carefully. With a serrated bread knife cut the strips on a sharp angle into cookies ½ inch wide. (These are more beautiful and, I think, even more delicious if they are extralong and extrathin. I cut them a scant ½ inch wide on an extremely sharp angle; the slices in the middle measure 8 inches or more in length.) Sometimes it is best to start each cut with the serrated knife and finish it with a straight knife.

Now the cookies will be baked again. Place them on a cut side, right next to each other, and bake them again for 35 to 45 minutes (depending on their width). After about 20 minutes, or when the cookies are half baked, turn them upside down and continue to bake until dry. Watch carefully, do not overbake. (While they are still warm they will feel a bit soft, but when they cool they will become crisp and hard.) They should be golden brown all over but should not look burnt.

Cool and store airtight.

VARIATIONS: Biscotti Cioccolato

To make stunning, dark (almost black), and intensely chocolate biscotti, *follow the above procedure but use the following ingredients and directions.*

7 ounces (1¼ cups) whole unblanched (skins on) almonds
3 eggs, graded "large"
½ packed cup light brown sugar
1 teaspoon vanilla extract
½ teaspoon almond extract, or ¼ teaspoon bitter almond extract
2 cups sifted unbleached flour
1½ teaspoons baking powder
¼ teaspoon salt
1¼ teaspoons white pepper, ground fine
1¼ teaspoons ground ginger
⅓ cup unsweetened cocoa powder (preferably Dutch-process)
2 tablespoons instant espresso or coffee powder
½ cup granulated sugar
4 ounces semisweet chocolate

Toast the almonds as above. Preheat the oven and prepare the cookie sheets. In a small bowl beat the eggs with the brown sugar and vanilla and almond extracts. Sift together into the large bowl of an electric mixer the flour, baking powder, salt, pepper, ginger, cocoa, espresso, and granulated sugar. Place the chocolate on a cutting board, and with a sharp knife, shred/chop it fine. Place the cut chocolate in the bowl of a food processor fitted with the metal chopping blade. Add about ½ cup of the sifted dry ingredients and process for about 1 minute until the chocolate is fine and powdery. Add this chocolate mixture and the egg mixture to the remaining dry ingredients in the large bowl of the mixer and mix as above. Beat in the nuts.

Shape, bake, and slice as above. (I cannot slice the chocolate *biscotti* as narrow as the others; they crumble or crack unless I slice them ⅔ to ¾ inch thick.) Bake again and cool as above.

Biscotti with Chocolate Icing

Some swanky *biscotti* have melted chocolate spread on one cut side of each cookie. They are extradelicious and extrawonderful; the hardened chocolate with the hard and dry cookie is a fabulous combination. I use Callebaut bittersweet chocolate (see page 13) or Ghirardelli bittersweet chocolate for this. I do not temper it—and it does not become streaked or discolored for at least several days.

Here's how to coat one side of some—or all—of the *biscotti* with chocolate: 4 ounces of chocolate will be enough to coat about half a batch of *biscotti;* plan on as much chocolate as you will need. On a board, with a long and heavy knife shred/chop the chocolate fine, and then place it in the top of a double boiler over warm water on low heat. Stir frequently until melted and smooth. Do not allow the chocolate to become very hot. Remove the top of the double boiler and transfer the chocolate to a small cup for ease in handling.

Line cookie sheets with wax paper.

With a small, narrow metal spatula or a table knife, spread a moderate layer of the chocolate on one cut side of a baked and cooled *biscotti* and place it, chocolate side down, on a lined cookie sheet. Continue to ice as many *biscotti* as you wish.

Then place the cookie sheet in the freezer or the refrigerator only until the chocolate is firm and the *biscotti* can be easily lifted from the wax paper. Remove all the *biscotti* from the paper and store airtight, in the refrigerator or at room temperature.

Cioccolati Affogati

Here is a delicious Italian dessert that means "drowned in chocolate." It can be put together in a minute if you have *biscotti* on hand. It can be made in a large serving bowl or in individual dessert bowls or wineglasses. Break or cut the *biscotti* into small pieces and place in the bottom of a large bowl or in individual bowls or glasses. Top with scoops of dark chocolate ice cream and a generous splash of Grand Marnier.

Raisin Oatmeal Cookies

Many of the letters I receive are requests for a soft cookie, specifically a soft oatmeal cookie. This is it! Huge, soft, and chewy—with peanut butter, raisins, oatmeal, and no flour. Oatmeal cookies simply do not get any better than these.

22 TO 24 LARGE
COOKIES

10 ounces (2 cups) raisins
4 ounces (1 stick) unsalted butter
12 ounces (1¼ cups) smooth peanut butter
1 teaspoon vanilla extract
1 teaspoon dark or light corn syrup
1 cup granulated sugar
½ packed cup dark brown sugar
3 eggs graded "large"
2 teaspoons baking soda
½ teaspoon mace
4 cups "old-fashioned" (not "instant") rolled oats

Adjust two racks to divide the oven into thirds and preheat the oven to 350 degrees. Line cookie sheets with baking-pan liner paper or aluminum foil, shiny side up, and set aside.

Place the raisins in a vegetable steamer over hot water on high heat, cover, and steam for about 10 minutes. Uncover and set aside.

In the large bowl of an electric mixer beat the butter until soft. Add the peanut butter and beat until mixed. Beat in the vanilla, corn syrup, and both sugars. Then add the eggs one at a time, beating until mixed. Through a fine strainer add the baking soda and mace. Then, on low speed, add the oats. Remove the bowl from the mixer and stir in the raisins.

To shape the cookies: Place a length of aluminum foil on the counter next to the sink. Use a ¼-cup measuring cup (the kind intended for dry ingredients), firmly packed, or use an ice cream scoop that is 2 inches in diameter and holds about ¼ cup, to measure the dough, and place the mounds any which way on the foil. Wet your hands, just shake off the water, pick up a mound of dough, shape it into a ball, and then press it to about ½-inch thickness and 2¾ inches in diameter. Place the round of dough on the lined cookie sheet. Keep your hands wet, continue to shape the cookies, and place them on the sheets at least 2 inches apart (these spread—place only four on a sheet).

Bake two sheets at a time, reversing the sheets, top to bottom and front to back, once during baking to ensure even baking. Bake for 16 to 17 minutes until the cookies are lightly browned but not until they feel firm when gently pressed with a fingertip. Do not overbake—these will firm up slightly as they cool and they are best when they are soft.

Let the baked cookies stand on the sheets for about a minute to firm up a bit. Then, with a wide metal spatula, transfer the cookies to racks to cool.

If these are not to be served soon they should be wrapped individually or two together (bottoms together) in clear cellophane, wax paper, or foil. Or place them in an airtight box with plastic wrap or wax paper between the layers. Just don't let them dry out.

VARIATIONS: Chocolate Chunk Raisin Oatmeal Cookies

You should use about 12 ounces of semisweet chocolate—preferably the kind that comes in thin bars, such as Tobler Tradition or Lindt Excellence. Cut the chocolate into pieces about ½ inch in diameter. The pieces will be uneven. Follow the above recipe and add the chocolate after adding the raisins. Shape as above. (If the cookies tend to crack on the edges, press the cracks together and, if necessary, move some of the pieces of chocolate from the edges to the top.) Bake as above. Serve while the chocolate is still soft (yummy) or let the cookies stand until the chocolate hardens before wrapping.

Peanut Raisin Oatmeal Cookies

Follow the above recipe for Raisin Oatmeal Cookies but add 1 cup salted peanuts (preferably dry roasted). Shake the nuts briefly in a strainer over the sink to remove excess salt. Then add the nuts when you add the raisins.

This variation with the peanuts is our favorite.

Ginger and Marmalade Fruit Bars

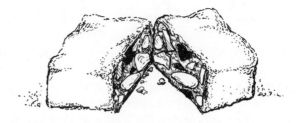

32 COOKIES

These are adapted from traditional Russian cookies called Mazurki. They are loaded with fruit and nuts—with barely enough batter to hold them together. The texture is moist, chunky, and chewy; the flavor is rich and not too sweet—the ingredients are unusual. They last, and last. At Christmas they seem like holiday cookies; on the Fourth of July they seem like picnic cookies. They are always popular.

> 5 ounces (1 cup) black raisins
> 5 ounces (1 cup) white raisins
> 6 ounces (1 loosely packed cup) dried apricot halves
> 5 ounces (scant ½ cup) stem ginger packed in syrup, drained (see Note)
> 12 ounces (1 cup) orange marmalade (may be sweet or Seville)
> 2 eggs graded "large"
> Finely grated rind of 1 large lemon
> ½ firmly packed cup light brown sugar
> 5 ounces (1 cup) unblanched almonds, whole
> 3 ½ ounces (1 cup) walnuts, halves and pieces
> 2 cups sifted unbleached flour
> Optional: confectioners sugar (to be used after baking)

Adjust a rack one-third up from the bottom of the oven and preheat the oven to 400 degrees. Generously butter a 13-by-9-by-2-inch baking pan (I use a Magic Line pan, see page 30). Set aside.

To steam the black and white raisins and the apricots, place them all together in the top of a vegetable steamer—or in a wide strainer resting on the rim of a deep saucepan—over hot water on high heat. Cover. Bring to a boil and let boil for about 5 minutes until the fruit is very moist. Then turn the fruit out in a thin layer on paper towels and let stand, uncovered.

Cut the ginger into 1/8-inch slices. In a bowl stir the marmalade to soften, stir in the ginger, and set aside.

In a small bowl stir the eggs to mix, stir in the lemon rind, and then stir in the sugar. Add to the marmalade mixture and stir to mix. Set aside.

To mix all the ingredients, place the steamed fruit in a very large bowl. Add the almonds and walnuts and then the marmalade mixture and stir well. Add the flour and stir—and stir—until completely absorbed.

Place the mixture by large spoonfuls all over the bottom of the pan.

The best way to form this thick dough into an even layer is as follows: Cover the dough with a length of plastic wrap and, with the palms of your hands and your fingertips, press down on the plastic wrap, forcing the dough into a smooth, even, and compact layer. (If you wish, also use a small square pan to press down with, moving the pan from one area to another until the top is smooth.)

Remove the plastic wrap. Bake for 35 to 40 minutes until the top of the cake is a rich golden color. Do not overbake.

Remove from the oven and let stand for about 5 minutes. Then cover the pan with a cookie sheet and carefully turn the pan and the sheet upside down. The cake will fall out of the pan. Remove the pan. Cover the cake with a large rack and turn the cookie sheet and rack upside down. Remove the sheet, leaving the cake right side up on the rack to cool.

Slide the cooled cake onto a cutting board. With a ruler and toothpicks mark the cake into fourths. Then, with a long, heavy, and sharp knife, cut the cake into fourths. Finally, cut each fourth into eight bars. These cut beautifully and their perfume is tantalizing.

To coat these with optional confectioners sugar, place the bars on a length of wax paper or baking-pan liner paper. Through a wide but fine strainer, strain confectioners sugar generously over the tops. Then turn each bar in the sugar to coat each side.

Wrap individually in clear cellophane, if you wish. Store airtight.

NOTE: The drained ginger syrup is not used in this recipe, but save it. Pour it over vanilla ice cream, or use it to sweeten and flavor whipped cream.

VARIATION: I have also made these with 1/2 cup unsalted green pistachio nuts, in addition to everything else in the recipe. If you have any unsalted green pistachio nuts, use them.

Browned Butter Shortbread

28 OR 30 COOKIES

I never ate shortbread better than this—and neither did you. Browned butter gives a totally different flavor (one that is difficult to identify and to describe). These are hard, dry, and crunchy—but tender, with a sandy texture and an irresistible "I-can't-stop-eating-these" quality.

Browning the butter is a slightly unusual step. You might wonder "How dark is brown?" but using a candy or sugar thermometer (as this recipe does) tells you exactly when the butter is done.

These are ice-box cookies, but they need only about 20 minutes in the freezer or a few minutes more in the refrigerator before they can be sliced and baked. (Of course they can wait much longer if you wish.)

8 ounces (2 sticks) unsalted butter
2 teaspoons lemon juice
1 cup unsifted unbleached flour
1 cup cornstarch
1 teaspoon baking powder
⅛ teaspoon salt
1 teaspoon vanilla extract
1 tablespoon milk
¾ cup granulated sugar

To stop the cooking immediately as soon as the butter is done, have ready a large bowl with some ice and cold water in it to place the pan of butter in.

Place the butter in a 6-cup heavy saucepan over moderate heat. Insert a sugar thermometer. Stir almost constantly with a wooden spatula (the butter will bubble up hard at first) until the thermometer registers 300 to 310 degrees. It will take about 10 minutes.

Remove from the heat, stir in the lemon juice (it will bubble up furiously), and immediately place the pan in the bowl of ice and water. Stir briefly to cool (now you will see many black specks in the butter and black sediment on the bottom). Then let stand in the ice and water until the butter becomes firm.

Meanwhile, adjust two racks to divide the oven into thirds and preheat the oven to 300 degrees. Line two cookie sheets with baking-pan liner paper or aluminum foil, shiny side up, and set aside.

Sift together the flour, cornstarch, baking powder, and salt and set aside.

When the butter is firm, use a wooden spatula or a large, heavy spoon to transfer it to the large bowl of an electric mixer. (When you remove the butter from the saucepan there will be a thin layer of black butter on the bottom. That's right, use every bit of it.) Add the vanilla and beat until pale and fluffy. Add the milk and sugar and beat well. Then, on low speed, add the sifted dry ingredients and beat until well mixed.

The mixture will probably be too dry to hold together. Turn it all out onto a large board or work surface and knead it (push it off with the heel of your hand) until it does hold together.

Lightly flour your hands and the work surface. With your hands form the dough into a long sausage shape, perfectly even and perfectly smooth, 14 or 15 inches long and 1 ¼ to 1 ½ inches in diameter. The sausage shape can be round, square, or oblong. (I think that a square or oblong shape is easier to do than a round shape.) Press the ends flat.

Wrap the shaped dough in plastic wrap. Slide a flat-sided cookie sheet under the package of dough and transfer it to the freezer or refrigerator. After about 15 or 20 minutes in the freezer or just a few minutes longer in the refrigerator the dough can be sliced.

Unwrap the firm dough. With a ruler and the tip of a small sharp knife mark the dough into ½-inch widths.

With a strong and sharp knife slice the cookies and place them at least 1 inch apart on the lined cookie sheets. (If the dough cracks while it is being sliced, it is too cold. Let it stand briefly at room temperature until it slices neatly.)

Bake two sheets at a time for about 40 minutes, reversing the sheets, top to bottom and front to back, once or twice during baking to ensure even browning.

When done the cookies will be a tan color.

With a wide metal spatula transfer the cookies to a rack to cool, and then store airtight.

NOTE: When I doubled this recipe the results were not as good. I can't explain it—but I will not do it again.

Buttercrisps

14 TO 18 COOKIES

A most amazingly crisp and crunchy cookie. Nobody will guess what is in them. Wonderful with fruit or ice cream for dessert, or with tea or coffee anytime. Actually, this is really a shortbread, but shortbread never had it so good. These have a surprise secret ingredient. They are unusual, quick, easy, and fun. They are fragile.

> 4 ounces (1 stick) unsalted butter
> ½ teaspoon vanilla extract
> ⅛ teaspoon salt
> ⅓ firmly packed cup light brown sugar
> 1 cup sifted unbleached flour
> 1 cup sweetened banana chips (the secret
>   ingredient—see Note)

Adjust two racks to divide the oven into thirds and preheat the oven to 350 degrees. Have ready two cookie sheets, not buttered.

In the small bowl of an electric mixer beat the butter until slightly soft. Add the vanilla, salt, and sugar, and beat to mix. On low speed gradually add the flour, and beat until the mixture holds together. Add the banana chips and beat briefly until incorporated.

Remove the bowl from the mixer. If the butter was cold when you used it, the dough may not be too soft to handle. But if the butter was at room temperature—or if the dough stood at room temperature for a while—the dough may be too soft to handle. If so, chill it in the bowl as necessary.

Flour a pastry cloth and a rolling pin. Turn the dough out onto the cloth, turn it over to flour all sides, and with your hands form it into a ball. Press down on the dough to spread the dough until it is about 5 inches in diameter.

It is too difficult to roll the dough because of the banana chips. It is best to pound the dough lightly with a floured rolling pin, working all across the dough, first in one direction and then in the opposite direction, turning the dough upside down occasionally. Continue to pound gently until the dough is 8 to 8½ inches in diameter and a generous ¼ inch thick. Reflour the cloth and pin as necessary. (Pounding the dough will break up the banana chips a bit, but not too much.)

Slide a flat-sided cookie sheet under the cloth and transfer the cloth and the dough to the freezer for 10 to 15 minutes until the dough is firm enough to be handled.

With a ruler and the tip of a small sharp knife mark the dough in one direction in 1-inch widths. With a long, heavy, sharp knife, cut the dough into strips 1 inch wide. And then cut the strips into 3- to 4-inch lengths, trimming the ends as you do.

Place the cookies at least 1 inch apart (these spread) on unbuttered cookie sheets.

Bake two sheets at a time for 20 to 23 minutes until golden brown all over (slightly darker on the rims), reversing the sheets, top to bottom and front to back, once during baking to ensure even browning. Do not under-bake.

Let the cookies cool on the sheets for a few minutes until firm enough to be handled. Then, with a wide metal spatula, transfer to racks to cool. Store airtight.

NOTE: Banana chips are fresh bananas that have been sliced and fried to a dramatically crisp consistency. They are available at health-food stores and fruit-and-nut shops, as well as at many grocery stores and newsstands. Although they are crisp to begin with, they seem to become even more crisp when baked in the cookies.

VARIATIONS: These two variations are outstanding. *Buttercrisps with Coconut:* Replace the banana chips with 3½ ounces (1 packed cup) shredded coconut, which may be sweetened or not, moist or dry. *Buttercrisps with Peanuts:* Replace the salt and banana chips with 4 ounces (1 cup) whole salted peanuts.

Tuiles aux Amandes

12 TO 20 PAPER-THIN
WAFERS

If these were easier to make—or quicker—they would not be as rare as they are. They are the thinnest, most fragile, most elegant, sophisticated, superspecial of all cookies. They take time and care—and love.

These cookies are draped over a rolling pin while they are still warm, to give them the shape of curved French roof tiles. They must be stored airtight from the moment they have cooled to the moment they are served. (Rubbermaid boxes do a good job of keeping them airtight and crisp, even overnight.) When you make these you will realize why the only restaurants that serve them are among the most expensive.

Question: "How do you serve these?"
Answer: "Carefully."

> 4 ounces (scant 1 cup) thin sliced natural or blanched almonds (I prefer the natural almonds that still have their skin)
> 1½ ounces (3 tablespoons) unsalted butter, at room temperature
> ¼ teaspoon almond or vanilla extract
> ½ cup granulated sugar
> ¼ cup egg whites (from 2 to 3 eggs, depending on their size; they may be whites that were frozen and then thawed)
> 4 tablespoons sifted cake flour (see Note)

Adjust a rack to the center of the oven and preheat the oven to 425 degrees.

Place the almonds in a jelly-roll pan and bake them in the oven, stirring frequently, for about 5 minutes until they are a pale golden color. Remove from the oven. Set aside ⅓ cup of the toasted almonds. On a large board, with a long, heavy knife chop the remaining almonds until they are semifine (they should not be powdered—and they may be uneven). Set aside.

You will use several cookie sheets, and you may butter them all beforehand or as you proceed. These are baked only one sheet at a time. The sheets must be generously buttered. Set the buttered sheets aside.

Have ready one or two long rolling pins and/or bottles or glasses (with at least a 2½-inch diameter) resting on their sides—to shape the baked cookies on.

In the small bowl of an electric mixer beat the butter until soft. Add the extract and sugar and beat to mix thoroughly. Gradually beat in the egg whites and then, on low speed, add the flour and beat only until incorporated. Remove the bowl from the mixer. Stir in the chopped nuts. Transfer to a small bowl for ease in handling.

I suggest that you bake only one cookie at a time, for the first few. When you get the hang of it, bake three at a time. Use a slightly rounded tablespoonful of the batter for each cookie. These spread considerably. After placing the mound (mounds) on the buttered sheet, dip a fork into a small cup of ice water and, with the back of the cold and wet fork, press each mound of the batter into an oval or round shape 3 to 4 inches in diameter (they will spread to about 5 inches during baking).

Sprinkle the tops with some of the reserved sliced almonds.

Bake in the center of the oven (at 425 degrees) for 5 to 6 minutes until the cookies are dark brown for at least ½ inch on the rims. Do not underbake (or the cookies will not become crisp). Remove the sheet from the oven.

Work quickly. (This is the most tricky part of making these.) With a wide metal spatula cut around the rim of a cookie, releasing the rim first, and then slide the spatula under the center to release the whole cookie. Immediately (and carefully), while the cookie is still hot and soft, transfer it to the rolling pin (or bottle or glass) and press down on the sides to shape the cookie.

Continue to bake and shape all of the cookies.

As soon as those on the rolling pin have cooled they should be carefully transferred to an airtight container.

If the cooled cookies become limp (from humidity or underbaking), they can be baked again. Place them top side up on an unbuttered cookie sheet. When they become warm they will flatten. Let them bake for a few minutes (at 425 degrees), transfer to the rolling pin, cool, and store airtight—again.

NOTE: Measuring cups and measuring spoons may vary. Although a ¼-cup measuring cup should equal 4 tablespoons, it might not. If you use a ¼-cup measuring cup you might be using too much flour, which would prevent the batter from spreading out as it should.

Tulipes

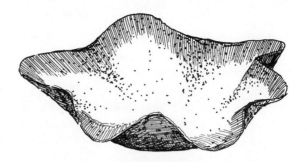

ABOUT 12 CUP-SHAPED
COOKIES

These cup- or bowl-shaped cookies are the height of swank and elegance. The classiest French restaurants serve these tulipes *holding a scoop or two (usually an oval-shaped scoop) of ice cream and/or sorbet, with a few fresh berries, and possibly a few fresh flowers, tenderly arranged on the plate. These are remarkably strong and firm (and they stay that way for weeks if the cookies are stored airtight).*

These take time and patience, but they are fun and exciting to make, and sensational to serve.

> 2 egg whites graded "large" (they may be
> whites that were frozen and thawed)
> ¼ teaspoon vanilla extract
> ½ cup sifted unbleached flour
> ¼ teaspoon salt
> ½ cup granulated sugar

Adjust a rack one-third up from the bottom of the oven and preheat the oven to 400 degrees. To generously butter a cookie sheet (or several sheets—although you will bake only one sheet at a time), spread the sheet with room-temperature butter. If the butter is cold it will not make a generous-enough coating. Use crumpled plastic wrap to spread the butter.

You will need something to shape the cookies on after they are baked. It is best to use glass custard cups, two for each *tulipe*. For each *tulipe*, place one cup upside down on a work surface close to the oven, and have an additional cup nearby.

In the small bowl of an electric mixer beat the egg whites with the vanilla until foamy. Add the flour, salt, and sugar and beat until smooth. It will be a thin and runny mixture. Transfer to a small bowl for ease in handling.

I suggest that you bake only one on a sheet for your first *tulipe*. After that, bake two on a sheet. Use a generous tablespoonful of the batter for each *tulipe*. When baking only one, place the mound of batter in the center of the sheet; when baking two, place the mounds of batter diagonally opposite each other on the sheet.

As soon as you have spooned out the batter (for one or two cookies), without waiting tilt the pan on a sharp angle in all directions to encourage the batter to run out into a round shape (or two round shapes) about 4 inches in diameter. Keep the shapes as round as possible, but if they do not stay completely round it is OK. Take your time. Be patient.

Bake for 6 to 7 minutes until the cookies have golden rims about ½ inch wide, or a little wider; the cookies will remain paler in the centers.

The baked cookies must be removed from the sheet and shaped quickly while they are still hot and flexible. When you take a cookie sheet out of the oven, use a wide, firm metal spatula to release the cookie quickly. And quickly place it upside down over the inverted custard cup. With your hands press down on the sides to mold the cookie a bit, and then place the additional custard cup upside down over the cookie to hold it in place.

If you have baked two cookies on a sheet, remove and shape the second one as soon as possible. Then, after a few minutes, when the cookies have just cooled, remove them from the cups and place in an airtight container (Rubbermaid boxes do a fine job of keeping these airtight and crisp).

Continue to bake and shape all the *tulipes*.

NOTE: If the cookies are not thoroughly crisp all over, including the centers, it means they were not baked enough. If you have trouble releasing a cookie from the sheet, it means the sheet was not buttered enough.

Cat's Tongues

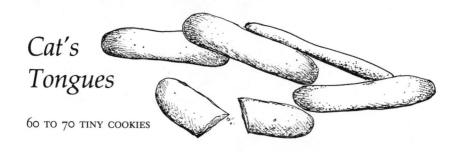

60 TO 70 TINY COOKIES

Exquisite. This is a charming and delicious classic little French cookie. Although it is plain, it is truly special and elegant. Bakeries do not generally make these. I can't recall ever seeing them in a bakery outside of France. They are extracrisp and not too sweet; a perfect bite to serve along with fruit, ice cream, or custard. Or with tea or coffee. When I serve these I never have enough; people eat them like popcorn.

These are shaped with a pastry bag, with care and patience. You will need a 10- to 15-inch pastry bag and a plain round tube with a 1/4-inch opening (number 3).

> 4 ounces (1 stick) unsalted butter
> 1/4 teaspoon salt
> 1/2 teaspoon vanilla extract
> 1/2 cup superfine or granulated sugar
> 3 egg whites graded "large" (they may be
>   whites that were frozen and thawed)
> 1 cup triple-sifted unbleached flour

Adjust two racks to divide the oven into thirds and preheat the oven to 400 degrees. Butter two cookie sheets. Dust them all over with flour through a sifter. Tilt and tap the sheets over the sink to remove excess flour.

To prepare the sheets, make guidelines directly on the cookie sheets for three rows of 3-inch cookies as follows (see illustration): You will mark the sheets with a ruler and a pencil. At each short side of a sheet mark a 1-inch border from each long side. From those marks, measure toward the middle 3 inches and make a mark. And then center a third 3-inch strip in the middle. Draw connecting lines from one short side of the sheet to the other. Set the sheets aside.

Prepare a 10- to 15-inch pastry bag as follows: Insert a tube that has a plain round 1/4-inch opening (number 3), and fold down a cuff about 2 inches wide on the outside of the bag. Twist the tube end of the bag and push it up a bit into the bag to prevent the batter from leaking out. Place the bag in a tall glass or jar to support it while you fill it. Set aside.

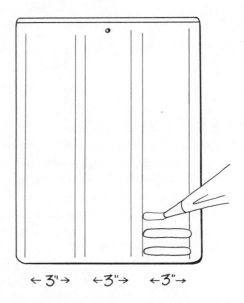

← 3″ →   ← 3″ →   ← 3″ →

In the small bowl of an electric mixer beat the butter until soft. Add the salt, vanilla, and sugar and beat until well mixed. Gradually beat in the unbeaten egg whites. On low speed add the sifted flour, scraping the bowl as necessary with a rubber spatula and beating only until incorporated.

Transfer the batter to the pastry bag. Unfold the cuff, gather the top of the bag closed, release the tube end of the bag, and then twist the top and press out thin strips of the batter, 3 inches long, from one guideline to another. The strips should be as thin as a pencil. When you press out a cookie, in order to cut the batter away from the tube (at the end of the cookie) without pulling the cookie out of shape, raise the bag very, very slowly (without leaving a tail of the batter). Allow 1 inch of space between the cookies; these spread. Form 10 to 12 cookies in each row.

Bake two sheets at a time, reversing the sheets, top to bottom and front to back, as necessary in order to ensure even browning. Bake for 12 to 15 minutes until the edges of the cookies are golden brown; the centers will remain pale. These will become crisp as they cool.

The cookies on the front and the back of the sheets will probably be done before those in the middle. They should be removed as soon as they are ready, and the remaining cookies should be baked longer. With a wide metal spatula transfer the cookies to racks to cool.

These must be stored airtight or they will not stay crisp.

VARIATION: Milanos

Milanos are Cat's Tongues sandwiched together with a small amount of melted semisweet chocolate. You will need about 3 ounces of semisweet chocolate for a full batch of the cookies, and you will need patience. Chop the chocolate fine, place it in the top of a small double boiler over warm water on low heat, and stir frequently until melted. Set aside.

Lay out the cookies in matched pairs, flat sides up.

The most efficient and professional way to apply the chocolate is with a small pastry bag and a small size tube (with any shape opening). All you want is a narrow strip of chocolate (1/8 to 3/16 of an inch wide) down the middle of half of the cookies. Then sandwich the cookies with their matched partners. Do not press the cookies together so hard that the chocolate runs out to the edges. Do not actually press them together at all. The chocolate should not really show on the edges.

Place the sandwiched cookies on a small tray in the freezer or refrigerator for a few minutes only until the chocolate is set.

Store airtight, and serve at room temperature.

In the absence of a small pastry bag and a small-enough tube, it is possible to apply the chocolate with a knife. First place the melted chocolate in a small cup for ease in handling. Use the tip of a table knife to place a rather thin line of chocolate in the middle of the flat side of half of the cookies. Keep the chocolate away from the edges of the cookies. Cover with the remaining cookies—do not press down so hard that the chocolate runs out to the edges—and chill as above.

Accordion Pleats

50 to 60 dainty cookies

In a kitchen shop recently the manager asked if I knew what a certain object was. It was about the size of a cookie sheet, probably made of aluminum, all pleated like an accordion. My memory is not always this good but I said, "Yes, it is a cookie sheet. Many years ago the people at Reynolds Wrap held a recipe contest and the winner was a recipe for a simple little butter cookie baked in a most unusual shape. A length of aluminum foil was folded like an accordion. The cookie dough was placed by the spoonful in the folds of the foil. As the cookie baked it took on an unusual shape." She was fascinated and asked if I had the recipe. I did not.

Strange things happen with recipes in our house. The Reynolds people had printed the recipe maybe thirty years ago in an ad; I had cut it out of a magazine. I never baked it or thought about it or even saw it after the first time. But the night after I was in the kitchen shop the recipe fell out of an old cookbook I was reading.

I promise you will be fascinated, amazed, and delighted. You do not have to buy the accordian sheet; you will make your own. The cookies are sensational—they are extremely unusual and, at the same time, plain. This is not quick, it is slow—but it is absorbing and easy and fun.

You will need Pam, or some other vegetable cooking spray.

1¼ cups sifted unbleached flour
¼ teaspoon salt
¼ teaspoon nutmeg
6 ounces (1½ sticks) unsalted butter
1 teaspoon vanilla extract
¾ cup granulated sugar
2 eggs graded "large"
Finely grated rind of 1 large lemon

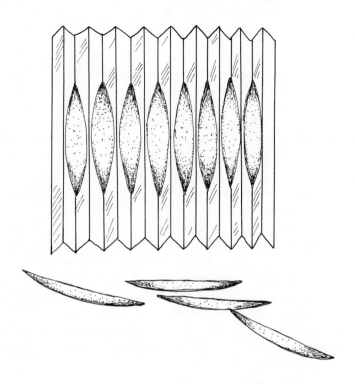

You will need two cookie sheets and aluminum foil folded as follows: Tear off a 36-inch length of foil. Place it, shiny side down, on a work area. Fold it in half like a book (the shiny sides will be on the outside—the length will now be 18 inches). With a ruler and a pencil, carefully mark 1-inch lengths on the top and the bottom, starting at the folded edge. Then, with the ruler and the pencil, make connecting lines from the top to the bottom of the foil. (The indentations from the pencil lines should be clear on both sides of the foil.) Open the folded foil to its full 36-inch length.

The folding must be done carefully. Make the first fold on the first pencil line next to the folded edge. Then turn the foil upside down and make another fold. Continue to turn the foil upside down and make accordianlike folds down the length of the foil on all the pencil lines.

Repeat the directions to make a second accordion-shaped strip of foil. Open each piece of folded foil slightly, making it a scant 15 inches long. Place each piece of foil on a cookie sheet. Spray Pam or some other nonstick cooking spray generously all over the foil. Set aside.

Adjust two racks to divide the oven into thirds and preheat the oven to 350 degrees.

Sift together the flour, salt, and nutmeg and set aside. In the small bowl of an electric mixer beat the butter until soft. Add the vanilla and sugar and beat until thoroughly mixed. Beat in the eggs one at a time, scraping the bowl as necessary with a rubber spatula. On low speed gradually add the sifted dry ingredients, beating only until incorporated. Remove the bowl from the mixer, stir in the grated lemon rind, and transfer the mixture to a shallow bowl for ease in handling.

Use two teaspoons, one for picking up with and one for pushing off with. Carefully place about 1 slightly rounded teaspoonful of the dough in the middle of one of the indentations in the foil. Continue to place one cookie in the middle of each fold. (The dough will spread out by itself during baking—each cookie will be 5 to 6 inches long and very narrow.)

Bake two sheets at a time, reversing the positions, top to bottom and front to back, once during baking to ensure even browning. Bake for 20 to 25 minutes until the cookies are richly browned on the tips and a pale golden color on the tops. Do not underbake; these are best if they are baked crisp.

Remove from the oven and let stand for about 5 minutes until the cookies can easily be removed with your fingers (and a small, narrow metal spatula, if necessary).

The foil can be reused. It is not necessary to wipe the foil after using it; it is necessary to respray it. And/or you can turn the used foil upside down and use the other side.

Store the cookies airtight.

Ladyfingers

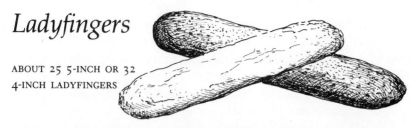

ABOUT 25 5-INCH OR 32
4-INCH LADYFINGERS

*Far superior to commercial ladyfingers; fragile, elegant, as light as air.
These are a first-rate accomplishment—one to be proud of. Shaping ladyfingers with even shapes and all alike (with a pastry bag) is an art, as is
making a perfect sponge cake batter, which is what these are made of (it
calls for folding in just enough but not too much). Once you get the
hang of this it takes only a few minutes to put ladyfingers together, and
only 15 to 18 minutes to bake.*

*If you have extralarge cookie sheets (about 17 by 14 inches), use
them for this recipe.*

> 1 cup sifted unbleached flour
> 4 eggs graded "large," separated
> 1 teaspoon vanilla extract
> ¼ teaspoon salt
> ⅛ teaspoon cream of tartar
> ½ cup plus 3 tablespoons superfine sugar
>   (see Note)
> Confectioners sugar (for sifting over the tops
>   before baking)

Adjust two racks to divide the oven into thirds and preheat the oven to 325
degrees. Lightly butter two cookie sheets (see above), dust them with flour
through a sifter, and over the sink shake off excess. Set aside.

Have ready a 15-inch pastry bag fitted with a plain round tube that has
a ⅝-inch opening (number 8). Fold down a cuff about two inches wide on
the outside of the bag. Twist the tube end of the bag and push it up a bit
into the bag to prevent the batter from leaking out. Place the bag in a tall
glass or jar to support it while you fill it. Set aside.

Resift the flour two or three times and set it aside in the sifter on a
piece of paper.

In a small bowl beat the yolks and vanilla with an egg beater to mix
well. Set aside.

Place the egg whites and salt in a clean small bowl of an electric mixer
and, with clean beaters, beat on medium speed until foamy. Add the cream

of tartar and beat on high speed until the whites hold a straight point when the beaters are raised. On moderate speed add the sugar 1 rounded tea-spoonful at a time. Then beat on high speed again until the whites are stiff but not dry. Remove the bowl from the mixer.

Add the beaten yolks all at once to the whites and fold together without being thorough about it. Turn into a large mixing bowl. In three additions, sift the flour over the top, folding it in with a rubber spatula. At first do not be completely thorough with the folding, and even at the end, fold only until you do not see any dry ingredients. Even if the mixture looks lumpy and not smooth, do not fold anymore.

Turn the mixture into the pastry bag. Unfold the cuff, gather the top of the bag closed, untwist the tube end, and press out ladyfingers onto the prepared sheets. Form the ladyfingers 4 or 5 inches long (unless they are to be used for lining a pan or bowl, in which case make them only as long as necessary to fit the pan or bowl), and about 1 inch wide. Allow ½ to ¾ inch of space between ladyfingers.

At the end of each ladyfinger lift the pastry bag slowly toward the other end of the ladyfinger to prevent leaving a tail of the batter.

Through a fine strainer, quickly strain confectioners sugar generously onto the ladyfingers and bake immediately.

Bake for 15 to 18 minutes, reversing the sheets once, top to bottom and front to back, to ensure even baking. Bake until the ladyfingers are lightly colored and feel dry and springy when gently pressed with a fingertip.

Let the ladyfingers stand on the sheets for about 10 minutes. Then remove them with a wide metal spatula.

Store the ladyfingers airtight, flat sides together. These are delicious either fresh and soft or after they have become dry and crisp. But for lining a container (as for an ice-box cake) they should be very fresh. They can be frozen.

NOTE: If you do not have superfine sugar, place plain granulated sugar in the bowl of a food processor fitted with the metal chopping blade and process for 30 seconds.

VARIATION: Chocolate Ladyfingers

Chocolate ladyfingers? Yes. They are unusual and delicious. Follow the above recipe with the following changes: Use only ⅔ cup plus 2 tablespoons of the flour. Add to the flour ¼ cup unsweetened cocoa powder (preferably Dutch-process) and an optional 3 teaspoons instant espresso or coffee powder. Sift together the flour, cocoa, and optional espresso or coffee until the color is smooth.

Plain ladyfingers *can't* be this good.

Royal Pecan Thins

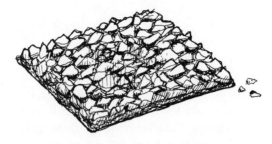

64 SMALL COOKIES

A fancy little cookie, elegant and swanky, although simple-looking. Thin and chewy-crunchy. The flavor is a seductive combination of browned butter, cinnamon sugar, and toasted pecans. Almost a candy. This cookie is said to have been a favorite of King Gustav of Sweden. It is a favorite of mine too.

Many years ago they baked these cookies at George's French Bakery in Rockville Center, New York, and people drove from miles around especially for these.

The recipe takes time and patience to mix and shape, and 1 ¾ hours to bake. The cookies are worth every minute.

You need two jelly-roll pans.

> 9 ounces (2½ cups) pecans
> 8 ounces (2 sticks) unsalted butter
> ¼ teaspoon salt
> ½ teaspoon vanilla extract
> ½ teaspoon almond extract, or ¼ teaspoon
>   bitter almond extract
> 1 cup granulated sugar
> 1 egg graded "large," separated, plus 1
>   additional egg white
> 1¾ cups sifted unbleached flour
> Generous ½ cup cinnamon sugar (see Note)
> 2 tablespoons additional granulated sugar (for
>   topping)

Adjust two racks to divide the oven into thirds and preheat the oven to 250 degrees. Generously butter two 15½-by-10½-by-1-inch jelly-roll pans (see page 30) and place them in the freezer (it will be easier to shape the dough in cold pans).

Place the pecans on a large chopping board, and with a long and sharp knife chop them until they are very fine; they must be fine but not ground.

If possible, no pieces should be larger than grains of rice. Set the chopped pecans aside.

In the large bowl of an electric mixer beat the butter until soft. Add the salt, vanilla and almond extracts, and sugar and beat to mix. Beat in the egg yolk (reserve both whites, separate from each other). On low speed gradually add the flour and beat until incorporated.

Remove the bowl from the mixer and divide the dough into two equal amounts (each half will be 1⅓ cups).

Work with only one pan at a time (reserve the other pan in the freezer). Since you have barely enough dough to cover the bottoms of the pans, it will be easiest if you first place the dough by small spoonfuls in an even pattern all over the bottom of the pan. Then, with floured fingers (keep a wide bowl of flour alongside the pan), press the dough all over to cover the bottom of the pan. The dough should not climb up on the sides. (Patience.) If you have placed the dough in the pan properly—by small amounts, and evenly spaced—this will be painless. But it will take time.

Prepare the dough in both of the pans.

Pour 1 unbeaten egg white over the dough in one of the pans and, with the palm of your hand, spread it all over the dough. Then, with your fingertips, slowly and carefully sprinkle half (¼ cup plus 2 teaspoons) of the cinnamon sugar evenly over the top. Then sprinkle half of the pecans over the top. Finally, sprinkle 1 tablespoon of sugar over the top.

Set aside and prepare the dough and topping in the other pan.

Now cover one of the pans with plastic wrap or wax paper and press down very firmly and carefully all over the pan to press all of the topping ingredients into the dough. Or place a smaller pan on the plastic wrap or wax paper and press down on that. Move the smaller pan as necessary to cover every bit of the topping.

Ditto, the other pan.

Remove the plastic wrap or wax paper. Bake both pans at the same time, reversing the positions, top to bottom and front to back, about every half hour. Bake for 1 hour. The cookies will not be done yet, but this is the time to cut them. With a small sharp knife—slowly and carefully—cut each cake into four strips in each direction, and cut around the sides to release. To cut, it is best to press the knife down and then raise it and move it—if you pull the knife through the dough it will not do as neat a job.

Continue to bake for about 45 minutes more (total baking time is about 1 hour and 45 minutes) until the cookies are nicely browned all over. Do not underbake. Turn off the oven. Remove one pan—leave the other in the oven to keep warm—and, without waiting (the cookies become crisp as they cool and it becomes difficult to remove them from the pans without breaking), carefully cut the cookies again. With a metal pancake turner, remove them from the pan (it is easiest to remove the first one from the middle rather than the edge), and immediately cut each cookie in half crosswise, making two smaller cookies. Cool on a rack.

Repeat with the second pan.

Store airtight. (These keep very well.)

NOTE: To make the cinnamon sugar mix ½ cup granulated sugar with 1 tablespoon cinnamon and ¼ teaspoon nutmeg.

Vanilla Meringue Flutes

ABOUT 30 MERINGUES

This is an unusual meringue. The egg whites are beaten stiff, a hot sugar syrup is added to the whites, which partially cooks them, making the mixture more stable and less fragile, and then confectioners sugar is folded in. When baked it is dry-dry-dry, hard, crisp, and crunchy, and it stays that way. It is very sweet.

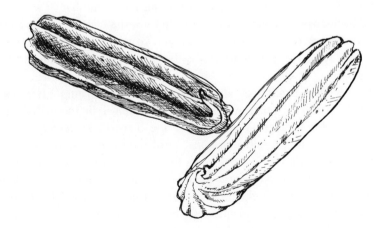

*The meringues are great with tea or cof-
fee, or served alongside fruit or ice cream. As a
matter of fact, a jar of these on our coffee
table disappears in no time, regardless of what
else is served.*

*You will need a 16-inch pastry bag, a
number 7 star-shaped tube, and a sugar thermometer. If you have extralarge cookie sheets
(17 by 14 inches), use them for this recipe.
Allow 2 hours baking time and a few hours
more for cooling in the oven.*

1 cup granulated sugar
½ cup water
4 egg whites (to equal ½ cup; they may be
     whites that were frozen and thawed)
⅛ teaspoon salt
⅛ teaspoon cream of tartar
¾ teaspoon vanilla
1 cup sifted or strained confectioners sugar

Adjust two racks to divide the oven into thirds and preheat the oven to 200 degrees (it is always best to check oven temperature with a portable thermometer, but it is especially important for such a low temperature).

Lightly butter and flour two cookie sheets, tap over the sink to remove excess flour, and set aside.

Have ready a 16-inch pastry bag fitted with a number 7 star-shaped tube. Fold down a 2- to 3-inch cuff on the outside of the bag. Twist the tube end of the bag (just above the tube) and push the twisted section back up into the bag a bit to hold it in place and to prevent the batter from running out. Place the bag in a tall glass or jar to support it while you fill it. Set aside.

Place the granulated sugar and water in a small saucepan. (It is important that the pan have a narrow base or the mixture will be too shallow for the thermometer to register correctly. I use a 3-cup saucepan with a 4½-inch base.) Stir over moderate heat until the sugar dissolves and the mixture comes to a boil. Cover the pan for 1 minute (to allow the steam in the pan to dissolve any sugar granules clinging to the sides). Then uncover, raise the heat to high, insert a sugar thermometer, and let boil until the thermometer registers 248 degrees (the stiff-ball stage).

However, before the syrup is ready, or when it registers about 240 degrees, place the egg whites, salt, and cream of tartar in the small bowl of an electric mixer and beat first on moderate speed until the whites hold a soft shape and then on high speed until the whites hold a firm shape when the beaters are raised. The syrup and the egg whites should be ready at the same time; if the whites are ready too soon, just reduce the speed and let the mixer beat on low speed.

As soon as the whites and the syrup are ready, gradually—in a thin stream—add the syrup to the whites on moderate speed, holding the pan about 6 to 8 inches above the whites. When necessary to prevent the whites from overflowing, transfer to the large bowl of the mixer and continue to beat and add the remaining syrup.

Then add the vanilla, increase the speed to high, and beat until the bottom of the bowl is almost cool and the meringue holds a straight point when the beaters are raised. Remove the bowl from the mixer.

In two or three additions, sift or strain the confectioners sugar onto the meringue and, with a large rubber spatula, fold together. Do not be too thorough with the folding in at first, and even at the end, fold only until you do not see unincorporated confectioners sugar—although the mixture might look lumpy and uneven. It is OK. Stop folding. The meringues will not be lumpy or uneven when baked.

Transfer the mixture to the pastry bag. Unfold the cuff, gather the top of the bag closed, untwist the tube end, and press out stick shapes about 5 inches long, 1 inch wide, and ½ to ¾ inch apart.

When you remove the pastry bag after shaping each stick, twist the bag gently and lift it toward the beginning of the stick to cut off the meringue and prevent a tail.

Bake for about 2 hours, reversing the sheets once, top to bottom and front to back, to ensure even baking.

Then turn off the heat and let the meringues stand in the oven with the door closed for a few hours until completely cool.

Before removing the meringues from the oven it is best to test one as follows: Remove one meringue from the oven and let it stand uncovered at room temperature for about half an hour. If it becomes a little soft or sticky, reheat the oven for only about 5 minutes and let the meringues stand in the warm oven to dry out a little longer.

When cool, store airtight. (If meringues lose their crispiness at any time, reheat them in a 200-degree oven for 15 or 20 minutes, although these particular meringues have always remained completely dry in our house, and I have made them over and over again.)

Follow the above recipe with the following additions: Add ⅓ cup sifted or strained unsweetened cocoa powder (preferably Dutch-process) and an optional 3 teaspoons powdered instant espresso or coffee. Sift or strain the cocoa and espresso or coffee with the confectioners sugar several times until the mixture is an even color.

Puff Pastry Devil's Tongues

48 COOKIES

In standard baking books the recipe for puff pastry takes many pages, and the list of do's and don'ts is frightening. This one is quick and easy and as delicious as any I have ever tasted.

This counterfeit puff pastry is from my first book. I am using it again not only because it is so good but because now I do it in a food processor—literally in seconds—and now I shape it differently. This charming shape was inspired by a recipe in Jacques Pépin's gorgeous book The Art of Cooking, Volume 2.

These are incredible; light, flaky, tender, gossamer. Elegant, simple, swanky. Serve (with love and pride) with tea or coffee, or along with ice cream, custard, or fruit.

After the dough is made it should be re-frigerated for about 2 hours (or overnight if you wish) before it is shaped and baked. As with all puff pastries, these are best when they are very fresh. But you have many options with this recipe. The Devil's Tongues can be baked and then frozen. Or they can be shaped, fro-zen, and then baked shortly before serving.

If the Devil's Tongues are more than a few hours old, reheat them before serving to re-store the original sensational flavor and tex-ture.

8 ounces (2 sticks) cold and firm unsalted butter
1½ cups unsifted unbleached flour
½ cup cold sour cream
Granulated sugar (to sprinkle on the board and over the tops)

The butter must be cut into small pieces ahead of time. (Handle the butter as little as possible to keep it cold.) On a board, with a long knife cut each stick of butter into four lengthwise quarters. Then cut the quarters (you can cut through four at once) into ½-inch slices. Refrigerate the cut butter for at least 10 minutes.

Place the flour in the bowl of a food processor fitted with the metal chopping blade. Add the cold butter. Be careful now. Pulse the machine only five times (the butter must remain in visible pieces). Remove the cover of the bowl. Add the sour cream, half on one side of the bowl and half on the other side. Pulse the machine again, thirteen to fifteen times; the mixture should not hold together or be smooth.

Turn the mixture out onto a lightly floured board. Flour your hands and press the ingredients together quickly, forming a compact brick about 3 by 8 inches and 1¼ inches thick, with square corners. Wrap in plastic wrap and refrigerate for 2 hours (or longer if you wish).

Voilà—puff pastry!

Line two cookie sheets with baking-pan liner paper or aluminum foil, shiny side up.

Cut the dough into two 4-by-3-inch rectangles 1 ½ inches thick. Work with one piece at a time; wrap and refrigerate the other piece.

Spread a moderate amount of granulated sugar on a large board or other work surface. Press both sides of the dough into the sugar to coat it well. Sugar a rolling pin. If the dough has been refrigerated overnight it will be necessary to pound it with the rolling pin until it can be rolled out. Keep the oblong shape of the dough and keep the corners as square as possible.

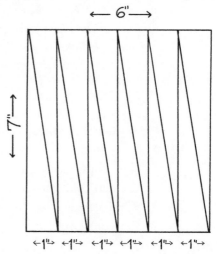

Roll out the dough gently and carefully, turning it upside down occasionally to keep both sides sugared. Pinch together any deep cracks in the edges. Roll the dough until it is about 6 by 14 inches and ⅛ inch thick.

With a long knife trim the edges carefully to make a perfect oblong. (The trimmings cannot be used unless some pieces are large enough for you to cut them into miniature triangles, but always remove uneven edges.)

Carefully cut the dough in half to make two 6-by-7-inch pieces. Place one piece on top of the other (the sugar will prevent them from sticking to each other).

Now you will cut through the two layers together, and then separate the pieces. Use a long and heavy knife. Cut the dough, forming triangles 7 inches long and about 1 inch wide at the base (see illustration).

Place the triangles about 1 inch apart on the lined cookie sheets. Refrigerate for 20 minutes to 4 hours.

(If you want to freeze these before baking, place them right next to each other on the sheet, freeze, and then remove from the sheet and wrap airtight. Thaw for about 10 minutes before baking.)

Adjust an oven rack one-third down from the top and preheat the oven to 400 degrees.

Bake one sheet at a time (keep the other refrigerated) for about 13 minutes until the tops of the Devil's Tongues are golden-colored and the bottoms are caramelized (but not burned). Do not underbake. The narrow points of the triangles will be darker than the rest.

Without waiting, with a wide metal spatula transfer the baked Devil's Tongues to a brown paper bag to cool.

Place in an airtight container.

To serve these if baked and then frozen, preheat the oven to 300 or 350 degrees. Simply place the frozen Devil's Tongues right out of the freezer onto cookie sheets and right into the oven until they are very hot. Cool and serve.

Hollywood Squares

40 TO 50 EXTRA THIN
COOKIES

Plain, extrathin, classy, elegant, sweet, crisp, and crunchy. Perfect with tea or coffee, or alongside ice cream or a fruit or custard dessert. These take time and patience, but they are actually easy and fun to make. The dough should be refrigerated overnight before it is shaped and baked. The finished cookies should be stored airtight; if so, they keep very well.

2 cups sifted unbleached flour
1 teaspoon baking powder
½ teaspoon salt
Scant ½ teaspoon mace
4 ounces (1 stick) unsalted butter
1 teaspoon vanilla extract
1 cup granulated sugar
1 egg plus 1 egg yolk graded "large"
Additional granulated sugar (to sprinkle on a
    pastry cloth while rolling out the dough
    with a rolling pin)

Sift together the flour, baking powder, salt, and mace and set aside.

In the large bowl of an electric mixer beat the butter until soft. Add the vanilla and 1 cup of sugar and beat to mix. Beat in the egg and yolk and then, on low speed, gradually beat in the sifted dry ingredients, beating only until smooth.

Turn the dough out onto a length of plastic wrap. Wrap the dough and then, with your hands, form the dough into a square shape about 1/2 inch thick. Transfer to the refrigerator and refrigerate overnight.

When you are ready to bake, line cookie sheets with baking-pan liner paper and set aside. Adjust two racks to divide the oven into thirds and preheat the oven to 350 degrees.

Spread out a pastry cloth and generously sprinkle granulated sugar onto the cloth. Unwrap the dough and cut it into equal quarters. Place one piece of the dough on the sugared cloth and wrap and refrigerate the remaining pieces. Turn the piece of dough on the sugared cloth to sugar both top and bottom.

With a rolling pin, start to roll the sugared dough gently, keeping the shape as square as possible. Turn the dough upside down frequently while rolling it to keep both top and bottom well sugared to prevent sticking.

Continue to roll out the dough in a square shape until it is extremely thin. As close as I can tell with an ordinary ruler, I roll it somewhere between 1/16 and 1/8 inch thick.

With a long, sharp knife trim the edges, cutting straight down with the full length of the blade (rather than pulling the tip of the blade through the dough). Then cut in one direction, forming strips about 2 1/2 inches wide. Next, cut in the opposite direction, forming squares about 2 1/2 inches wide.

With a wide metal spatula transfer the cookies to the lined cookie sheets, placing the cookies at least 1/2 inch apart.

Roll and cut remaining dough.

Press scraps together, wrap, chill, and then roll and cut into squares.

Bake two sheets at a time, reversing the sheets, top to bottom and front to back, as necessary to ensure even browning. Bake about 10 minutes until the cookies are just sandy-colored or a delicate beige color. If you bake only one sheet at a time, adjust the rack to the center of the oven.

If some of the cookies are done before others (depending on their thickness), use a wide metal spatula to transfer them to racks to cool. If the cookies are all done at one time, let them cool on the sheets, and then just lift them off with your fingers. If the cookie sheets have three flat sides (and the cookies are all done at one time), you can just slide the paper off the sheet and slide the sheet (even if it is warm) under another piece of paper with unbaked cookies on it.

As soon as the cookies are cool, store them airtight. If it should become necessary to recrisp the cookies, just spread them out on a cookie sheet and reheat in a 350-degree oven for about 5 minutes.

English Butter Cookies

30 TO 35 LARGE
COOKIES

When Martha Washington made these English cookies they were called Shrewsbury Biscuits. They are large, plain, and dry, somewhat like Scotch Shortbread. They last remarkably well; they seem to get better—and better. Great for a camping trip—or a cookie jar. (To hang on a Christmas tree, make a small hole for a thin ribbon with a small cutter or the tip of a pastry tube. Bake one as a sample to be sure that the hole doesn't close up.) Although these are plain, they are irresistible.

5 cups sifted unbleached flour
½ teaspoon salt
1½ teaspoons cinnamon
¾ teaspoon cloves
¾ teaspoon allspice
½ teaspoon ginger
12 ounces (3 sticks) unsalted butter
1 teaspoon vanilla extract
1½ cups granulated sugar
3 eggs graded "large"

Adjust two racks to divide the oven into thirds and preheat the oven to 350 degrees. Line cookie sheets with baking-pan liner paper or aluminum foil, shiny side up, and set aside.

Sift together the flour, salt, cinnamon, cloves, allspice, and ginger and set aside.

In the large bowl of an electric mixer beat the butter until soft. Add the vanilla and sugar and beat to mix. Beat in the eggs. On low speed gradually add most of the sifted dry ingredients; it will probably be necessary to add the last of the dry ingredients by hand with a heavy wooden spatula.

Turn the mixture out onto a lightly floured board.

The dough will be soft but not too sticky to handle. Knead it briefly until perfectly smooth.

Then work with about one third of the dough at a time. (Do not chill the dough before rolling and cutting it.)

On a lightly floured pastry cloth, with a lightly floured rolling pin roll out the dough until it is a scant ¼ inch thick. With a large (about 3½ inches wide), plain or scalloped round cutter, cut out the cookies. (The cookies may be smaller, thinner, or a different shape if you wish.) Cut the cookies around the rim of the dough first, just barely touching each other. With a wide metal spatula place the cookies 1 inch apart on the lined sheets.

Reserve all the scraps of dough, knead them together, roll out, and cut more cookies; do not incorporate any more flour than necessary.

Bake two sheets at a time, reversing the sheets, top to bottom and front to back, as necessary to ensure even browning. Bake for 20 to 25 minutes until the cookies are golden on the rims, paler in the centers.

With a wide metal spatula transfer the cookies to racks to cool.

Peace-and-Plenty Granola Cookies

36 COOKIES

You start by making your own deluxe granola. And you wind up with thick, crunchy, chewy drop cookies that are loaded—packed solid—bursting out—with all kinds of nuts and seeds and oats and sugar and spice and everything nice.

You can make the granola ahead of time—or not. It's no big deal either way. Some of the ingredients—the seeds and some of the nuts—may necessitate a shopping trip to the health-food store.

1 cup "old-fashioned" (not "instant") rolled oats (or organic oat flakes from the health-food store)

¾ cup wheat germ (may be toasted or not)

2½ ounces (½ cup) whole natural (with the skins on) almonds

2½ ounces (¾ cup) walnuts, in large pieces, or pecan halves

1½ ounces (⅓ cup) cashew nuts or blanched hazelnuts

2½ ounces (½ cup) pignolias (pine nuts)

2 ounces (⅓ cup) sesame seeds

2 ounces (⅓ cup) untoasted, unsalted pumpkin seeds

2 ounces (⅓ cup) untoasted, unsalted sunflower seeds

3½ ounces (1 firmly packed cup) sweetened or unsweetened shredded coconut

⅓ cup vegetable oil (i.e., safflower, corn, or canola oil)

⅓ cup honey

¼ cup water

¼ cup maple syrup

Adjust a rack to the center of the oven and preheat the oven to 350 degrees. In a large bowl stir together the oats, wheat germ, almonds, walnuts or pecans, cashew nuts or hazelnuts, pignolias, sesame seeds, pumpkin seeds, sunflower seeds, and coconut.

In a small bowl whisk or beat together the vegetable oil, honey, water, and maple syrup.

Add the liquids to the dry ingredients and stir to mix.

Turn into a large jelly-roll pan or shallow roasting pan and spread smooth.

It is important to stir this mixture frequently while it is baking. For the first half of the baking, stir every 10 minutes, then stir every 5 minutes, for a total of 45 to 50 minutes of baking time. (Especially watch the ingredients along the edges of the pan; that part wants to burn.) When it is done it should all have a nice golden color and should be evenly toasted.

When done, pour into a large mixing bowl and stir occasionally until cool.

Then continue with the recipe, or store airtight and continue some other time.

¾ cup unsifted unbleached flour
1¼ cups unsifted whole wheat flour
½ teaspoon salt
½ teaspoon baking soda
½ teaspoon baking powder
1½ teaspoons cinnamon
¼ teaspoon allspice
¼ teaspoon cloves
¼ teaspoon nutmeg
4 ounces (1 stick) unsalted butter
½ firmly packed cup dark brown sugar
1 egg graded "large"
2 tablespoons molasses
½ cup milk
Sesame seeds (to sprinkle on top of the cookies)

Adjust two racks to divide the oven into thirds and preheat the oven to 350 degrees. Line cookie sheets with baking-pan liner paper or aluminum foil, shiny side up.

Sift together the unbleached flour, whole wheat flour, salt, baking soda, baking powder, cinnamon, allspice, cloves, and nutmeg and set aside.

In the small bowl of an electric mixer beat the butter until soft. Add the sugar and beat to mix. Beat in the egg and then about half of the sifted dry ingredients. Stir the molasses into the milk and add to the dough, beating until mixed. Finally mix in the remaining dry ingredients.

Add the dough to the bowl of granola (nuts and seeds, et cetera). It will be a thick and stiff mixture; stir and stir and stir until evenly mixed.

Place a large piece of aluminum foil next to the sink. Use a heaping tablespoonful (actually, it is the same amount as ¼ cup) of the dough for each cookie, and place them any which way on the foil. Wet your hands with cold water, shake off but do not dry, and with wet hands roll a mound of the dough into a ball. Then flatten the ball between your hands until it is about ½ inch thick and 2¼ to 2½ inches wide.

Place on a lined cookie sheet. Continue to shape all the cookies, placing them a scant 1 inch apart from each other.

Sprinkle the tops lightly with sesame seeds.

Bake two sheets at a time, reversing the positions of the sheets, top to bottom and front to back, once during baking to ensure even baking. Bake for about 20 minutes until the bottoms are lightly colored and the tops are only barely colored (if at all).

With a wide metal spatula transfer to racks until completely cool.

Store airtight.

Date-Nut Spice Cookies

ABOUT 40 COOKIES

After the manuscript for this book went through many stages of editing, copyediting, and proofreading, it finally went to the compositor. I thought I was finished with it. And then my sister-in-law, Connie Heatter, sent me this recipe from Rangeley, Maine. When I made it, my husband and our neighbors devoured the whole batch in record time, and said that they were scrumptious, delicious, yummy, and super duper. I thought it was too late to include the recipe in the book, but I called my publisher and told them about these, and how good they are. They said that if the cookies were all that good, they would make the necessary arrangements in order to include the recipe.

These are very old-fashioned, semisoft, and remarkably chewy drop cookies. (They are first dropped, then rolled between your hands and flattened.) Their mildly spiced flavor is seductive and addictive. Their perfume during baking can turn strong men into pussycats.

1 pound (2 generous firmly packed cups) pitted dates
8 ounces (2¼ cups) walnuts
3 cups sifted unbleached flour
1 teaspoon cinnamon
1 teaspoon nutmeg
¼ teaspoon cloves
¼ teaspoon salt
8 ounces (2 sticks) unsalted butter
2 cups granulated sugar
3 eggs graded "large"
1 teaspoon baking soda
2 teaspoons water

Adjust two racks to divide the oven into thirds and preheat the oven to 350 degrees. Cut baking-pan liner paper or aluminum foil to fit cookie sheets.

(You will need many pieces, but you can cut more as you need them.) Line two sheets with the paper or foil (shiny side up). Set aside.

With scissors cut the dates crosswise or lengthwise into 1/4- to 1/2-inch pieces, and set aside. Cut or break the walnuts into medium-size pieces, and set aside.

Sift together the flour, cinnamon, nutmeg, cloves, and salt, and set aside.

In the large bowl of an electric mixer beat the butter until soft. Add the sugar and beat to mix. Beat in the eggs one at a time.

In a small cup dissolve the baking soda in the water (see Note), and beat into the dough. On low speed add the dates and beat until mixed. Then, on low speed, gradually beat in the sifted dry ingredients. Remove the bowl from the mixer and stir in the walnuts.

Place a large piece of aluminum foil alongside the sink. Use two kitchen tablespoons for dividing the dough, one for picking up with and one for pushing off with. Form about forty mounds of the dough, each one a heaping tablespoonful, and place them any which way on the foil. They can be right next to each other.

Place a lined cookie sheet close to you. Wet your hands under cold running water, pick up a mound of the dough, roll it between your wet hands into a round shape, and then flatten it between your hands to 1/2-inch thickness (each cookie should be about 2 to 2 1/2 inches in diameter). Place it on the lined cookie sheet. Now the cookies should be placed about 2 inches apart (I get eight cookies on a sheet). Your hands must be held under the cold running water before shaping each cookie.

Bake two sheets at a time, reversing them top to bottom and front to back once or twice during baking to insure even browning. Bake for 18 to 20 minutes until the cookies are golden brown all over and spring back when gently pressed with a fingertip. Do not underbake.

Use a wide metal spatula to remove the cookies, and transfer them to racks to cool.

Continue to shape and bake all of the cookies.

When cool, store in an airtight container (a wide, plastic freezer box works best for me) with wax paper between the layers. Store at room temperature or freeze.

NOTE: As closely as I can tell, diluting the baking soda in water is a very old-fashioned step that was done, I think, to be sure that the soda was dissolved. The very first recipe for Toll House chocolate chip cookies included this step.

Y. O.
Ranch Date
Bars

24 BAR COOKIES

From Kerrville in the beautiful hill country of west Texas. A soft and juicy filling of dates and nuts between crisp and crunchy layers of whole wheat, oatmeal, coconut, honey, butter, wheat germ, pumpkin seeds, and sunflower seeds (somewhat like a delicious and firm granola).

These are very good for you, they last well, they are good for mailing, and they are fun to make.

1 pound (2 packed cups) pitted dates
Finely grated rind of 2 lemons
Finely grated rind of 1 orange
3 tablespoons lemon juice
Orange juice
4 ounces (generous 1 cup) walnuts, cut or
    broken into medium-sized pieces
3 ounces (¾ stick) unsalted butter
⅓ cup mild honey
1 cup unsifted whole wheat flour
¼ teaspoon salt
1 teaspoon cinnamon
½ teaspoon nutmeg
Scant 2 ounces (½ packed cup) shredded
    coconut
1 cup "quick" (not "instant") rolled oats
2 tablespoons raw or toasted wheat germ
¼ cup untoasted, unsalted pumpkin seeds
¼ cup untoasted, unsalted sunflower seeds

Adjust a rack to the middle of the oven and preheat the oven to 350 degrees. Line an 8-inch square pan as follows: Turn the pan upside down, center a 12-inch square of aluminum foil, shiny side down, over the pan, fold down the sides and corners of the foil to shape it to the pan, remove the foil, turn the pan right side up, place the shaped foil in the pan, and press it into place.

Then, to butter the foil, put a piece of butter in the lined pan and put it in the oven to melt. With a piece of crumpled plastic wrap or a pastry brush spread the butter all over the foil and set the pan aside.

With scissors cut the dates into halves and place in a heavy covered saucepan with about a 2-quart capacity. Add the grated rinds. Pour the lemon juice into a 1-cup glass measuring cup and add orange juice (or orange juice and water) to the 1-cup line. Pour the liquids over the dates. Place on moderate heat, cover, bring to a boil, reduce the heat a bit, and simmer for 5 minutes. Then uncover and cook slowly, stirring with a wooden spatula for about 15 minutes until the mixture resembles a thick, chunky jam or conserve.

Remove the pan from the heat, stir in the walnuts, and set aside.

Place the butter and honey in a small pan over low heat and cook until the butter melts.

Meanwhile, into a large mixing bowl, sift together the flour, salt, cinnamon, and nutmeg. Any flour that is too coarse to go through the sifter should be stirred back into the sifted ingredients. Stir in the coconut, oats, wheat germ, pumpkin seeds, and sunflower seeds. Add the hot honey and butter. With a rubber spatula stir and press down on the mixture until all the dry ingredients are moistened. The mixture will not hold together; it will be crumbly.

Place half (a scant 2 cups) of the mixture in the prepared pan. With your fingertips distribute the mixture all over the bottom of the pan. Then, with your fingertips, press down firmly on the ingredients to form a firm and compact layer.

Place the date mixture (which may still be warm) over the bottom layer and spread it smooth. Then, with your fingertips, sprinkle the remaining oatmeal mixture evenly over the date mixture. With your fingertips press down firmly to make a compact layer.

Bake for 40 minutes until the top is brown and feels firm and dry to the touch.

Remove from the oven and let stand until the bottom of the pan is cool or just tepid. Cover the pan with a rack, turn the pan and rack upside down, remove the pan, peel off the foil, cover with another rack and turn upside down again, leaving the cake right side up on the rack.

The cake must be chilled before it is cut. Place it in the refrigerator for an hour or more, or in the freezer until cold.

Cut the cold cake into quarters gently with a strong and heavy serrated French bread knife. Then cut each quarter into two bars, and finally cut each bar into three small bars.

Wrap individually in clear cellophane or wax paper, or package in an airtight box with wax paper between the layers.

Bizcochitos

36 TO 42 COOKIES

Bizcochito is an old Mexican anise-seed cookie recipe traditionally made at Christmastime. There are many variations; this one with bourbon is unusual. These are old-fashioned and homey, thin, crisp, and buttery drop cookies. Incidentally, in 1989 bizcochito was named the official state cookie of New Mexico.

2 cups sifted unbleached flour
½ teaspoon baking powder
¼ teaspoon salt
Generous ½ teaspoon anise seeds
8 ounces (2 sticks) unsalted butter
½ cup plus 2 tablespoons granulated sugar
½ cup bourbon
Additional anise seeds (to sprinkle on top)

Adjust two racks to divide the oven into thirds and preheat the oven to 375 degrees. Line cookie sheets with aluminum foil (see Note), shiny side up, and set aside.

Sift together the flour, baking powder, and salt and set aside.

With a mortar and pestle crush the generous ½ teaspoon of anise seeds only until coarse, or crush them in a blender or in a Cuisinart chopper/grinder, and set aside.

In the large bowl of an electric mixer beat the butter until soft. Add the sugar and crushed anise seeds and beat until thoroughly mixed. On low speed, in several small additions, add the sifted dry ingredients alternately with the bourbon. Beat until mixed.

Use a rounded teaspoonful of the dough for each cookie. Place the mounds carefully at least 1½ inches apart on the foil-lined sheets (twelve cookies on a sheet).

Dip a fork into flour and then use it to press down once on the top of a cookie, flattening it to ¼- to ½-inch thickness. Repeat dipping the fork and flattening all the cookies.

With your fingertips sprinkle a few of the additional anise seeds (which should be left whole) on each cookie.

CINNAMON SUGAR

This will make more than you need, but it is hard to measure less. Reserve the leftover for another use.

3 tablespoons granulated sugar
½ teaspoon cinnamon
¼ teaspoon nutmeg

In a small bowl mix the sugar, cinnamon, and nutmeg.

With a teaspoon sprinkle some of the cinnamon sugar over all the cookies.

Bake two sheets at a time, reversing the sheets, top to bottom and front to back, once during baking to ensure even browning. Bake for about 18 minutes until the outside rims are golden brown. Do not underbake.

With a wide metal spatula transfer the cookies to racks to cool. Then store airtight.

NOTE: These do not bake as well on baking-pan liner paper as they do on aluminum foil.

Jumbo Raisin-Nut Cookies

18 HUGE COOKIES

Moist, soft, chewy, spicy, old-fashioned, and wonderful. Quick and easy to make. Great to take on a picnic or in a lunch box. (Boiling the raisins first makes the cookies especially yummy.)

6 ounces (1¼ cups) raisins
¾ cup water
6 ounces (1½ cups) walnuts
1¼ cups unsifted unbleached flour
¾ cup unsifted whole wheat flour
½ teaspoon baking soda
½ teaspoon baking powder
½ teaspoon salt
1 teaspoon cinnamon
¼ teaspoon nutmeg
¼ teaspoon allspice
4 ounces (1 stick) unsalted butter
1 teaspoon vanilla extract
1¼ firmly packed cups dark brown sugar
2 eggs graded "large"

Adjust two racks to divide the oven into thirds and preheat the oven to 375 degrees. Line cookie sheets with baking-pan liner paper or aluminum foil, shiny side up. Set aside.

Place the raisins and water in a small heavy saucepan over high heat. Cover, bring to a boil, reduce the heat a bit, and let simmer for about 5 minutes. Then uncover and continue to simmer, stirring occasionally, for about 10 minutes more until the liquid is almost but not completely evaporated (there should be a teaspoon or two remaining). Transfer the raisins and remaining liquid to a bowl to cool.

Toast the nuts: In a small pan bake the walnuts for about 8 to 10 minutes until they are very hot to the touch. Set aside to cool.

Sift together the unbleached flour, whole wheat flour, baking soda, baking powder, salt, cinnamon, nutmeg, and allspice and set aside.

In the large bowl of an electric mixer beat the butter until soft. Add the vanilla and sugar and beat to mix. Beat in the eggs one at a time. On low speed gradually add the sifted dry ingredients and beat until incorporated.

Remove the bowl from the mixer. With a heavy wooden spatula stir in the raisins and any remaining liquid and then the walnuts (the raisins and nuts may still be slightly warm—it is OK).

To form drop cookies: Use about a ¼-cup measuring cup of the dough for each cookie. Place only five cookies on a sheet.

Bake two sheets at a time for 15 to 18 minutes, reversing the sheets, top to bottom and front to back, once during baking to ensure even baking. Bake until the tops of the cookies just barely spring back when gently pressed with a fingertip.

Transfer the cookies with a wide metal spatula to racks to cool.

Store two cookies together, flat sides together.

Almond Macaroon Slices

This is more like a French pastry than a cookie. It is a classic almond-macaroon mixture, shaped into one long strip; a trench is formed in the middle, and the strip stands overnight (this helps it hold its shape during baking). The following day the trench is filled with apricot preserves (or any other thick preserves) and topped with sliced almonds. Then the strip is baked. The preserves will soak into the macaroon mixture a bit, making it extra-moist, juicy, chewy, and yummy. After it is baked and cooled, the strip is covered with confectioners sugar and then cut into slices. They are elegant, classy, and fancy—although easy.

7½ ounces (1½ cups) blanched almonds
⅓ cup granulated sugar
2 egg whites graded "large," separated from each other (they may be whites that were frozen and then thawed)
About ⅓ cup apricot preserves
Sliced natural (not blanched) almonds (for topping)
Confectioners sugar (for topping)

Line a cookie sheet with baking-pan liner paper and set aside.

Place the blanched almonds and granulated sugar in the bowl of a food processor fitted with the metal chopping blade. Process until fine and powdery. Through the feed tube add one of the egg whites and process briefly. Beat the remaining white slightly in order to be able to add only part of it (if it is not beaten, too much of it will slip into the feed tube). Gradually add the second egg white, just a bit at a time, until the mixture holds together and forms a paste firm enough to hold its shape. (Actually, it is better for the mixture to be a bit too wet rather than too dry.) You will most probably not use all of the second egg white.

Turn the mixture out onto a floured surface, form it into a ball, turn it over to flour all sides, and then, with your hands, mold it into a sausage shape about 11 inches long and about 1¾ to 2 inches in diameter.

Transfer to the lined cookie sheet. With a pastry brush, brush off excess flour.

To form a trench down the middle, dip your middle finger in water and, with the wet fingertip, press a trench in the dough. The long sides and the ends of the strip must remain high or the preserves will boil over during baking. The trench should be about 1 inch wide and about ¾ inch deep. To perfect the shape, support the outside of the strip with one hand while you shape the trench with the middle finger of the other hand.

Let stand uncovered overnight.

Before baking adjust an oven rack to the middle of the oven and preheat the oven to 350 degrees.

Stir the preserves well to soften. Then, with a small spoon, place the preserves in the trench. The preserves should just about fill the trench but they should not be higher than the sides anywhere or they will run over during baking.

Then, with your fingertips, place a generous layer of sliced almonds all over the preserves, placing them casually every which way.

Bake for 25 to 28 minutes until the macaroon mixture is lightly colored and the preserves start to bubble. Keep an eye on this toward the end in order not to allow the preserves to run over.

Remove from the oven. Handle gently now as the whole strip is soft and tender while it is hot. Slide a long, narrow metal spatula under the strip to make sure it is not stuck anywhere. Let stand until cool and firm. Then place on a cutting board.

Generously sprinkle confectioners sugar through a fine strainer on the top. Then, with a sharp knife, cut the strip on an angle into slices a scant 1-inch wide.

Blondies

24 BAR COOKIES

This nonchocolate brownie (a.k.a. Butterscotch Brownies) is made with an unusual technique: The eggs and sugar are cooked together before the other ingredients are added. This makes the cookies deliciously chewy.

6 ounces (1½ cups) pecans
4 eggs graded "large"
1 pound lump-free light brown sugar (strain if necessary)
2 cups triple-sifted unbleached flour
1 teaspoon baking powder
½ teaspoon salt
1 teaspoon vanilla extract

Adjust a rack one-third up from the bottom of the oven and preheat the oven to 375 degrees. Prepare a 13-by-9-by-2-inch pan (see page 30) as follows: Place the pan upside down on the work surface. Center a 17-inch length of aluminum foil, shiny side down, over the pan. Fold down the sides and corners to shape it. Remove the shaped foil. Pour a little cold water into the pan and then pour it out. Do not dry the pan (the wet pan will hold the foil in place). Place the pan right side up and place the shaped foil in the pan; press it into place gently and carefully. To butter the foil, place a piece of butter in the pan, place the pan in the oven to melt the butter, and then brush the butter all over the foil with a pastry brush or spread it with crumpled plastic wrap or wax paper. Set the pan aside.

To toast the nuts: Place them in a shallow pan in the oven for about 10 minutes until very hot. Cool, then break into coarse pieces and set aside.

In the top of a large double boiler, whisk or beat the eggs to mix. Add the sugar, place over warm water on moderate heat, and stir with a rubber spatula until the ingredients are mixed. Then cook for 20 minutes, stirring and scraping the sides occasionally.

Meanwhile, sift together the flour, baking powder, and salt and set aside.

After cooking the egg mixture for 20 minutes, transfer the mixture to the large bowl of an electric mixer. Without cooling the mixture add the vanilla, and then, on low speed, add the sifted dry ingredients, scraping the bowl and beating only until incorporated. Remove the bowl from the mixer. Stir in the nuts. Turn into the prepared pan and smooth the top.

Bake for 20 minutes or until the top has a hard golden-colored crust and a toothpick gently inserted in the middle comes out only slightly sticky.

Let stand at room temperature until cool. Then cover with a cookie sheet and turn the pan and the sheet upside down. Remove the pan and gently peel off the foil. Cover the cake with wax paper and another cookie sheet. Carefully turn both cookie sheets and the cake upside down, leaving the cake right side up.

These will cut much better if the cake is chilled. Place it in the refrigerator for at least an hour or in the freezer for a little less time.

Mark the cake into quarters with a ruler and toothpicks. With a serrated French bread knife cut it into quarters, cut each quarter in half, and finally cut each piece into three bars. Wrap individually in clear cellophane or wax paper. Or pack in an airtight box with wax paper or plastic wrap between the layers.

Corn Lace

13 TO 15 LARGE, THIN
CRACKERS

It is not a dessert. It is anything but. It is a cracker. The thinnest, crispest, crunchiest cracker I have ever had. It takes just a moment to mix the batter; it takes longer to shape and bake the crackers. They last; that is, they remain crisp. And they are not as fragile as they look. Fantastic describes them. Like a designer tortilla; elegant and wispy thin.

This recipe is written for a small volume. You can double it, but it is so easy to mix up a batch that I suggest you try this amount the first time.

1 ounce (1/4 stick) unsalted butter
1/2 cup yellow cornmeal (see Note)
1/2 teaspoon salt
3/4 cup boiling water

Adjust two racks to divide the oven into thirds and preheat the oven to 350 degrees. Butter two cookie sheets; they must be buttered generously or the crackers will stick. Place the cookie sheets in the freezer (the crackers can be spread thinner on frozen sheets).

Melt the butter and set aside.

In a small bowl stir the cornmeal and salt. Add the boiling water to the butter, add to the cornmeal mixture, and stir until smooth. (That's all there is to it.)

Use a rounded tablespoon of the batter for each cracker. As you place one on the cookie sheet, dip a teaspoon in ice water and use the bottom of the spoon to spread the batter as thin as possible. Each cracker should be spread to 4 or 5 inches in diameter. There may be—in fact, there should be—thin, lacy sections where the batter does not quite cover. I mean, actual holes in the crackers. The crackers do not change shape during baking; therefore they may be placed close to each other. I make four on each cookie sheet.

Bake for 20 to 30 minutes (depending on the thickness) until the crackers are lightly colored all over. Reverse the positions of the pans, top to bottom and front to back, as necessary during baking to ensure even browning. Do not underbake.

With a wide metal spatula transfer the crackers to a brown paper bag to cool.

Store airtight.

NOTE: When I have it, I use cornmeal from a health-food store. I generally have one labeled "stone-ground coarse meal," but I have also used one labeled only "organic," and they work the same.

Texas
Pecans

1 POUND

The pecans are toasted, then mixed with a sweet meringue and baked with butter until golden. They come out dry and crisp, crunchy and irresistible. In Minnesota they call these Swedish Nuts and in California they are Meringue Nuts. Other nuts can be used in place of pecans, or you can use a combination of nuts. I have made this with just pecans, as well as with an exotic combination of macadamias, almonds, cashews, hazelnuts, and walnuts. Delicious either way.

These keep very well. They are fun to make, and a jar or a box of them is a gorgeous gift.

1 pound (4 to 5 cups) pecans (or other untoasted, unsalted nuts)
4 ounces (1 stick) unsalted butter
3 egg whites (they may be whites that were frozen and then thawed)
¼ teaspoon salt
1 cup granulated sugar
1 teaspoon vanilla extract

Adjust a rack to the middle of the oven and preheat the oven to 325 degrees. Spread out the nuts in a 15½-by-10½-inch jelly-roll pan (or use an even larger pan if you have one) and place in the oven for about 12 minutes until very hot but not darker in color.

Remove from the oven and let cool completely. Do not turn off the oven.

When the nuts have cooled, place them in a very large mixing bowl and set aside.

Place the butter in the 15½-by-10½-inch jelly-roll pan (or a pan even larger if you have it) and place in the oven to melt the butter.

Meanwhile, in the small bowl of an electric mixer, at high speed beat the egg whites and the salt until the whites hold a soft point (one that bends over) when the beaters are raised. Reduce the speed to moderate and gradually add the sugar, about 1 tablespoon at a time, beating briefly between additions. Then, on high speed again, beat until the whites are very stiff. Add the vanilla and continue to beat for a few seconds (if the vanilla thins the meringue a bit, just beat a little longer).

Add the meringue to the nuts and stir to mix just a bit.

Place the mixture by large spoonfuls over the melted butter in the jelly-roll pan; it is not necessary to cover all the butter or to spread the nuts and meringue.

Bake for 10 minutes, remove from the oven, and, with a wide metal spatula, turn the mixture over, any which way. Bake for 10 minutes more. Then turn the nuts over again and stir just a bit. Continue to bake and stir a bit every 10 minutes until the meringue is golden and the butter is all absorbed. The total baking time will be about 45 minutes. (The first few times you stir this you will feel frustrated and pessimistic; it will look and feel like a mess. But just wait.)

When done, turn the nuts out onto a large brown paper bag and let stand until cool. When cool, you can either break this apart to separate the nuts or leave it in clumps.

Store airtight.

This will keep well for many days (and probably for weeks), but for longer storage it may be refrigerated or frozen, and may be freshened by heating for a few minutes in a wide pan in a hot oven.

The Georgia Pig Peanut Brittle

3 POUNDS

We bought a little bag of peanut brittle at The Georgia Pig, a barbecue restaurant in Brunswick, Georgia. The brittle had been made by The Nut House in De Soto, Georgia, in the heart of peanut country. I have made peanut brittle since I was a teenager, and I always thought it was great. But this Georgia brittle was something else. It was crisp and brittle, but at the same time more tender than others; on the broken edges I could see an open, airy texture like a honeycomb. For several days I made peanut brittle from morning till night, trying to duplicate this one. I finally got it. This is it. The best ever.

You need a sugar thermometer. And a saucepan with a 5- to 6-quart capacity. The saucepan must have a handle so that you can lift the pan with one hand to pour out the brittle quickly without hesitating for even a few seconds as soon as it is ready.

1 pound (3⅓ cups) salted peanuts
3 cups granulated sugar
1 cup light corn syrup (Karo)
½ cup water
1 tablespoon butter
2 tablespoons baking soda

Place a piece of heavy-duty aluminum foil (18 inches wide) about a yard long, shiny side up, on a work surface near the stove. Spread a thin layer of vegetable oil (I use peanut oil) over the foil (spread it with paper toweling, which makes a really thin layer). Let stand.

With additional butter to that called for, butter the sides of a 5- to 6-quart saucepan (see above) and set aside.

Adjust a rack to the middle of the oven and preheat the oven to 200 degrees.

Place the peanuts in a shallow pan about 9 by 13 inches and place in the oven to heat.

Meanwhile, place the sugar, corn syrup, and water in the buttered saucepan. With a long wooden spatula stir over moderate heat until the sugar is dissolved and the mixture comes to a boil.

Clip a sugar thermometer to the side of the pan and let boil over moderate heat without stirring until the thermometer registers 275 degrees.

Meanwhile, melt the butter in a small saucepan and set aside.

When the thermometer registers 275 degrees, add the warm peanuts and continue cooking, now stirring frequently to prevent burning, until the thermometer reaches 300 degrees. (The mixture will carmelize and darken as it cooks. But if it smells the least bit burned, lift the pan quickly from the heat and stir well.)

NOW WORK QUICKLY. Remove the pan from the heat. Stir in the butter and then the baking soda (this is the secret of this recipe), and stir very briskly for only 2 or 3 seconds until the mixture becomes foamy, pale in color, and rises to the top of the pan. Do not wait or the foam will settle down and the brittle will not be airy. Quickly pour the foamy mixture onto the oiled aluminum foil. Do not smooth over the top or spread thin or you will deflate the brittle.

Let stand for about 30 minutes or until cool and crisp. Then, with a wide metal spatula, turn the brittle upside down and dry the bottom with a paper towel.

Then break the brittle into pieces and store airtight.

NOTE: This lasts remarkably well as long as it is airtight. I successfully carried a cellophane bag of it in the car from Florida to California. For mailing, wrap large pieces airtight and pack them in layers with crumpled paper between the layers.

Cheesecakes, Bread Puddings, and a Hot Chocolate Soufflé

All cream cheeses do not work the same in baking. Some have more stabilizers (gums), or different stabilizers, than others. I always use Philadelphia
cream cheese.

All three of these cheesecakes freeze very well. I have served them after
weeks in the freezer—and I could not see or taste any difference.

If you have some cheesecake left over, freeze it as it is—and then wrap
it. But if you plan to freeze the whole thing, hold the glaze until after freezing
and thawing; glaze before serving.

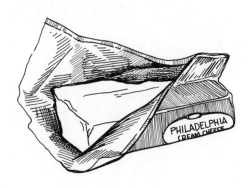

Rum and Espresso Chocolate Cheesecake

16 TO 20
PORTIONS—5 ½ POUNDS

Spectacular! Stark—simple—dramatic. As smooth as honey, deliciously custardy, extremely chocolate (but not heavy), with a rum and espresso flavor. The cake cuts like a dream. It is huge (2 ½ inches high), and should be made a day or two before serving. Everything about this makes it the perfect dessert for a large and important party.

You need a 9-by-3-inch springform pan (see page 30).

CRUST

> 10 packages (20 cookies) amaretti macaroons (or ¾ cup graham-cracker crumbs)
> 2 ½ ounces (½ cup) blanched and toasted hazelnuts or almonds
> 2 tablespoons granulated sugar
> 2 ounces (½ stick) unsalted butter, melted
> 4 ounces semisweet chocolate (to be used after the crust is baked)

Adjust a rack one-third up from the bottom of the oven and preheat the oven to 375 degrees.

In the bowl of a food processor fitted with the metal chopping blade process the macaroons until the crumbs are about as fine as graham-cracker crumbs. Transfer the crumbs (or graham-cracker crumbs) to a mixing bowl.

Place the nuts and sugar in the processor and process until rather fine (although slightly visible pieces of nuts may remain—they add a nice crunch to the crust).

Transfer to the bowl of crumbs and mix well. Add the melted butter and stir to mix and to moisten the crumbs evenly (the ingredients will not hold together).

The sides should be fastened to the bottom of a 9-by-3-inch springform pan (both parts unbuttered).

Turn the crust mixture out onto the bottom of the pan. With your fingertips distribute the crumbs evenly all over the bottom. Then, with your fingertips, press down on the crumbs firmly to make a compact layer on the bottom only. (To smooth the layer, you can cover it with a piece of plastic wrap about 10 inches long, and then place an 8-inch layer-cake pan on the plastic wrap and press all over. Remove the pan and the plastic wrap.)

Bake for 8 minutes. Set aside and let cool.

Then place the pan in the freezer; the crust should be cold for the next step.

Cut the chocolate into small pieces and place it in the top of a small double boiler over warm water on low heat. Stir frequently until melted and smooth. Remove from the heat, pour the melted chocolate over the cold crust, and, before the chocolate sets, spread it with the bottom of a teaspoon all over the crust, stopping about 1/4 inch away from the edges. Let stand until firm; if necessary, replace in the freezer to set the chocolate. (This layer of chocolate will protect the crust and keep it crisp, aside from adding additional chocolate flavor.)

Now butter the sides of the pan carefully with a pastry brush and melted butter (using additional butter to that called for).

The cake will bake in a larger pan of hot water. To be sure that no water seeps into the cake pan, it should be wrapped carefully in a double layer of heavy-duty aluminum foil as follows: Tear off two 18-inch lengths of the foil. Place one on top of the other. Place the cake pan in the center of the foil. Be very careful now not to tear the foil (even a small hole would allow water through). Carefully bring all the sides up around the pan, and gather the excess together at the rim of the pan. With scissors cut away the foil that extends above the rim of the pan. Press firmly all around the pan to make the foil fit as close as possible. Set aside.

You will need a pan larger than the cake pan but not deeper for the hot water; just have it ready.

CHEESE MIXTURE

1 pound semisweet chocolate
1½ cups heavy cream
3 tablespoons unsweetened cocoa powder
    (preferably Dutch-process)
3 tablespoons instant espresso or coffee
    powder
¼ teaspoon salt
½ cup dark rum
4 eggs graded "large"
2 pounds (4 8-ounce packages) cream cheese
    at room temperature
1 cup granulated sugar

Adjust a rack one-third up from the bottom of the oven and preheat the oven to 350 degrees.

On a board, with a long and heavy knife shred/chop the chocolate fine. Place it in the top of a large double boiler over warm water on low heat. Cover the pot with a folded paper towel (to absorb steam) and the pot cover. Let cook until almost completely melted. Then uncover and stir until completely smooth. Remove the top of the double boiler and set aside, uncovered.

In a 1-quart saucepan over moderate heat scald ½ cup of the cream (reserve remaining 1 cup cream). When you see a wrinkled skin on top, strain in the cocoa, espresso or coffee powder, and salt. Whisk until smooth. Cook for a few minutes, stirring constantly. Then remove from the heat and stir in the rum and the remaining 1 cup of cream. Set aside.

In a small bowl beat the eggs lightly just to mix and set aside.

In the large bowl of an electric mixer beat the cheese until it is completely soft and smooth. There must not be any lumps in the cheese. It is best to remove the beaters once during mixing, scrape them clean with a fingertip, then replace them and continue beating.

Add the sugar and beat, scraping the bowl occasionally with a rubber spatula, until the mixture is perfectly smooth. Then add the chocolate and, without waiting, on low speed gradually add the cream mixture, and finally the eggs. While beating, frequently scrape the bowl with a rubber spatula. After adding the eggs beat as little as possible.

Turn the mixture into the prepared pan, pouring it over the crust. It will fill the pan almost to the top.

Gently rotate the pan a bit in opposite directions to level the batter; do not be so rough that the mixture clings unevenly to the sides of the pan.

Place the cake pan in the larger pan. Add ½ to 1 inch of hot water to the larger pan.

Bake for 1 hour. Then turn off the heat and let the cake stand in the oven with the oven door closed for 1 hour.

Then remove the cake pan. Carefully remove the foil wrapping. Let the cake stand in the pan on a rack at room temperature for several hours until the pan is completely cool.

With a small sharp knife cut around the sides—all the way to the bottom—to be sure the cake and/or crust are not stuck to the sides of the pan.

Then release the spring and remove the sides. If necessary, smooth the sides with a small, narrow metal spatula. Place the cake (still on the bottom of the pan) on a cookie sheet or a small board (for ease in handling) and refrigerate uncovered overnight.

To remove the cake from the bottom of the springform, insert the tip of a wide, heavy, sharp knife at one edge of the crust. Cut all around the crust. Gently raise the knife to release the crust from the pan. Then, with a wide metal pancake turner or using a flat-sided cookie sheet as a spatula, transfer the cake to a serving plate or a cutting or serving board and glaze the top of the cake.

GLAZE

3 to 4 tablespoons seedless red or black
currant or blackberry jam

In a small pan over moderate heat stir the jam until melted and smooth. If necessary, add a few drops of water to help melt the jam. Then boil briefly to reduce. Brush a generous layer all over the top of the cake. Brush on two layers if you wish. Gorgeous! Refrigerate until serving time.

It is necessary to use a hot and wet knife for serving this. Use a strong, heavy, sharp knife, with a blade preferably 8 or 9 inches long. Either work in the kitchen and hold the knife under hot running water or dip it in a deep saucepan of boiling water before making each cut. Or, to serve this in the dining room, have a deep pitcher of boiling water and dip the blade before each cut.

This may be served as is. Or, preferably, with soft whipped cream and fresh raspberries on the side.

Prune Armagnac Cheesecake

12 PORTIONS

Prunes in Armagnac—coal-black and as shiny as wet tar—baked in a ring on top of a divine white cheesecake. Spectacular to look at, fantastic to serve and to eat.

Hediard is one of the most elegant French specialty food stores. I have had several memorable treats there. One was the inspiration for this cake. They have huge, tender, and juicy sweet prunes stuffed with a puree of prunes mixed with Armagnac. You never forget the first bite into one of them.

Prepare the prunes a day or more ahead of time.

You will need an 8-by-3-inch one-piece round cheesecake pan (which is generally available now in most kitchen shops—see page 30), and a wider but not deeper pan (for hot water).

> Prunes in Armagnac (see page 396)
> 2 pounds (4 8-ounce packages) cream cheese
>   (at room temperature)
> 1 teaspoon lemon juice
> 1 teaspoon vanilla extract
> Pinch of salt
> 1¾ cups granulated sugar
> 4 eggs graded "large"
> ⅓ cup graham-cracker crumbs (to be used
>   after the cake is baked)

For this cheesecake it is best to use prunes that are medium or large, rather than extralarge or jumbo. Prepare the prunes and let them stand.

Before mixing the cake, remove 12 prunes from the syrup. With a small sharp knife cut them in half. Open and flatten each half and place them, skin side down, on a plate or board. Let stand.

Place the remaining prunes and the syrup in a frying pan (preferably nonstick) over moderate heat. Let cook, uncovered, until the syrup becomes thick, dark, and reduced in volume to about 3 tablespoons. (The syrup will be bubbling hard all over when it is ready.)

Pour the prunes and syrup into a strainer set over a bowl. Transfer the prunes to the bowl of a food processor fitted with the metal chopping blade. Process until pureed. Through the feed tube add 2 to 3 tablespoons of the reduced syrup and process until smooth. You will have a scant 1 cup of a thick puree; transfer it to a small bowl.

Now, to make prune-puree sandwiches on prunes: Use 1 slightly rounded teaspoonful of the puree (as a filling) on top of 12 prune halves. And then cover the puree with the remaining halves, skin side up. With your fingers shape each prune sandwich to elongate it slightly, and to make it a bit more narrow. (If the prunes are too wide there will not be room for all of them around the top of the cake.) Let the prune sandwiches stand.

You will have some leftover puree that you will not need for this recipe. It is a delicious spread for toast (thin with Armagnac if necessary), or serve it with ice cream.

Now proceed with the cake. Adjust an oven rack one-third up from the bottom and preheat the oven to 350 degrees. Butter an 8-by-3-inch one-piece round cheesecake pan—carefully and thoroughly—all the way up to and including the rim. Set aside.

In the large bowl of an electric mixer beat the cheese until it is soft and smooth. Add the lemon juice, vanilla, salt, and sugar, and beat until the mixture is thoroughly smooth. (With your fingertip scrape the beaters to remove any chunks of cheese that are not incorporated, and beat them into the mixture.)

Then, on rather low speed, beat in the eggs one at a time, scraping the bowl and beating only until incorporated after each addition. Do not beat any more than necessary; the mixture should not become airy.

Turn the mixture into the prepared pan. Rotate the pan briefly to level the top of the batter.

Place the 12 prune sandwiches on the top of the cake, carefully, as follows: Place them ½ inch away from the rim of the pan with their length at a right angle to the rim. Place them like numerals on a clock. First place one at twelve o'clock, one at six o'clock, one at three o'clock, and one at nine o'clock. Then place two more between each two. There should be a small space between the prunes, or they can just barely touch each other. And for the time being they will only barely sink down into the cake—do not push them down.

Place the cake pan in a wider (but not deeper) pan and place it in the

oven. Carefully pour hot water about 1½ inches deep into the wider pan.
Bake for 1½ hours.

Then remove the cake pan from the hot water and let cool on a rack. (During baking the top of the cake will become golden brown and it will rise to the top of the pan. The prunes will sink slightly but will remain visible. During cooling the top of the cake will sink to its original level.)

Let the cake stand at room temperature for about 3 hours. Then tilt the pan gently from side to side to be sure the cake is not clinging to the sides of the pan.

Cover the pan loosely with a piece of wax paper and then with a flat cake plate or a small plastic cutting board. Turn the pan and the plate or board upside down. Remove the pan.

Sprinkle the graham-cracker crumbs generously over the cake. Cover the cake with another flat plate or board and carefully turn upside down again, leaving the cake right side up. Remove the wax paper.

GLAZE

About ⅓ cup apricot preserves
1 tablespoon Armagnac, cognac, or brandy

In a small pan over low heat stir the preserves to soften and melt. Strain through a fine strainer. Return to the pan. Stir in the Armagnac, cognac, or brandy, and bring to a boil.

With a soft, pointed paint brush or a small spoon, apply the hot glaze to cover each prune generously and to fill in the indentations. Glaze over the prunes only, and not over the cake itself.

Refrigerate for a few hours or overnight.

To serve, dip a sharp knife into very hot water before making each cut, and wipe the blade after making each cut.

NOTE: This cake, made without the prunes, is the original—and famous—and wonderful—Craig Claiborne Cheesecake.

Apricot Cheesecake

6 TO 8 PORTIONS

A shallow cake made in a loaf pan. The cheese mixture has pureed apricots mixed into part of it, and the two parts are layered in the pan. The tart flavor of apricots is perfect with the smooth, sweet, and rich flavor of the cheese.

This is smaller than most cheesecakes. It is attractive, unusual, irresistible, and easy (but not quick).

> 6 ounces (1 loosely packed cup) dried
>   apricots
> 1 pound cream cheese, at room temperature
> 1 cup plus 4 tablespoons granulated sugar
> 1/2 teaspoon vanilla extract
> 2 eggs graded "large"
> 3 tablespoons sour cream
> 1/4 cup apricot preserves (to be used after the
>   cake is baked and cooled)

Adjust a rack one-third up from the bottom of the oven and preheat the oven to 300 degrees. You will need a loaf pan that measures about 10½ by 4½ by 3 inches (see page 29). The cake will not fill the pan; the cake should be only 1 ½ inches deep. (In a smaller pan the cake would be too deep.) Butter the pan generously, and set it aside.

Place the apricots in a vegetable steamer or in a strainer over boiling water and steam, covered, for about 10 minutes or until very tender.

Place the steamed apricots in the bowl of a food processor fitted with the metal chopping blade and process until smooth. Let the processed apricots remain in the processor.

In the large bowl of an electric mixer beat the cream cheese until it is very smooth. Add 1 cup plus 2 tablespoons of the sugar (reserve remaining 2 tablespoons sugar) and beat very well until perfectly smooth. (During beating, stop the machine once and, with your finger, scrape the beaters clean to be sure there are no lumps of cheese.) Beat in the vanilla and the eggs, one at a time, beating only until incorporated. Remove the bowl from the mixer.

Transfer 1 cup of the cheese mixture to the apricot puree. Add the remaining 2 tablespoons of sugar and the sour cream, and process for a few seconds until smooth.

Carefully place the apricot mixture in the buttered pan, avoiding any uneven smears on the sides of the pan. Smooth the top. Then carefully pour the white cheese mixture evenly over the apricot mixture. Wiggle the pan just a bit to smooth the top, again avoiding any uneven smears on the sides.

Place the pan in a larger (but not deeper) pan. Add 1 inch of hot water to the larger pan.

Bake for 1 hour and 40 minutes. Then turn off the heat but do not open the oven door. Let the cake stand in the oven for about 45 minutes.

Then remove the pan from the water and let stand at room temperature for about 2 hours.

To remove the cake from the pan, cover the pan with a flat serving plate or a cutting board. Turn the plate or board and the pan upside down. If the cake does not fall right out of the pan, bang the plate or board and the pan on the counter a few times until the cake comes out.

Refrigerate for at least an hour or overnight.

Anytime before serving (it can be hours before), stir the apricot preserves in a small, heavy saucepan over moderate heat to melt. Strain through a fine strainer. Pour the hot preserves in a wide ribbon on the length of the cake. With a long, narrow metal spatula smooth over the preserves to cover only the top (not the sides).

Refrigerate and serve cold.

To serve: This cuts beautifully if you use a hot and wet knife. Hold the blade under hot running water, or dip it into a pitcher of boiling water. Wipe the blade and wet it before each cut. Then use a pie server or a metal spatula to transfer the portions.

This cake does not need a thing, but the color of fresh strawberries with the color of the apricot mixture is gorgeous. If you use some, either slice a few for each plate, or use them whole (with the green hulls on if they are nice and fresh).

Lemon Bread Pudding

12 PORTIONS

In many popular restaurants around the country the newest and most talked about dessert for the last few years has been bread pudding. It is surely one of the greatest custard desserts we have, and it is receiving the respect it deserves—it is not just a way of using up stale bread.

There are many kinds of bread pudding. A friend recently asked me if I had a recipe for a lemon bread pudding. She wanted to make it for her boyfriend, who remembered it from his childhood. It sounded new and fascinating to me, and while I worked on the recipe, we didn't mind having it for breakfast, lunch, and dinner.

This is a taste thrill when served at any temperature, but it is most spectacular right out of the oven. The lemon curd can be prepared days or even weeks ahead; the bread can be sliced and toasted a day or so ahead if you wish; the pudding can be put together (in about 5 minutes) one hour before it is baked, and it can bake while dinner is being served. It is an easy and foolproof recipe.

The recipe calls for one loaf of French bread. A standard loaf of French bread weighs 8 ounces; most other white breads weigh more. It is best to use French bread.

Although this is a simple, homey dessert, it is also elegant and appropriate for a fancy and important occasion.

Serve this plain or with Raspberry Sauce (see page 411).

Prepare the Lemon Curd first.

LEMON CURD

3 eggs plus 1 egg yolk graded "large"
1 cup granulated sugar
Finely grated rind of 2 large lemons
⅓ cup lemon juice
4 ounces (1 stick) unsalted butter, cut into
    1-inch pieces

In the top of a large double boiler beat the eggs, yolk, and sugar to mix. Stir in the rind and juice. Add the butter. Place over hot water on moderate heat. Cook uncovered, stirring and scraping the pan frequently with a rubber spatula, for 15 to 20 minutes until the mixture is as thick as mayonnaise; it will register 180 degrees on a sugar thermometer.

Remove the top of the double boiler and set aside to cool, stirring occasionally.

You can use the curd as soon as it has cooled, or you can refrigerate it for several weeks.

BREAD PUDDING

1 loaf (8 ounces) French bread
10 eggs graded "large"
1¼ cups sugar
1 quart milk
¼ teaspoon salt
1½ teaspoons vanilla extract
Lemon Curd (above)

Butter a shallow, oblong 3-quart baking dish (13 by 8 [or 9] by 2 inches) and set it aside. Preheat the oven to 350 degrees.

With a serrated French bread knife slice the bread ½ inch thick. Place the slices on cookie sheets and bake for 10 to 15 minutes until dry but not brown; turn the slices over when half-done. Set aside.

In a large bowl beat the eggs and 1 cup of the sugar (reserve the remaining ¼ cup sugar). Beat in the milk, salt, and vanilla and set aside.

In the bottom of the baking dish place a layer of the bread slices touching each other. If necessary, break a few of the slices to fill in spaces. Spread half of the cooled or cold lemon curd over the bread. Then make a second layer of the bread slices, these slices at right angles to the first slices. Again, break a few slices if necessary to fill in spaces. You may have a few slices left over that you will not need. Spread the remaining curd over the top.

Now ladle the egg-and-milk mixture slowly all over the top. Let stand at room temperature for 1 hour.

Before baking, adjust a rack to the center of the oven and preheat the oven to 350 degrees.

Sprinkle the remaining ¼ cup sugar evenly over the pudding.

Place the baking dish in a large, shallow pan, place in the oven, and then pour hot water into the pan to about half the depth of the baking dish.

Bake for about 45 minutes until the top is puffed and just barely colored. Testing this with the point of a knife (the way custard is generally tested) is not good, because the lemon curd will cling to the blade even after the custard is done. It is better to tap the side of the baking dish lightly, and when the middle of the pudding moves only slightly, it is done. (I have made this many times, and now all I do is test the oven temperature with a portable thermometer and watch the clock carefully.)

If necessary, you may place the baking dish under the broiler for just a few seconds to darken the top, but only until barely golden.

Serve piping hot—right away, or at room temperature.

To serve the pudding, use wide, flat dessert plates. If you serve this with the above-mentioned Raspberry Sauce, spoon or pour the sauce onto each plate and tilt the plate to run the sauce toward the rim. With a small sharp knife cut the pudding into squares and, with a pancake turner, place a portion of the pudding on each plate.

For a gorgeous decoration (if you are using the raspberry sauce) that takes just a minute, place about 1 teaspoon of unwhipped whipping cream on the sauce alongside the pudding. With the tip of a sharp knife or the side of a fork, pull curved lines of the cream into the sauce.

Cream-Cheese-and-Jelly-Sandwich Bread Pudding

10 TO 12 PORTIONS

Cream cheese and jelly sandwiches in a smooth and creamy vanilla custard—divine! The taste might remind you of cheese blintzes—or cheese strudel. You need an oven-proof baking dish that measures about 9 by 13 by 2 inches and has a 3-quart capacity. This is served with Vanilla Custard Sauce and/or Raspberry Sauce. It is served hot, warm, or at room temperature; try it hot if possible.

16 slices (a 1-pound loaf) Pepperidge Farm sandwich bread (see Notes)
8 ounces cream cheese
1 cup plus 3 tablespoons heavy cream
⅔ cup (about 8 ounces) strawberry preserves (see Notes)
1 quart milk
5 eggs plus 4 egg yolks graded "large"
⅓ cup plus 1 tablespoon granulated sugar
¼ teaspoon salt
2 teaspoons vanilla extract
Optional: scant ½ teaspoon almond extract
¾ teaspoon cinnamon
¾ teaspoon nutmeg

Adjust two racks to divide the oven into thirds and preheat the oven to 300 degrees. Butter a 9-by-13-by-2-inch ovenproof baking dish and set aside.

Stack the bread in piles of four or five slices and trim the crusts. Place the slices on cookie sheets and bake for 15 minutes, turning the slices upside down once during baking; the slices should become partially dry—not completely—and they should not brown.

In the small bowl of an electric mixer beat the cream cheese until soft, add 3 tablespoons of the heavy cream (reserve the remaining 1 cup cream) and beat until smooth. Set aside. In a small bowl stir the preserves with a fork to soften a bit and set aside.

Spread the cheese on eight of the slices of baked bread (it should be a generous layer of cheese) and spread the preserves on the remaining eight slices of bread. Place a slice that is spread with preserves upside down over each cream cheese slice.

Now use a serrated French bread knife—hold a sandwich so that the filling does not ooze out—and one at a time cut all but one of the sandwiches in half crosswise. Place the cut sandwiches touching each other in a single layer in the casserole. It will be necessary to cut the last sandwich (the one that was left whole) in different sizes to fill in all the empty spaces on the edge of the dish; cut gently with the serrated knife. You may have a bit more sandwich than you need.

In the top of a large double boiler over hot water on moderate heat or in a heavy saucepan over low heat scald the milk and the remaining 1 cup cream (that is, cook until tiny bubbles form around the edges and a wrinkled skin forms on top).

Meanwhile, in the large bowl of an electric mixer beat the eggs and yolks, 1/3 cup of the sugar (reserve remaining 1 tablespoon sugar), salt, vanilla, and optional almond extract at low speed only to mix.

When the milk and cream are ready, ladle the hot mixture slowly into the egg mixture while beating at low speed.

Then gradually—only a little bit at a time—ladle the mixture over the sandwiches. At first, the sandwiches will rise to the top of the custard. To keep them submerged, cover the pudding with a length of plastic wrap and place something lightweight (for instance, a folded kitchen towel or two) on top of the plastic. As the sandwiches absorb the custard, you will be able to use a heavier weight (a few more towels or a lightweight box), but be careful—a bit too much weight will make the custard run over. Let stand for about 1 hour.

Before baking adjust an oven rack one-third up from the bottom of the oven and preheat the oven to 350 degrees.

Just before baking, in a small cup mix the cinnamon and nutmeg with the remaining 1 tablespoon sugar. Through a fine strainer sprinkle the mixture all over the top of the pudding.

Place the baking dish in a large, shallow pan that must not be deeper than the dish. Place in the oven and pour hot water into the large pan to a depth of 1 inch.

Bake for 40 to 45 minutes until a small sharp knife gently inserted in the middle comes out clean (a bit of the cheese may cling to the blade, but as long as the custard is set it is OK—do not underbake).

Remove from the oven, remove from the hot water, and serve hot, warm, or at room temperature. To serve, cut the pudding into oblongs with a small sharp knife and use a wide metal spatula to transfer to dessert plates.

Serve with Vanilla Custard Sauce (see page 409) and/or Raspberry Sauce (see page 411). Pour or ladle the sauce or sauces onto the plates alongside the pudding.

NOTES: This bread, labeled "Distinctive White," measures about 4 inches square; if you use a different bread—larger slices—you will need fewer slices. It is best to use bread of a standard thickness—not thin-sliced. The "Distinctive" loaf has a few more slices than you will need.

Use some other preserves if you wish, but use one that is thick (not runny) and preferably not too sweet.

Wolfgang's Individual Bittersweet Chocolate Soufflés

6 PORTIONS

This is from my very good friend Wolfgang Puck, of California restaurant fame. Wolfgang is one of the nicest people I know, and one of the world's greatest chefs. (A caviar pizza, champagne, and a hot chocolate soufflé at Spago are worth driving from Florida to California for, which we have done many, many times.)

A hot soufflé is the most elegant and posh of all desserts, but it is surprisingly quick and easy to make. Although this must be served immediately when it is done, the preparation can be completed (in 10 to 15 minutes) up to about 2 hours before serving. It is not necessary to wait until the last minute to beat the egg whites.

It would take all of Hollywood's hyperboles to properly describe this. It has more chocolate than most soufflés, with a lush, rich texture and a densely bittersweet and extravagant flavor.

It has a dynamite white chocolate and dark rum sauce that is divine with the soufflé and takes only a few minutes to make.

You need individual soufflé dishes that have a 2/3-cup capacity. I use the white porcelain ones made by Pillivuyt in France. (See page 31.)

DYNAMITE WHITE CHOCOLATE AND DARK RUM SAUCE
½ CUP

This can be made ahead of time, if you wish.

3 ounces white chocolate
¼ cup dark rum

On a board, with a long and heavy knife shred/chop the chocolate fine. Place it in the top of a small double boiler over warm water on low heat. Add the rum, cover, and let stand briefly only until warm. Then whisk until smooth. If necessary, transfer the mixture to a blender and blend until smooth. It will be a thin sauce. Set aside and let stand at room temperature.

The sauce may be served at room temperature or slightly warm. The cocoa butter will separate as the sauce stands; whisk it briskly until smooth just before serving. (The sauce can stand for days or weeks in a covered jar at room temperature.)

SOUFFLÉS

2½ ounces unsweetened chocolate
2½ ounces semisweet chocolate
⅓ cup whipping cream
2 eggs graded "large," separated, plus 3
    additional egg whites (the additional
    whites may have been frozen and
    thawed)
⅓ cup granulated sugar
1 teaspoon lemon juice
Confectioners sugar (to sprinkle on top just
    before serving)

Prepare individual soufflé dishes with a ⅔-cup capacity (they will measure 3 ¼ by 1 ½ inches). It is important to butter the dishes well or the soufflés will not rise properly. With room-temperature butter and a piece of crumpled plastic wrap, butter the dishes all over, including the tops of the rims. Sprinkle a generous amount of granulated sugar into one of the dishes and, over paper, tilt and turn the dish to coat it all over. Turn the excess sugar into the next dish. Repeat to prepare all the dishes. Place the prepared dishes aside.

Also prepare a flat dessert plate for each soufflé dish by placing a folded napkin on each plate and set aside.

Place the chocolates in the top of a small double boiler over warm water on low heat. Cover with a folded paper towel (to absorb steam) and the pot cover for a few minutes. Then uncover and stir until smooth.

Meanwhile, heat the cream in a small pan over low heat until hot but not boiling.

When the chocolates are melted, remove the top of the double boiler, add the hot cream all at once, and stir with a small wire whisk until smooth. Whisk in the 2 egg yolks and half of the sugar (reserve the remaining sugar). Transfer to the large bowl of an electric mixer. The mixture will look uneven; whisk until beautifully smooth and shiny. Set aside.

In the small bowl of the electric mixer beat the 5 egg whites with the lemon juice (Wolfgang always adds lemon juice when beating egg whites— it stabilizes the whites and makes them firmer but not dry) until they hold a soft shape—or a mound—when the beaters are raised. On moderate speed gradually add the remaining sugar, and then, on high speed again, beat until the whites hold a straight shape when the beaters are raised. Do not overbeat.

Remove the bowl of whites from the mixer. Place the large bowl with the chocolate mixture on the mixer stand. Since the chocolate mixture is thick, it is best to actually beat in some of the whites. On low speed beat in a scant one fourth of the beaten whites. Remove the bowl from the mixer and, in three or four additions, gently fold in the remaining whites. Do not handle any more than necessary.

Pour the mixture into the prepared dishes, filling each to the top (or slightly mounded) and refrigerate uncovered.

About 20 minutes before serving adjust a rack to the lowest position in the oven and preheat the oven to 425 degrees.

Place the soufflés on a cookie sheet and bake for 13 minutes. The tops of the soufflés will be dry but delicate and tender; about 1 inch in the centers will be soft and slightly saucelike.

While the soufflés are baking, check the sauce. If necessary, whisk it a bit, or heat it slightly if it has become firm.

As soon as the soufflés are done, remove the cookie sheet from the oven, quickly sprinkle confectioners sugar over the tops through a fine strainer, and quickly place the soufflés on the napkin-lined plates. (For ease in handling, use a wide metal spatula.)

Work quickly. With a teaspoon remove a teaspoonful of the top of each soufflé—right in the center—pour in about a teaspoonful of the sauce, replace the teaspoonful of soufflé that was removed, and serve.

The remaining sauce should be poured into a small pitcher and passed at the table.

NOTE: This Dynamite White Chocolate and Dark Rum Sauce is spectacular over dark chocolate ice cream or ice milk.

Ice Cream, Ice Milk, Ice, et Cetera

ICE CREAM—THE BEST
IN THE WORLD

A few years ago I received a phone call from two men—one a public relations man and one an advertising man—representing a group of multimillionaires who had moved to Europe from South Africa. They told me that the men they represented wanted to manufacture ice cream in America; it was to be the best ice cream in the world. They wanted to know if I would be interested in creating recipes for them and letting them use my name and my picture on the ice cream containers. The containers, incidentally, were a great new invention for which these men held the patent. They claimed the containers would keep the ice cream from melting for four or five hours without refrigeration, even in the sun. I should have suspected something fishy then. But I didn't.

Three of the top would-be executives had come from South Africa to Florida, where we live. They were charming. One of them could have given Don Johnson lessons in charm. They told me that their investors had vast financial resources. They offered me a million dollars plus a percentage of the business. They had their lawyers draw up a lengthy and incredibly detailed and restrictive contract for me. We had meetings with their lawyers and our lawyer. We had ice cream tastings at our home about once a week. We invited them to our home for dinner. I worked full time every day on recipes for them. They did not care how much the ice cream would have to sell for—this was to be the Tiffany of ice cream.

There were endless delays in their signing the contract (one of the negotiators was out of town, or they had to talk to investors in Europe, or it was raining), delays that dragged out the negotiations for almost a year. I lost track of time because I was having such fun making ice cream.

The bottom line is that nothing ever came of it (the moral is that if something sounds too good to be true, it usually is), except that I wound up with a glorious collection of recipes for the best ice cream in the world.

My husband's last memory of this affair was of the evening they invited us out to dinner, but made no move to pick up the check. My husband picked it up.

Many connoisseurs and ice cream experts (especially French chefs) say that ice cream should be served almost immediately after it is churned, at least within an hour or two. That means soft. I was brought up to question the experts. I think that ice cream is best when it is firm. Häagen-Dazs ice cream cones have the right consistency for me. Softer is too soft—and if it is hard to scoop it is too hard. When I plan ice cream for company I like to make it a day ahead, or no less than ten hours ahead. But just between you and me, I have served ice cream several days after it was churned (and longer) and it was perfect. Much depends on the temperature in your freezer. Check the ice cream ahead of time and, if necessary, transfer it from the freezer to the refrigerator briefly before serving.

Today, the classiest restaurants serve ice cream compositions: one or two flavors of ice cream, one or two of sherbert or ice, some fresh fruit, and a sauce or two. (Often the variety is all based on one theme—peach, pear, or chocolate, for instance.) All carefully arranged with a designer's eye, on wide dinner plates. The ice creams are most often shaped with an oval ice cream scoop. (Oval scoops are generally available in kitchen shops.)

Recently I asked my friend Craig Claiborne what the exact difference is between ice, granita, and sorbet (sherbert). Here is what he said: "The French word for an ice is *granite;* in Italian it is *granita.* These are classically made with nothing but pure fruit juice or pulp combined with a simple syrup and, sometimes, only with sugar. A sorbet is almost identical although a true sorbet contains the addition of cream, an Italian meringue, or, simply, beaten egg whites. A sorbet is, naturally, a bit smoother than an ice. I prefer sorbets."

All of the recipes in this section, except the last two, are made with an ice cream churn.

Incidentally, Häagen-Dazs stores their ice cream at eight degrees above zero for serving, and at twenty below for storage.

Tahitian Vanilla Ice Cream

1 ½ QUARTS

The Chino Nojo family (affectionately known as the Chinos) in Rancho Santa Fe in Southern California are wonderful people whom we admire and love. We are proud that they are friends of ours. They are Japanese-Americans whose sense of family—whose togetherness—is beautiful to see. The mother and father are in their nineties. The children have all been educated at the best universities. The punch line is that they have a farm and most of them (including the father) work on it. The farm is an outstanding example of the finest of everything. Nobody but nobody grows such sweet strawberries (deep and bright red all the way through to the center) and such tomatoes in a variety of colors and sizes I never saw before (some almost as small as green peas) and flavors I never tasted before. Their corn is so sweet and tender that when a restaurant serves their corn the menu only has to say "Chino's corn" and everyone orders it.

I could go on and on.

The luxurious limousines lined up at their farm stand, The Vegetable Shop (6123 Calzada del Bosque), and the groups of patient customers waiting their turn to buy salad greens, herbs, edible flowers, jalapeño peppers, and baby vegetables, are testimony to the quality of what the Chinos grow. So is the fact that Wolfgang Puck (Spago and Chinois, et cetera) uses almost only Chino produce.

And what's more, the Chinos can cook.

We visit them every chance we get. Once, Fred, one of the sons, treated us to a variety of fresh ice creams he had just made. I never had such a vanilla ice cream. I felt that I had never really tasted vanilla before. I was honored that he gave me the recipe.

Here it is. I warn you that vanilla ice cream will never be the same after this.

The Licor 43 called for in the recipe is a
Spanish liqueur that I had never heard of
before. It has a great vanilla flavor. (The liquor
stores here in Miami all carry it.)
You will need a sugar thermometer.

2 whole Tahitian vanilla beans (see page 31),
    split and scraped (see page 10)
4 cups whipping cream
1 cup granulated sugar
⅛ teaspoon cream of tartar
½ cup water
8 egg yolks graded "large"
Pinch of salt
3 tablespoons Licor 43
1 teaspoon vanilla extract

Place the prepared vanilla beans and their seeds in a small saucepan that
has a tight cover. Add 1 cup of the cream (reserve the remaining 3 cups
cream). Place over moderate heat until the cream comes to a low boil, then
cover, remove from the heat, and let stand for about 30 minutes.

Then, in a small, narrow saucepan (with only a 2- to 3-cup capacity),
stir the sugar, cream of tartar, and water over moderate heat until the sugar
dissolves and the mixture just comes to a boil. Cover for 1 minute to allow
steam to dissolve any sugar granules that are clinging to the sides. Then
increase the heat to high, uncover the saucepan, place a sugar thermometer
in the saucepan, do not stir anymore, and let boil until the thermometer
registers 234 degrees (the thread stage).

Meanwhile, in the small bowl of an electric mixer beat the egg yolks
just to mix. As soon as the syrup is ready add it in a thin, threadlike stream
while beating at moderate speed. Add the salt. Then continue to beat at
high speed for about 10 to 15 minutes until the mixture is almost as thick
as whipped cream and very pale. Beat in the Licor 43 and the vanilla.

Meanwhile, remove the vanilla beans from the warm cream and scrape
them between your thumb and forefinger to get every bit of the seeds. (You
will not use the beans anymore for this recipe.) Transfer the flavored cream
to a large bowl.

With a large wire whisk, whisk in the egg-yolk mixture and the remaining cream.

Chill in the freezer, refrigerator, or over ice and water, stirring occasionally, until very cold.

Freeze in an ice cream churn according to the manufacturer's directions.

Place in a covered container and freeze for at least a few hours before serving.

White Chocolate Ice Cream

2 QUARTS

Many food writers say that UHT (ultra-high-temperature pasteurized) cream does not work—and that we must track down "natural" heavy cream. Easier said than done. Of course I agree that natural is wonderful—but I made this ice cream (as well as all the others in this collection) with UHT cream, and I simply do not think this could be any better even if I milked my own cow. The white chocolate taste is mild and mellow and the texture is ultra-smooth. It does not get too hard even after a few days in the freezer.

You will need a sugar thermometer.

10 ounces white chocolate
2 cups whipping cream
2 cups half-and-half
8 egg yolks graded "large"
⅔ cup granulated sugar

Chop the chocolate fine, place it in a large mixing bowl, and set aside.

In a 2½- to 3-quart saucepan over moderate heat scald the cream and half-and-half until you see tiny bubbles around the rim.

Meanwhile, in the small bowl of an electric mixer beat the yolks and sugar at high speed for a few minutes until the mixture is pale and forms a wide ribbon when the beaters are raised.

On low speed gradually ladle about a cup or two of the hot-cream mixture into the yolk mixture, scraping the bowl occasionally with a rubber spatula. Then pour the yolk mixture into the remaining hot-cream mixture and whisk until smooth.

Now, to make an extralarge double boiler, place the saucepan with the mixture in it into a larger pan of shallow hot water. If possible, the pan of cream mixture should fit the larger pan so that it is raised above the water.

Insert a sugar thermometer. Stir and scrape the pan constantly over moderate heat until the mixture coats a spoon and registers 170 degrees on the thermometer.

Remove the top pan from the hot water. Pour the hot mixture into the bowl of chopped chocolate and whisk until melted and smooth. Then stir occasionally until cool.

Now, if possible, the mixture should be covered and refrigerated overnight. If that is not possible, refrigerate it for at least a few hours, or stir it over a bowl of ice and water until it is icy cold.

Then transfer to an ice cream churn and freeze according to the manufacturer's directions.

Transfer to a covered freezer container and freeze for at least 3 or 4 hours before serving.

Serve as is, or sprinkle the top with unsweetened cocoa powder through a fine strainer. Or serve with any dark chocolate sauce.

VARIATION: Double White Chocolate Ice Cream

Cut 3 to 4 ounces of white chocolate into ¼-inch pieces and stir into the ice cream when it is removed from the churn. Double yummy.

NOTE: Strawberries are wonderful with white chocolate ice cream—and vice versa. To each basket of berries, washed, hulled, drained, and sliced, add about 1 tablespoon of granulated sugar and about 1 tablespoon of kirsch. Toss gently to mix and let stand at room temperature for an hour or so. Serve the berries and their juice as a sauce either over and/or under the ice cream. Be prepared with a generous amount of the berries.

Rum-Raisin Chocolate Ice Cream

Luxurious and voluptuous. Made with bitter-sweet (or semisweet) chocolate and cocoa. And honey. This is as good as chocolate ice cream gets.

If possible, marinate the raisins in the rum overnight.

(Omit the raisins and rum entirely if you wish for a sensational plain chocolate ice cream.)

You will need a sugar thermometer.

GENEROUS 1½ QUARTS

5 ounces (1 cup) raisins
½ cup dark rum
12 ounces bittersweet (or semisweet)
    chocolate (I use Callebaut bittersweet
    chocolate—see page 13)
2 cups whipping cream
2 cups milk
¼ cup unsweetened cocoa powder
    (preferably Dutch-process)
6 egg yolks graded "large"
¼ cup granulated sugar
⅓ cup mild honey
1 teaspoon vanilla extract

Marinate the raisins in the rum in a small covered jar for at least several hours or, preferably, overnight.

On a large board, with a long knife shred/chop the chocolate medium-fine and set aside.

In the top of a large double boiler over hot water on moderate heat scald 1½ cups of the cream (reserve the remaining ½ cup cream) and 1 cup of the milk (reserve the remaining 1 cup milk) until a wrinkled skin forms on top of the cream.

Meanwhile, in a 2½- to 3-quart saucepan bring the remaining 1 cup of milk to a simmer over moderate heat. Add the cocoa and whisk to dissolve. Add the chocolate, reduce the heat to low, and whisk until perfectly smooth. Set aside.

At the same time, place the yolks, sugar, and honey in the large bowl of an electric mixer and beat just to mix. Let stand.

When the cream-and-milk mixture is scalded, ladle it gradually, on low speed, into the egg-yolk mixture, scraping the bowl and beating until mixed.

Return the mixture to the top of the double boiler over hot water on moderate heat and cook, scraping the pan almost constantly with a rubber spatula, until the mixture thickens enough to coat a spoon and registers 180 degrees on a sugar thermometer.

Immediately remove the top of the double boiler from the heat and stir in the remaining ½ cup of cream to stop the cooking.

Gradually whisk the yolk mixture into the chocolate mixture. Stir occasionally until cool.

Meanwhile, drain the raisins in a strainer set over a bowl. Stir the drained rum into the ice cream mixture (reserve the raisins until after the ice cream is churned). Stir in the vanilla.

Chill the mixture in the freezer, refrigerator, or over a bowl of ice and water, stirring occasionally until very cold.

Then churn in an ice cream machine following the manufacturer's directions.

When churned, stir the raisins into the ice cream.

Transfer to covered containers and place in the freezer.

VARIATION: Chocolate-covered Rum-Raisin Chocolate Ice Cream

This ice cream is so good it is almost a crime to do anything to it. But as Mae West said, "Too much of a good thing is wonderful." This is quick and easy, and does not detract from the ice cream. It just adds another chocolate dimension. For each serving of ice cream use ½ to 1 ounce of bittersweet (or semisweet) chocolate. On a board, with a long and heavy knife shred/chop the chocolate into uneven pieces, some fine and powdery and some as much as ¼ inch in width. The chocolate can be cut up ahead of time and can wait at room temperature or in the refrigerator.

Just before serving, sprinkle each portion generously with the chocolate, and/or pass a small bowl of the chopped chocolate.

Serve with a spoonful of whipped cream on top.

This was inspired by *tartufo,* an Italian dessert. *Tartufo*—the real thing—is a ball of chocolate ice cream coated with chopped chocolate, with a glacéed cherry in the center of the ice cream. (The word *tartufo* is Italian for "truffle.")

Chocolate Obsession

1½ PINTS

The darkest, the most densely chocolate, the smoothest and creamiest (although it is made without cream), one of the most voluptuous and irresistible of all. This could spoil you forever.

You will need a sugar thermometer.

2 cups milk
3 tablespoons mild honey
2 ounces semisweet chocolate
6 egg yolks graded "large"
⅓ cup granulated sugar
¾ cup strained unsweetened cocoa powder
(preferably Dutch-process)

In a small saucepan over moderate heat bring the milk and honey just to a simmer. Meanwhile, chop the chocolate into rather small pieces. Remove the pan from the heat, add the chopped chocolate, and stir until melted.

In the small bowl of an electric mixer beat the yolks and sugar at high speed until thick. On low speed add the cocoa and beat until incorporated.

Then transfer the hot-milk mixture to a pitcher and, on low speed, gradually add it to the yolk mixture, scraping the bowl with a rubber spatula as necessary.

Transfer the mixture to the top of a large double boiler. Place over hot water on moderate heat. Cook, scraping the bottom and sides with a rubber spatula, for about 10 minutes until the mixture registers 170 degrees on a sugar thermometer.

Strain through a fine but wide strainer set over a bowl. Place in a larger bowl of ice and water or chill in the freezer or refrigerator, stirring occasionally until cold.

Freeze in an ice cream churn according to the manufacturer's directions. Transfer to a covered container and place in the freezer.

Frozen Chocolate Yogurt

1 ½ QUARTS

Several years ago at an ice cream stand named Johnston's (not Howard) in Westwood Village, California, next door to Beverly Hills, I had a frozen chocolate yogurt that I lost my heart to and have since thought of every time I see the sign FROZEN YOGURT. There is frozen yogurt and there is frozen yogurt. I have tried too many to count and never had another like the one I fell in love with. I don't know why it took me all these years to try to make it myself.

Frozen chocolate yogurt (the real stuff) is strange and exotic and divine. It is both sweet and sour. Most of us have never had frozen chocolate yogurt that really tasted like chocolate—and really tasted like yogurt. The ones that are generally available are pale in both color and flavor. This one, however, is dark-colored and strong-flavored, and it has a spectacular silky-smooth texture. And it is beautifully shiny.

Nothing could be easier, but allow at least 5 hours or more for it to freeze after it is churned.

4 8-ounce containers low-fat coffee yogurt (I use Dannon)
1½ cups granulated sugar
⅔ cup plus 4 tablespoons unsweetened cocoa powder (preferably Dutch-process)
Pinch of salt
2 tablespoons instant espresso or coffee powder
1 tablespoon dark rum

Place the yogurt, sugar, cocoa, salt, espresso or coffee powder, and rum in a large bowl and, with a large whisk, whisk until thoroughly mixed and smooth. Stir for about 10 minutes until the sugar is dissolved. If the mixture is not smooth, strain it.

Freeze in an ice cream churn according to the manufacturer's directions. But these ingredients will take longer than most—about 20 to 30 minutes longer—to reach the proper consistency.

Then place in a covered container and freeze for at least 5 hours or overnight before serving.

Café Liègeoise

1 ½ QUARTS

Café Liègeoise is from the city of Liège in Belgium. Traditionally it is a drink, a thick, rich, semisoft drink, possibly the world's best iced coffee.

This is the traditional recipe, which may be served as a thick drink, as it is in Belgium, or frozen firm like American ice cream. The ice cream is especially delicious with a bittersweet chocolate sauce (see page 404 or page 357), or marbelized with Dutch Chocolate Sauce (see page 403).

The first time I ever had this was at Angelina's elegant tea room in Paris. I ordered it without any idea of what it was, along with a chocolate pastry. The Café Liègeoise, topped with whipped cream, was served in a tall, narrow, frosted glass and accompanied with both a straw and a long-handled spoon.

I was in seventh heaven.

You will need a sugar thermometer to make this.

8 egg yolks graded "large"
1 cup granulated sugar
½ cup water
4 tablespoons instant espresso or coffee powder (see Note)
2 tablespoons boiling water
4 cups cold whipping cream

In the small bowl of an electric mixer beat the egg yolks to mix well.

Meanwhile, in a small, narrow saucepan over moderate heat stir the sugar and ½ cup water until the sugar is dissolved, occasionally washing down the sides with a brush dipped in water to remove any undissolved grains of sugar. When the mixture comes to a boil, increase the heat to high and insert a sugar thermometer. Let boil until the thermometer registers 234 degrees (the thread stage).

Then, with the mixer on moderate speed, add the hot syrup, pouring it slowly in a thin stream. Increase the speed to high and continue to beat for 10 to 15 minutes until the mixture is thick and completely cool. Meanwhile, dissolve the instant espresso or coffee in the boiling water, and add to the yolk mixture.

When the mixture is thick and cool, transfer it to a larger bowl and mix in the cold whipping cream.

Freeze in an ice cream churn according to the manufacturer's directions.

To serve this as an ultrathick drink, or soft frozen ice cream, or whatever-you-call-it, serve it right out of the churn before it has frozen solid.

To freeze it solid, transfer to a covered container and place in the freezer.

NOTE: I use Medaglia D'Oro instant espresso.

Prune Armagnac Ice Cream

1 ½ QUARTS

Très chic! With a powerful punch of Armagnac. Elegant. Luxurious. Sophisticated.

The prunes can be prepared a week or more ahead of time, or (for this ice cream) only 1 hour ahead if you wish.

You will need a sugar thermometer.

Prunes in Armagnac (see page 396)
2 cups milk
4 egg yolks graded "large"
Pinch of salt
1 cup whipping cream
Optional: Armagnac (to be drizzled over each serving)

Prepare the prunes and set aside.

In the top of a large double boiler over hot water on moderate heat scald the milk, uncovered, until tiny bubbles form around the edge.

Meanwhile, in the small bowl of an electric mixer beat the yolks just to mix. On low speed gradually add the hot milk and the salt, beating only to mix.

Return to the top of the large double boiler over hot water on moderate heat. Insert a sugar thermometer. Cook, scraping the pan almost constantly with a rubber spatula, until the mixture thickens enough to coat a spoon and registers 180 degrees on the thermometer.

Remove the top of the double boiler and stir in the cream to stop the cooking. Set aside.

Pour the prunes through a strainer set over a bowl; reserve the juice. Transfer the prunes to the bowl of a food processor fitted with the metal chopping blade and process until pureed. Then, through the feed tube, add all the prune juice and process to mix.

Transfer the prune puree to a large mixing bowl and gradually stir in the egg-yolk mixture.

Stir occasionally until cool. Then place in the freezer, refrigerator, or over a bowl of ice water, and stir occasionally until very cold.

Freeze in an ice cream churn according to the manufacturer's directions.

Transfer to a covered container and place in the freezer for at least a few hours before serving.

Drizzle a bit of the optional Armagnac over each serving.

Kumquat Ice Cream

1 ½ QUARTS

This has a mellow kumquat flavor and a most remarkable silky-smooth texture. It is unusual, elegant, extraordinary, and superdelicious. The texture will remain sensational for weeks (I am nonplussed by how long this maintains its perfect consistency).

This takes longer to freeze than most ice creams; it is best to allow it to stand in the freezer overnight before serving.

You will need a sugar thermometer.

1 10-ounce jar kumquats in syrup (I use Raffetto brand)
4 tablespoons Grand Marnier
1 cup milk
2 cups whipping cream
8 egg yolks graded "large"
1 cup granulated sugar

Drain the kumquats (you will not use the syrup). With a small sharp knife cut the kumquats lengthwise into quarters. Pick out and discard the seeds. Some of the seeds are transparent and difficult to see; examine carefully.

Place the kumquats in the bowl of a food processor fitted with the metal chopping blade. With the motor running add the Grand Marnier through the feed tube and process, scraping down the sides as necessary, until pureed. Kumquats resist being pureed, but if you gradually add a few spoonfuls of the milk you might be able to convince them. Continue to process for at least a minute or more, until you believe that the kumquats will not become any finer. Stop the machine, but let the mixture remain in the bowl and let stand.

In the top of a large double boiler over hot water on moderate heat scald the milk and cream until a wrinkled skin forms on the top and small bubbles appear around the edge.

Meanwhile, in the small bowl of an electric mixer beat the egg yolks with the sugar at low speed for a minute or two. With a ladle gradually add about half of the hot-milk mixture to the egg-yolk mixture and beat on low speed to mix. Then stir the egg-yolk mixture into the remaining milk mixture.

With a rubber spatula stir over hot water on moderate heat, scraping the pan constantly, until the mixture coats a spoon and registers 180 degrees on a sugar thermometer.

Transfer the mixture to a mixing bowl. Place in a larger bowl of ice and water. Stir until cool.

Add about 1 cup of the cool mixture to the kumquats in the processor bowl and process for about half a minute.

Pour the kumquat mixture through a wide but fine strainer set over a bowl. Press down hard with a wooden spoon or with the bowl of a ladle to force as much of the mixture as possible through the strainer.

If more than a tablespoon or so of the kumquats remains in the strainer, put it back in the processor, add the strained ingredients, process well again, and strain again.

Stir in the remaining milk mixture.

Chill in the freezer, refrigerator, or over ice.

Then freeze in a churn according to the manufacturer's directions.

Transfer to a covered container and place in the freezer.

Tropical Lime Ice Cream

Although this is much lighter than other ice creams, it is creamy and smooth. It is cool and refreshing, with a tart, tropical flavor. This is quick and easy—and one of the most popular; everyone raves about it.

1 QUART

1 cup milk
¾ cup whipping cream
1 cup granulated sugar
Finely grated rind of 2 or 3 limes
¾ cup lime juice

In a bowl stir the milk, cream, and sugar for a few minutes until the sugar is dissolved. (If it is not completely dissolved it is OK; it will continue to dissolve during churning.)

Add the rind and juice and stir once or twice to mix. (It does not curdle.)

Transfer to an ice cream churn and freeze according to the manufacturer's directions. Then place in a covered container in the freezer.

Tahitian Vanilla Ice Milk

1 QUART

This is astonishing. Read the ingredients. It is light-light-light, but also creamy. It is elegant and exquisite. A divine dessert to serve after a swanky meal, as well as the perfect end to a chili dinner—or a pizza party. It can be served a few hours after it is churned or many days later; the texture remains great. Be prepared with a generous amount.

The recipe calls for a Tahitian vanilla bean, but another variety can be used. The ice milk will still be delicious, but the flavor might not be as intense.

1 Tahitian vanilla bean (see page 31), split
    and scraped (see page 10)
1 cup granulated sugar
4 cups milk

Place the vanilla bean and seeds, the sugar, and the milk in a saucepan over moderate heat. Stir occasionally until the mixture just barely comes to a boil. Cover. Remove from the heat and let stand for about half an hour.

Remove the vanilla bean and scrape it between your thumb and forefinger to get every bit of the seeds and flavor. (You will not use the bean anymore for this recipe.)

That's it. Now cool, then chill in the refrigerator or freezer, and then churn in an ice cream churn according to the manufacturer's directions.

Taste. Happy?

Transfer to a covered container and freeze.

Serve plain. Or sprinkled with unsweetened cocoa powder through a fine strainer. Or serve with fresh berries.

Chocolate Ice Milk

1 ½ QUARTS

How can these few simple and light ingredients taste so rich and so wonderfully chocolate? Trust me—they do. This is one of the easiest of all these frozen desserts to prepare. And the frozen mixture does not get icy or too hard.

1 ½ cups granulated sugar
⅔ cup plus 4 tablespoons unsweetened cocoa
    powder (preferably Dutch-process)
Pinch of salt
2 tablespoons instant espresso or coffee
    powder
1 quart (4 cups) cold milk

Place the sugar, cocoa, salt, and espresso or coffee powder in a blender jar or in the bowl of a food processor fitted with the metal chopping blade. Add 1 to 2 cups of the milk (reserve the remaining milk) and blend or process until the sugar and cocoa are dissolved. Then mix in the remaining milk.

Cover and refrigerate for a few hours or overnight; even if the mixture is cold to begin with, it will churn better if it is refrigerated for at least a few hours.

Freeze in an ice cream churn according to the manufacturer's directions.

Then place in a covered container and freeze for at least a few hours before serving.

Milk Chocolate Ice Milk

GENEROUS 1 QUART

I would like to say this in letters 6 inches high, to be sure to get your attention. If you have an ice cream maker, make this. It is hard to believe. As rich, smooth, and creamy as ice cream made with heavy cream and many egg yolks, yet look at the ingredients. I made this up because I thought of the name and the sound pleased me. I had no idea that the result would be—could be—so delicious. Amazing.

If possible, refrigerate the mixture overnight before you churn it.

1 pound milk chocolate (I use Hershey's)
3 cups milk

Break up the chocolate and place it in the top of a large double boiler. Add ½ cup of the milk (reserve the remaining 2½ cups milk). Stir over hot water on moderate heat until melted and smooth.

Gradually add the remaining milk, whisking it in until smooth.

Cook uncovered over moderate heat, stirring and scraping the pan frequently, for 30 minutes. Then remove the top of the double boiler and stir occasionally until cool.

Place in a covered container and refrigerate for at least several hours or overnight.

The chocolate will form a heavy layer on top; whisk to incorporate the ingredients. Then freeze in an ice cream churn following the manufacturer's directions.

Transfer to a covered container and place in the freezer.

Caramel Ice Milk

A true caramel flavor—simply the pure taste of caramelized sugar—and a voluptuously smooth texture. This is luscious just as it is, or with fresh peaches, or with a bittersweet chocolate sauce (see page 404 or page 357). Or with Creamy Milk Chocolate Sauce (see page 402).

SCANT 1 QUART

Plan to use this within a day or two; it separates slightly if it stands longer.

2⅓ cups milk
1½ cups granulated sugar
⅔ cup water

Before you start to caramelize the sugar, place the milk in a bowl next to you. And have a long-handled ladle (a must) nearby.

Place the sugar and water in a wide and heavy frying pan or a sauté pan. (I use a heavy pan 11 inches wide and 2¼ inches deep. It has a 2½-quart capacity and a nonstick finish. Do not use anything smaller, or anything with a narrow diameter.) With a wooden spatula stir over moderate heat until the sugar has dissolved and the mixture comes to a boil. Wash down any sugar crystals from the sides with a pastry brush dipped in cold water. Or cover the pan airtight and let boil for 1 minute (the steam will wash down the sides). Increase the heat to high and boil the syrup, stirring almost constantly until it caramelizes to a rich honey color. (If it is too pale it will not have any flavor; if too dark it will taste burned.)

Remove the pan from the heat and, without waiting, ladle the milk into the syrup; the mixture will foam up and bubble (the long-handled ladle is to prevent you from burning yourself). Stir to mix.

Adding the milk will probably solidify some of the syrup. If so, stir over moderate heat until melted and smooth.

Transfer to a large bowl. Place the bowl in a larger bowl of ice and water and stir occasionally until cool. Then chill in the freezer for an hour or so or longer in the refrigerator. Or just let the bowl continue to sit over ice and water until very cold (adding more ice as necessary).

Freeze in an ice cream churn according to the manufacturer's directions. Transfer to a covered container and place in the freezer.

Chocolate Ice

As smooth as butter—as shiny as wet tar—as dark as midnight—not too sweet and not too rich—with an enticing bittersweet flavor. And easy.

ABOUT 3 CUPS

6 ounces unsweetened chocolate
1 cup granulated sugar
2 teaspoons instant espresso or coffee powder
2 cups boiling water
½ teaspoon vanilla extract
2 tablespoons dark rum

Chop the chocolate into medium-fine pieces. Then place it in the bowl of a food processor fitted with the metal chopping blade. Process until fine. Add the sugar and espresso or coffee powder and process for about 10 seconds. Then, with the motor running, add about 1 cup of the boiling water through the feed tube and continue to process for about 10 seconds more.

Transfer the mixture to a heavy saucepan. Add the remaining 1 cup boiling water and stir over moderate heat until the mixture comes to a boil. Reduce the heat and simmer the mixture—stirring occasionally—for 5 to 6 minutes. Remove from the heat.

Let cool to room temperature. Stir in the vanilla and rum. Refrigerate for at least an hour or longer, if possible.

Freeze in an ice cream churn according to the manufacturer's directions for 20 to 30 minutes or until semifirm. Transfer to a covered container and place in the freezer for at least 1 hour before serving. This will be at its best up to 6 to 8 hours in the freezer. After that it becomes very hard (although still smooth—never icy). However, if it is necessary to freeze this until it becomes very hard, it will soften nicely if transferred to the refrigerator about an hour before serving.

Banana Ice

1 ½ QUARTS

I am bananas about this. It tastes almost like ice cream—the bananas give it a richness, a creamy appearance, and a lush taste.

Bananas must be fully ripe to give the ice their flavor. The skins should be quite well-darkened—the fruit itself should be soft and should have a strong banana smell. If there are any brown spots on the fruit they should be cut away.

1 cup granulated sugar
1 cup water
Scant 2 pounds (3 ½ large) ripe bananas (to make 2 cups puree)
2 ½ tablespoons lemon juice (or more to taste)
¼ cup orange juice
2 tablespoons dark rum

In a saucepan over moderate heat stir the sugar and water until the sugar is dissolved. Turn the heat to high, bring the mixture to a boil, cover, and let boil for 1 minute (in order to dissolve any sugar granules clinging to the sides of the pan). Uncover. Set aside and cool to room temperature. Then refrigerate until cold.

Peel the bananas, break into pieces, and process in a food processor fitted with the metal chopping blade (or in a blender, half at a time) until smooth and pureed.

Transfer to a bowl. Stir in the juices and then the sugar syrup and the rum.

Refrigerate for about an hour or more until the mixture is very cold.

Then freeze the mixture in an ice cream churn according to the manufacturer's directions.

Transfer to a covered container and place in the freezer for a few hours before serving.

Green Apple Ice

1 QUART

Wonderfully refreshing and delicious—and it does not freeze too hard even after a few days.

1½ pounds (4 medium-large) tart apples (preferably Granny Smith)
1 cup unsweetened apple juice
1 cup granulated sugar
2 tablespoons lemon juice
1 teaspoon vanilla extract
Optional: Calvados or applejack

Peel the apples with a vegetable parer. Cut them in half from top to bottom. With a melon baller remove the cores. With a small sharp knife cut a small grove above and below the cores to remove the stems and fibers. Cut each piece in half, making quarters. Place in a heavy saucepan with the apple juice and sugar.

Cover and cook over moderate heat, stirring occasionally, for about 10 minutes or until tender.

With a slotted spoon transfer the apples to the bowl of a food processor fitted with the metal chopping blade. Process until pureed. Through the feed tube gradually add the syrup remaining in the saucepan, and process until smooth.

Strain through a wide but fine strainer set over a bowl. Stir in the lemon juice and vanilla. Cool.

Chill, preferably in the refrigerator for a few hours or overnight.

Freeze in an ice cream churn according to the manufacturer's directions.

If you wish, serve with a bit of the optional Calvados or applejack spooned over the top.

Rhubarb and Strawberry Ice

This is a glorious shade of pink, identical to the color of the pink flamingos at Hialeah racetrack. The flavor is mild and mellow, a combination of rhubarb and strawberries with a hint of cinnamon and lemon.

This is a seasonal recipe to be made in the early spring, when fresh young rhubarb is available.

GENEROUS 2 QUARTS

Unless your ice cream churn is large enough for this volume, churn it in batches.

1 1/4 pounds fresh rhubarb (to make 4 cups when cut)
1 cup granulated sugar
1 cup water
1/2 teaspoon cinnamon
Pinch of nutmeg
1/2 pound (2 cups) fresh strawberries
1/2 teaspoon vanilla extract
2 tablespoons lemon juice

Discard any leaves on the rhubarb. Trim the ends. Wash the rhubarb and cut it into 1/2-inch slices.

Place in a heavy saucepan. Add the sugar, water, cinnamon, and nutmeg. Place on moderate heat and stir frequently until the liquid comes to a boil. Then reduce the heat to allow the mixture to simmer. Cover and let simmer for 10 to 15 minutes until the rhubarb falls apart when stirred.

Meanwhile, wash and hull the strawberries. Cut them into halves or quarters. When the rhubarb is ready, remove the pan from the heat, add the strawberries, cover, and let stand for about 10 minutes. Then uncover, stir, and let cool.

Stir in the vanilla and lemon juice. Puree through a food mill, or in a blender or food processor.

Chill in the freezer, refrigerator, or over a bowl of ice and water, stirring occasionally, until very cold.

Freeze in an ice cream churn according to the manufacturer's directions.

Transfer to a covered container and place in the freezer.

This is delicious served with a generous amount of sliced fresh strawberries. Or just by itself.

Plum Ice

1 ½ QUARTS

The color varies from a gorgeous rosy pink to a deep magenta, depending on the variety of plum. The texture is smooth and the flavor is mellow and delicious. Plums are seasonal; you can prepare the mixture and freeze it before churning. Then thaw and churn even months later. Extraordinary.

2 pounds (8 large) dark plums (i.e., Black Diamond or Santa Rosa)
1 cup water
1 cup granulated sugar
Pinch of salt
1 teaspoon vanilla extract
1 tablespoon lemon juice

Halve and pit the plums and set aside.

In a saucepan stir the water and sugar over moderate heat until the sugar is dissolved and the mixture comes to a boil. Add the salt and the plums. Cover and simmer, stirring occasionally, for 10 to 20 minutes until the plums are completely tender. During cooking the skins will separate and float off the plums—it is OK.

In two batches puree the plums (including the skins—they add color—and the liquid) in a food processor fitted with the metal chopping blade until completely smooth.

Then strain through a wide strainer set over a bowl. Stir in the vanilla and lemon juice.

Cool, and then chill in the freezer or refrigerator, stirring occasionally, until very cold.

Freeze in an ice cream churn according to the manufacturer's directions.

Then transfer to a covered container and place in the freezer for at least several hours or overnight before serving.

NOTE: This plum mixture, not churned, makes a wonderful sauce, especially over Tahitian Vanilla Ice Milk (see page 328).

Fresh or Frozen Fruit Ice

This can be made with almost any fresh fruit or fruit frozen without sugar. I have made it with raspberries, strawberries, blackberries, pineapple, apricots, peaches, pears, and mangoes.

Generally speaking, 1 pound of fruit—without pits, peel, or rind—will make the 2 cups of puree called for.

ABOUT 1 QUART

2 cups puree of fruit
1 cup water
1 cup granulated sugar
Optional: lemon or lime juice to taste
Optional: dark rum to taste

In a food processor fitted with the metal chopping blade or in a blender (in two batches), puree the fruit and set aside.

Make a simple syrup as follows: In a saucepan over moderate heat stir the water and sugar until the sugar is dissolved and the mixture comes to a boil. Cover the pan for 1 minute (to allow steam to wash down any undissolved sugar granules clinging to the sides). Then uncover and let boil over high heat for 2 minutes. (You will have 1½ cups of syrup.)

Stir the hot syrup into the fruit puree. Stir in the optional lemon or lime juice and rum, just to perk up the flavor a bit. (Most fruits are better with about 2 tablespoons of lemon or lime juice, and mango, pineapple, peach, and apricot are better with about 1 tablespoon of rum also.)

Strain through a wide but fine strainer set over a bowl.

Let cool, and then chill in a freezer, refrigerator, or over a bowl of ice and water until icy cold.

Then freeze in an ice cream churn according to the manufacturer's directions.

Place in a covered container in the freezer for at least a few hours before serving. (Paul Bocuse says, "Serve immediately, when you remove the mixture from the churn." At that point I think the consistency is nearly that of a drink. However, do serve within a day or two.)

Check this ice ahead of time. If it is too firm, transfer it to the refrigerator for 10 to 20 minutes before serving.

NOTE: In mango season I puree the fruit and freeze it in 2-cup quantities. I see no reason why the same thing could not be done with any seasonal fruit. It is great to serve a fresh fruit ice when the fruit is out of season.

Frozen Irish Whiskey Mousse

Marvelous. Wonderful. Deluxe. Elegant. Make this at least a day ahead. It does not need an ice cream churn. And it does not become too firm to serve easily.

You will need a sugar thermometer.

2 QUARTS

⅔ cup granulated sugar
⅔ cup water
8 egg yolks graded "large"
1 cup whipping cream
1 cup Irish whiskey

Place the sugar and water in a 5- to 6-cup saucepan over moderate heat and stir until the sugar is dissolved and the mixture comes to a boil. Raise the heat to high. Cover for 1 minute (to allow steam to dissolve any undissolved sugar granules). Insert a sugar thermometer and let boil without stirring until the thermometer registers 234 degrees.

Meanwhile, in the small bowl of an electric mixer beat the egg yolks until pale.

When the syrup is ready, with the electric mixer going, pour the syrup in a thin stream into the yolks and then continue to beat for 15 minutes or until completely cool. Remove the bowl from the mixer.

In a chilled bowl with chilled beaters whip the cream until it holds a shape.

With a rubber spatula gradually fold half of the whiskey into the whipped cream and half into the beaten egg-yolk mixture.

Then, in a large bowl, fold the two mixtures together, folding only until incorporated.

Pour into a covered container and place in the freezer overnight or for a few days.

Serve this simply, as you would serve ice cream (although this will be slightly softer), preferably in well-chilled glasses or bowls. It does not need a thing with it, but I have served it over sliced bananas and it was glorious.

Frozen Rum-Raisin Chocolate Fudge

1½ QUARTS—12 PORTIONS

Calling all chocolate lovers!

This is slightly related to ice cream, but is more rich, dense, and intense, darker, and more chewy. It is like a frozen fudge-truffle-caramel combination. It is made without an ice cream churn.

This needs at least 6 hours in the freezer before it is served, but then it can stay in the freezer for a week or more with no change—it does not become too hard to serve easily.

Sensational is the word. And sexy.

The raisins have to be prepared (marinated) at least a day ahead, but they can be prepared a week ahead if you wish.

Occasionally there can be too much of a good thing. Serve this in small portions, with a generous amount of Brandied Custard Sauce (see page 409).

½ cup raisins
⅓ cup dark rum
8 ounces semisweet chocolate
4 ounces (1 stick) unsalted butter
4 eggs graded "large," separated
⅓ cup granulated sugar
¼ cup unsweetened cocoa powder
(preferably Dutch-process)
5 tablespoons boiling water
Pinch of salt
Brandied Custard Sauce, to serve alongside

A day or more ahead, steam the raisins in a vegetable steamer or a strainer, covered, over boiling water for 5 minutes. Drain on paper towels. Place in a jar with a leak-proof cover, add the rum, cover, and let stand, occasionally turning the jar from end to end.

Chop or break the chocolate into coarse pieces. Place the chocolate and butter in the top of a large double boiler over hot water on moderate heat.

Cover and let cook until partially melted, then uncover and stir until smooth. Remove the top of the double boiler and set aside.

While the chocolate is melting, beat the yolks (reserve the whites) with half of the sugar (reserve remaining sugar) in the small bowl of an electric mixer; beat until pale. Remove from the mixer and set aside.

In a small bowl whisk the cocoa and boiling water until smooth.

Whisk the warm cocoa mixture into the warm chocolate mixture. Transfer to the large bowl of an electric mixer. Add the beaten egg-yolk mixture and beat on low speed until smooth. Remove the bowl from the mixer.

Stir in the raisins and any remaining rum. Set aside.

The chocolate mixture will be thin at this stage, and when you fold in the beaten egg whites the raisins might sink. But if you chill the chocolate mixture briefly it will thicken and will prevent the raisins from sinking. Therefore, place the bowl in the freezer for about 5 minutes or in the refrigerator for 10 to 15 minutes, stirring the mixture every few minutes in order to chill it evenly. Do not let it actually harden (it should only thicken a bit).

While the chocolate is chilling, beat the egg whites as follows: In a clean small bowl of the electric mixer, with clean beaters beat the egg whites and the salt until the whites hold a soft shape. On moderate speed gradually add the remaining sugar. Then beat on high speed until the whites just barely hold a straight shape when the beaters are raised. Remove the bowl from the mixer.

Remove the bowl of chocolate mixture from the freezer or refrigerator. Fold about a cup of the chocolate mixture into the beaten whites, and then fold the beaten whites into the remaining chocolate mixture.

Transfer to a covered container and place in the freezer. Freeze until firm, or longer.

To serve, use a large spoon or an ice cream scoop. A portion should not be more than a level standard-sized scoop (or ⅓ cup) of the frozen fudge. Place each portion in a bowl-shaped dish, and pour the sauce (which should be very cold) around the sides of the frozen fudge.

Refrigerator Desserts

Banana Rum Terrine

8 PORTIONS

This is the dessert I served at a small party the night I signed the contract for this book.

Run—don't walk—to the kitchen to make it.

When I served it recently to close friends I heard two comments: "I don't believe it"; and "I would kill for this." Then, complete silence, until, "Can we have more?"

A loaf pan is lined with ladyfingers and then filled with the most delicious, it-can't-get-any-better-than-this, light but creamy, rich rum and banana filling. After adequate refrigeration the loaf is turned out onto a serving plate, covered with sliced bananas, and served with whipped cream. It could be called an ice-box cake, or a charlotte, or a terrine, but by any name this is happiness.

Make this at least 8 hours before serving—or make it the day before.

You need a loaf pan with a 10-cup capacity; preferably a long and narrow pan rather than a short, wide one. The pan that measures 13 3/4 by 4 1/4 by 2 3/4 inches is just right (see page 29).

The bananas should be just perfection, not the least bit overripe or underripe.

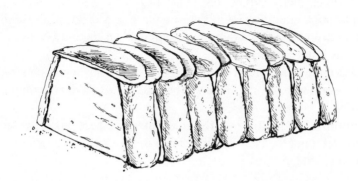

2 large bananas (about 1 pound)
Fresh and soft ladyfingers (see Note)
1 envelope unflavored gelatin
¼ cup cold water
¾ cup dark rum (i.e., Myers's)
5 egg yolks graded "large"
¾ cup granulated sugar
Pinch of salt
¼ teaspoon vanilla extract
1 cup whipping cream

Prepare a 10-cup loaf pan (see above) as follows: Fold or cut two lengths of aluminum foil, one that will cover the bottom and two short sides of the pan and another for the bottom and two long sides. Turn the pan upside down on the counter. Center one piece of the foil over the pan and press down on the sides to shape the foil to the pan. Remove the foil and set aside. Then shape the second length of foil and remove it. Turn the pan right side up. Carefully place both lengths of foil in the pan (one on top of the other in the bottom) and press into place. Do not butter the foil. Set aside.

Place the bananas in the refrigerator to chill while preparing the pan and the rum mixture.

To line the pan with ladyfingers: First, you will place ladyfingers against the long sides of the pan. Trim one rounded end of the ladyfingers (enough for the two long sides) so that they can stand up straight. Then trim the other end, making them the same length as the height of the pan. Press a row of these trimmed ladyfingers, rounded side against the pan, along the two long sides of the pan. Place them very close to each other—the closer the better (trim the long edges a bit if necessary to make a tight fit). Do not line the short sides of the pan with ladyfingers.

Then cut both ends of enough ladyfingers to fill in the bottom of the pan, placing them crosswise in the pan and rounded side against the pan. Chop or crumble a few ladyfingers to sprinkle on the bottom in order to fill in any empty spaces.

Place the remaining trimmings and/or a few ladyfingers on a sheet in a very low oven to dry out; these will be used to make a dry crumb topping. Set aside.

Sprinkle the gelatin over the cold water in a heat-proof glass custard cup and let stand for a few minutes. Then stir in ¼ cup of the rum (reserve remaining ½ cup rum).

Let stand for 5 minutes. Then place the cup in a shallow pan of hot water over low heat and stir occasionally until the gelatin is dissolved. Remove from the hot water and set aside.

In the top of a small double boiler—off the heat—beat the yolks with a portable electric mixer or a manual egg beater for a minute or so. Then gradually add the sugar, beating constantly. Place over warm water on low-medium heat and continue to beat without stopping for 3 minutes (no longer).

Remove the top of the double boiler and, without waiting, transfer the mixture to the large bowl of an electric mixer.

On low speed gradually beat in the warm gelatin mixture and then beat in the reserved ½ cup of rum along with the salt and vanilla. Let stand.

In a chilled bowl with chilled beaters whip the cream until it holds a shape that is almost but not quite stiff. Set aside.

Place the bowl of egg-yolk mixture into a larger bowl of ice and water and stir and scrape the bowl constantly until the mixture thickens to the consistency of a medium cream sauce; it takes 12 to 13 minutes.

When the mixture has thickened, remove the bowl from the ice and water (but reserve the bowl of ice and water) quickly before the mixture thickens too much. Fold one fourth of the yolk mixture into the whipped cream, fold in another fourth, and then fold the cream into the remaining yolk mixture. If necessary, gently pour the mixture from one bowl to the other to ensure thorough blending, finally leaving the mixture in the large bowl.

Peel the refrigerated bananas and slice them into rounds ½ inch thick. Gently fold the bananas into the yolk-and-rum mixture. Return the bowl to the ice and water and fold gently for a few minutes to chill and thicken the mixture a bit more in order to prevent the bananas from sinking.

Pour the mixture into the prepared pan. Smooth the top.

With your fingers or in a food processor crumble a few of the dried ladyfingers to make crumbs. Then sprinkle the crumbs over the top (to prevent the dessert from sticking to the serving plate when it is inverted).

Refrigerate uncovered until the mixture becomes firm, and then cover the pan with plastic wrap. If the filling does not reach to the top of the ladyfingers, wait until the filling becomes firm, and then, with the tip of a small sharp knife, trim the ladyfingers level with the filling.

Complete the folowing presentation up to an hour or two before serving.

TOPPING

⅓ cup apricot preserves
1 teaspoon water
2 to 3 medium-to-large bananas

In a small saucepan stir the preserves and water over moderate heat until melted. Strain through a strainer over a small bowl. Set aside briefly.

Cover the terrine with a long serving plate or a chocolate-roll board (see page 31) and turn the pan and plate or board upside down. Remove the pan and the foil.

Peel the bananas. On a cutting board slice the bananas about ¼ inch thick on a sharp angle, making slices 3 inches long or even longer (the long slices are stunning).

Brush a thin layer of the apricot glaze on the top of the terrine. Place the banana slices crosswise (the length of the banana slice should be at a right angle to the length of the terrine) on the top, deeply overlapping each other. If some of the banana slices actually extend over the edge of the terrine, leave them that way—the look is gorgeous. Now pour or brush a generous layer of the remaining glaze over the bananas (the glaze will prevent the bananas from discoloring for a few hours).

Refrigerate uncovered.

WHIPPED CREAM

1½ cups whipping cream
¾ teaspoon vanilla extract
3 tablespoons confectioners sugar

In a small chilled bowl with chilled beaters whip the cream with the vanilla and sugar until it just barely holds a definite shape. It should hold a mound but not a point when the beaters are raised. Serve, or cover and refrigerate.

If the cream has been prepared ahead of time, it will probably separate a bit while standing. If so, whisk it a bit with a wire whisk just before serving.

Spoon a mound of the cream alongside each portion.

NOTE: The recipe for homemade ladyfingers is on page 257. If you plan to use bought ladyfingers, buy 3 packages or 6 to 9 ounces.

Tiramisu

12 PORTIONS

This old Italian favorite just recently became popular in America, and it took the country by storm. It reminds me—vaguely—of an American ice-box cake. It is made with ladyfingers and a light chiffonlike mixture (the ladyfingers and chiffon mixture are layered together in a shallow casserole). But Mamma Mia—*this is something else! It is totally irresistible. An important dessert for an important event. Magnificent. Exciting. Although it can be made with bought ladyfingers, you might like to try it (and I hope you will) with homemade chocolate ladyfingers. The ladyfingers are soaked in a mixture of strong espresso and Grand Marnier, and the chiffon mixture is made with mascarpone (see Note), dark rum, whipped cream, and beaten egg whites. The top is sprinkled generously with unsweetened cocoa powder.*

Make this one to two days before serving. Serve it from the kitchen. Even with adequate chilling time the texture will not be firm (not as firm as a gelatin mixture), but it should not be soupy or runny. The texture of a perfect tiramisu *should be semifirm; it should almost but not quite hold its shape when you serve it.*

Incidentally, tiramisu *means "pick me up," as in "This will pick me up—it will give me a lift. It will put me on cloud nine."*

Chocolate Ladyfingers (see page 258) or 6 to
8 ounces bought ladyfingers, to make
two layers in a casserole that measures
about 13 by 9 inches
1¼ cups prepared unsweetened strong
espresso (I use 5 tablespoons instant
espresso powder in 1¼ cups hot water;
it is stronger than brewed espresso)
6 tablespoons Grand Marnier
16 to 17½ ounces (about 2 cups)
mascarpone (see Note)
¼ cup dark rum
5 eggs graded "large," separated
6 tablespoons granulated sugar
2 cups whipping cream
½ teaspoon vanilla extract
⅛ teaspoon salt
Unsweetened cocoa powder (preferably
Dutch-process)

You will need an oblong casserole that measures about 13 by 9 by 2 inches; it should have at least a 14-cup capacity. Set the casserole aside.

Set the ladyfingers aside.

Mix the espresso and the Grand Marnier. Place half of the mixture in a shallow bowl large enough to dip the ladyfingers into (reserve the remaining half of the mixture).

One at a time place a ladyfinger in the espresso mixture. Turn it upside down two or three times until it is well moistened but not until it starts to fall apart. Place the ladyfingers flat side down in the casserole. Place them close together to make a fairly solid layer; if necessary, cut some of the ladyfingers to fill in large empty spaces. If some of the espresso mixture is left over in the shallow bowl, drizzle it onto the moistened ladyfingers.

Reserve enough of the ladyfingers to make a second layer (you will form two layers of ladyfingers alternating with two layers of the mascarpone mixture). Set the casserole aside.

Place the mascarpone in a large bowl. Add the rum and beat or whisk until smooth. Set aside.

In the top of a small double boiler over warm water on medium-low heat beat the yolks using a manual or hand-held electric mixer with 3 tablespoons of the sugar (reserve the remaining 3 tablespoons sugar) for 3 minutes or until light and foamy. Remove from the heat and, without waiting, stir or beat the yolk mixture into the mascarpone mixture. Set aside.

In a chilled bowl with chilled beaters whip the cream with the vanilla until the cream just holds a firm shape.

In two small additions fold about one third of the mascarpone mixture into the whipped cream. Then fold the whipped cream into the remaining mascarpone mixture. Set aside.

In the small bowl of an electric mixer, with clean beaters beat the egg whites with the salt on moderate speed until foamy. Increase the speed to high and beat until the whites hold a soft shape. Gradually add the remaining 3 tablespoons of sugar and continue to beat on high speed only until the whites just hold a straight shape when the beaters are raised but not until dry. Do not overbeat. Add the beaten whites all at one time to the mascarpone-and-cream mixture and fold together.

Pour half of this mixture over the layer of ladyfingers. Smooth the top.

Pour the remaining espresso mixture into the shallow bowl. To make a second layer of ladyfingers, dip them one at a time—as above—and place them flat side down close together on top of the mascarpone layer.

If any of the espresso mixture is left over, drizzle it onto the ladyfingers.

For the top layer, pour the remaining mascarpone mixture over the ladyfingers. Smooth the top. (The dish will be very full.)

Refrigerate uncovered.

After a few hours in the refrigerator (or longer if more convenient), sift or strain a dense layer (no white showing through) of the cocoa all over the top. Wipe the rim of the casserole. Cover with plastic wrap and continue to refrigerate at least overnight.

Just before serving sift or strain a little more cocoa on top.

The *tiramisu* should be served very cold, preferably on chilled plates.

To serve: You can't be "chicken" when you serve this; you have to be gutsy. Cut the *tiramisu* into oblongs with a small sharp knife. Then, courageously, slide a wide metal spatula under a portion, lift it and move it over a dessert plate, and with another wide metal spatula push it off, trying to keep it top side up as much as possible.

NOTE: Mascarpone is an unsalted Italian cheese similar to cream cheese, but smoother, richer, and softer. It is extremely perishable and should be used soon after it is purchased. It is available in some Italian markets and some cheese shops, and from Dean & DeLuca (see page 29). Five hundred grams equal $17\frac{1}{2}$ ounces; that is the amount I use. However, if you buy 1 pound, or 16 ounces, you can make the recipe with that amount.

Strawberry Trifle-Charlotte

8 PORTIONS

A trifle is an English dessert prepared in a glass bowl with pieces of sponge cake or ladyfingers coated or sandwiched with jam, soaked in sherry, and topped with a soft custard. A charlotte is a French dessert prepared in a charlotte mold (a round container, rather deep, with a flat bottom), lined with ladyfingers, filled with a custard-and-gelatin mixture, and turned out of the mold before serving.

This half-breed is a combination of a creamy custard made with gelatin and diced strawberries—and bite-sized jelly sandwiches on chocolate sponge cake—layered together in a clear glass bowl. It is served at the table spooned onto dessert plates.

It is simple-looking, but gorgeous; the almost-black sandwiches against the almost-white custard look fancy and festive. This is not a quickie, but it is not difficult.

The chocolate sponge cake can be made ahead of time; it can be wrapped and refrigerated overnight or it can be frozen. The finished dessert should be refrigerated for at least 5 or 6 hours, but overnight is best (it will be heavenly either way, but will hold together a little better while serving after being refrigerated overnight).

You will need a clear glass serving bowl with an 8-cup capacity. I use a 6½-by-3½-inch straight-sided glass soufflé dish (see page 31). And you will need a sugar thermometer.

Chocolate Sponge Roll (see page 35)
¾ to 1 cup seedless strawberry or raspberry
jam
½ pound fresh strawberries (to make a
generous 1 cup, diced), plus 1 large
berry to place on top just before serving
2 tablespoons plus ⅔ cup granulated sugar
2 tablespoons kirsch
1 envelope unflavored gelatin
3 tablespoons cold tap water
1 cup milk
4 egg yolks graded "large"
Pinch of salt
1 cup whipping cream
1 teaspoon vanilla extract

Prepare the cake for chocolate sponge roll up to and including turning the cake out of the pan and removing the foil lining. Then, with a long sharp knife, cut the cake in half, cutting through both of the long sides.

In a small bowl stir the jam until it is soft and smooth, and spread it over half of the cake, spreading it on a side that was the bottom of the cake. Smooth with a long, narrow metal spatula. Sandwich with the other half of the cake, bottoms together.

The cake will now be cut into 1-inch squares. It will be easier to cut the squares if you freeze the cake a bit first; slide a flat-sided cookie sheet under the cake and place it in the freezer for approximately 30 minutes (it is not necessary to cover the cake while it is in the freezer). Then cut the cold cake into 1-inch squares. Wrap airtight and set aside.

Wash, hull, and drain the berries. Dice them into ¼-inch pieces. Place in a small bowl with 2 tablespoons of the sugar (reserve remaining ⅔ cup sugar) and the kirsch. Let stand at room temperature, turning occasionally with a rubber spatula.

In a small cup sprinkle the gelatin over the water, stir with a knife to mix, and let stand.

In a small heavy saucepan over moderate heat scald the milk uncovered until it just starts to bubble around the edge.

Meanwhile, in the small bowl of an electric mixer beat the yolks at high speed to mix well. Gradually add the remaining ⅔ cup of sugar and continue to beat for a few minutes until pale and thick. Reduce the speed to low and gradually—only a small amount at a time at first—add the hot milk and the salt, scraping the bowl as necessary with a rubber spatula.

Transfer this custard mixture to the top of a large double boiler over hot water on moderate heat. Insert a sugar thermometer. Stir and scrape the bottom and sides constantly with a rubber spatula until the mixture thickens enough to coat a spoon and the thermometer registers 180 degrees. Add the softened gelatin, remove the top of the double boiler, and stir for a minute or two until the gelatin is completely dissolved. Transfer to a larger bowl and set aside.

In a chilled bowl with chilled beaters whip the cream just until it holds a shape and set aside.

Strain the diced strawberries through a strainer set over a small bowl. Set the berries aside. Pour the strained juice into a small saucepan. Place over high heat and let boil uncovered until the juice is reduced to 1 tablespoon. Stir the reduced juice into the custard mixture.

Place this bowl of custard mixture into a larger bowl of ice and water, add the vanilla, and stir constantly until the mixture begins to thicken. When you see the first signs of thickening raise the bowl from the ice and water and stir briskly. If the mixture still looks thin (like milk), return it to the ice and water and stir. However, when it begins to have a thicker consistency (more like a heavy cream or a light white sauce), work quickly (the cold bowl will continue to set the mixture) and, in two additions, fold half of the custard into the whipped cream and then fold the whipped cream into the remaining custard. Do not handle any more than necessary. Pour back and forth from one bowl to another if necessary to incorporate the mixtures thoroughly.

Then, gently, fold in the diced and drained strawberries.

Without waiting, pour a very thin layer of the custard into the serving dish—barely enough to cover the bottom of the dish—and place a layer of the jelly sandwiches on top. Place some of the sandwiches right up against the side of the dish, carefully, in order to make an attractive pattern. Pour on half of the remaining custard. Make a second layer of the sandwiches, and cover that with the balance of the custard.

Cover airtight with plastic wrap and refrigerate for at least 5 or 6 hours, or overnight.

Just before serving, slice the reserved strawberry to fan it out (see page 22) and place it in the middle on top.

Serve at the table with a large serving set; spoon out the portions and serve on flat dessert plates.

Additional strawberries may be served alongside each portion if you wish.

Ethereal Chocolate Mousse Cake with Bittersweet Chocolate Sauce

24 PORTIONS

Chocolate on chocolate on chocolate, sprinkled with cocoa, and served with a bittersweet chocolate sauce. All gossamer—as light as air. Extravagant and luxurious—and yet simple. This consists of two sheets of incredible, flourless chocolate sponge cake (one baked after the other) with a 1 1/2-inch-deep filling of exquisite chocolate mousse. Although it takes time, it is so exciting and the results are so great that the time will fly (it does for me).

The whole thing can be made a day ahead, or two or three days ahead if you wish (it must be finished at least one day before serving), and must be refrigerated until serving time. Or it can be frozen (see Note).

This is perfect for a large and wonderful party.

You need a 15 1/2-by-10 1/2-by-1-inch jelly-roll pan (see page 30) for baking the sponge cakes. And you need a 13-by-9-by-2 or 2 1/2-inch pan with a 16-cup capacity in which to put the layers and the filling together. The standard pan with these dimensions has only a 14-cup capacity, but the Magic Line pan (see page 30) has straight sides (that do not flare out at the top) and perfectly square corners (as opposed to rounded corners), and it has a 16-cup capacity. This is the pan I use. (If you do not have a large enough pan, you can use one slightly smaller. Simply use only as much of the filling as you have room for; chill the remainder in small cups and serve separately.)

FLOURLESS CHOCOLATE SPONGE SHEET

The lightest of all sponge cakes. Actually, this is a flourless chocolate soufflé. But since it is not served immediately when it has risen, it falls—as it should—wonderfully.

6 eggs graded "large," separated
¾ cup granulated sugar
1 teaspoon vanilla extract
¼ cup plus 1 tablespoon sifted unsweetened
    cocoa powder (preferably Dutch-process),
    plus additional cocoa to sprinkle on
    before serving
¼ teaspoon salt

Adjust a rack one-third up from the bottom of the oven and preheat the oven to 400 degrees. Prepare a 15½-by-10½-by-1-inch jelly-roll pan as follows: Turn the pan upside down. Center an 18-inch length of regular-weight aluminum foil over the pan—shiny side down. With your hands press down on the sides and corners to shape the foil to fit the pan. Remove the foil and turn the pan right side up. Use a piece of crumpled plastic wrap to spread soft (not melted) butter all over the pan. Place the shaped foil in the pan, pressing against the foil with a pot holder or folded towel to make a perfect fit. Butter the foil all over with the crumpled plastic wrap and more soft butter. Then sift flour lightly all over the pan. Over the sink, turn the pan from side to side to shake the flour all over the bottom and sides, and then turn the pan upside down and tap to remove excess flour. Set the pan aside.

In the small bowl of an electric mixer beat the egg yolks with half of the sugar (reserve remaining half of the sugar) and the vanilla at high speed for 5 minutes or until the mixture is pale and thick and forms a ribbon when the beaters are raised.

On low speed add the cocoa and beat, scraping the bowl with a rubber spatula, only until thoroughly mixed. Remove the bowl from the mixer and set aside.

Unless you have an additional pair of beaters for the mixer, wash and dry the beaters. In the large bowl of the electric mixer, with clean beaters beat the egg whites with the salt until the whites hold a soft shape. Reduce the speed to moderate and gradually add the remaining half of the sugar.

Then, on high speed again, beat the whites until they just hold a straight shape when the beaters are raised (but do not beat until too stiff and/or dry).

In a few additions, small at first, fold about half of the whites into the chocolate mixture. Then fold the chocolate mixture into the remaining whites. Do not handle any more than necessary.

Turn into the prepared pan. With the bottom of a large spoon smooth the batter lightly, making it the same thickness all over. Place the cake in the oven and immediately reduce the temperature to 375 degrees.

Bake at 375 degrees for 30 minutes or until the top just springs back when lightly pressed with a fingertip. (The cake will rise dramatically while baking, and then it will sink. It is supposed to.)

While the cake is baking, spread out a dry kitchen towel, preferably smooth cotton, flour sacking, or linen.

As soon as the cake is done, invert the pan onto the towel and remove the pan. Let the cake stand as is for 20 minutes.

Then peel off the foil as follows: First, slowly and gently, remove the foil from the four sides of the cake. Then, in several large pieces, remove the rest of the foil. Let the cake stand.

Repeat directions to make a second sponge sheet.

To prepare a pan for putting the layers together with the filling, place a 9-by-13-by-2- or 2½-inch pan upside down. Tear off a piece of aluminum foil large enough to line the bottom and all four sides. (If the pan has sharp, square corners, you may prefer heavy-duty foil for this—there is less chance that the sharp corners will tear it.) Center the foil shiny side down over the pan. With your hands press down on the sides and corners to shape the foil to fit the pan. Remove the foil. Turn the pan right side up. Place the foil in the pan and press against the foil with a pot holder or a folded towel to make it fit perfectly. Set the pan aside.

Cut both layers of the cake as follows: If you have used a pan with straight sides, center the pan right side up on one of the cakes, and cut around the pan to make the cake fit securely in the pan. Repeat with the second cake. But if you have used a pan that flares out at the top, cut one layer to fit the bottom of the pan, and then turn the pan upside down to make the second layer fit in the top of the pan. Always center the pan over the cake.

Place one layer of cake, smooth side (top side) down, in the pan. Reserve the second layer of cake. Prepare the filling.

CHOCOLATE MOUSSE FILLING

2 cups whipping cream

3 tablespoons sour cream (this simply adds to the flavor)

12 ounces semisweet or bittersweet chocolate

2 ounces (½ stick) unsalted butter

¼ cup dark rum

4 eggs, separated, plus 2 egg yolks, graded "large"

1 tablespoon instant espresso or coffee powder or granules

¼ cup boiling water

1 teaspoon vanilla extract

⅛ teaspoon salt

¼ cup granulated sugar

In the large bowl of an electric mixer beat the whipping cream (which must be very cold) with the sour cream until the mixture is the consistency of soft whipped cream and refrigerate.

Cut the chocolate into pieces and place it in the top of a large double boiler over warm water on moderate heat. Cut the butter into pieces and add it to the chocolate, along with the rum. Cook, covered, until almost melted. Then stir until melted and smooth.

Remove the top of the double boiler. Then, with a portable beater, beat in the 6 egg yolks, one or two at a time. Dissolve the espresso or coffee in the boiling water and add to the chocolate mixture along with the vanilla. Beat gently with the beater until perfectly smooth.

Transfer the mixture to a large mixing bowl (use an 8-quart bowl—see page 16—if you have one), and let stand until cool.

In the clean small bowl of the electric mixer, with clean beaters beat the 4 egg whites with the salt until the whites hold a soft shape (a point that bends over). Reduce the speed to moderate and gradually add the sugar. Then beat on high speed again just until the whites hold a straight point when the beaters are raised but not until they are stiff or dry. Remove the bowl from the mixer.

Remove the whipped cream from the refrigerator. Whisk it briskly a bit with a large wire whisk to be sure it is all smooth; it should be firm enough to almost but not completely hold a shape.

Add about one third of the whipped cream to the chocolate mixture and fold together. Then add the remaining whipped cream and the beaten egg whites at the same time and fold together just until the color is even.

Pour the mousse over the layer of cake in the pan. With the bottom of a spoon, smooth the mousse. Cover the mousse with the remaining layer of cake; this time place the smooth side (top side) up. Press on the cake very gently with your hands. The cake should fit the pan tightly.

Cover the cake and pan with plastic wrap, folding it down around the sides. Refrigerate overnight, or for 2 or 3 days, if you wish.

BITTERSWEET CHOCOLATE SAUCE WITH COCOA
1½ CUPS

1 cup strained unsweetened cocoa powder
    (preferably Dutch-process)
¾ cup granulated sugar
1¼ teaspoons instant espresso or coffee
    powder or granules
Pinch of salt
1 cup boiling water
1 tablespoon plus 1½ teaspoons dark rum

In a heavy 5- to 6-cup saucepan stir the cocoa, sugar, espresso or coffee, and salt to mix. Add the water and stir with a wire whisk to mix.

Place over moderate heat and stir and scrape the pan constantly with a rubber spatula until the mixture comes to a boil. Immediately reduce the heat to low and let barely simmer, stirring and scraping the pan constantly with a rubber spatula, for 3 minutes.

Remove from the heat. Strain. Stir in the rum. Place in a covered jar and refrigerate.

Check the sauce ahead of time. If it has become too thick to serve, let it stand at room temperature and stir it a bit.

Hours before serving (or just before), remove the plastic wrap from the cake. Cover the cake pan with a large serving board or cutting board, turn the pan and board upside down, remove the pan and the foil.

Cover the top of the cake with a generous layer of unsweetened cocoa powder, sprinkling it on through a wide but fine strainer. Refrigerate.

To serve: Work next to the sink so that you can hold the knife under hot running water before making each cut. With a long and sharp knife cut the cake into fourths. Cut each fourth into six portions. Since the filling is so light and delicate, work carefully. With a wide metal spatula transfer the pieces to cake plates.

Pour the sauce into a pitcher and pour some of the sauce on each plate along one side of the cake.

Serve quickly while it is cold.

NOTE: To serve this after freezing, thaw it covered in the refrigerator for at least 5 or 6 hours.

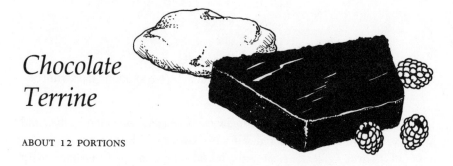

Chocolate Terrine

ABOUT 12 PORTIONS

Although this is a cake, I am putting it in the section of refrigerated desserts because it must be served refrigerated.

Terrine is a French word that originally meant an earthenware container for cooking in; it was round or oval, and deep, with a cover. Then the word came to mean the food that was cooked in the earthenware container—fish, meat, or a vegetable—frequently a combination of foods, often layered in a pattern. It is only recently that the food prepared in the terrine might be a dessert—most often chocolate. Sometimes cooked and sometimes not cooked. The shape most often used today is an oblong bread shape.

This divine dessert terrine may be served with either an elegant or a casual meal. It is an important dessert, but easy. It may be prepared days or weeks ahead and frozen. If so, transfer it from the freezer to the refrigerator for an hour or more before serving.

This is made in a metal loaf pan with an 8-cup capacity, preferably one that is long and narrow rather than short and wide. Mine measures 10¼ by 3¾ by 3¼ inches (see page 29). The loaf pan is placed in a larger pan of shallow hot water; therefore the loaf pan must be waterproof. The baked and cooled terrine is refrigerated or frozen before it is removed from the pan. It is served with Brandied Custard Sauce (see page 409) or whipped cream; today many popular restaurants sprinkle unsweetened cocoa powder, through a fine strainer, onto the whipped cream.

The terrine is dense, intense, fudgelike, caramellike, compact, concentrated, chewy, and rich—but not too sweet.

It is best to cut this with a hot and wet knife; therefore it is easiest to serve it from the kitchen.

> 8 ounces (2 sticks) unsalted butter, cut or
>   sliced
> 8 ounces semisweet or bittersweet chocolate,
>   cut or broken
> 1½ tablespoons unsweetened cocoa powder
> 1½ tablespoons instant espresso or coffee
>   powder
> ⅛ teaspoon salt
> 1¼ cups sugar
> 3 eggs plus 1 yolk, graded "large"
> 1½ tablespoons dark rum or whiskey
> ⅓ cup sifted cake flour

Adjust a rack one-third up in the oven and preheat the oven to 375 degrees.

To prepare the 8-cup loaf pan (see above): Place the pan upside down on a work surface. Cut or fold two strips of aluminum foil, one to fit the length of the bottom and the two short sides and another to fit the width of the bottom and the two long sides. Measure and cut or fold the foil carefully—it must fit perfectly (if the foil is wrinkled the dessert will be as well). To shape the foil to fit the pan, carefully place one piece shiny side down over the upside down pan and fold it down on the sides of the pan. Remove the foil and set it aside. Repeat the procedure with the second piece of foil. Let cold water run into the pan, pour out the water, but do not dry the pan (a wet pan holds the foil in place). Place the pan right side up. Carefully place one piece of the foil in the pan and press it into place. Then place the other piece in the pan and press it into place. There will be two thicknesses of foil in the bottom of the pan. The sides of the foil may be even with the top of the pan or they may extend half an inch or so above the pan (if so, fold the foil down over the rim of the pan). Since most pans flare at the top, the upper corners of the pan will probably be unlined—it is OK. To butter the pan: Place a piece of butter (additional to that called for) in the pan, place the pan in the oven to melt the butter, and then, with a pastry brush, brush the butter all over the foil and exposed corners. Set the pan aside.

Place the butter and chocolate in the top of a large double boiler over hot water on low or moderate heat and let cook, stirring occasionally, until melted. Transfer to the large bowl of an electric mixer and, without waiting—while the mixture is still hot—mix in the cocoa, espresso or coffee, salt, and sugar. And then the eggs and yolk, one at a time. Beat on low speed only until mixed. Still on low speed (air must not be beaten into this mixture), beat in the rum or whiskey and the flour. Beat only until smooth.

Pour into the prepared pan. Place the pan in a larger (but not deeper) pan and add about an inch of hot water to the larger pan.

Fold a length of aluminum foil in half, making a piece large enough to cover the loaf pan, place it loosely on top of the pan, and let it just rest on the pan.

Bake for 1½ hours. There is no way to test this; just check your oven temperature with a portable oven thermometer and watch the clock.

Then uncover the pan. The dessert will look slightly dry along the rim of the pan—it will look uncooked in the middle—and it will not have risen. Don't think of this as a cake or you will be sure it is not done. Instead, think of it as a rich custard. (Since the terrine will not rise during baking, it will appear that the pan is too large. It might be, but I have had better luck with this recipe in a pan this size than in one that just fits.)

Remove the pan from the hot water and let cool to room temperature. Then refrigerate for at least 4 hours or longer. Or freeze the terrine for 2 hours or longer. If the terrine has been frozen for more than a few hours, transfer it from the freezer to the refrigerator for about an hour before serving.

The terrine can be removed from the pan hours before serving: Dip the pan carefully in a dishpan of hot water and hold it there for 30 seconds. Dry the pan. With a small sharp knife cut around the cake in the unlined corners of the pan. Cover the pan with a serving board or platter. Turn the pan and board or platter upside down. If necessary, tap the pan lightly against the board or platter to release the cake. Remove the pan and gently peel off the foil lining. Return to the refrigerator until serving time.

To slice, hold a strong and sharp knife under hot running water or dip it into boiling water, and with the hot and wet blade slice the terrine ½ to ¾ inch thick. The portions should be small.

Pour or ladle the Brandied Custard Sauce on each plate alongside the terrine. Or place a mound of soft whipped cream alongside the terrine.

WHIPPED CREAM

1½ cups whipping cream
1 teaspoon vanilla extract
3 tablespoons confectioners sugar

In a chilled bowl with chilled beaters whip the cream with the vanilla and sugar only until the cream holds a soft shape. If it is whipped ahead of time, cover and refrigerate, and then stir lightly with a whisk just before serving.

White Chocolate Mousse with Raspberry Sauce

8 GENEROUS PORTIONS

Rich, smooth, luscious. Elegant.
   This can be made in a large glass bowl, one with at least a 10-cup capacity, or in individual large wineglasses.
   You will need a sugar thermometer.

10 ounces white chocolate
¼ cup cold tap water
1 envelope unflavored gelatin
3 eggs, separated, plus 2 whole eggs, graded "large"
⅔ cup granulated sugar
2 tablespoons cornstarch
1½ cups milk
3 tablespoons dark rum
1 teaspoon vanilla extract
1 cup whipping cream

On a large board, with a long and heavy knife shred/chop the chocolate into fine pieces. Place it in the top of a large double boiler over warm water on low heat. Cover and let cook until partially melted. Then stir with a rubber spatula until completely melted and smooth. Remove the top of the double boiler and set aside uncovered.

Place the water in a small Pyrex cup, sprinkle on the gelatin, and let stand for about 5 minutes or more to soften.

Place the 3 egg yolks (reserve the 3 whites) and the 2 whole eggs in the small bowl of an electric mixer. Add ½ cup of the sugar (reserve remaining sugar). Beat at high speed for a few minutes until the mixture is pale and thick.

In a small cup mix the cornstarch with 2 tablespoons of the milk (reserve remaining milk) and beat into the egg mixture. Transfer the mixture to the large bowl of the electric mixer.

Scald the remaining milk in a saucepan over moderate heat until it forms small bubbles around the edge. (This next step is easiest if you transfer the hot milk to a small pitcher.) Then, on low speed, gradually beat the hot milk into the egg mixture.

Transfer the mixture to a heavy 3-quart saucepan. Place over low heat and insert a sugar thermometer. Stir and scrape the bottom constantly with a rubber spatula for about 10 minutes until thickened, at which point the thermometer should register 180 degrees.

Remove from the heat. Add the softened gelatin and stir to dissolve. Whisk about a cup of the hot mixture into the chocolate, and then another cup. Then whisk the chocolate mixture into the remaining hot mixture and stir until thoroughly mixed. Transfer to a large bowl.

Let stand until cool. Or place the bowl in a larger bowl of ice and water and stir constantly until completely cool. (Do not leave the mixture over the ice water so long that it starts to set.)

Stir in the rum and vanilla.

In a small chilled bowl with chilled beaters whip the cream until it holds a shape and set aside.

In a clean small bowl with clean beaters whip the remaining 3 egg whites until they hold a soft shape. Gradually add the remaining sugar and continue to beat only until the whites just barely hold a shape, but not until they are stiff/dry.

Fold about 1 cup of the cooled white-chocolate mixture into the whipped cream and another into the beaten whites. Then, using a large rubber spatula if possible, fold the whipped cream and the beaten whites at the same time into the remaining chocolate mixture.

Gently transfer the mixture to a large serving bowl, or transfer it to a pitcher and pour into large wineglasses.

Cover the bowl or glasses lightly with paper towels, not touching the mousse. (Sometimes when you cover a dessert like this airtight with plastic wrap, condensation forms and drips back onto the dessert. The paper towels will absorb it.)

Refrigerate for about 4 to 6 hours.

Serve with a generous amount of Raspberry Chambord Sauce. If the mousse is in a large bowl, use a large serving spoon and place mounds of mousse on flat dessert plates. Pour the sauce around it. If the mousse is in glasses, pour the sauce over the tops. Pass additional sauce.

RASPBERRY CHAMBORD SAUCE
2½ CUPS

They said of some sauce, and the chef who created it, "In this sauce he could enjoy his own grandmother."

2 12-ounce packages dry-pack frozen
    raspberries
5 tablespoons Chambord (raspberry liqueur)

Thaw the berries, then puree them in a food processor, blender, or food mill. Strain through a wide but fine strainer set over a wide bowl (the strainer must be fine enough to remove all the tiny seeds).

Stir in the Chambord, and refrigerate.

NOTE: This sauce is specifically for the White Chocolate Mousse. It is a tart sauce that goes perfectly with the rich sweetness of the mousse. To use this for another dessert, you might want to add some honey to sweeten it a bit.

Cognac Espresso Mousse

6 PORTIONS

Quick and easy, rich, smooth, and creamy. This may be served as dessert, coffee, and brandy all in one because that is what it is. But you don't drink this; you eat it with a spoon. It can be made about 4 hours before serving, or the day before.

Prepare this in 6-ounce coffee cups (first choice) or wine glasses.

3 tablespoons granular or powdered instant espresso or coffee
⅓ cup granulated sugar
1 envelope unflavored gelatin
⅛ teaspoon salt
1½ cups milk
3 tablespoons cognac
1 teaspoon vanilla extract
1 cup whipping cream
Optional: semisweet chocolate or unsweetened cocoa powder or white chocolate curls (to use just before serving)

Place the espresso or coffee, sugar, gelatin, salt, and milk in a 6-cup saucepan. Stir to mix and let stand for about 3 minutes to soften the gelatin. Then whisk and stir over moderate heat for a few minutes only until the milk is warm and the espresso or coffee, sugar, and gelatin are dissolved. (Test by dipping a metal spoon in and out of the mixture; undissolved granules will show up against the metal.) Remove from the heat, pour into a rather wide bowl, and set the bowl into a larger bowl of ice and water. Stir occasionally until cool. Mix in the cognac and vanilla.

Meanwhile, in a chilled bowl with chilled beaters whip the cream until it just barely holds a shape. Set aside.

When the gelatin mixture has cooled it must be stirred constantly with a rubber spatula, and the bottom and sides of the bowl must be scraped constantly with the spatula, until the mixture thickens to the consistency of unwhipped heavy cream.

Remove the bowl from the ice and water a few seconds too soon because the bowl will remain cold and the mixture will continue to set.

(Optional: As a safety precaution, you may, if you wish, quickly pour the mixture into another bowl that is not cold.)

In about three additions—quickly but carefully—fold the gelatin mixture into the whipped cream. Then gently pour it back and forth from one bowl to another until the two mixtures are incorporated. (If there is a bit of the darker mixture that is still not incorporated, leave it as it is; it will give a slightly marbelized effect that is lovely.)

Pour the mixture into a pitcher that is easy to pour from and pour it into six 6-ounce coffee cups or wineglasses. Cover with plastic wrap or aluminum foil and refrigerate for 4 hours or longer until set.

The cups or glasses may be topped with grated semisweet chocolate if you wish. (Use a standing metal grater placed over a large piece of wax paper. Use the side that has small round—not diamond-shaped—openings: Look from the inside or the underside of the grater to tell the shape of the openings. But try different sides and use whichever you like. Grate the chocolate onto the paper and then use a teaspoon to sprinkle it over the mousse.) Or, through a fine strainer, strain unsweetened cocoa powder over the tops. Or, with a vegetable parer, scrape a few white chocolate curls over the tops.

Double Chocolate Pots de Crème

8 TO 10 PORTIONS

Quick, easy to prepare. It can be made a day ahead. Dense, dark, delicious—elegant, classy, classic. This rich custard is not baked; the texture is creamy and almost—but not really—firm. (This recipe has more than twice as much chocolate as other similar recipes I have made.)

This can be made in individual pots de crème cups with covers (3-ounce capacity), individual soufflé dishes (4-ounce capacity), or demitasse cups or wineglasses (5- to 6-ounce capacity). The recipe can be divided or multiplied.

1 pound semisweet or bittersweet chocolate
2 cups milk
1 tablespoon dry instant espresso or coffee
Pinch of salt
6 egg yolks graded "large"
1 ½ teaspoons vanilla extract

Chop the chocolate fine and set aside. In a large heavy saucepan over moderate heat, stir the milk occasionally until it just barely starts to boil. Add the chocolate and whisk until smooth. Add the espresso or coffee and the salt and whisk until the mixture just comes to a boil again.

Meanwhile, in a bowl, beat the yolks just to mix. Ladle the boiling mixture slowly into the yolks, beating on low speed only to mix. Mix in the vanilla. The mixture should be as smooth as honey; pour the hot mixture through a fine strainer into a pitcher.

Pour into 10 *pots de crème* cups or 8 soufflé dishes, demitasse cups, or wineglasses.

Refrigerate uncovered for about half an hour only until chilled, and then cover and refrigerate a few hours longer (3 to 4 hours minimum) or until the next day. (If this is not covered a skin will form on the top.)

This does not need much, but a small spoonful of soft whipped cream on each portion is nice, with a light sprinkling of unsweetened cocoa powder over the cream, if you wish.

Rancho Lemon Mousse

8 GENEROUS PORTIONS

Light, airy, fluffy, lemony, and creamy (with both whipped cream and sour cream)—a lemon cloud in lemon heaven. Simple and elegant. This recipe is from lemon country, Rancho Santa Fe in Southern California, where they can just step out the back door and pick them as they need them.

This can be made the day before serving, or at least 4 hours before. Make it in large wineglasses, if possible.

6 eggs graded "large," separated
1 envelope unflavored gelatin
3 tablespoons plus ⅓ cup cold tap water
½ cup plus ⅓ cup granulated sugar
Finely grated rind of 2 large lemons
¾ cup lemon juice
1 cup sour cream
1 cup whipping cream
⅛ teaspoon salt

In the small bowl of an electric mixer beat the egg yolks at high speed for about 5 minutes until they are pale-lemon–colored. Let stand.

In a small cup sprinkle the gelatin over 3 tablespoons of the water (reserve remaining water) and let stand.

In a 4- to 6-cup saucepan over high heat stir ½ cup of the sugar (reserve the remaining ⅓ cup sugar) with the remaining ⅓ cup of water until the mixture comes to a boil. Let boil for 3 minutes. Add the softened gelatin and remove from the heat. Stir to dissolve the gelatin. Stir in the lemon rind and juice.

In a large bowl beat the sour cream with a whisk until it is soft and smooth. Gradually whisk in the lemon mixture (which may still be warm).

Then gradually, on low speed, add the sour-cream mixture to the egg yolks, adding about ½ cupful at a time (it is handy to use a ladle for adding the sour-cream mixture). After a few additions add the yolk mixture to the remaining sour-cream mixture. Mix well.

Place the bowl of sour-cream-and-egg-yolk mixture into a larger bowl of ice and water. Stir and scrape the bowl frequently with a rubber spatula until the mixture just begins to thicken—do not let it actually set.

Meanwhile, in a chilled bowl with chilled beaters beat the whipping cream until it just holds a soft shape but not until it is stiff. Set aside.

Also meanwhile, in the large bowl of the electric mixer, add the salt to the egg whites and beat until the whites hold a soft shape. Reduce the speed to moderate and gradually add the remaining ⅓ cup of sugar. Then, at high speed again, beat briefly only until the whites hold a definite shape but not until they are stiff or dry.

When the sour-cream-and-egg-yolk mixture has started to thicken, remove it from the ice and gradually fold almost half of it into the whipped cream. Then gradually fold the whipped cream and the remaining yolk mixture (at the same time) into the beaten whites. Handle as little as possible.

Ladle or pour the mousse into eight 10- to 12-ounce wineglasses or dessert bowls, or into a serving bowl with at least a 12-cup capacity.

Refrigerate for 4 hours or more.

I think this is divine just as it is—it does not need a thing (except a spoon). Maybe a few crisp cookies on the side. Or, if you wish, pass a bowl of fresh blueberries, raspberries, strawberries, or blackberries.

Fruit

Glacéed Dried Fruit

ABOUT 30 PIECES OF
FRUIT

We had a delicious dinner at Remi, a small and lovely Venetian restaurant in Manhattan. It started with a hot garlic and chèvre cheese spread and whole wheat pasta with anchovies, onions, and caviar—and it wound up with an array of outstanding desserts. The one I rushed into our kitchen to make when we returned home was this glacéed dried fruit.

Fabulous! The only "but" is the fact that the glacéed fruit does not hold up for more than 2 or 3 hours (see Notes). Just after glacéing the fruit it will look as though it has a thin, clear coating of glass. It will sparkle like a jewel—the coating will be hard and crisp. But after standing too long the glacé coating will become sticky. Therefore, plan the timing carefully. At Remi they glacé the fruit to order.

This is a perfect way to wind up a casual dinner, or a formal banquet, or a big Thanksgiving or Christmas feast. It can be served as dessert—preferably with a few crisp cookies—or after dessert with coffee. I recently made and served a variety of glacéed dried fruit and nuts (see following recipe)—to raves—to friends who were watching an afternoon football game with us on television.

This is simple and plain, and at the same time it is chic and classy; the height of elegance. And it is fun and quick, and an exciting challenge.

You can use one or more varieties of fruit: pitted prunes, pitted dates, apricots, and/or figs. This recipe is written for about thirty pieces of fruit. You must have a sugar thermometer that gives a true reading (I use a Taylor sugar thermometer from a hardware store). And you will need a wide, airtight container to hold the glacéed fruit in a single layer. (A Rubbermaid rectangular freezer box with a lid that snaps on tight works very well).

About 30 pieces of dried fruit
About 30 strong toothpicks
1 cup granulated sugar
½ cup water
¼ cup light corn syrup

You will make a sugar-and-water syrup. While you dip the fruit in this syrup you must work alongside the stove, because it will be necessary to return the syrup to the burner occasionally or the syrup will cool off and become too thick. You will need a large surface covered with aluminum foil on which to put the glacéed fruit. Therefore, line one or two large cookie sheets with aluminum foil, shiny side up (it is not necessary to oil the foil). Place the sheet or sheets as close as possible to the stove.

Spear each piece of fruit on a toothpick, and place them on a tray next to your work area. (Instead of simply placing a toothpick in an apricot half, it is better to insert the toothpick in an edge and weave it in and out once to make the fruit secure. The prunes, figs, and dates are simply speared.)

Place the sugar, water, and corn syrup in a 6-cup heavy saucepan (the saucepan must not be too wide, or the syrup will be so shallow that the thermometer will not register). Place on moderate heat. Stir frequently with a wooden spatula until the sugar dissolves. Raise the heat to high.

When the syrup comes to a boil, cover the saucepan for 1 minute, then uncover, insert the thermometer, and let the syrup boil without stirring until the thermometer registers 300 degrees. Remove the pan from the heat. The temperature will quickly go up to 310 degrees, just from the heat of the pan; 310 degrees is the temperature for dipping.

Tilt the pan to make the syrup deep on one side. Without waiting, quickly dip a piece of the fruit, covering it completely with the syrup. Wipe the bottom of the fruit lightly against the rim of the pan to remove excess syrup. (When you place the dipped fruit on the foil, a large puddle of syrup should not form around the fruit. A small puddle is OK.) Continue to dip the fruit and place it on the foil. After several pieces are dipped, return the pan to the heat briefly to keep the syrup from cooling and thickening.

Be very careful while dipping the fruit—the syrup is extremely hot.

As soon as you have finished dipping all the fruit, place the saucepan in the sink and let hot water run into it to dissolve the remaining syrup.

Just a few minutes after the fruit is dipped, the glaze will harden and the fruit can easily be lifted from the foil.

Place the pieces of fruit in a single layer, not touching each other, in an airtight plastic freezer box. Cover the box and let stand at room temperature until serving time.

To serve, at the last moment place the fruit in a single layer, not touching each other, on a glass or china dish (not in paper candy cases and not on a paper doily—they might stick).

NOTES: I hesitate to say this, because I don't want you to count on it, but if it is a dry day, and if the fruit is in an airtight box until just before serving, the chances are that the fruit will hold up longer than 2 or 3 hours; I have served this successfully 5 hours after making it.

Glacéed Toasted Almonds

1 CUP OF GLACÉED
ALMONDS

This is a variation of the above recipe for glacéed dried fruit.

This past Christmas, Fouquet in Paris sold glacéed assorted nuts in a classy turquoise tin at an astronomical and ridiculous price, and many hundreds of the tins were shipped to customers around the world. The ones I know of arrived in New York, Colorado, and Florida in perfect condition. The magic word is airtight.

It is best to store these in an attractive glass or acrylic jar (the ones I use have a hinged lid and a rubber seal between the jar and the cover). This way, they can be served right in the jar, and the top can be reclosed quickly. In this airtight jar I have kept the nuts several days and they were still fine (even here in Florida, where it is always humid).

You will toast the almonds in the oven and make the sugar syrup from the preceding recipe. Then, working as fast as possible, you will dip the almonds in the syrup and place them singly or in mounds on aluminum foil. As soon as the coating sets and barely cools, transfer the nuts to an airtight container, and do not uncover until you are ready to serve.

5 ounces (1 cup) blanched almonds

Adjust an oven rack to the center and preheat the oven to 350 degrees. Place the almonds in a shallow metal cake pan and bake, stirring occasionally, for 10 to 12 minutes until the nuts are lightly colored and have a nutty smell.

Meanwhile, line two cookie sheets with aluminum foil, shiny side up, and place them as close as possible to the stove.

Prepare the syrup as in the preceding recipe.

Be prepared with a proper fork. If possible, the fork should have long prongs that are rather close to each other. I use a stainless-steel serving fork.

Pour about one third of the nuts into the syrup. It is important not to stir the nuts (stirring has a tendency to make the glaze opaque instead of clear). To submerge the nuts, just push them down into the syrup. Work as quickly as you can. With the long-pronged fork, lift a mound of the nuts (covered with the syrup), and wipe the bottom of the fork against the side of the pan to remove excess syrup. Use a table knife or a table fork to push the nuts off the serving fork and onto the foil, either individually or in mounds. (I do it both ways; I let the nuts go as they wish.) Quickly repeat with the remaining nuts, reheating the syrup a bit once or twice, if necessary. You must work quickly.

As soon as the glaze is dry to the touch (although the nuts may still be warm), place the nuts in an airtight container.

Vanilla Bourbon Peaches

6 TO 8 PORTIONS

This is just as good with cognac. It is a delicious dessert to serve after a formal or a casual meal. Serve with a few crisp cookies on the side. It can be made a few hours before serving, or a day before. The peaches must be freestone—and wonderful.

6 to 8 medium-large freestone peaches, ripe but firm
1 cup granulated sugar
1 vanilla bean, split and scraped (see page 10)
1½ cups water
¼ cup bourbon
Optional: fresh raspberries

To peel the peaches: Have ready a large bowl of ice-cold water, a slotted spoon, and a saucepan of boiling water deep enough to cover the peaches.

With the slotted spoon place one or two of the peaches in the boiling water. If the peaches are really ripe they will need only about 15 seconds in the boiling water; if not quite ripe they will need longer. Test one to be sure of the timing.

With the slotted spoon transfer the peach or peaches to the ice water. Peel with your fingertips, starting at the stem end. Return the peeled fruit to the ice water. Partially peeled peaches may be returned to the boiling water for additional boiling if necessary. Continue to blanch and peel all the peaches, leaving the peeled peaches in the ice water.

In a saucepan large enough to hold the peaches in a single layer, mix the sugar, vanilla bean and seeds, and the water. Over high heat bring the mixture to a boil. Boil for 5 minutes to make a syrup.

Then, with the slotted spoon, gently add the peaches to the syrup. Reduce the heat to moderate. Cover the pan and cook, turning the peaches a few times with a rubber spatula. (Or use a cake tester to turn the peaches. It does a good job without leaving any marks.) Test for doneness with a cake tester. Do not overcook. When just tender transfer the peaches with a slotted spoon to a wide, shallow bowl.

Then, over high heat, boil the syrup uncovered for 10 minutes until it is reduced to a scant 1 cup. Remove from the heat.

Add the bourbon to the hot syrup and pour over the peaches. Baste occasionally with the syrup, or ladle it over the top, until cool. Do not remove the vanilla bean.

Cover with plastic wrap and refrigerate for at least a few hours or overnight.

The peaches may be served whole or they may be halved and pitted before serving. (Whole peaches with the pits in may be a bit more work to eat, although there is no problem if they are freestone. If you serve the peaches whole, serve with a fork and spoon. You hold the peach with the fork while you use the spoon to cut it.) Whole peaches are much more special than halves.

Serve in chilled dessert bowls. Divide the syrup over the peaches.

Serve as is or with a few fresh raspberries.

NOTE: This has a strong bourbon taste shortly after it is made. But as the peaches stand in the bourbon, the flavor mellows. If you will not serve these until the following day, you might want to pass a bottle of bourbon—or simply add a bit of it to the syrup before serving.

Today's Peach Melba

When Dame Nellie Melba, the great Australian singer, gave a party at the Hotel Savoy in London in 1892, Escoffier, who was then the chef at the Savoy, created the famous Pêche Melba in her honor. A swan—symbolic of the swan in Lohengrin—carved of ice was in the center of this work of art, and around it were arranged poached peaches on a layer of vanilla ice cream. Later he improved upon this by adding a puree of fresh raspberries and a sprinkling of green (not dried) almonds.

I had my first Peach Melba many years ago at Maxim's in Paris and I'll never forget it. It was served in a wide, shallow dish like a spaghetti bowl. There was a whole (pit in) peeled stewed peach and a scoop of vanilla ice cream the same size as the peach. The peach and the ice cream were each dazzling perfection. There was a bit of sauce that seemed to be simply pureed and strained fresh raspberries, and also a few whole fresh raspberries, and a sprinkling of almonds. If the almonds were green—as opposed to dried—I didn't know it, but I have been told by a French chef, "If you can't get green almonds, then do without them; never use the dried ones for Pêche Melba" (a dictate I take with a grain of salt).

This version of Peach Melba is contemporary and timely, untraditional, and extremely delicious. This is the way I make it—today.

Vanilla Bourbon Peaches (see page 375)
Tahitian Vanilla Ice Milk (see page 328)
Bourbon
Fresh raspberries
Optional—a few toasted sliced almonds

The peaches and ice milk can be prepared a day ahead if you wish, or they can be prepared in the morning to serve that evening.

Serve in wide-topped, stemmed glasses (margarita glasses or wide champagne glasses) or in any dessert bowls.

For each portion: Drain a peach, cut it in half, separate the halves, remove the pit, cut the fruit into bite-sized pieces, and place in the glass or bowl. Add 1 to 2 tablespoons of the peach syrup (not any more). Drizzle 1 to 2 teaspoons of bourbon over the peach. Top each portion with 1 or 2 scoops of Tahitian Vanilla Ice Milk.

Sprinkle each portion with a few fresh raspberries.

And a few toasted sliced almonds if you wish.

Hot Brandied Cherries

1 PORTION

You need fresh black Bing cherries—and a cherry pitter (see page 31). After the cherries are pitted (they can be pitted ahead of time) it takes only 2 or 3 minutes to make this; if you take more time you are overcooking the cherries. They should be cooked only until they are hot, not until they are soft or lose their crispness. Serve immediately while piping hot—either in small dessert bowls or wineglasses or over vanilla ice cream.

Multiply the recipe by the number of portions you want. If you are serving this over ice cream it would appear that you could use fewer cherries, but in our house there is never enough, no matter how much I start with.

1 cup large fresh black Bing cherries
1 teaspoon unsalted butter
1 tablespoon granulated sugar
2 tablespoons kirsch
1 tablespoon cognac or Armagnac

Pit the cherries. They can wait at room temperature for a few hours or can be refrigerated for longer.

In a wide frying pan (preferably nonstick) over high heat melt the butter. Add the sugar and cherries, and stir and/or twirl the pan for about a minute until the sugar is dissolved and the cherries are hot. Do not overcook. Stir in the kirsch and cognac or Armagnac and serve immediately.

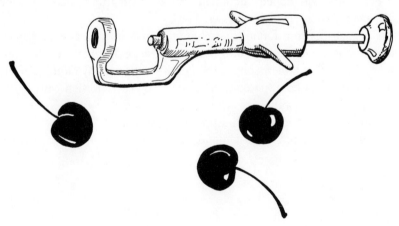

Peppered Peaches in Port

6 PORTIONS

The success of this recipe—as with all fresh fruit recipes—depends on the quality of the fruit. Do not use underripe or overripe peaches. Taste them first. Then, if the fruit is extraordinary, you might say, as I often do, "Why cook it—it is perfect as it is." One reason to cook it is that when it is cooked it can be frozen. Just picture these in the middle of winter. For a Christmas dinner. With a variety of cookies.

The peaches are stewed whole, pits in. Just before serving they can be halved and pitted, if you wish. But if they are truly freestone and if they are cooked perfectly, it is not difficult to eat the peach whole, cutting the fruit off the pit with a spoon. They look so gorgeous it is a shame to cut them before serving. And I have been told that the pits add flavor.

Serve in small bowl-shaped dishes, or in wide champagne glasses.

The flavor is pleasantly sharp—peppery, but not hot.

1 bottle (3⅓ cups) port wine (see Notes)
1 cup water
¼ cup granulated sugar
¼ cup plus 1 tablespoon mild honey
1 teaspoon finely ground black pepper (see Notes)
1 vanilla bean, split and scraped (see page 10)
2 cinnamon sticks
Optional: 2 whole cloves
6 large freestone peaches, firm but ripe

In a saucepan that will hold the peaches in a single layer, mix the wine, water, sugar, honey, and pepper. Add the vanilla bean, cinnamon sticks, and optional cloves. Let stand.

To peel the peaches: Have ready a large bowl of cold water, a slotted spoon, and a saucepan of boiling water deep enough to cover the peaches one or two at a time.

With the slotted spoon, place one or two of the peaches in the boiling water. If the peaches are fully ripe they will need only about 15 seconds; if not quite ripe they will need longer.

With the slotted spoon transfer the peach or peaches to the cold water. Peel the peach or peaches with your fingers, starting at the stem end. Return the peeled fruit to the cold water. Partially peeled peaches may be returned to the boiling water for additional boiling if necessary. Continue to blanch and peel all the peaches, leaving the peeled peaches in the cold water.

Over high heat bring the wine mixture to a boil, stirring occasionally. Then reduce the heat so that the mixture simmers.

With the slotted spoon add the peaches to the wine mixture. Cover and let simmer. Turn the peaches occasionally, either with two rubber spatulas or by inserting a cake tester into a peach and using that to turn it over. Test the peaches frequently with a cake tester. Do not overcook. The fruit should feel just barely tender. Then, with the slotted spoon, gently transfer the peaches to a wide and shallow bowl.

Over high heat boil the wine syrup uncovered for about 5 minutes to reduce slightly. Taste the syrup and continue to boil until it tastes right—not watery.

Pour the hot syrup over the peaches. Do not remove the vanilla bean or cinnamon sticks until serving time. Let cool, basting occasionally.

Cover with plastic wrap and refrigerate. Serve very cold with a generous amount of the syrup.

And serve some cookies alongside. Both the Vanilla and Chocolate Meringue Flutes (see pages 261–264) or Cat's Tongues (see page 251) are especially good with stewed fruit.

To freeze these peaches, place one or two of them in a small covered freezer container with enough—or almost enough—of the syrup to barely cover the fruit.

NOTES: Ficklin Vineyards or Gallo Livingston Cellars tawny port, both from California, work well here.

In place of the vanilla bean you can use 1½ teaspoons of vanilla extract added to the syrup after it has been reduced.

The amount of pepper can be reduced according to your taste. One teaspoon makes quite a peppery peach (it is the way we like it), ½ teaspoon is more moderate (but still delicious), or omit the pepper entirely if you wish (still delicious).

Peppered Pears in Port

6 PORTIONS

Gingered—and peppered, with a punch. These pears may be served as a dessert, or along with an entrée. As dessert they may be served with a generous amount of their delicious syrup, or drained and served alongside ice cream. We have had the pears with White Chocolate Ice Cream (see page 317), and at other times with Tahitian Vanilla Ice Milk (see page 328). The sharp and spicy pears with a sweet and bland cream is a gorgeous combination.

These stewed pears freeze well.
The pears should be just barely ripe.

1 bottle (about 3⅓ cups) port wine (see Note)
1 cup water
3 tablespoons honey
2 tablespoons syrup from preserved ginger in syrup
2 knobs preserved ginger in syrup, drained
1 teaspoon finely ground black pepper (see Notes)
1 teaspoon cinnamon
¼ teaspoon mace
6 medium-large pears, firm but ripe

In a wide and heavy saucepan stir the wine, water, honey, and syrup. Slice the ginger very thin and add it, along with the black pepper, cinnamon, and mace. (Wait until after the syrup is cooked before tasting it; it is different and better after it is cooked.)

Peel the pears with a vegetable parer. Cut them in half from top to bottom. With a melon baller remove the cores, and with a small sharp knife cut a small groove above and below the cores to remove the stems and fibers.

Place the pears in the saucepan, place over moderate heat, cover, and bring to a boil. Adjust the heat so that the syrup just simmers, and let simmer only until the pears feel tender when tested with a cake tester. The cooking time takes about 20 to 30 minutes, depending on the ripeness of the pears.

With a slotted spoon transfer the pears and sliced ginger to a wide and shallow serving bowl.

Over high heat let the syrup boil, uncovered, for about 10 minutes to reduce slightly. Pour the hot syrup over the pears. Baste frequently until cool.

Cover with plastic wrap touching the pears and the syrup. Refrigerate.

These are at their best after a few hours in the refrigerator. Serve cold.

NOTES: I have made this recipe many times with great success with inexpensive port. I have used Ficklin Vineyards as well as Gallo Livingston Cellars tawny port.

The amount of pepper can be reduced according to your taste. One teaspoon makes quite a peppery pear (it is the way we like it), ½ teaspoon is more moderate (but still delicious), or omit the pepper entirely if you wish (still delicious).

Marmalade and Grand Marnier Baked Apples

2 PORTIONS

Make baked apples only when you can get fresh and crisp baking apples, preferably Rome Beauties. Preferably not too large. Although the very large ones look dramatic, they are often mealy and blah. With good apples this is wonderful.

Multiply the recipe by any amount you wish.

2 baking apples (preferably Rome Beauties)
½ cup sweet orange marmalade
1 cup water
6 tablespoons Grand Marnier

Adjust a rack one-third up from the bottom of the oven and preheat the oven to 400 degrees. You will need a shallow ovenproof casserole that will hold the apples and have plenty of space around the sides, so that you can spoon the liquid over the apples. Butter the casserole and set aside.

Wash the apples. With a vegetable parer remove the skin from the top third of each apple. With an apple corer remove the cores from the stem end to about three fourths of the way down; do not cut through the bottoms. Place the prepared apples in the baking dish.

In a small saucepan over moderate heat stir the marmalade and water until mixed and very hot. Pour the hot mixture over the apples.

Bake for about 30 minutes, basting frequently with the syrup, using a bulb baster or a large spoon.

Test the apples with a cake tester and bake only until they are just barely tender all the way through. (Do not overbake or they will fall apart.)

As soon as you remove the casserole from the oven, pour the Grand Marnier over the apples, and baste frequently with the syrup.

These can be served warm or chilled. (If you are not familiar with warm baked apples, try them—they are delicious.)

Divide every bit of the sensational sauce over the apples.

Serve plain or with sour cream or vanilla ice cream. Or with Cream Ooh-la-la (page 392), Bittersweet Sour Cream (page 393), or Vanilla Yogurt (page 394).

Apricot-
Apple
Crumble

6 PORTIONS

A delicious casserole of juicy sliced apples and poached dried apricots (a great combination), with a hint of rum and a crisp and crunchy walnut crumb topping. This can wait at room temperature for an hour or two before it is baked. And then it can be served hot, right out of the oven, when it is most sensational. Or it can be served at room temperature.

You need a shallow ovenproof casserole with a 3-quart capacity.

CRUMB TOPPING

¾ cup unsifted unbleached flour
¼ cup unsifted whole wheat flour
½ firmly packed cup dark brown sugar
4 ounces (1 stick) unsalted butter, cold and
    cut into small pieces.

Place both flours and the sugar in a large bowl. Rub the ingredients between your fingertips until mixed. Add the butter and, with a pastry blender, cut the mixture until it resembles coarse crumbs and the pieces of butter are about the size of corn kernels. The ingredients should not hold together. Refrigerate.

FILLING

3½ ounces (1 cup) walnuts
6 ounces (1 cup) dried apricots
⅔ cup water
⅓ cup apricot preserves
4 tablespoons dark rum (or apple juice or
    orange juice)
3 pounds (about 8 medium-large) tart apples
    (preferably Granny Smith)
¼ firmly packed cup dark brown sugar

Adjust a rack to the center of the oven and preheat the oven to 350 degrees. Butter a shallow 3-quart ovenproof casserole (13 by 9 by 2 inches) and set aside.

To toast the walnuts, place them in a shallow cake pan and bake for

10 minutes, stirring occasionally, until very hot. Cool and then break them into medium-sized pieces and set aside.

Place the apricots and water in a small heavy saucepan. Bring to a boil over high heat. Then cover, reduce the heat to moderate, and let cook, stirring occasionally, until the apricots are completely tender when tested with a cake tester or a toothpick. Uncover and stir constantly until there is no liquid remaining. (While stirring, press the apricots against the sides of the pan, breaking them into coarse chunks.) Add the apricot preserves and stir until melted. Remove from the heat. Stir in the rum (or juice) and set aside.

With a vegetable parer, peel the apples. Cut them from top to bottom into halves. With a melon baller remove the cores. With a small sharp knife cut a small groove in the top and bottom of each half, removing the fibers and stems. (Or quarter the peeled apples and remove the cores and stems with a small knife.)

Cut each half into about 8 wedges and place in a large mixing bowl. Add the apricot mixture and the sugar. With a rubber spatula stir to mix well. (Each wedge should be coated with the preserves.)

Turn into the buttered casserole. With your fingers arrange the apples to level the top layer.

Sprinkle the walnuts evenly over the apples.

Then, with your fingers, sprinkle the crumb topping over the nuts.

If you are not ready to bake the casserole now, cover it with plastic wrap and let it wait at room temperature.

When you are ready to bake, adjust a rack to the center of the oven and preheat the oven to 400 degrees.

Bake the casserole, uncovered, for 30 to 40 minutes until the apples in the center are tender when tested with a cake tester or a toothpick, and the juices are bubbling, and the crumb topping is slightly browned.

Serve hot, warm, or at room temperature in bowl-shaped dishes. Serve as is or with vanilla ice cream.

Ginger Apple Betty

6 PORTIONS

This has a crisp and crunchy whole wheat bread-crumb topping over diced apples mixed with preserved ginger. Delicious, quick, and easy. It can be put together just before baking, or early in the day if you wish. Then it can be baked just before serving and can be served piping hot—right out of the oven (wonderful)—or at room temperature, or refrigerated.

You need a shallow ovenproof casserole with a 3-quart capacity.

About ½ pound whole wheat bread (preferably a light-textured bread rather than a dense and heavy loaf)
4 ounces (1 stick) unsalted butter
1 cup granulated sugar
8 knobs of stem ginger preserved in syrup (to make ⅓ cup chopped)
2 tablespoons syrup from the preserved ginger
3 pounds (6 medium-large) firm and tart apples (preferably Granny Smith)
¼ teaspoon salt
½ teaspoon cinnamon
⅛ teaspoon cloves
¼ teaspoon nutmeg
2½ ounces (½ cup) raisins
5 tablespoons Calvados, applejack, apple juice, cider, or water

Adjust a rack one-third up from the bottom of the oven and preheat the oven to 400 degrees. Butter a shallow ovenproof casserole with a 3-quart capacity (13 by 9 by 2 inches) and set aside.

To prepare the crumb topping, break the bread into coarse pieces, place it in the bowl of a food processor fitted with the metal chopping blade, and pulse to make coarse crumbs (not fine).

In a large frying pan over moderate heat melt the butter. Add all the crumbs and 2 to 3 tablespoons of the sugar (reserve remaining sugar). Stir almost constantly until the crumbs become crisp and crunchy but only slightly darker. It is important to cook the crumbs long enough or the topping will not be crisp. Set aside.

On a board, with a heavy and sharp knife chop the ginger into pieces about the size of corn kernels. Transfer to a small bowl, add the ginger syrup, and set aside.

Peel the apples with a vegetable parer, cut them in half vertically, with a melon baller remove the cores, and with a small sharp knife cut a small groove above and below the cores to remove the stems and fibers. Place the apples flat side down and cut into ½-inch dice (no smaller). Place in a large bowl.

In a small bowl mix all but 2 tablespoons of the remaining sugar with the salt, cinnamon, cloves, and nutmeg. Add to the apples and stir to mix. Mix in the raisins and ginger.

Then place the mixture in the casserole, smooth the top, sprinkle with the Calvados, applejack, apple juice, cider, or water, and then—with your fingers—sprinkle the crumb topping evenly over the apples. Sprinkle the remaining 2 tablespoons of sugar over the top.

Cover airtight with heavy-duty aluminum foil (the foil should be large enough to fold down the sides and a bit under the casserole).

Bake for 40 to 50 minutes until the apples are tender when tested with a cake tester.

Remove the foil and continue to bake, uncovered, for 10 to 15 minutes. (Total baking time is 50 to 65 minutes.)

Spoon the pudding out onto dessert plates or into dessert bowls. Serve as is, or with ice cream, sour cream, or Crème Fraîche (see page 412).

Chunky Applesauce

Many people are surprised at how quick and easy it is to make applesauce, and at how good homemade applesauce is.

5 TO 6 CUPS

3 pounds (about 9 medium) firm and tart apples (I use Granny Smith apples)
2 cups apple juice, apple-raspberry juice, or water
Optional: about ⅓ cup honey, maple syrup, or sugar

Peel the apples with a vegetable parer. Cut them in half vertically and remove the cores with a melon baller. With a small sharp knife cut a groove above and below the cores to remove the stems and blossom ends. Place flat side down on a board and cut into 1-inch squares. You will have 10 to 12 cups of apples.

Place the apples in a large, wide, and heavy saucepan. Add the juice or water. Cook, covered, over moderate heat until the liquid comes to a boil, and then simmer (reduce the heat if necessary) for 5 to 10 minutes until the apples are just barely tender. Uncover and mash with a potato masher or break up the apples with a large wooden spatula; leave some chunky pieces.

Add the optional honey, maple syrup, or sugar and stir to mix. Taste for sweetness, and add more sweetening if you wish.

The mixture should not be cooked until the liquid evaporates; it should be a little soupy—it thickens as it stands.

Applesauce can be left perfectly plain or it can be flavored with vanilla, cinnamon, nutmeg, mace, brandy, Calvados or applejack, et cetera. Raisins and/or walnuts can be mixed in or sprinkled on top.

Applesauce can be frozen.

Rhubarb and Bourbon Applesauce

Tart and chunky, with a fabulous flavor. Serve this plain, with crisp cookies on the side, or as a thick sauce with vanilla ice cream. Deep-colored rhubarb has more flavor than the pale.

SCANT 4 CUPS

2 pounds Golden Delicious apples (to make about 5 cups sliced)
1½ pounds fresh rhubarb (to make about 4 cups cut up)
½ cup maple syrup
¼ cup bourbon

Peel the apples, cut into halves from top to bottom, remove the cores with a melon baller, and, with a small sharp knife, cut small grooves above and below the cores to remove stems and fibers. Slice the apples crosswise about ¼ inch thick, and then, cutting through the slices, cut once from top to bottom. Set aside.

Wash the rhubarb, cut off the leaves, and trim the ends. Peel only if necessary (that is, if the skin is tough and stringy). Cut the rhubarb stalks into ½-inch slices.

Place the apples, rhubarb, maple syrup, and bourbon in a wide skillet or a shallow saucepan. Place over moderate heat, cover, and cook for 5 minutes. Then increase the heat to high, uncover, and stir constantly for about 10 minutes or less until the fruit is tender (the rhubarb will fall apart) and the liquid is almost completely evaporated. But a bit of the liquid should remain; it will be absorbed into the fruit as it cools.

Taste for sweetening; if necessary add more maple syrup.

If the mixture becomes too dry, add more bourbon.

Serve this either warm, at room temperature, or chilled.

NOTE: The apples should not be very tart because the rhubarb adds a good deal of tartness.

Nantucket Blueberry Crunch

A favorite recipe in blueberry season. Everyone loves it and it is quick and easy to make. You can prepare it even hours ahead of time, leave it at room temperature, and then bake it at the last minute and serve piping hot (great). Or it can be served at room temperature.

You need a shallow ovenproof casserole with a 3-quart capacity.

6 PORTIONS

3 ounces (scant 1 cup) walnuts
2 pints fresh blueberries
½ cup granulated sugar
½ teaspoon cinnamon
¼ teaspoon mace or nutmeg
Finely grated rind of 1 large and firm lemon
1 tablespoon lemon juice
¾ cup sifted unbleached flour
¼ teaspoon salt
½ firmly packed cup dark brown sugar
3 ounces (¾ stick) unsalted butter, cold and firm

Adjust a rack to the middle of the oven and preheat the oven to 350 degrees. Butter a shallow ovenproof casserole with a 3-quart capacity (13 by 9 by 2 inches) and set aside.

Place the walnuts in a shallow pan and bake for 8 to 10 minutes until very hot. Cool and then break or chop the nuts into medium or medium-small pieces and set aside.

In a large bowl of cold water wash the berries, drain, and then spread out on a paper towel. Pat the tops with a paper towel to dry. Turn the berries into a large bowl.

In a small bowl mix the granulated sugar, cinnamon, and mace or nutmeg and add to the berries. Sprinkle the rind all over and add the lemon juice. Toss gently with a rubber spatula until well mixed.

Turn the blueberry mixture into the prepared casserole. Sprinkle the walnuts evenly all over the top. Set aside.

In a bowl mix the flour, salt, and brown sugar. Cut the butter into small pieces and add to the dry ingredients. With a pastry blender cut the mixture until the mixture resembles coarse meal. Then, with your fingertips, work the ingredients to a crumbly texture.

Sprinkle the crumbs evenly all over the casserole.

Bake the casserole in the middle of the oven for 30 minutes or until the juices bubble all around the sides and the top is crusty. If necessary, to brown the top, adjust the rack high in the oven (the hottest part) and bake in that position for the last 5 or 10 minutes—do not overbake.

Serve hot or at room temperature, plain or with vanilla ice cream or Banana Ice (see page 333). To serve, use a large serving spoon and place in bowl-shaped dishes; it is gorgeous in wide spaghetti bowls.

Strawberries and Cream Ooh-la-la

6 PORTIONS

This is marvelous. The cream mixture looks like whipped cream but is lighter and has a delicious sweet-and-sour taste. Make the cream mixture not more than 2 or 3 hours before serving. Actually, the strawberries are best if they are also prepared about 2 to 3 hours before serving.

Incidentally, the cream mixture is also delicious with fresh blueberries, raspberries, or sliced peaches. Or with apple tart or baked apples. I could go on and on.

About 1½ pounds (6 cups) fresh strawberries
2 tablespoons plus ¼ cup granulated sugar
2 tablespoons Grand Marnier
¼ cup sour cream
½ cup whipping cream
2 egg whites graded "large" (they may be
    whites that were frozen and thawed)

Wash, hull, and drain the berries. Cut them lengthwise into quarters. Place in a bowl and sprinkle with 2 tablespoons of the sugar (reserve remaining ¼ cup sugar) and the Grand Marnier, and refrigerate until serving time.

No more than 2 hours before serving, prepare the Cream Ooh-la-la as follows: In a small bowl stir the sour cream until soft and set aside.

In a small chilled bowl with chilled beaters whip the cream until it just holds a shape and set aside.

In a clean small bowl with clean beaters whip the egg whites until they hold a soft shape. On moderate speed gradually add the remaining ¼ cup of sugar, and then, on high speed, continue to beat until the whites are thick and shiny and hold a soft peak (a peak that bends over).

Add the sour cream and beaten whites to the whipped cream and fold together. Refrigerate.

To serve, place the fruit in individual dessert bowls or large wineglasses and pour the Cream Ooh-la-la generously over the tops.

Strawberries with Bittersweet Sour Cream

3 PORTIONS

Multiply this recipe as you wish. Prepare it an hour or so before serving, or immediately before. It is wonderful.

12 ounces (generous 3 cups) fresh strawberries
1 tablespoon granulated sugar
2 tablespoons Grand Marnier
¾ cup sour cream
¼ cup bitter orange marmalade (made with Seville oranges)

Wash, hull, and drain the berries. Cut them in quarters and place in a bowl. Sprinkle with the sugar and Grand Marnier. Stir gently with a rubber spatula to mix, and refrigerate until serving time.

In a small bowl stir the sour cream and marmalade to mix, and refrigerate.

To serve, place the berries in individual dessert bowls or large wineglasses and pour the sour-cream mixture generously over the tops.

VARIATION: Use a mixture of cut strawberries and sliced bananas instead of only strawberries.

Strawberries with Vanilla Yogurt

Multiply this recipe as you wish. Prepare it hours before serving, or immediately before. Delicious.

3 PORTIONS

12 ounces (generous 3 cups) fresh
    strawberries
1 tablespoon granulated sugar
2 tablespoons Grand Marnier
2 cups plain yogurt
1 teaspoon vanilla extract
⅔ cup strained confectioners sugar

Wash, hull, and drain the berries. Cut them in quarters and place in a bowl. Sprinkle with the sugar and Grand Marnier. Stir gently with a rubber spatula to mix, and refrigerate until serving time.

In a small bowl whisk the yogurt with the vanilla and sugar. Refrigerate.

To serve, place the berries in individual dessert bowls or large wine-glasses and pour the yogurt mixture generously over the tops.

Strawberry-Rhubarb Compote

6 PORTIONS

Fresh rhubarb is available in the spring and early summer. This is a lovely dessert as it is— or use it as a sauce with vanilla ice cream or bread pudding. Generally, in all fresh rhubarb recipes, it is better to use thin stalks rather than thick, fibrous ones (but this is delicious even with the thick and old stalks). The leaves of rhubarb are poisonous and should never be eaten. If the stalks are thin and tender they should not be peeled, only washed. If they are thick and have a tough and stringy exterior they should be peeled with a vegetable parer (as you would peel celery).

2 pounds fresh rhubarb
    (about 5 cups, cut up)
1 vanilla bean, split and scraped
    (see page 10)
2 cinnamon sticks
Pinch of salt
¾ cup granulated sugar
Pinch of nutmeg
12 ounces (generous 3 cups) fresh
    strawberries

Adjust a rack one-third up from the bottom of the oven and preheat the oven to 375 degrees. Wash the rhubarb, cut off the leaves, and trim the ends. Peel only if necessary (that is, only if the skin is tough and stringy). If the stalks are thin, cut them into 1-inch pieces; if the stalks are thicker than 1 inch, cut them into ¾-inch pieces. Place the rhubarb in a heavy saucepan or casserole with a cover. Bury the vanilla bean and the seeds and cinnamon sticks in the rhubarb. Sprinkle with the salt, sugar, and nutmeg. (Do not add any water; rhubarb gives off a large amount of juice.)

Cover airtight and bake for 30 to 40 minutes until tender (test early— do not overbake).

Meanwhile, wash and hull the berries, and cut them into halves or large pieces.

As soon as the rhubarb is tender, remove the casserole from the oven, add the strawberries, and cover so that the berries will soften without actually cooking. Let cool.

Refrigerate for several hours or overnight.

Remove the vanilla bean and cinnamon sticks just before serving.

Prunes in Armagnac

1 QUART

Although these may be served as they are for dessert, I find that on many more occasions I use them with something else. They are wonderful with vanilla ice cream, or with Peppered Pears in Port (see page 381), or with Peppered Peaches in Port (see page 379). I have diced about 1/2 cup or more of the prunes and added them to Ginger Apple Betty (see page 386) before baking, and I have also served them alongside baked apples (a big hit). I have put them in a cheesecake (see page 297) and in ice cream (see page 325). I pureed the prunes and added the puree to brownies (see page 195). Alongside a chocolate cake (any chocolate cake) they are spectacular.

Armagnac is the name of a brandy distilled from wines in southwest France. It has a highly prized, distinctive flavor. However, cognac can replace Armagnac in this recipe—it will be slightly different but equally delicious.

There is practically nothing involved with preparing the prunes. And they last—and last. (They should stand for at least a week before they are served. However, for a puree to use in other recipes an hour is enough if you are in a hurry.) A jar of these is a great gift (especially at Christmas).

1/2 cup granulated sugar
1/3 cup port wine
12 ounces (2 cups) pitted prunes
1/2 cup Armagnac

In a 1-quart heavy saucepan over moderate heat stir the sugar and port until the sugar is dissolved and the syrup comes to a boil. Add the prunes, stir gently, and reduce the heat so that the syrup simmers. Cover and let simmer, stirring occasionally, until the prunes are completely tender when tested with a cake tester or a toothpick. Most prunes today are moist and tender to begin with and do not need more than 15 minutes.

Then cool to tepid, add the Armagnac, stir gently, and transfer to a jar with a cover. Press down on the prunes to submerge them all. Cover. Refrigerate. Let stand; I have kept them for many months.

Shake the jar occasionally and press down on the prunes, or turn the jar occasionally from end to end.

Sauces

Tahitian Vanilla Chocolate Sauce

SCANT 1½ CUPS

This is a favorite recipe of my friend Marilyn Evins. Basically, it is a classic recipe, but it calls for a whole vanilla bean, which is most unusual in a chocolate sauce. The flavor is intense, rich, and complex. Seductive. The sauce may be refrigerated for several days before using. It should be reheated in a double boiler if it becomes too thick. (Don't go near it with a spoon when it is cold and very thick if you want any left to serve.)

1 Tahitian vanilla bean (see page 31) split
and scraped (see page 10)
Granulated sugar (as necessary to prepare the
vanilla bean)
1 cup whipping cream
1 teaspoon unsalted butter
Tiny pinch of salt
4 ounces semisweet chocolate

Prepare the vanilla bean.

Place the cream in a small heavy saucepan and add the vanilla pod and seeds. Slowly bring the cream to a boil over moderate heat. Add the butter and salt, then cover and remove from the heat. Let stand for about half an hour.

Meanwhile, chop the chocolate into medium-sized pieces and place in the top of a small double boiler over warm water on moderate heat. Stir occasionally until melted and smooth.

When the cream is ready, remove the bean pod and scrape it between your fingers to get every bit of flavor into the cream. Then gradually whisk the cream into the chocolate.

Serve slightly warm or at room temperature. Stir well before serving.

Creamy Milk Chocolate Sauce

This is an unusual and delicious sauce. It is easy although it cooks for half an hour, and it has whipped cream is folded in before serving. It can be made a day or two ahead if you wish. It must be served cold. Over vanilla ice cream it is stupendous.

2½ CUPS

8 ounces milk chocolate
1 cup warm tap water
½ cup whipping cream

Break up the chocolate and place it in the top of a large double boiler over hot water on moderate heat. Add 3 tablespoons of the water (reserve remaining water) and cook, stirring frequently until melted and completely smooth.

Very gradually whisk in the remaining water. Increase the heat to high and cook, uncovered, for half an hour, frequently stirring and scraping the pan with a rubber spatula. (The mixture will thicken only slightly.)

Remove the top of the double boiler and let the sauce cool, stirring occasionally.

Transfer to a covered container and refrigerate until cold, or for a few days if you wish.

Either just before serving or a few hours before, whip the cream in a small chilled bowl with chilled beaters until it holds a semifirm shape when the beaters are raised.

Stir the chocolate to mix and gradually, in small additions, fold the chocolate into the whipped cream. Pour the sauce from one bowl to another once or twice to ensure thorough blending.

Cover and refrigerate until serving time. The sauce should always be served ice cold. If the sauce has been refrigerated overnight after folding in the whipped cream, some of the chocolate might settle. If so, pour gently from one bowl to another to blend.

Dutch Chocolate Sauce

2 CUPS

Thick and deliciously gooey.

During the time that I worked on the recipes for "Ice Cream—the Best in the World" (see page 312) I wanted a sauce that could be stirred into any ice cream and then frozen in an ice cream container. Or poured over the top of the ice cream in the container and then frozen. Most of the sauces I tried were too hard when they were frozen.

This yummy stuff seems to stay just right when it is frozen.

Try this: Make the sauce, cool it, and make Café Liègeoise (see page 323). After the Café Liègeoise has been frozen in an ice cream churn, add the sauce, drizzling it into the ice cream and stirring only slightly so that the sauce remains in thick globs. Then freeze. (I think that this sauce and Café Liègeoise are wonderful together, but of course any other ice cream can be used.)

1 cup light cream (light cream has 18 percent butterfat)
¼ cup water
1 cup granulated sugar
1 cup strained unsweetened cocoa powder (preferably Dutch-process)

In a saucepan with at least an 8-cup capacity bring the cream to a boil. Add the water and sugar, stir over moderate heat until the mixture comes to a boil, and boil, stirring, for 2 minutes.

Then, in the top of a large double boiler, whisk the hot cream mixture with the cocoa until perfectly smooth. Place over boiling water on moderate heat and let cook, stirring and scraping the sides frequently for 20 minutes.

If the sauce is not absolutely smooth, strain it.

This may be served hot, cool, or cold, although I love it best mixed into an ice cream and frozen (see above). When frozen, it has a remarkably delicious consistency.

Bittersweet Chocolate Sauce

You can use semisweet chocolate in place of the bittersweet. The sauce will be equally wonderful (even though it may be a tiny bit sweeter). But if you have Callebaut bittersweet chocolate (see page 13), use it for this. The best!

¾ CUP

4 ounces bittersweet chocolate
2 tablespoons unsalted butter
1 tablespoon unsweetened cocoa powder
5 tablespoons boiling water
1 tablespoon cognac

Chop the chocolate and place it in a small heavy saucepan over low heat. Add the butter. Stir occasionally until almost melted.

Meanwhile, place the cocoa in a small cup. Add about 2 tablespoons of the boiling water and stir to mix. Then gradually stir in the remaining water and the cognac.

Add to the chocolate mixture and whisk until smooth.

Remove from the heat.

This should be served at room temperature, but if it thickens too much as it stands, it should be warmed briefly over low heat until fluid.

NOTE: After this stands at room temperature for an hour or two it thickens to a heavenly consistency that is just right for an icing. It will be gloriously shiny and glossy. It can be spread smooth or swirled into peaks. This amount is right for a single-layer 8- or 9-inch round cake.

Mocha Caramel Sauce

2 CUPS

Thick, smooth, dark, rich, yummy. Spectacular over vanilla ice cream. You will need bought caramels.

½ cup milk
2 teaspoons dry instant coffee
4 ounces milk chocolate
14 ounces plain caramels (for instance, Kraft)

In the top of a small double boiler over warm water on moderate heat, heat the milk until warm. Add the coffee and stir to dissolve.

Cut or break the chocolate into medium-sized pieces and add, along with the caramels. Cover and let cook over moderate heat until the caramels and chocolate are melted (see Note). Stir with a heavy wire whisk until smooth.

Serve slightly warm or at room temperature.

NOTE: Occasionally some caramels resist melting. If that happens, with a slotted spoon transfer the hot caramels to a blender and blend until smooth. Gradually add the hot-milk-and-melted-chocolate mixture and blend until smooth.

Grand Marnier Chocolate Sauce

1 1/4 CUPS

Intensely chocolate with a Grand Marnier and mocha flavor.

This may be made ahead of time and reheated in the top of a double boiler if it becomes too thick.

8 ounces semisweet chocolate
2 teaspoons dry instant espresso or coffee
1/4 cup boiling water
3 tablespoons whipping cream
1/4 cup Grand Marnier

Chop the chocolate into coarse pieces and then place it in a food processor fitted with the metal chopping blade. Pulse the machine 8 to 10 times until the chocolate is fine. Transfer the chocolate to a small heavy saucepan.

Dissolve the espresso or coffee in the boiling water and add to the chocolate. Add the whipping cream. Place on low heat and stir frequently with a small wire whisk until melted and smooth.

Remove from the heat and stir in the Grand Marnier.

Serve slightly warm or at room temperature.

Butterscotch Sauce

2 CUPS

Creamy, rich, smooth. Serve slightly warm or at room temperature. This can be refrigerated for a week or so and can be reheated in a double boiler. Serve over and/or under vanilla ice cream or any apple dessert.

1 cup granulated sugar
1½ cups water
1½ cups whipping cream
2 ounces (½ stick) unsalted butter

Place the sugar and water in a 2½- to 3-quart saucepan and stir frequently with a wooden spatula over high heat until the mixture comes to a boil. Cover and let boil for 10 minutes. Then uncover, reduce the heat to moderate, and let boil without stirring for 10 to 13 minutes until the syrup caramelizes and becomes a rich medium-brown. When the syrup starts to color you can twirl the pan gently a few times to encourage even browning.

Meanwhile, scald the cream in a saucepan over moderate heat, uncovered, until a wrinkled skin forms on top. Reduce the heat to low and keep the cream warm.

As soon as the caramel syrup is ready, remove it from the heat. Gradually add the hot cream, beating briskly with a long-handled wire whisk. The mixture will boil up furiously; if the saucepan is not large enough it will boil over.

When the cream is all added, cut the butter into pieces and add, stirring until melted and smooth.

Clear Caramel Sauce

A gorgeous shade of amber, sparkling clear. This is a perfect combination with baked apples, apple tart, or apple tartlets. It lasts indefinitely.

¾ CUP

1 cup granulated sugar
1⅓ cups water
2 tablespoons dark rum

Place the sugar in a wide, heavy frying pan (preferably one with a 12-inch diameter, and preferably one with a nonstick finish). Add ⅓ cup of the water (reserve the remaining 1 cup water).

Stir with a wooden spatula over moderate heat. Wash down the sides occasionally with a brush dipped in water to remove any sugar granules that cling to the sides. When the sugar is dissolved and the mixture comes to a boil, increase the heat to high, do not stir anymore, and let boil until the sugar turns a caramel color. When the syrup begins to color, swirl the pan occasionally to prevent the syrup from burning or coloring unevenly.

Meanwhile, in a small pan over moderate heat bring the remaining 1 cup of water to a boil, reduce the heat, and keep the water hot until you are ready for it.

When the syrup is an even caramel color, remove the pan from the heat. With a long-handled wooden spatula gradually stir in the hot water (the syrup will boil up hard—keep your distance).

Now return the pan to moderate heat and let the syrup simmer for 5 to 10 minutes to reduce to ¾ cup.

Let cool. Stir in the rum. Transfer to a container.

Serve at room temperature, in small portions.

Brandied Custard Sauce

2⅓ cups

Great with any fresh berries or sliced bananas, and/or cheesecake. Or with chocolate cake.
It is best to use a sugar thermometer when you make this.

¾ cup milk
1 cup whipping cream
4 egg yolks graded "large"
¼ cup granulated sugar
Pinch of salt
¼ cup Armagnac, cognac, or brandy (or rum)
½ teaspoon vanilla extract

In a small heavy saucepan over moderate heat scald the milk and cream until you see a wrinkled skin on the top or tiny bubbles around the edge.

Meanwhile, in the top of a large double boiler off the heat, beat the yolks lightly with a small wire whisk just to mix. Gradually stir in the sugar and salt.

When the milk-and-cream mixture is ready, very gradually whisk it into the yolks. Place over hot water on moderate heat. Insert a sugar thermometer.

Cook, scraping the pan constantly with a rubber spatula, until the mixture thickens enough to coat a spoon and registers 180 degrees on the thermometer.

Remove from the heat and strain into a bowl immediately to stop the cooking. Stir in the Armagnac, cognac, or brandy (or rum) and the vanilla.

Cool, uncovered, stirring frequently. Then transfer to a covered container and refrigerate. Serve very cold.

VARIATION: Vanilla Custard Sauce
Omit the liquor and increase the vanilla to 1½ teaspoons.

Sour Cherries in Kirsch and Cognac

1 ¼ CUPS

Unless you live in Michigan or the state of Washington, the chances are that dried pitted sour cherries are new to you. They have been sold commercially around the country for only the last two or three years. They look like large raisins; they have a sweet/tart flavor and a chewy texture, and can be used anyway you use raisins. Some cherry connoisseurs say that the best ones are the Chukar cherries from Washington. These are sold in bulk by Dean & DeLuca (see page 29).

Serve this divine sauce with ice cream, fresh or stewed peaches or pears, quartered fresh strawberries (see Note), or sliced fresh figs. Serve this generously. This amount will serve four people (if I am not one of them).

A jar of this makes a very special gift for a very special person.

Making this is a snap. And it will keep well for a long long time (refrigeration is not necessary).

Generous 4 ounces (1 cup) dried pitted sour
    cherries
1 cup water
¼ cup granulated sugar
2 tablespoons kirsch
2 tablespoons cognac or Armagnac

Place the cherries, water, and sugar in a small, heavy saucepan. Stir to mix. Place over moderate heat, uncovered, and bring to a boil. Stir occasionally and let boil for about 8 minutes until the liquid has reduced by half and is just below the top of the cherries (if you drain the cherries through a strainer set over a bowl, the liquid should measure ½ cup).

Remove from the heat and without waiting stir in the kirsch and cognac or Armagnac.

Let cool and transfer to a covered jar.

Serve at room temperature or slightly warmed.

NOTE: When you serve this with fresh strawberries, a light sprinkling of black pepper and a bit of balsamic vinegar mixed into the berries and sour cherries is wonderful—and not as strange as it sounds.

Raspberry Sauce

2 CUPS

2 10-ounce packages frozen raspberries in light syrup

Thaw the berries. Place the berries and syrup in a blender and blend to puree. Force through a wide but fine strainer set over a bowl to remove the seeds.

Serve cold.

Crème Fraîche

It takes no time to mix your own, but then it has to stand for a few days. The finished crème can be refrigerated for about 4 weeks. When this is served with fruit as dessert, plan on 1 cup for every 3 portions.

I have read that this cannot be made with UHT (ultra-high-temperature pasteurized) cream. Don't believe it. I make this frequently, most often with UHT cream.

1 cup whipping cream
1 teaspoon buttermilk

Pour the cream into a jar with a cover. Add the buttermilk and stir to mix. Cover the jar and let stand at room temperature for from 1 to 3 days, until it is as thick as commercial sour cream.

Refrigerate for at least 24 hours or up to 4 weeks. Or for as long as it still tastes good. In the refrigerator, after a day or so, it will thicken quite a bit more and will become very firm. Use it as it is, or whisk it a bit to soften.

VARIATION: Yogurt Crème Fraîche (2 cups) is made the same way, substituting 1 cup of unflavored yogurt for the 1 teaspoon of buttermilk. The flavor will be more tart/sour; it can be sweetened after it has thickened. Stir in about 1 teaspoon of granulated sugar for each half-cup of Yogurt Crème Fraîche for a delicious flavor. (Wonderful with fresh strawberries.)

Index

apricot(s) (cont'd)
  glaze
    for apple tart, 157
    for cheese and fruit tartlets,
      161–62
  preserves
    homemade, 140–41
    rum, 148–49
  rum cake, 138–42
  rum jelly roll (variation), 148–49
  steaming, 241–42, 300
  and walnut applesauce cake, 100–101
Armagnac brandy:
  and apricot glaze, for prune
    Armagnac cheesecake, 299
  in brandied custard sauce, 409
  cheesecake; prune, 297–99
  espresso brownies; prune (variation),
    195
  ice cream; prune, 325
  prunes in, 396–97
The Art of Cooking, Volume 2 (Pépin),
  264

baking parchment:
  source for, 29
baking soda:
  diluting, 275
banana(s):
  and apricot topping, for banana rum
    terrine, 346
  cookies; double chocolate, 224–26
  ice, 333
  rum terrine, 343–46

  and strawberries with bittersweet
    sour cream (variation), 393
  and white chocolate cake, 62–63
  see also banana chips
banana chips:
  about, 246
  in buttercrisps, 245–46
The Barnard Nut Company, 10
biscotti:
  about, 234
  with chocolate icing (variation),
    237–38
  in cioccolati affogati (variation), 238
  cioccolato (variation), 236–37
  honey, 234–36
bishop's bread, 59–61
bittersweet chocolate sauce, 404
  with cocoa, 357
bizcochitos, 278–79
black-and-white angelfood cake
  (variation), 134–35
black pepper: see pepper, black
blackberry jam:
  glaze, for rum and espresso chocolate
    cheesecake, 296
blondies, 284–85
blueberries:
  crunch; Nantucket, 390–91
  preparing, 22–23
bourbon:
  in bizcochitos, 278–79
  and hazelnut chocolate cake, 74–76
  and rhubarb applesauce, 389
  vanilla peaches, 375–76
brandied custard sauce, 409

cheese, mascarpone: *See* mascarpone
     cheese
cheesecakes:
     about, 292
     apricot, 300–301
     Craig Claiborne (variation), 299
     prune Armagnac, 297–99
     rum and espresso chocolate, 293–96
cherries:
     hot brandied, 378
     sour, in kirsch and cognac, 410
     topping, for tartlets, 161
chiffon cakes:
     about, 142
     rum mocha, 142–45
Chinois (restaurant), 315
Chino Nojo family, 315
chocolate:
     about, 12–13
     banana cookies; double, 224–26
     in biscotti cioccolato (variation),
          236–37
     brownies, Santa Fe, 191–93
     in brownstone icing, 54–55
     cakes, 35–81
          banana and white, 62–63
          bishop's bread, 59–61
          date, 77–78
          French, with two sauces, 48–50
          Gustaf Anders's, 45–47
          hazelnut and bourbon, 74–76
          Hôtel de Crillon's, 39–41
          intrigue, 51–52
          Irish whiskey, 64–66
          layer, Creole, 67–69
          layer, Mexican, 70–73

New York City brownstone front,
          53–55
     panforte cioccolato, 79–81
     rum chocolate truffle roll, 35–38
     Sonrisa, 42–44
     sour cream black fudge loaf, 56–58
     sourdough, 184–87
     very small, 201–204
Callebaut, 13
     source for, 29
cheesecake; rum and espresso,
          293–96
chocolate chunk cookies; the newest,
          218–19
chunk peanut cookies, 220–21
chunk raisin oatmeal cookies
          (variation), 240
cioccolati affogati (variation), 238
cookies
     Pennsylvania Dutch, 214–15
     raisin and peanut butter, 221–23
covered rum-raisin chocolate ice
          cream (variation), 320
crumbs, 21
date cake, 77–78
in espresso brownies, 194–95
flour, 21
fudge; frozen rum-raisin, 339–40
fudge pie; Joe's, 166–68
ginger sandwich cookies, 196–98
glaze, 147–48
     honey, 49
hazelnut macaroons, 215–17
ice, 332
ice cream
     plain (variation), 319–20

marmalade:

and ginger fruit bars, 241–42

and Grand Marnier baked apples, 382–83

mascarpone cheese:

about, 349

source for, 29

in tiramisu, 347–49

Maxim's, 377

measuring techniques, 18

Medaglia D'Oro espresso powder, 11

Melba, Nellie, 376

meringues:

coffee Pavlova, 149–52

flutes

chocolate (variation), 264

vanilla, 261–63

with walnuts and chocolate, 199–201

Mexican chocolate layer cake, 70–73

Mexican chocolate mousse icing, 72–73

Miami vice, 211–13

milanos (variation), 253

mile-high cinnamon bread, 178–80

mile-high sponge cake, 129–31

milk chocolate: *See* chocolate

mixers, electric, 14

mixing bowls, 16

source for, 29

mocha angelfood cake (variation), 133

mocha caramel sauce, 405

The Model Bakery, 211

mousse:

cognac espresso, 364–65

frozen Irish whiskey, 338

lemon, Rancho, 367–68

white chocolate, with raspberry sauce, 361–63

muffins, Texas, 106–107

Munter, Bruce, 42

Nantucket blueberry crunch, 390–91

Napa Valley prune cake, 96–97

Nassikas, Jim, 211

New York City brownstone front cake, 53–55

The newest chocolate-chocolate chunk cookies, 218–19

The Nut House, 289

nut(s):

about, 8–10

date loaf; espresso, 94–95

date raisin prune cake, 123–24

date spice cookies, 274–75

and fruit brioche loaf, 175–78

gingercake; rum-raisin and, 102–103

raisin cookies; jumbo, 280–81

storing, 8

Texas, 287–88

wholesale, 10

see also individual names

oatmeal cookies:

chocolate chunk raisin (variation), 240

peanut raisin (variation), 240

raisin, 239–40

orange marmalade: *See* marmalade

walnut(s):

    and apricot applesauce cake, 100–101

    buttermilk lemon cake, 113–14

    and chocolate; meringues with,
        199–201

    date spice cookies, 274–75

    in espresso brownies, 194

    in espresso date-nut loaf, 94–95

    in fruit and nut brioche loaf, 175–78

    in Hungarian coffee cake, 181–83

    in prune Armagnac espresso
        brownies, 195

    in Miami vice, 211–13

    raisin cookies; jumbo, 280–81

    in raisin date-nut prune cake,
        123–24

    in rum-raisin and nut gingercake,
        102–103

    in Santa Fe brownies, 191–93

    in Texas muffins, 106–107

    toasting, 194, 384–85

West, Mae, 320

whipped cream: *See* cream, whipping

whipping cream: *See* cream, whipping

whiskey, Irish: *See* Irish whiskey

white chocolate: *See* chocolate

wine, port: *See* port wine

Wolfert, Paula, 11

Wolfgang's individual bittersweet
    chocolate soufflés, 307–10

Wood's Cider Mill, 145

Y.O. Ranch date bars, 276–77

yogurt:

    crème fraîche (variation), 412

    frozen chocolate, 322–23

    vanilla, strawberries with, 394

A Note About the Author

Maida Heatter, author of *Maida Heatter's Book of Great Desserts*, *Maida Heatter's Book of Great Cookies*, *Maida Heatter's Book of Great Chocolate Desserts*, *Maida Heatter's New Book of Great Desserts*, and *Maida Heatter's Book of Great American Desserts* is the daughter of Gabriel Heatter, the radio commentator. She studied fashion illustration at Pratt Institute and has done fashion illustrating and designing, made jewelry, and painted. But her first love has always been cooking. She taught it in classes in her home, in department stores, and at cooking schools across the country. For many years she made all the desserts for a popular Miami Beach restaurant owned by her husband, Ralph Daniels.

She prepared desserts for the 1983 Summit of Industrialized Nations at Colonial Williamsburg, Virginia, for President Reagan and six other heads of state.

Ms. Heatter's late daughter, Toni Evins, a painter and illustrator, did the drawings for all of Ms. Heatter's books.